Lincoln's
Political Generals

Lincoln's Political Generals

The Battlefield Performance of Seven Controversial Appointees

BENTON RAIN PATTERSON

McFarland & Company, Inc., Publishers
Jefferson, North Carolina

Photograph research by Victoria Harlow

LIBRARY OF CONGRESS CATALOGUING-IN-PUBLICATION DATA

Patterson, Benton Rain, 1929–
Lincoln's political generals : the battlefield performance of seven controversial appointees / Benton Rain Patterson.
pages cm.
Includes bibliographical references and index.

ISBN 978-0-7864-7857-6 (softcover : acid free paper) ♾
ISBN 978-1-4766-1681-0 (ebook)

1. United States—History—Civil War, 1861–1865—Biography.
2. United States—History—Civil War, 1861–1865—Campaigns.
3. Command of troops—History—19th century. 4. Generals—United States—Biography. 5. United States. Army—Biography. 6. Lincoln, Abraham, 1809–1865—Military leadership. 7. Patronage, Political—United States—History—19th century. I. Title.
E467.P37 2014   973.7'1—dc23   2014027782

BRITISH LIBRARY CATALOGUING DATA ARE AVAILABLE

© 2014 Benton Rain Patterson. All rights reserved

No part of this book may be reproduced or transmitted in any form or by any means, electronic or mechanical, including photocopying or recording, or by any information storage and retrieval system, without permission in writing from the publisher.

On the cover: Maj. Gen. John McClernand, Maj. Gen. Lew Wallace, Maj. Gen. John Frémont, Maj. Gen. Benjamin F. Butler, Maj. Gen. Nathaniel Banks, Maj. Gen. Stephen Hurlbut, Maj. Gen. Franz Sigel (Library of Congress)

Printed in the United States of America

McFarland & Company, Inc., Publishers
Box 611, Jefferson, North Carolina 28640
www.mcfarlandpub.com

To the memory of
Robert T. Patterson,
William B. Patterson,
Benton C. Rain and
James B. Roberts.
They served.

Table of Contents

Introduction   1

   1. Major General Benjamin Franklin Butler   5

   2. Major General Nathaniel Prentice Banks   64

   3. Major General Franz Sigel   102

   4. Major General John Charles Frémont   128

   5. Major General John Alexander McClernand   140

   6. Major General Stephen Augustus Hurlbut   186

   7. Major General Lewis Wallace   196

Chapter Notes   223

Bibliography   229

Index   231

Introduction

Civil War history ultimately leads readers to detailed accounts of the battles, and those accounts often cause wonder about the armies' commanders, raising in the minds of readers questions such as "How the heck did *he* ever become a general?"

The answer lies in the fact that when Fort Sumter was fired on and President Lincoln immediately issued a call for 75,000 volunteers to go to war, he created an instant army that required officers of all grades, including generals. The generals would be appointed by the president and confirmed, or not, by the U.S. Senate. It's been argued—in Lincoln's defense for having made some outstandingly poor appointments—that he, having been in office but thirty-nine days when Fort Sumter was attacked, had no knowledge of officers, active or inactive, who had the right stuff to make effective generals. He was not completely blind in creating generals, however, for he had at least one veteran officer who knew the army inside and out, a person to whom he could turn for recommendations and advice. That was seventy-four-year-old Lieutenant General Winfield Scott, the army's general in chief, who had been in every U.S. war since the War of 1812 and who knew the officer corps' personnel well enough to propose Colonel Robert E. Lee as the officer who should organize and command that instant army, a proposal made before Lee committed to the side of the rebellion.

Whatever else can be said about Abraham Lincoln, he was, first of all, a politician, one who understood that continuation in high office requires making deals and doing favors, not all of them to his liking. At the beginning of the war he treated generalships as political plums or sops. He seemed possessed of the notion that since generals were to be leaders of men, the place to look for generals was among *political* leaders of men. Training and experience in the art of war and in the profession of arms were not to him important considerations. There was some justification for his holding that view. The nation had a tradition of citizens untrained in military matters stepping forward, or being called forward, in times of need and becoming successful soldiers and successful leaders of soldiers.

In the beginning of his experience as a wartime president Lincoln seemed to have the idea that running a war was something almost anyone with intelligence and a will to win could do. He thought he could do it. He shared a trait of many successful men whose superior abilities in one area lead them to believe their abilities in all areas are superior. When he at last realized that winning the war was beyond his ability, beyond even *his* ability combined with that of Secretary of War Edwin Stanton, he conceded. "You and I," he told Stanton in March of 1864, "have been trying to boss this job and we have not succeeded very well with it. We have sent across the mountains for Mister Grant, as Mrs. Grant calls him, to relieve us, and I think we had better leave him alone to do as he pleases."[1]

Then there is the argument that it was okay for Lincoln to choose political leaders as generals because they, better than most others, could rouse public support of the war and inspire the enlistment of volunteers to fight it. Unfortunately, the political generals—those appointed, promoted or kept in command for political reasons—saw themselves as warriors, as leaders in battle, not as recruiting officers, and they used whatever political power they had, which in some cases was considerable, to put themselves in the field, not in recruiting campaigns. Major General Benjamin Butler, the most vociferous of the political generals and who had to be relieved of his duties in the occupation of New Orleans, let Lincoln know he wouldn't accept the recruiting role that had been offered him. "Sending Banks to command in my place," he told the president, "and then sending me down the Mississippi to enlist troops, would be simply saying that I was not fit to command troops, but only fit for a recruiting sergeant."

Lincoln, of course, had his purposes in maintaining the political generals for the help they could provide in supporting the war and in supporting his presidency. And although those generals he used for those purposes knew they were being used, they still insisted on being battlefield leaders and used their political connections and constituencies as leverage to keep themselves in field commands.

Major General Henry Halleck, a West Point graduate and the army's general in chief before being superseded by Grant, had no use for Lincoln's political generals and was forcefully frank about his opposition to them. In a letter to General Sherman in April 1864, following Major General Nathaniel Banks's shameful defeats and disastrous campaign in Louisiana, Halleck wrote that "Banks' operations in the West are about what should have been expected from a general so utterly destitute of military education and military capacity. It seems but little better than murder to give important commands to such men as Banks, Butler, McClernand, Sigel, and Lew. Wallace, and yet it seems impossible to prevent it."[2]

Some who were politicians first and generals second proved themselves perfectly competent to perform as army commanders, men such as John A. Logan, who at the start of the war was a U.S. congressman from Illinois and resigned his seat to serve in the U.S. Army. He had served as a lieutenant in the Mexican War and at the outbreak of the Civil War became a colonel commanding a regiment of volunteers, soon rising to the rank of major general. Grant had naught but good to say about Logan, who, he wrote, served "from the battle of Belmont to the fall of Atlanta ... having passed successively through all grades from colonel commanding a regiment to general commanding a brigade, division and army corps, until upon the death of [Major General James] McPherson the command of the entire Army of the Tennessee devolved upon him in the midst of a hotly contested battle.... I can bear testimony, from personal observation, that he had proved himself fully equal to all the lower positions which he had occupied as a soldier."[3]

Logan fell victim to Sherman's bias against political generals. Sherman peremptorily removed him from command of the Army of the Tennessee: "I regarded both Generals Logan and [Frank] Blair as 'volunteers,' that looked to personal fame and glory as auxiliary and secondary to their political ambition, and not as professional soldiers."[4] Sherman may have had a point. Grant explained that "Generals Logan and Blair commanded the two corps composing the right wing [of Sherman's army on its march to the sea]. About this time [September 1864] they left to take part in the presidential election, which took place that year, leaving their corps to Osterhaus and Ransom. I have no doubt that their leaving was at the earnest solicitation of the War Department. General Blair got back in time to resume his command and to proceed with it throughout the march to the sea.... General Logan did not return to his command until after it reached Savannah."[5] Logan, although competent in the field, had demonstrated a major fault of political generals. He had put political activity—campaigning for Lincoln's reelection—ahead of his military duties.

Almost to a man the political generals shared another fault bothersome to professional officers. As one biographer observed, they understood the chain of command from themselves *down* the chain, but not from themselves *up* the chain. Some considered obedience to orders from their superiors to be optional. Nearly all appealed to their political contacts, including to President Lincoln, for special consideration or for the decisions of their superiors they found disagreeable to be countermanded in Washington. Their insubordination and refusal to follow orders seemed to their commanders, such as Grant, offenses even more objectionable than ineffectual performance in the field.

The purpose of this book is not to analyze the actions of the seven generals presented on these pages and then to pass judgment on their worthiness as commanders. It is instead to *show* them—to let readers see them—in action and allow readers to judge for themselves the political generals' competence for the tasks of leading troops in mortal combat. Five of the seven generals presented here are those cited by General Halleck as being almost criminally inept. Readers can decide for themselves if he was right.

1

Major General Benjamin Franklin Butler

Before the War: Born November 5, 1818, in Deerfield, New Hampshire. Graduated from Waterville College in Waterville, Maine. Studied law in the law office of William Smith of Lowell, Massachusetts. Admitted to the bar, September 4, 1840. Entered private practice, 1840. Married Sarah Hildreth, an actress, May 16, 1844. Children: three sons (one of whom died at age five), one daughter. Gained prominence as an advocate for workers' rights and for the institution of the ten-hour workday in Massachusetts. Political affiliation: Democrat. Elected to the Massachusetts house of representatives, 1853. Elected to the Massachusetts senate, 1859. Supported the candidacy of Jefferson Davis as Democratic nominee for U.S. president in 1860. Military experience: Third lieutenant in the Massachusetts militia, 1839, eventually rising to the grade of colonel as a regimental commander; elected brigadier general and brigade commander by the field officers of his brigade, 1855.

On Friday, April 19, 1861, exactly one week after a Confederate army commenced a massive artillery assault on Fort Sumter, thereby beginning the Civil War, U.S. troops were being rushed to Washington, D.C., to defend the city against a Confederate assault expected to be launched from Virginia. Among the troops was the Sixth Massachusetts Infantry Regiment, a militia unit commanded by Colonel Edward F. Jones and traveling by train from Boston through New York, Philadelphia and Baltimore to reach the stricken nation's capital. In Baltimore the troops' urgent journey was abruptly interrupted.

To continue on the last leg of the trip, from Baltimore southwest to Washington, the troops would have to move ten blocks along Pratt Street in Baltimore, from the President Street depot of the Philadelphia, Wilmington & Baltimore Railroad westward to the Baltimore & Ohio's Camden Station, the railroad cars being drawn down the tracks by horses rather than steam locomotives because a city ordinance prohibited the operation of trains through the city. It was the same station-to-station transfer President Lincoln had been forced to make furtively in the middle of the night to prevent a possible assassination attempt on his way to Washington for his inauguration ten weeks earlier. The route through Baltimore was believed to be the quickest way to Washington, one of the two major accesses to Washington from the north, one being the Baltimore & Ohio's rail line from Baltimore to the capital, the other being the Potomac River, on which vessels now had become vulnerable to Confederate artillery mounted on the banks where the river was narrowest.

In 1861 Baltimore had a population of 212,000 residents, making it the nation's fourth largest city. Although many, if not most, of its citizens were loyal to the U.S. government, a considerable number were rabidly secessionist and pro–South. The city's mayor, George Brown, and its police marshal, George Kane, both expected trouble when it was learned that federal troops would be passing through Baltimore on their way to Washington. The trouble soon materialized, a mob estimated at between 8,000 and 10,000 having gathered along Pratt Street to harass the soldiers and attempt to block the railroad cars in which they were traveling.

The troop train's first seven cars, to which teams of horses were quickly hitched, managed to get past the mass of protesters. By the time the last three cars of the train[1] began to move toward Camden Station, however, the tracks had become so obstructed by logs, timbers, anchors and debris that the cars could not proceed, and some two hundred and fifty men of the Sixth Regiment were forced to cover the distance on foot while the mob taunted and threatened them and threw paving stones and bricks at them. Pistol shots as well were fired at them. Four soldiers were killed, and thirty-six were injured, the first casualties of what was to be the bloody, fiercely fought, four-year-long Civil War.

The troops were at last ordered to defend themselves by opening fire on the menacing mob. In the melee twelve members of the mob were killed and an unknown number were wounded. The troops at last reached Camden Station and with police protection were hurried aboard the train waiting to take them to Washington. As the train made its way down the tracks, members of the mob ran alongside it, keeping up a constant stream of shouted threats and invective, pelting the cars with rocks and placing obstructions on the tracks, which the Baltimore police cleared off almost as quickly as they were placed. Gathering speed, the train finally outran the tiring mob and steamed off to Washington.

The embattled Sixth Regiment had left Boston a day earlier than the Eighth Regiment, which also had been ordered to Washington by Massachusetts governor John Andrew, following the U.S. secretary of war's request for troops. The Eighth Regiment was in Philadelphia when news of the Baltimore mob's attack on the Sixth reached the brigade commander,

Maj. Gen. Benjamin Butler entered the war as a brigadier general in the Massachusetts militia, elected to that rank by the field-grade officers (major and above) of his brigade (Library of Congress).

Brigadier General Benjamin Butler, who was traveling with the Eighth. The two other regiments of his brigade, the Third and Fourth, had been ordered to Fort Monroe and were on their way. By the time the news of the Baltimore riot reached Butler, Baltimore's mayor Brown and Maryland governor Thomas Hicks had warned President Lincoln that no more federal troops would be able to pass through Baltimore without fighting their way through uncontrollable mobs.

Butler consulted with the commandant of the Philadelphia Navy Yard and with the president of the Philadelphia, Wilmington & Baltimore Railroad and decided to circumvent Baltimore and move swiftly on to Washington by way of Annapolis. Butler and his troops would take a train from Philadelphia to Perryville, Maryland, where the Susquehanna River debouches into the northern end of Chesapeake Bay. There, with the permission of the railroad's president, they would commandeer the PW&B's railroad ferry, the *Maryland*, and take it down Chesapeake Bay to Annapolis, from which they would travel the last thirty-odd miles over the branch rail line to Washington.

At Annapolis, the capital of Maryland and home of the U.S. Naval Academy, Butler met a new obstacle—Maryland governor Hicks, who warned Butler against landing his troops in Annapolis. In a written message, Hicks told Butler, "The excitement here is very great, and I think it prudent that you should take your men elsewhere. I have declared to the Secretary of War advising against your landing your men here."[2]

Rioters in Baltimore attack the troops of the Sixth Massachusetts Infantry Regiment on their way to Washington, D.C., on April 19, 1861, one week after Fort Sumter had been fired on. The regiment was part of Butler's brigade, and he quickly took forceful steps to suppress rioters and other secession sympathizers in Baltimore (Library of Congress).

Governor Hicks had a lot to learn about Butler, a man practiced in defiance. Forty-two years old, not tall, but stout, nervous-seeming in his movements, with thin lips, sparse hair combed back over his ears, a large head and one eye noticeably bigger than the other, Butler was by nature and background an autocrat, much better at giving orders than taking them. He wrote back to Hicks, telling him, "I am sorry that your excellency should advise against my landing here. I am not provisioned for a long voyage. Finding the ordinary means of communication cut off by the burning of railroad bridges by a mob, I have been obliged to make this detour, and hope that your excellency will see, from the very necessity of the case, that there is no cause of excitement in the mind of any good citizen."[3]

Undeterred, Hicks, on the morning following the *Maryland*'s arrival at Annapolis, came to meet with Butler at the naval academy, bringing with him the mayor of Annapolis. The two men "exhorted me," Butler related, "not to think of landing." They told Butler that all of Maryland was ready to rush to arms and that the people of Annapolis could not be long restrained. When they told him that he would be unable to buy provisions in Annapolis, that no patriot would sell to Yankee troops, Butler finally had to lay it out in plain language. He was going to land his troops, he told the governor and mayor, and if merchants in Annapolis refused to sell the provisions his troops required, "a thousand hungry, armed men have other means of getting what they want to eat besides buying it."[4] He also warned that he intended to stay in Annapolis as long as it was convenient for his troops and that if they were attacked, they would repel the attack.

While the governor was chewing on that threat, Butler's troops ate what the naval academy could spare. But the governor and mayor had got Butler's message, and within days of their meeting with him, the mayor applied for the job of sutler for the regiment. And the governor, although he shifted meetings of the legislature from Annapolis to Frederick, turned over to Butler the great seal of Maryland, without which the legislature could not enact laws, particularly one that attempted to take Maryland out of the Union.

Before Butler's troops could be carried by rail from Annapolis to Washington they first would have to repair the tracks, which had been torn up by secession sympathizers, repair the bridge that secessionist saboteurs had crippled, and find the locomotive that secessionists had hidden. The locomotive was found partly dismantled in a locked shed that the railroad agent refused to unlock. Butler ordered the door forced open and then had a detail of volunteers who had built train engines to see if they could put the locomotive back together. One of the volunteers spotted the manufacturer's name plate on the locomotive and realized he had helped assemble it when it was new. He and the other volunteers gathered up the parts they found in the shed and soon had the engine reassembled and running.

Butler ordered a detail of two companies of the Eighth Regiment to march out two miles toward Washington and hold the rail line against all comers. Another detail, twenty men who had answered Butler's call for volunteers "who had ever had anything to do with laying railroad track,"[5] was assigned the task of rounding up the rails that had been ripped up and scattered in the nearby countryside and returning them to the rail bed to restore the line. Still another detail went to work to add supporting timbers to the crippled bridge over the South River, some six miles out from Annapolis. The bridge's original timbers had been partly sawn through, weakening the structure to the point that the bridge may have collapsed under the weight of the locomotive.

It was during those assignments that Butler first showed his disdain for West Point officers. By this time the Seventh Infantry Regiment of the New York state militia had arrived in Annapolis by steamer after giving up an attempt to reach Washington via the Potomac River. It was commanded by Colonel Marshall Lefferts, a militia officer who, in Butler's words, "had picked up somewhere a man who had once been at West Point, to accompany and cosset him in his command. Lefferts never called upon me without him."[6] Butler decided to have Lefferts, shortly after his arrival, immediately march his regiment out to repair the broken rail line. Lefferts refused, claiming that he had consulted his officers and they had declined to march.

Butler then attempted to explain the facts of military life to Lefferts. "Colonel Lefferts," he said, "war is not carried on in this way. A commander doesn't consult his regiment as to the propriety of obeying his orders. He must judge of what those orders should be. Now, by the Articles of War, I am in command, as brigadier general of the United States militia, called into service, and actually in service. I take the responsibility of giving you an order to march and shall expect it to be obeyed."

Lefferts' tag-along civilian advisor, whom Butler described as "officious and not always too courteous" and as having a red nose, presumably because of his drinking habits, then interjected, saying, "General Butler, you don't appear to be aware that a general of United States militia has no right to command New York state troops."

"No, sir," Butler, the eminent lawyer, responded, "I am not aware of that, and it is not the law. Have you got a copy of the Articles of War in your pocket?"

"No, sir."

"Have you examined them?" Butler asked.

"No, sir, but I was educated at West Point."

In his account of the incident, Butler interrupted his narrative to make a significant comment. "That was the first time in carrying on war," he wrote in his autobiography, "that West Point had ever interfered to render my movements abortive, but not the last time by a great deal, as we shall see hereafter. It stirred me then, as it always has stirred me since."[7] Shortly after making that comment, he criticized Jefferson Davis for not moving on Washington and making an easy capture of it right after the assault on Fort Sumter. "I know not what prevented him save his education at West Point, where the necessity of a rapid movement in warlike operations is taught in the negative."[8]

In the end, Butler could not move Lefferts to follow his order and he turned to his own men to repair and guard the railroad, telling the commander of the Massachusetts Eighth Regiment, in the presence of Lefferts, that "Colonel Lefferts with his whole regiment is afraid to go, colonel, but you will obey orders."

When Lefferts' advisor objected to Butler's language, Butler told him, "Oh, well, as far as Colonel Lefferts is concerned, I shall be entirely satisfied with him if he shows a disposition to fight anybody anywhere. Let him begin with me. But as for you, if you interrupt this conversation again, and if you do not leave the room instantly, I will direct my orderly to take you out." Then turning to Lefferts, he dismissed him by saying, "Good afternoon, Colonel Lefferts." That was the last communication Butler had in person with Lefferts.[9]

The tracks had been restored, but rails kept disappearing and had to be hunted for and replaced. Butler decided the railroad's superintendent had something to do with the continuing harassment. He arrested the superintendent. He also posted armed guards every 500 feet along the tracks and gave them orders to shoot on sight anyone found tampering with the rails.

Butler's militia troops managed to put the rail line back in service and secure it, allowing the movement to Washington of not only the Sixth Massachusetts Regiment and Lefferts' New York Seventh Regiment but also more than 7,000 others who were sent to reinforce the troops protecting the nation's capital. Butler, however, stayed behind. On April 25 Lieutenant General Winfield Scott, the U.S. Army's general in chief, ordered him to remain at Annapolis and take command of the newly created Department of Annapolis, which embraced an area twenty miles on either side of the railroad that ran from Annapolis to Washington and which was created to keep that rail line open.

General Scott was so impressed with Butler's initiative and effectiveness in Annapolis that on May 3, eight days after appointing him commander of the new district, Scott summoned him to Washington and gave him orders to lead an assault on Baltimore and take back the city from the secessionists. That assignment left little to Butler's discretion or original thinking. He was to first reinforce the garrison at Fort McHenry, just south of Baltimore, and after that, he was to march four columns of 3,000 men each in the attack on Baltimore. One column was to advance from Washington, one from York, Pennsylvania, one from Perryville and the fourth one was to come from Annapolis by ship. The four columns would converge at Baltimore and overwhelm whatever resistance the city offered. That was the plan the general in chief of the U.S. Army handed Butler for execution.

Butler came up with a different plan. One of his aides, Captain Peter Haggerty, had dressed in civilian clothes and spent three days undercover in Baltimore, then had reported to Butler that Baltimore could be taken without the large force and elaborate plan Scott had ordered. So many of the rabid secessionists had left Baltimore and gone south that opposition to a Union attack would be minimal, Haggerty said. After conferring with a number of sympathetic community leaders, Butler accepted Haggerty's appraisal of the situation but thought he would not suggest to Scott a change of plans, believing Scott would reject any change.

About 4:00 p.m. on Monday, May 13, 1861, Butler put his new plan into operation. He boarded a thousand troops onto a train at Annapolis, loaded several artillery pieces onto flatcars and set the train in motion toward Harpers Ferry, to the west, to make it appear an attack on Harpers Ferry, not Baltimore, was under way. About two miles out, the train stopped, then began backing toward Baltimore, which it reached an hour later, about 6:00 p.m. At Camden Station Butler formed up a column and issued detailed instructions about their march through the city, which he would lead mounted on a white horse. No halt in the march should be made or any shot fired except to repel an attack; if a shot was fired from a house and a man was hit by it, the column should halt and burn the house, the column waiting until the house was destroyed. The column's destination was Federal Hill, on the south side of Baltimore. Butler described the march:

> We had gone forward but a few rods when a most violent thunderstorm set in, with furious wind and gusts. The flashes were incessant, and the thunder rolled almost a continuous volley. At one moment the flashes of lightning would light up everything with an intense brilliancy, and in the tithe of a second the darkness was equally intense. In that storm nobody could hear us. In the darkness nobody could discern the column, and nobody knew we were there. As I looked back from my horse, while the column slowly wound up the hill, the effect of the rolling thunder and playing lightning that made for an instant the point of every bayonet a glittering torch, was gloriously magnificent.[10]

Butler led the troops down Light Street and on to Federal Hill, where they established a fortified position, emplacing the artillery pieces. In the tavern at the top of the hill Butler took over one of the rooms to set up his headquarters. He then notified the commandant of Fort McHenry, which guarded the harbor entrance about two miles east of Butler's position, of his troops' presence and he requested support if needed. "If I am attacked tonight," he wrote in a note to the commandant, "please open upon Monument Square with your mortars. I will keep the hill fully lighted with fires during the night so that you may know where we are and not hit us."[11]

The night passed tensely but uneventfully. The men dried their clothes and kept themselves warm and brewed coffee by the fires they had lighted to illuminate their position. Butler dried his clothes in front of a fire at the tavern and took time to compose a proclamation to the citizens of Baltimore, which he published the next morning. In it he let the citizens know that he was in command of the city and he set forth the rules of his military government. He stated that he intended to protect "every good citizen" and "deal properly with every enemy of the United States."[12] That morning he also set about to discover and confiscate whatever arms and ammunition could be discovered and, with the cooperation of the mayor and the police chief, he rounded up some 3,000 muskets, which were hauled off to Fort McHenry for safekeeping. On the morning of the second day of his occupation of the city, May 15, he received a message from General Scott:

> Sir:
> Your hazardous occupation of Baltimore was made without my knowledge, and, of course, without my approbation. It is a godsend that it is without conflict of arms. It is also reported that you have sent a detachment to Frederick; but this is impossible. Not a word have I received from you as to either movement. Let me hear from you.[13]

Butler thought that because he had pulled off a remarkable coup and had done so without bloodshed he deserved appreciation and respect from his commanding general. He was miffed at Scott's failure to recognize his success and was further irritated at being addressed merely as "sir." He ignored Scott's demand for an answer. "Knowing that I could hold Baltimore as easily as I could my hat, and knowing also that Scott knew all I could tell him," he wrote in explanation, "I thought I was not the 'sir' to answer the communication of the commanding-general so addressed."[14]

On May 15 Scott relieved Butler of command of the Annapolis department. To give him something to do, Scott put him in command of Fort Monroe, an old masonry fortification built to protect Hampton Roads and the entrance to the James River. Butler didn't take the reassignment without protest. On May 18 he wrote to the secretary of war, Simon Cameron:

> Sir: I have just received an order from General Scott transferring the command of the Department of Annapolis to General Cadwallader, and ordering me to Fortress Monroe. What does this mean? Is it a censure upon my action?...
> If my services are no longer desired by the Department [of War], I am quite content to be relieved altogether, but I will not be disgraced. In all I have done, I have acted solely according to what I believed to be the wishes of the President, General Scott, and yourself.
> I am not disposed to be troublesome to you, but I wish this matter might be laid

before the President. To be relieved of the command of a department and sent to command a fort, without a word of comment, is something unusual at least, and I am so poor a soldier as not to understand it otherwise than in the light of a reproof.

At least, I desire a personal interview with you and with the President before I accept further service....[15]

In the meantime, Butler's service had been noticed with approbation in government offices other than General Scott's. The secretary of war, apparently with the president's concurrence, had offered Butler a promotion to major general, the highest rank in the U.S. Army other than the rank of lieutenant general held by Scott as general in chief. Butler was so stressed out by the quarrel with Scott that he considered refusing the promotion and leaving the army. When he met with Secretary Cameron on May 18, Butler told him, according to Butler's account, that "if I was no longer needed, I intended to report home."

Cameron urged him not to resign. "He said," Butler wrote, "that I had come into the service a leading Democrat, and others who were prominent Democrats had followed my example, and my action [in leaving the army] might tend to make the war a partisan one."[16] Cameron, Butler said, "kindly begged" him to stay in the army for that political reason. Cameron also assured Butler that Scott, then seventy-four years old and in poor health, would not remain as general in chief much longer.[17]

Commissioned a Major General

On the same day that he met with Cameron, Butler later met with President Lincoln, who presented him with his commission as major general. Butler told Lincoln that he had doubts about accepting the commission because he felt he had been reproached by being relieved of command of the Annapolis department. Supported by his wife's advice and Lincoln's assurance that his administration had done everything to remove any hint of reproach, he decided he would accept the commission and stay in the army.

Before leaving for Fort Monroe on his new assignment, Butler was summoned to Scott's office and handed the general in chief's detailed instructions, carefully setting forth the limits of Butler's authority to act. "He [Scott] seemed to have entirely forgotten our late interview," Butler reported, "and became quite companionable." The interview to which Butler referred was one where Scott had chewed him out for his actions in capturing Baltimore and Butler had responded with a frank and forceful rebuttal. Now Scott had turned amiable. "General," he remarked, according to Butler, "you are very fortunate to be assigned to duty at Fortress Monroe. It is just the season for soft-shelled crabs." From that time on, Butler reported, "I never had the least objectionable communication from General Scott."[18]

On the afternoon of May 22 Butler arrived at Fort Monroe, an eighty-acre site enclosed by a moat and a low wall of stone and brick inside which were barracks to quarter the fort's 300-man garrison. There was also a hospital, a chapel, a parade ground, a garden and the commodious house that quartered the fort's commandant, Colonel Justin Dimick. Butler quickly commandeered the house for his own use.

The problems with which he would have to deal surfaced immediately. He would have to find room for twelve additional regiments—some three thousand men—that Scott had promised him. He would also have to find a water supply to supplement what the cisterns

1. Major General Benjamin Franklin Butler   13

Fort Monroe, Virginia. Butler was placed in command of the fort on May 15, 1861, an assignment he considered a demotion and a censure, prompting him to appeal to the U.S. secretary of war and to President Lincoln (John Clark Ridpath).

provided. He would have to devise some logistics that would allow expeditious transport of provisions and supplies from the wharf into the fort. Other than his own horse and those of some of his officers, there were no horses or mules to pull loaded drays or wagons, and the garrison's troops had to roll barrels of food from dockside through sand into the fort.

Never without ideas, Butler soon came up with solutions to his major problems. Over the objections of his engineering officer, and borrowing an expert from the Pennsylvania Railroad, he had track laid across the sand and cars put on the track to carry freight to and from the fort, his men towing the cars with ropes. For additional drinking and cooking water he had a pipe laid from the spring from which Colonel Dimick had directed his men to haul water across a causeway to supplement the cisterns' supply. Butler also put details to work digging a well inside the fort. To house the additional troops that were on their way to him, he had the first arrivals, the troops of the Third Massachusetts Regiment, set up tents within the fort's walls. He had later arrivals take over an area between the community of Black River and the town of Hampton, and there in dusty wheat fields the arriving troops set up their encampment, connected to the fort by the causeway.

The day after Butler's arrival at Fort Monroe a new problem presented itself. Three Negro men were brought into the fort at their own request after escaping from their owner, Colonel Charles K. Mallory of the Virginia militia, commander of the rebel troops positioned around Hampton. Brought before Butler, the men said Mallory intended to send them to

North Carolina to help build Confederate fortifications and they didn't want to leave their families, perhaps never to see them again. Butler needed laborers and he decided to take them in. He pronounced them contraband of war, enemy property confiscated by agents of the U.S. government. In so doing he took a big step toward emancipation of the rebel South's slaves. Mallory's reaction was fast coming. On Friday, May 24, Butler received a note that read, "Be pleased to designate some time and place when it will be agreeable to you to accord me a personal interview." It was signed, "J.B. Carey, major-acting, Virginia volunteers."[19] Carey was acting for Colonel Mallory. He was known to Butler, as they were fellow Democrats who had been allies at two national Democratic conventions.

Not wishing to allow Carey to see what was going on inside the fort, Butler proposed meeting him on the road to Hampton, about a mile from the fort. Butler took two of his staff officers with him, and Carey was also accompanied by two aides. After an exchange of pleasantries, Carey got down to business. He wanted to know whether the families of Virginia citizens would be allowed passage through the U.S. Navy's blockading fleet. With a roundabout answer, Butler told him they would not. Carey then moved to the subject of the escaped slaves:

"I am informed," Carey said, "that three negroes, belonging to Colonel Mallory, have escaped within your lines. I am Colonel Mallory's agent and have charge of his property. What do you intend to do with regard to those negroes?"

"I propose to retain them," Butler answered forthrightly. To do so could be construed as a violation of the 1850 Fugitive Slave Law.

"Do you mean, then, to set aside your constitutional obligations?" Carey asked.

"I mean to abide by the decision of Virginia, as expressed in her ordinance of secession, passed the day before yesterday. I am under no constitutional obligations to a foreign country, which Virginia now claims to be," lawyer Butler answered.

"But you say we *can't* secede and so you cannot consistently detain the negroes," Carey argued.

"But *you* say," Butler replied, "you *have* seceded and so you cannot consistently claim them." Butler then set out his position. "I shall detain the negroes as contraband of war. You are using them upon your batteries. It is merely a

Troops at Fort Monroe. In June 1861 Butler's force at Fort Monroe totaled some 7,000 men, half of whom were raw recruits who had to be trained and who were poorly clothed, poorly equipped and poorly armed (Library of Congress).

question whether they shall be used for or against the government. Nevertheless, though I greatly need the labor which has providentially fallen into my hands, if Colonel Mallory will come into the fort and take the oath of allegiance to the United States, he shall have his negroes, and I will endeavor to hire them from him."[20]

The meeting then ended. After speaking polite farewells, the two men turned their mounts around and rode off in their separate directions.

Two days later, on Sunday morning, eight more Negroes came to the fort and were taken in. On Monday morning forty-seven more arrived, including men, women and children. On Monday afternoon twelve more men came. Over the next few weeks more came each day, until their number grew to more than nine hundred. Under the supervision of a commissioner appointed by Butler to see to them, the escaped slaves were put to work and were taught and fed. Butler reported them to be gentle, careful and efficient workers.[21] To house them, he established a camp outside the fort.

Butler reported the situation to General Scott and asked for instructions. He also sent a copy of his report to secretary of war Cameron. Cameron responded with a letter approving Butler's actions and telling him to employ the Negroes to do the work they were best suited for and to keep an account of their work and the value of it and the cost of their maintenance. "The question of their final disposition," Lincoln's secretary of war told Butler, "will be reserved for future determination."[22]

Butler's declaring the escaped slaves to be contraband brought a widespread positive response in the North. Abolitionists especially were delighted. Others in the North were simply glad to see that Butler, whose publicized military exploits by now had gained him a large civilian following, had devised a way of getting back at the slave-holding secessionists. Butler himself was pleased with the effects and in his autobiography took credit for advancing the cause of emancipation. "The effect upon the public mind," Butler wrote, "was most wonderful. Everybody seemed to feel a relief on this great slavery question. Everybody thought a way had been found through it. Everybody praised its author by extolling its great use, but whether right or wrong it paved the way for the President's proclamation of freedom to the slaves within eighteen months afterwards."[23] Even so, officials in Washington dithered and delayed over an official policy on the Negro refugees.

Washington also seemed to dither over the prosecution of the war, lacking an aggressive plan for putting down the rebellion. Butler, though, was eager to take the war to the Confederates. By the end of the first week of June 1861 Butler's force posted at Fort Monroe totaled nearly 7,000 men, about half of whom were three-month volunteers whose term of service was about to expire. The other half were raw recruits who had enlisted for three years and who were being trained, however inadequately, by the regulars of Colonel Dimick's garrison. Many were poorly clothed and equipped; most were poorly armed, having to depend on outdated muzzle-loading muskets. Butler's entire command was handicapped by a shortage of ammunition and by a lack of horses. Butler had brought from home nine horses of his own, mounts for him and his chief officers but hardly enough to fill the need for mounted pickets and scouts.

Nevertheless, now designated commander of the Department of Virginia, Butler had sent a force to occupy the lightly defended town of Newport News and establish a fortification, later named Camp Butler, to guard with artillery the entrance to the Kanawha ship canal and the mouth of the Nansemond River. That mission had been completed by May 29. Impatient then to use his three-month volunteers before their enlistment term ended

Butler's troops on the night of June 10, 1861, attempted to capture the Confederate position at Big Bethel, Virginia, and suffered a humiliating defeat. Butler was criticized for the failure of the operation but shifted blame to Brig. Gen. Ebenezer Pierce, whom he had put in command of the expedition (Library of Congress).

and to initiate an offensive against the Confederate capital, Butler decided to move a force toward it. His troops' first obstacle on the way to Richmond was a fortified position the Confederates had established at the church known as Big Bethel, halfway between Fort Monroe and Yorktown.

Butler's plan was to advance two or more regiments from his forward positions under cover of darkness on the night of June 10 and have them join forces in the nearby forest, then strike the Confederate forward post just east of Big Bethel at a church called Little Bethel. "If we bag the Little Bethel men," Butler wrote in his orders, "push on to Big Bethel, and similarly bag them. Burn both the Bethels, or blow up if brick." Because of the shortage of ammunition, he instructed that "men will fire one volley, if desirable; not reload, and go ahead with the bayonet."[24]

The Confederates had placed some 1,400 troops and a howitzer at Big Bethel, and Butler sent 3,500 men, supported by field artillery, to make what was planned to be a surprise attack on them. He decided not to go along on the expedition, for whatever reason, and instead designated Brigadier General Ebenezer W. Pierce, another Massachusetts lawyer and politician without military training, to lead the operation. The plan began to go awry when Butler's two forces, moving toward their rendezvous in the dark, mistook each other to be Confederates and opened fire on their comrades. The operation ended with Pierce ordering a retreat and troops turning and fleeing back to their original positions, discarding equipment and clothing in their rush to escape. Casualties in the disaster amounted to 18 U.S. soldiers killed, 53 wounded and five missing. The Confederates who responded to the botched assault reportedly lost one man killed and three wounded.

Not surprisingly, Butler blamed Pierce, who had issued the order to retreat. "If Pierce had given the order for them [his troops] to sit down and take lunch," Butler remarked, "the enemy would have run away ... because they would have supposed we had come to stay."[25] As for the reason he placed Pierce in command, Butler explained that with three regiments participating in the expedition, he was bound to give command to his lone brigadier general, Pierce. "Yet while no blame could seem to attach to me," he wrote, exonerating himself, "a senseless cry went out against me."[26] That "senseless cry" was the wave of public and official criticism that struck him for not leading the attack himself or at least being on the scene of the action to assume command when difficulties arose. The fault-finding nearly cost him his major general's commission; the required U.S. Senate confirmation of his promotion, when put to a vote on July 21, passed by a mere two votes.

There were other repercussions from the expedition's failure, in the South as well as in the North. Southern spokesmen exulted in the Confederates' repulse of the Union attack, the Confederacy's president, Jefferson Davis, boasting that Big Bethel was a "bright augury of more important victories in the future."[27] In the North, the influential *Philadelphia Inquirer*, reacting to the death of Philadelphian Lieutenant John T. Greble, who was killed in the disastrous attack, decried Butler's leadership, editorializing that Greble had been sacrificed "in order that Butler might be made a Major-General, without possessing the rudiments of military skill."[28]

President Lincoln was among those who saw that Butler presented a problem. In early August he instructed General Scott to call from retirement seventy-two-year-old Major General John E. Wool, second in seniority only to Scott himself, and place him in command of the Department of Virginia, superseding Butler. "The President well knew that General Wool could not do anything, simply because he was too old and infirm," Butler remarked about the move.[29] Scott, Butler said, knew it as well. Nevertheless, on August 17 Wool arrived at Fort Monroe, and Butler turned over to him the command of the department.

In his autobiography Butler professed that he had "nothing to complain of" in being replaced by Wool, whom he described as "a very much older soldier, and a very efficient military officer when he was younger."[30] However, Butler seemed puzzled over the reason for his loss of the command. His guess, as he told his wife, was that his removal had been brought on by his policy of freeing and harboring those slaves, including women and children, who came into his lines seeking refuge. He was positive, though, that freeing them was the right thing to do, even though it had become a political issue. To Montgomery Blair, the postmaster general and Lincoln confidant, he wondered if his removal was "a move on the part of the President." "I am in the dark," he told Blair. "Please give 'more light.'"[31]

When Wool showed up at Fort Monroe, Butler was all outward graciousness, giving him a full military welcome, allowing him the use of Butler's own favorite mount and charming the old general into an amicable arrangement by which Butler would be in charge of troops in the field while Wool would be in over-all command. "I told all my friends that I did not feel aggrieved at all," Butler wrote in his autobiography. "Wool wanted all the work done by some one else while he had a nice place in the camp, and I wanted to do all the work I could do and have somebody else take the responsibility."[32]

Determined to neuter Butler by depriving him of troops, Scott by then had ordered four regiments and part of another to be moved from Fort Monroe to Baltimore, ostensibly to replenish the Union force that was protecting the U.S. capital and had suffered nearly 3,000 casualties at the first Battle of Bull Run (First Manassas) on July 21. Within days of sending off those regiments, Butler learned they were not headed for Washington but had been halted at Baltimore, where they were encamped.

The loss of those troops failed to defeat Butler in his quest for action and fame. He soon became involved in a plan that would gain him both. He had received, he said, intelligence about two fortifications, Fort Hatteras and Fort Clark, that the Confederates were building at Hatteras Inlet, the entrance through North Carolina's Outer Banks that provided a way from the Atlantic Ocean into Pamlico Sound. "I proposed, as soon as I could," he wrote, "to take the forts, for they were very important." The two forts indeed were important, for they guarded Hatteras Inlet to keep it open to Confederate raiders that preyed on Northern shipping and to blockade runners that ferried supplies to the Confederates, using Pamlico Sound and its inlets as a safe haven. U.S. Admiral David D. Porter, then a Union blockade commander at the mouth of the Mississippi River and later author of *The Naval History of the Civil War*, described the situation: "There is in this region a network of channels communicating with the Chowan, Neuse and Roanoke rivers by which any amount of stores and munitions of war could be sent by blockade runners to supply the South. The numerous inlets are navigable for light draft vessels, but owing to their shallow water our vessels of war could not penetrate them. The main channel for entering the Sounds [Pamlico and Albemarle] was Hatteras Inlet, and here the enemy had thrown up heavy earthworks to protect the most important smuggling route then in operation."[33]

Butler took credit for conceiving the plan to capture the forts, but the credit apparently belonged to U.S. Navy commodore Silas H. Stringham. Butler claimed that he, himself, described the planned operation to General Wool to get his approval, artfully neglecting to tell Wool how many men he intended to take from the fort's diminished garrison. "He was an officer in the regular army," Butler explained, "and I knew [he] would never attempt such an expedition without a great many men with him." He assured Wool, he said, that there would be no danger of a Confederate attack on Fort Monroe while the operation was being executed. He had sent up a tethered observation balloon, a recent innovation in warfare, more than a thousand feet to spy out the Confederate troop positions and learned that the force being assembled for an assault on Newport News had been withdrawn to Yorktown and Bethel. "This, by the way," he wrote in his autobiography, "was the first balloon reconnoissance [sic] of the war."[34]

Butler's claim of being the first to use balloon reconnaissance was accurate, although little else in his vainglorious account was. On August 13 General Scott ordered Wool to "prepare a sufficient detachment to accompany an expedition, under Commander [H.S.] Stellwagen, against some batteries on Hatteras Inlet, North Carolina."[35] Wool was to do so, according to the order, "after consultation with Commodore Stringham."[36] There was neither reason nor need for Butler to persuade Wool, since Wool already had his orders from the general in chief. And in the order he issued to execute Scott's order, Wool specified the number of troops to be used in the operation. Furthermore, in a message from Scott's headquarters on August 21 Wool was told "the expedition originated in the Navy Department, and is under its control."[37] Butler was a supporting player, not the star. On August 25, 1861, General Wool issued the order to commence the army's part of the operation:

> 1. Major-General Butler will prepare 860 troops for an expedition to Hatteras Inlet, North Carolina, to go with Commodore Stringham, commanding Home Squadron, to capture several batteries in that neighborhood. The troops will be as follows: 200 men from Camp Butler and 600 from Camp Hamilton, with a suitable number of commissioned officers, and one company (B) of the Second Artillery from Fort Monroe. They will be provided with 10 days' rations and water and 140 rounds of ammunition. General Butler will report as soon as he has his troops prepared to Flag Officer Stringham, and he will be ready to embark at 1 o'clock to-morrow. As soon as the object of the expedition is attained the detachment will return to Fort Monroe.
>
> 2. Captain Tallmadge, chief quartermaster, will provide a detachment of 860 men for the expedition to Hatteras Inlet, with a suitable quantity of water for 10 days' consumption, and the chief commissary of subsistence, Captain Taylor, will provide it with rations for the same length of time. These officers will report the execution of these orders by 10 o'clock to-morrow if possible.
>
> By command of Major-General Wool.[38]

Butler embarked his troops on two transport steamers, which, escorted by Stringham's squadron of six navy warships, plus a cutter of the U.S. Revenue Service and an army tugboat, steamed off on Monday, August 26, 1861, leaving about 1:00 p.m. The last ship of the expedition fleet arrived off Hatteras Inlet about 4:00 p.m. the next day, and there the vessels anchored to await daylight on August 28, when the first troops would be sent ashore in flatboats. Their landing would be covered by the guns of Stringham's fleet. The inlet was at the southwestern end of Hatteras Island, and the two forts stood on opposite shores of a shallow bay at the tip of the island, about half a mile apart, Fort Clark on the east and Fort Hatteras, the larger of the two, on the west. Together the two forts mounted twenty-five guns. The vessels of Stringham's fleet together mounted 158 guns, the USS *Wabash* alone carrying fifty guns.[39]

The attack on Confederate forts at Hatteras Inlet, North Carolina. Both were captured in a joint army-navy operation, and Butler quickly took credit for conceiving the plan, which had originated with the navy, and hurried to Washington, D.C., to tell Lincoln about his success (Library of Congress).

At 8:45 on the morning of August 28 the assault commenced. Braving the huge swells heaved up by gale-force winds, landing boats carried the first of Butler's troops to the beach about two miles north of Fort Clark. After some 315 men, including Marines from Stringham's fleet, were put ashore, the landing craft swamped in the heavy surf, and the steam tug, *Fanny*, grounded in an attempt to land more troops. Further landings then were called off while the wind continued to rise.

In the meantime, the fleet began bombarding Fort Clark using a tactic that put the vessels in continuous motion, one behind the other, moving in an ellipse, firing broadsides as they came abreast of the fortification and then circling seaward to reload and deliver another broadside as they passed again. "The people in the forts," Admiral Porter related, "were almost smothered by the fire from the frigates, and their aim made so uncertain that little damage was done to the ships. Shortly after noon the Confederate flags had disappeared from both forts, and the enemy were evidently abandoning Fort Clark, on which our troops moved up the beach and hoisted the Union flag on that work. Fort Hatteras still kept up the fire, and at night the squadron hauled off. At 7:30, on the morning of the 29th, the ships again opened on Fort Hatteras, and continued the fire with vigor until 11:10, when a white flag was displayed by the enemy."[40]

Aboard the refloated *Fanny*, Butler ordered an aide to go ashore and "demand the meaning of the white flag," as he put it. The commander of Confederate naval defenses of Virginia and North Carolina, Captain Samuel Barron, a former U.S. Navy officer, offered to surrender the fort with terms. Butler rejected that offer and in a written response demanded "full capitulation; the officers and men to be treated as prisoners of war. No other terms admissible. Commanding officers to meet on board the flag-ship *Minnesota* to arrange details."[41] Barron and two other Confederate officers—Colonel Martin, commander of the Seventh North Carolina Infantry Regiment, and Colonel Andrews, commander of forts Hatteras and Clark—came aboard the *Fanny* and met with Butler. Then they were taken aboard the *Minnesota* and at 2:30 p.m. on August 29 they surrendered to Commodore Stringham and General Butler. The Confederate troops of the two forts were then taken prisoner, disarmed and put aboard the *Minnesota*, bound for a prisoner-of-war camp, leaving both forts to be occupied by U.S. troops. Confederate losses in the engagement amounted to four killed, twenty wounded and 691 taken prisoner. U.S. casualties were one killed and two wounded.[42]

Admiral Porter pronounced it a victory of immense importance. "This was our first naval victory," he wrote in his naval history of the war, "indeed our first victory of any kind, and should not be forgotten. The Union cause was then in a depressed condition, owing to the reverses it had experienced. The moral effect of this affair was very great, as it gave us a foothold on Southern soil and possession of the Sounds of North Carolina, if we chose to occupy them. It was a death-blow to blockade running in that vicinity, and ultimately proved one of the most important events of the war."[43]

The Race for Recognition

General Butler was quick to claim credit and take advantage of the success. He hurried off to Washington to crow. "Reporting to General Wool, I got leave immediately to go to Washington," he wrote in his autobiography, "or, as he [Wool] expressed it, he sent me to Washington to report the matter."[44] In a race, apparently, to beat Stringham to Washington, Butler "immediately made requisition for a train to take myself and staff to Washington, and we started at eleven o'clock at night," as he reported it. When the train arrived in Washington, he made a dash for the White House. "Dropping a twenty-dollar gold piece in the hands of the [train's] engineer," he recounted, "I got off, woke a sleeping negro in a carriage, and told him to drive up to Postmaster-General Blair's house, opposite the White House, as fast as he could."[45]

When he reached Blair's house, he found Blair and Gustavus Fox, the assistant secretary of the navy and an old acquaintance from Lowell, sitting in Blair's study. "I went in," Butler reported in his account:

> Fox knew that I had gone on the expedition to Hatteras, for it was one in which he was much interested. When he saw me, he cried out: "Where from?"
> "Direct from Hatteras."
> "What news?"
> I stated the result of the expedition. He was very much elated, and asked me to go right over and tell the President about it.

Butler protested that the president would be sleeping and that he didn't want to wake him. "He will sleep enough better for it," Fox insisted, according to Butler, "so let us go and wake him up." They walked over to the White House, got the night watchman to let them in and made their way to the Cabinet Room. "The President was called," Butler reported, "and when our errand was hinted to him, he immediately came in in his night shirt." Butler described the scene that followed:

> Everybody knows how tall Lincoln was, and he seemed very much taller in that garment; and Fox was about five feet nothing. In a few hurried words, without waiting for any forms or ceremonies, Fox communicated the news, and then he and Lincoln fell into each other's arms. That is, Fox put his arms around Lincoln about as high as his hips, and Lincoln reached down over him so that his arms were pretty near the floor apparently, and thus holding each other they flew around the room once or twice, and the night shirt was considerably agitated. The commanding general was entirely overcome by the scene, and lying back on the sofa roared with the most irresistible merriment.[46]

In Butler's account, President Lincoln shook Butler's hand "very warmly" and when Butler tried to tell him what he had *not* done, Lincoln said, "You have done all right," and instructed him to come to the White House at 10 o'clock the next morning to make a report to the Cabinet. What Butler was referring to when he mentioned what he had not done was a mysterious—perhaps phantom—order that he claimed he had received and rejected:

> The wonderful stupidity at Washington, desired Hatteras Inlet stopped up, so that nothing could get into or out of it. So the fleet had supplied itself with two sand-laden schooners to sink in the inlet, where the sands floating around would have soon made dry land. When I came there I saw the importance not only of having the inlet open but of guarding and defending it. I had positive orders from Washington to sink the sand vessels. With my usual "hazardous bravado" I came to the conclusion to disobey orders and not sink the vessels. I could do that with some safety, I thought, provided I got to Washington and carried the news of the capture myself.[47]

Perhaps Butler did receive such an order, although a search of the *Official Records* concerning the Hatteras Inlet matter did not discover it. Furthermore, the orders to Butler from Wool dated August 25 specified that Butler's mission was to "capture several batteries," no mention being made of scuttling vessels to block the inlet. Wool's orders to Butler also seemed to make clear that Commodore Stringham was in charge of the operation. Stringham reportedly opposed stopping up the inlet (a recommendation made to Secretary Gideon Welles by a board considering how best to blockade Southern ports) from the outset of his mission and likely had decided early that the old ships the navy had acquired for that purpose would not be used. The decision was not only not Butler's to make but had already been made by the officer in charge. And even if the ships were to be scuttled, what would be the need for Butler's soldiers rather than Stringham's sailors to perform the task?

Most important in Butler's attempt to glorify himself, though, was the revelation—made in his own words—of his arrogance and willfulness. His I-know-best attitude and his belief that obedience to orders was optional for him would eventually end his military career, but for now his brashness was working for him. While the president was in such a buoyant mood, Butler decided to make a couple of requests. He asked for leave to go home to Lowell and he asked for authority to recruit troops in Massachusetts and elsewhere in New England. Both requests were granted. "You have a right to go home, general, for a little rest," Lincoln told him, according to Butler, "but study out another job for yourself."[48] Perhaps with that encouragement in mind, Butler then asked Secretary of War Cameron to give him a command of his own, a command comprising the men he would recruit. That request was also granted. He would become commander of the Department of New England, with a headquarters in Boston.

At this point Butler was completely satisfied with himself. "I had opened the way through Annapolis for the troops to save the capital," he wrote, congratulating himself. "I had fulfilled my mission at Fortress Monroe; and by taking Hatteras I had atoned for capturing Baltimore and wiped out Big Bethel, all in a campaign of four months and fifteen days, besides showing the administration and the country the best way out of the slavery question. In all this time nobody else had done anything except to get soundly thrashed at Bull Run."[49] His newly won fame preceded him to Lowell. "When I got to Lowell," he reported, "my friends and neighbors insisted upon showing me every honor and attention, which were accepted as tokens of personal friendship and regard.... But now persons whom I had known would halt on the sidewalk to see me pass; would get in my way to examine me and look me over (and this refers to both sexes).... I think I at last came to know what hero worship meant."[50]

Among those resisting any urge to worship Butler was the Massachusetts governor, John Andrew. The governor insisted Butler produce a written authorization to recruit in Massachusetts before he would recognize Butler's right to do so, and Butler couldn't come up with the authorization document Lincoln had signed. It somehow had been lost. Butler promptly sped to Washington to get a new authorization document. Secretary Cameron told him to write his own authorization, and Cameron would sign it. Never at a loss for words, lawyer Butler wrote out the enabling order, dated September 10, 1861, and Cameron signed it:

> Major-General B.F. Butler is hereby authorized to raise, organize, arm, uniform, and equip a volunteer force for the war, in the New England states; not exceeding six (6) regiments of the maximum standard, of such arms, and in such proportions, and in such manner as he may judge expedient; and for this purpose his orders and requisitions on the quartermaster, ordnance, and other staff departments of the army, are to be obeyed and answered; provided the cost of such recruitment, armament, and equipment does not exceed, in the aggregate, that of like troops, now or hereafter raised, for the service of the United States.[51]

Butler's recruiting began, competing in Massachusetts with recruitment campaigns being conducted not only by the state's own recruiting officer but also by Brigadier General William T. Sherman. Sherman's campaign made Butler's recruiting all the more objectionable to Governor Andrew and to the state's recruiting officer, Brigadier General W.W. Bullock, who issued a declaration that Butler's recruits would not be eligible for the financial benefits that his own recruits would receive. Butler countered that move by announcing that he would, from his own fortune, guarantee his recruits the same benefits as those received by the state's recruits.

Andrew's next move to thwart Butler was to refuse to honor Butler's requests for commissions for those whom he had appointed officers in his newly recruited regiments. Even an appeal by President Lincoln failed to gain Andrew's cooperation. Butler's influence in Washington finally resolved the matter in his favor. The army's adjutant general on January 16, 1862, declared that the commissions Butler sought were approved.

By then Washington had come up with a strategy that would put General Butler's new army to good use. The plan originally was for Butler to lead his troops on a campaign to capture the eastern shore of Virginia, but in November 1861 the navy's assistant secretary, Gustavus Fox, and (then) Commander David Dixon Porter hatched a plan to grab the Confederacy's major seaport, the city of New Orleans, gateway to and from the nation's vast midlands. On November 7 a U.S. fleet commanded by Captain Samuel DuPont had performed a feat thought impossible by much of the navy's brass. His seventeen wooden warships had steamed into Port Royal Sound in South Carolina and, as Commodore Stringham had done at Hatteras Inlet, had turned huge ellipses in single file and blasted the sound's two protective forts into submission and had captured Port Royal, which would become an important base for the Navy's Atlantic blockading squadron. Fox, a former navy officer, believed a similar feat could be achieved against the two forts guarding the lower Mississippi River—Fort St. Philip and Fort Jackson, protecting New Orleans from an attack coming up the river. Porter, who like Fox was familiar with the two forts, agreed.

Fox and Porter won Secretary Welles over to the plan to capture New Orleans by storming past the two forts, and the three men then sold it to President Lincoln. Porter described the plan: "A naval expedition was to be fitted out, composed of vessels mounting not fewer than two hundred guns, with a powerful mortar-flotilla, and with steam transports to keep the fleet supplied. The army was to furnish twenty thousand troops, not only for the purpose of occupying New Orleans after its capture, but to fortify and hold the heights above Vicksburg. The navy and army were to push on up the river as soon as New Orleans was occupied by our troops, and call upon the authorities of Vicksburg to surrender. Orders were to be issued to Flag-Officer Foote, who commanded the ironclad fleet on the upper Mississippi, to join the fleet above Vicksburg with his vessels and mortar-boats."[52] It was going to be an immense and immensely important expedition. Once it had passed the forts, the powerful fleet bearing more than two hundred guns would stand in the river at the New Orleans waterfront, poised to pound the city into ruins, and New Orleans would have no choice but to surrender. The city would then be occupied by the U.S. troops carried aboard the fleet's transports.

To include the troops in the expedition required bringing into the loop the army's new general in chief, Major General George B. McClellan, whom Lincoln had appointed on November 1 following General Scott's resignation on October 31. Upon being briefed, McClellan expressed doubts about the navy's wooden-hulled ships being able to survive the guns of Forts Jackson and St. Philip, but he acquiesced after navy secretary Welles huffily told him that the ships were the navy's concern and that the army was being asked only to provide troops for the occupation of New Orleans. To command the expedition, Welles, Fox and Porter settled on sixty-year-old Captain David Glasgow Farragut, who had begun his naval career at age nine as an acting midshipman and had been informally adopted by Porter's father, also named David Porter and also a career navy officer and who commanded the ship aboard which young Farragut had served.

McClellan decided to turn the occupation task over to Butler's recent recruits, whom Butler had been training. Butler, however, was not to be told the objective of the mission yet. It was to be kept secret for the time being, and Butler was led to believe his objective would be Mobile or Texas. After the first batch of Butler's troops, under the command of Brigadier General John W. Phelps, arrived at the expedition's marshaling point on Ship Island on December 3, 1861, McClellan had new thoughts about the use of Butler's army and fired off a telegram to Butler, ordering him not to send a second batch of troops, 2,200 men who were already embarked on a transport at Boston, ready to leave for Fort Monroe. "Don't sail," the telegram commanded, "disembark the troops."[53] Never one to readily accept orders to which he objected, Butler quickly set out for Washington to find out what was going on and to have the order countermanded. What he discovered in Washington was that a new crisis had arisen.

A U.S. Navy blockading ship, the USS *San Jacinto*, on November 8 had stopped a British mail packet, the RMS *Trent*, which, along with the mail, was carrying two Confederate emissaries, James Mason and John Slidell, on a mission to seek diplomatic recognition of the Confederate States of America by England and France. The *San Jacinto*'s boarding party seized Mason and Slidell as contraband of war and took them aboard the *San Jacinto*. Soon after the *San Jacinto* arrived in Hampton Roads on November 15, news of the Confederates' seizure was published in newspapers and spread abroad, setting off an international *cause célèbre*, to the extent that some in Washington feared a war with England, in which case Butler's troops would be needed somewhere other than Ship Island, Mississippi.

The *Trent* Affair, as it became known, was settled several weeks later when President Lincoln disavowed Captain Wilkes's action and released Mason and Slidell from the prison in Boston where they were being held. The two Confederates were taken aboard a British navy vessel and carried to St. Thomas in the Virgin Islands, where on January 14, 1862, they boarded a British mail packet and sailed off to Southampton to resume their quest for diplomatic recognition of the Confederacy—which in the end proved fruitless

As the *Trent* Affair crisis waned, Butler, on January 1, 1862, loaded the waiting 2,200 troops onto a transport at Boston and sent them to Fort Monroe, whence they would move to Ship Island, first needing, however, an order from McClellan to continue the journey to the island. Weeks passed without the order being issued. Impatient with the delay, Butler again went to Washington to see—and fix—whatever was wrong. The problem, he discovered, was McClellan. "I found," Butler reported, "that General McClellan was very much averse to having the number of men I needed taken away from the army around Washington."[54]

McClellan had the idea that there were more than 200,000 Confederate troops, perhaps as many as 270,000, opposing the Union forces around Washington, which, according to Butler, amounted to 190,000 men. "He [McClellan] very much wanted two hundred thousand men there," Butler claimed.[55] Butler's estimate was that the Confederates had no more than 65,000 effective troops opposite Washington, dramatically fewer than the numbers McClellan feared.[56] McClellan had already been ordered to move against the Confederate force but had ignored the order, apparently hoping to collect more troops before taking on the enemy.

While Butler waited for McClellan to authorize sending the 2,200 waiting troops to Ship Island, he became a frequent visitor to Washington, talking to the president—who, Butler claimed, was always willing to listen to him—talking to McClellan, talking to members of Lincoln's cabinet, particularly the new secretary of war, Edwin Stanton, who was a fellow Democrat and an old friend of Butler. Around the middle of January Butler was in a long conference with Stanton. Near the end of their discussion, Stanton, apparently having heard arguments against the New Orleans expedition, asked Butler, "Why can't New Orleans be taken?" Butler replied, "It can!" That was the first time New Orleans as the objective had been mentioned in Butler's presence.[57] Stanton then asked Butler to draw up a plan for the capture of the city. About that same time, Stanton asked McClellan for his opinion on the New Orleans expedition. McClellan reported that a force of 50,000 troops would be required and that no such force was available for that purpose.[58]

Butler, on the other hand, was enthusiastic about such an expedition, with himself at the head of it. He proposed to execute the mission with a force of 15,000. He already had under his command 12,700 men—2,000 at Ship Island, 2,200 at Fort Monroe and 8,500 in New England awaiting orders to embark. The remainder of a 15,000-man army could come from regiments posted at Baltimore.[59]

Anticipating approval of the New Orleans expedition, Butler returned to Boston in late January to oversee the embarkation of the 8,500 troops awaiting orders to board transports.[60] In the third week of February he was back in Washington, where he learned that McClellan had issued an order for Butler's troops to be disembarked at Fort Monroe and then moved to Baltimore.[61] "I determined to bring the matter to a focus at once," Butler related:

> I went to General McClellan and told him about the order and asked him to revoke it.
> "Why are you so anxious about this expedition?" he said to me.
> "Because I think I can do a great deal of good for the country. Besides, I want to get away from Washington. I am sick of the intrigues and cross purposes that I find here. Mr. Lincoln and Mr. Stanton seem to me to be about the only persons who are in dead earnest for a vigorous prosecution of the war" [Butler said he told McClellan].[62]

He also told McClellan that he had an appointment to discuss the matter with the president on the day after next, the next day being February 22, the George Washington's birthday holiday. "I looked General McClellan in the eye," Butler related, "and said, 'General, shall I call on you before or after I call on the President?'"[63] McClellan understood the threat. "Better come before," he replied.

On the morning of February 23 Butler took a carriage and drove to army headquarters, arriving shortly after ten o'clock. "I was admitted to the general's [McClellan] presence, and he met me very cordially, and handed me a sealed envelope," Butler reported. "Therein," McClellan told Butler as he handed him the envelope, "you will find your instructions about your expedition to New Orleans, and you may go as soon as you can get ready to do so."[64] By stubborn persistence and the force of his personality, Butler had got his way.

From McClellan's office Butler walked to Secretary Stanton's office and found President Lincoln conferring with Stanton there. "I stated to them the facts," Butler reported. "Mr. Stanton was overjoyed. The President did not appear at all elated, but shook hands with me with a far-off, pensive look." (Lincoln's twelve-year-old son, Willie, had died of typhoid fever three days earlier.) Butler let them know he was eager to get started and have his troops ship out. "To be honest with you," he told Stanton, explaining his eagerness, "my orders cannot be countermanded after I get to sea, for I am going to take New Orleans or you will never see me again." In reply, Stanton told him (according to Butler's account), "Well, you take New Orleans and you shall be lieutenant-general." At that, Butler bowed and left.[65]

Butler taking his army to play its role in the plan to capture New Orleans was not regarded as entirely bad news for McClellan. McClellan's chief of staff, Brigadier General Randolph Marcy, whose daughter Ellen Mary was McClellan's wife, was reported to have remarked, following Butler's departure, "I guess we have found a hole to bury this Yankee elephant in."[66]

The New Orleans Mission

Butler left Washington on the night of February 24. On the evening of Tuesday, February 25, he stood with his wife, Sarah, on the deck of the steamer *Mississippi*, his staff officers beside him and 1,600 troops quartered aboard, and, as he said, gave the order to "up anchor for Ship Island." The orders McClellan had handed him in that sealed envelope were dated February 23 and read:

> General: You are assigned to the command of the land forces destined to co-operate with the navy in the attack upon New Orleans. You will use every means to keep the destination a profound secret, even from your staff officers, with the exception of your chief of staff, and Lieutenant Weitzel, of the engineers.
>
> The force at your disposal will consist of the first thirteen regiments named in your memorandum handed to me in person.... The cavalry force already *en route* for Ship Island, will be sufficient for your purposes. After full consultation with officers well acquainted with the country in which it is proposed to operate, I have arrived at the conclusion that three light batteries fully equipped and one without horses, will be all that will be necessary.
>
> This will make your force about 14,400 infantry, 275 cavalry, 580 artillery, total 15,255 men....
>
> The object of your expedition is one of vital importance—the capture of New Orleans. The route selected is up the Mississippi river, and the first obstacle to be encountered, perhaps the only one, is in the resistance offered by Forts St. Philip and Jackson. It is expected that the navy can reduce the works; in that case, you will, after their capture, leave a sufficient garrison in them to render them perfectly secure....
>
> Should the navy fail to reduce the works, you will land your forces and siege train, and endeavor to breach the works, silence their fire, and carry them by assault.... If these works are taken, the city of New Orleans necessarily falls.
>
> In that event it will probably be best to occupy Algiers [directly across the river from New Orleans] with the mass of your troops, also the eastern bank of the river above the city—it may be necessary to place some troops *in* the city to preserve order; though if there appears sufficient Union sentiment to control the city, it may be best for purposes of discipline to keep your men out of the city.
>
> After obtaining possession of New Orleans, it will be necessary to reduce all the works guarding its approaches from the east, and particularly to gain Manchac Pass.
>
> Baton Rouge, Berwick Bay, and Fort Livingston will next claim your attention....
>
> Allow nothing to divert you from obtaining full possession of *all* the approaches to New Orleans. When that object is accomplished to its fullest extent, it will be necessary to make a combined attack on Mobile, in order to gain possession of the harbor and works, as well as to control the railway terminus at the city.... [I]n the mean time you will please give all the assistance in your power to the army and navy commanders in your vicinity, never losing sight of the fact that the great object to be achieved is the capture and firm retention of New Orleans.
>
> Very respectfully, your obedient servant,
GEORGE B. MCCLELLAN,
Major-General Commanding, &c., &c.[67]

After narrowly escaping disaster when the transport steamer *Mississippi* ran aground off the North Carolina coast and suffered a puncture in its hull below the waterline, Butler and his entourage and the troops on board with him arrived within sight of Ship Island on March 20, 1862. Butler's nineteenth-century biographer, James Parton, described the setting: "A gale was blowing as the ship steamed into the harbor, and huge waves were seen rolling up, apparently among the tents [of General Phelps' 2,000 troops, encamped there since early December], and no man could tell which was water and which was land. For two days and more the gale continued, and the men, unable to land, looked out upon the island dolefully."[68]

Finally, on March 25, a month after the transport had left Fort Monroe, the troops were able to disembark and go ashore.

Butler remembered the following in his autobiography:

> Ship Island is an island of white sand thrown up by the winds and waves. It is between five and six miles long, and is about ten miles distant from the Mississippi coast. At the upper part of it [the eastern end] there is some soil on which is a growth of pine which serves at once for the fuel and for the timber required. This eastern end of the island rises to some considerable height above the waters of the Gulf. The western end is more flat and rises only a little above the sea, in places less than two feet, and in case of any considerable sea, the waves wash over it. It was [in] 1845, if I recollect aright, a place of seaside resort for the people of New Orleans, many of whom had built cottages there and occupied them, when a storm, accompanied by rain and lightning, drove the water over the island and washed off substantially all the inhabitants.
>
> The United States, at the breaking out of the war, had partly finished a fort upon the island called Fort Massachusetts. At the time of the arrival of my troops, there was not a house on the island. We brought some section houses to be put up for hospital purposes and to cover stores and supplies, but we relied for shelter upon our tents.[69]

Farragut had sailed from Hampton Roads in his flagship, USS *Hartford*, on February 2 and reached Ship Island on February 20. As Farragut's fleet arrived, Butler, growing anxious to move his troops out, asked Farragut how soon he could be ready to launch the assault on the forts. Farragut replied that he would sail at once for the mouth of the Mississippi and he thought he could be ready to commence the advance up the river in seven days. His estimate proved overly optimistic. In the first place, he discovered that his ships, equipped with both steam engines and sails but relying on steam power to make their way up the river, were running short of coal and had no new supply from which to draw.

Butler had a solution for that problem. Instead of ballasting his transports with stones, the usual ballast, he had ballasted them with anthracite coal: "I saw that anthracite coal was steadily rising in the market when our equipment was forwarded from Boston, and I assumed that if I ballasted all my ships with anthracite coal, the coal would be worth more when it got back to Boston after having gone down to Ship Island, than it was when I put it on board, and so something very considerable might be saved to the government."[70] He told Farragut that he had between 2,500 and 3,000 tons of anthracite and would lend it to him. Overjoyed by that news, Farragut told Butler, "Why, this is almost providential." "Yes," Butler told him. "I provided it." Farragut next had a question about the propriety of taking the coal. "But how can you in the Army let the Navy have the coal? Your Army regulations are against it, are they not?" Butler gave a revealing answer. "I never read the Army regulations," he said, "and what is more, I shan't, and then I shall not know I am doing anything against them."[71]

The next problem, insoluble by the resourceful general, was getting Farragut's big warships over the bars at the mouths of the Mississippi River. With great difficulty and the strenuous exertions of men and towboats, the assembled fleet at last crept over the bar at Southwest Pass, one by one, except for the USS *Colorado*, the mammoth frigate that drew twenty-three feet of water. It was sent back to Ship Island because it became obvious it would never make it across the mud at any of the passes that gave access to the river. Some of the *Colorado*'s guns were removed and distributed among the other vessels. The USS *Mississippi* and USS *Pensacola*, two other deep-draft warships, also returned to Ship Island, where they were lightened by removing whatever weight could be spared. They then rejoined the fleet.

All of that took time. It was not until April 7 that Farragut had his fleet together and across the bar. More days were then consumed with gaining intelligence on the obstructions the Confederates had placed in the river and mapping the river near the forts and planting markers to indicate where Porter's mortar boats should be anchored to bombard the forts. By April 16, Farragut, Porter and the fleet were at last ready to commence their assault.

On the morning of Friday, April 18, Porter gave the order to commence firing, each mortar boat being instructed to fire once every ten minutes. During the night the firing slackened, a shell being fired only once every thirty minutes. The bombardment by Porter's mortars went on for six days, which Butler considered mostly a waste of time. "The first day's bombardment," he recounted, "set fire to the wooden barracks and officers' quarters, which burned all night. Porter ceased firing while the burning was going on, supposing that the fort would be destroyed. But that fire had the same effect as when the enemy fired on Fort Sumter and set fire to the same class of buildings. They supposed that Sumter must surrender on account of that fire. But that fire, and this one, too, only cleared the fort of obstructions and obstacles."[72]

The forts' commander, Confederate brigadier general Johnson K. Duncan, reported the damage to his commander after the first night's bombardment, confirming Butler's assessment, but with some exaggeration: "Heavy and continued bombardment all night and still progressing. No further casualties except two men slightly wounded. God is certainly protecting us. We are still cheerful, and have an abiding faith in our ultimate success. We are making repairs as best we can. Our barbette guns are still in working order.... Twenty-five thousand thirteen-inch shells have been fired by the enemy, one thousand of which fell in the fort. They must soon exhaust themselves; if not, we can stand it as long as they can."[73]

Referring to General Duncan's report, Butler took the occasion not only to point out the exaggeration but also to again denigrate West Point-trained officers. "Not twenty-five thousand shells were thrown altogether," Butler contended, "but five thousand only. Not one thousand struck inside the fort, but only three hundred during the whole bombardment.... Duncan's report reads exactly like some of the magazine war articles written by our officers who wish to establish reputations for bravery and endurance, but are somewhat economical of truth. As Duncan was educated at West Point he was taught in the same way as were these officers who write magazine articles and war books."[74]

After managing to sever the chain barrier that the Confederates had stretched across the width of the river and dodging blazing fire rafts meant to set Farragut's wooden vessels alight, the fleet got under way about 2:00 a.m. on Thursday, April 24. Two red lights hoisted high atop the *Hartford*'s mast signaled the thirteen other ships as they waited in the darkness, ready to haul up their anchors and steam ahead. The vessels would be moving no faster than four miles an hour against the Mississippi's three-and-a-half knot current. From where the ships would start it was about two miles to the forts, where they would be under the forts' guns for a mile, and it would be another two miles before the ships were out of range of those guns, a total distance of five miles and a time of more than an hour to reach success and safety.

The arrangement of the fleet put seven ships comprising the first division in single file on the east side of the river, nearest Fort St. Philip, five ships comprising the third division in single file on the west side of the river, nearest Fort Jackson, and three ships, including Farragut's flagship, USS *Hartford*, in the middle of the river. As the vessels steamed ahead, the mortar boats were to move forward from their position two miles below Fort Jackson and pound the heavy guns of Fort Jackson's water battery, considered the most dangerous of the Confederate guns, while the fleet of warships attempted to get past the forts.

About 3:00 a.m., when the moon had lightened the sky and spread a dim glow on the river, the forts' guns opened fire, the gun crews aiming at the shadowy shapes moving slowly toward them. The first division advanced for nearly a mile under the rebel barrages and suffered considerable damage while returning fire as its guns came to bear on Fort St. Philip, finally blasting the fort with broadsides of grape and canister shot. Meanwhile, Porter's mortars opened fire on Fort Jackson, the bombardment so intense that no fewer than five of their huge shells were in the air at the same time, sometimes as many as eleven. Commander (later Admiral) Porter described the scene:

> No grander or more beautiful sight could have been realized than the scenes of that night. From silence, disturbed now and then only by the slow fire of the mortars—the phantom-like movements of the vessels giving no sound—an increased roar of heavy guns began, while the mortars burst forth into rapid bombardment, as the fleet drew nearer the enemy's works. Vessel after vessel added her guns to those already at work, until the very earth seemed to shake from their reverberations. A burning raft adding its lurid glare to the scene, and the fiery tracks of the mortar-shells as they passed through the darkness aloft, and sometimes burst in mid-air, gave the impression that heaven itself had joined in the general strife.[75]

An hour and ten minutes after Farragut's vessels had weighed anchor to storm their way up the river, all guns fell silent. The gallantly defiant fleet had passed the forbidding forts, had destroyed or chased off the defending Confederate gunboats and rams and had lost but one ship in the process. Now it was steaming toward the grand prize, the storied city of New Orleans.

Two days after Porter had begun the mortar bombardment, Butler's transports were standing in the river with 6,000 troops aboard, ready to move against the forts and attempt to capture them. Additional troops were aboard another steamer, the *Great Republic*, which was too large and heavy to get over the bar.[76] As they waited to proceed with their part of the mission, they knew nothing of how Farragut's fleet was faring. "But as the sun rose up in the heavens in the clear calm of a beautiful April morning [April 24]," Butler reported, "Farragut flashed back the signal of his triumph and victory by covering his entire fleet with flags and signals, as in the celebrations of a gala day. That told the story."[77]

From the transports Butler's troops were ferried in yawls up a canal as far as the vessels could go. They then got out of the boats and, according to Butler's account, waded for miles to reach Fort St. Philip, on the east bank, and attack it from the rear, which was unprotected. "To get there," Butler wrote, "I myself waded in the water above my hips for nearly two miles—which was not unsafe but unpleasant."[78] A detachment of Butler's force, having reached the vicinity of Fort St. Philip, was then taken aboard the USS *Mississippi*, which Farragut had posted to keep its guns trained on the forts, and carried to the west side of the river, which landed the troops several miles above Fort Jackson, where they entrenched, preparatory to attacking the fort.

Not waiting for the army, Commander Porter, whom Farragut left to command the forts, on April 25 sent Lieutenant Commander John Guest aboard one of the gunboats to Fort Jackson under a flag of truce to seek surrender of the forts. Confederate General Duncan, commanding the two forts, refused to surrender before hearing from authorities in New Orleans. Upon receiving Guest's report of Duncan's refusal, Porter ordered his mortar crews to renew the bombardment of Fort Jackson. "The effect was such as to cause a mutiny among the garrison," Porter related, "who refused to longer undergo the probability of useless slaughter, and many deserted from the works and retreated up river out of range. The remainder refused to fight the guns, and reasoned that they had unflinchingly borne the terrible six days' bombardment, and had exposed themselves to the night ordeal of the fire of the passing fleet, it was time the fort should be surrendered without further loss of life."[79] "On April 27," Butler related, "the majority of the garrison of Fort Jackson mutinied against their officers, either spiked the field-pieces or turned them against their officers, and deserted and came up five miles and surrendered themselves to my pickets. The day afterwards the officers surrendered the forts, having substantially no garrison, to Captain Porter."[80] As soon as the forts surrendered, Butler ordered General Phelps to move the troops into the forts and take possession of them. Butler then boarded the USS *Wissahickon*, which was posted at the quarantine station above Fort Jackson, and was taken to New Orleans to confer with Farragut.

Farragut had run into problems at New Orleans. Having moored his ships in the river in front of the city, Farragut on the afternoon of April 25 had sent two of his officers, Captain Theodorus Bailey and Lieutenant George Perkins, ashore in a rowboat to demand the surrender of the city. They were met on the wharf by a taunting, threatening mob and on the way to city hall, some ten blocks distant, they were assailed with shouts of "Hang them! Hang them!" as well as objects thrown at them. At city hall the mayor, John T. Monroe, surrounded by other city officials, responded to Farragut's demand for surrender by telling Bailey and Perkins, "I am not the military commander of the city. I have no authority to surrender it and would not do so if I had. There is a military commander now in the city. I will send for him to receive and reply to your demand."[81]

The military commander was Confederate major general Mansfield Lovell, a former U.S. Army officer who, as New Orleans was under Confederate martial law, was in nominal charge of the city. His 2,800 troops, however, along with a few thousand militiamen, had fled the city after learning that the U.S. fleet had passed the forts. When he arrived at city hall, Lovell introduced himself and told Bailey and Perkins that he would not surrender the city. Neither would he allow it to be surrendered. He said he was overpowered by a superior naval force, but that his army would continue to fight on land. He said he had withdrawn his troops from New Orleans to prevent the city from being bombarded by the U.S. fleet, despite pleas from women of the city for him and his troops to stay and fight. He said that if Flag Officer Farragut decided to bombard the city, despite the large number of women and children within it, there was nothing to stop him. He concluded by saying that he intended to leave New Orleans and allow city officials to do whatever they thought proper.

The mayor then told Bailey and Perkins that he would discuss with city council members what should be done next and that he would report the council's decision to Flag Officer Farragut. Bailey and Perkins then decided to return to the *Hartford* and report the situation to Farragut. By then the mob outside city hall had grown so large and threatening that Lovell instructed two of his officers to accompany Bailey and Perkins to the waterfront. They were led out of the rear entrance of city hall, ushered into a waiting carriage and hurriedly driven back to the wharf, where the crewmen of their small boat were silently and anxiously enduring the harassment of a new mob. Bailey and Perkins were speedily rowed back to Farragut's flagship, where they gave their report.

Around six-thirty the next morning, Saturday, April 26, Mayor Monroe's secretary and the New Orleans chief of police came up to the *Hartford* in a small boat and informed Farragut that the city council would meet at ten o'clock that morning to determine what the city's response to Farragut's demands would be and that the decision would be promptly delivered to Farragut. In response to that message, Farragut wrote a message of his own to the mayor: "I, therefore, demand of you, as its representative, the unqualified surrender of the city, and that the emblem of the sovereignty of the United States be hoisted over the City Hall, Mint and Custom-House, by meridian of this day, and all flags and other emblems of sovereignty other than that of the United States be removed from all the public buildings by that hour."[82]

On Sunday morning, April 27, Farragut received Mayor Monroe's promised reply to Farragut's demands:

> I am no military man, and possess no authority beyond that of executing the municipal laws of the city of New Orleans. It would be presumptuous in me to attempt to lead an army in the field, if I had one at command; and I know still less how to surrender an undefended place, held, as this is, at the mercy of your gunners and your mortars. To surrender such a place were an idle and unmeaning ceremony. The city is yours by the power of brutal force, not by my choice or the consent of its inhabitants. It is for you to determine what will be the fate that awaits us here.
>
> As to hoisting any flag not of our own adoption and allegiance, let me say to you that the man lives not in our midst whose hand and heart would not be paralyzed at the mere thought of such an act; not could I find in my entire constituency so desperate and wretched a renegade as would dare to profane with his hand the sacred emblem of our aspirations.[83]

Realizing that if the United States flag was going to be raised on any buildings in New Orleans, his men would have to be the ones to raise it, Farragut sometime before eight o'clock Sunday morning ordered the captain of the USS *Pensacola*, moored off Esplanade Avenue, at the edge of the French Quarter within sight of the U.S. mint that been seized by the Confederates, to send a party ashore and hoist the Stars and Stripes atop the building. By eight o'clock that mission was accomplished.

Desecration of the U.S. Flag

Shortly after eleven o'clock, while worship services were being held on the deck of the *Pensacola*, the ship's crew, alerted by a lookout atop the main mast, looked toward the mint, which had been left unguarded, and saw four men on the roof of the building. The men

U.S. mint at New Orleans. It was here that a rebel civilian, William Mumford, hauled down the U.S. flag that Admiral Farragut had ordered raised atop the building following the city's capture by a U.S. naval fleet in April 1862. Mumford then dragged the flag through the muddy streets and finally ripped it to shreds in an act of defiance. Butler, commanding the occupation troops in New Orleans, had Mumford arrested and hanged in front of the mint while a crowd watched (Library of Congress).

pulled down the U.S. flag, grabbed it and hurried off with it. They then dragged the flag through the muddy streets as a crowd cheered them on. They paraded it to the accompaniment of a fife and drum and finally tore it to shreds and handed out the pieces to people in the crowd. For what they did they were praised as heroes in the New Orleans newspapers. The *Picayune* discovered their names and in its Monday morning edition rewarded them with an editorial tribute: "The names of the party that distinguished themselves by gallantly tearing down the flag that had been surreptitiously hoisted, we learn, are W.B. Mumford, who cut it loose from the flag-staff amid the shower of grape, Lieutenant N. Holmes, Sergeant Burns and James Reed. They deserve great credit for their patriotic act."[84] The editorial writer had not got all the facts straight, there having been no "shower of grape," the *Pensacola*'s guns then being temporarily incapable of firing.[85] But he had the name of the group's ringleader right. And that would prove important.

With feelings of both exasperation and desperation Farragut decided to threaten the city with bombardment and to order that women and children be evacuated from the city. He penned a note to Mayor Monroe warning him against anymore incidents such as the tearing down of the U.S. flag. "The fire of this fleet may be drawn upon the city at any moment," he wrote, "and in such an event the levee would ... in all probability, be cut by the shell, and an amount of distress ensue to the innocent population which I have heretofore endeavored to assure you that I desired by all means to avoid. The election ... is with you, but it becomes my duty to notify you to remove the women and children from the city within forty-eight hours, if I have rightly understood your determination."[86]

The note was delivered to the mayor the next day by two of Farragut's officers, who suffered from the mob in the streets the same harassments that Farragut's earlier emissaries had endured. Like the others, they escaped through the rear entrance of city hall and were swiftly driven to the waterfront. The city council, being apprised of Farragut's threatening letter and evacuation order, authorized Pierre Soule, a former U.S. senator from Louisiana and a secessionist firebrand, to write a reply to Farragut, to be signed by the mayor:

> Sir, you can not but know that there is no possible exit from this city for a population which still exceeds 140,000 and you must therefore be aware of the utter inanity of such a notification. Our women and children can not escape your shells if it be your pleasure to murder them on a question of mere etiquette; but if they could, there are but few among them that would consent to desert their families and their homes and the graves of their relations in so awful a moment....
>
> You are not satisfied with peaceable possession of an undefended city, opposing no resistance to your guns, because of its bearing its doom with something of manliness and dignity; and you wish to humble and disgrace us by an act against which our nature rebels. This satisfaction you can not expect to obtain at our hands.
>
> We will stand your bombardment, unarmed and undefended as we are. The civilized world will consign to indelible infamy the heart that will conceive the deed and the hand that will dare to consummate it.[87]

Soule and the mayor's secretary delivered the letter to Farragut early the next morning, Tuesday, April 29. Soule tried to take the occasion to lecture Farragut on international law, but Farragut turned him away by telling him that he, Farragut, was just a sailor trying to do his duty as commander of a navy fleet and he had no knowledge of the fine points of the law. The meeting ended shortly after that.

About eleven o'clock that morning Farragut sent a force of a hundred of his Marines ashore with two howitzers. While a crowd gathered to watch, the Marines marched up Canal Street to the custom house, three blocks from the river, raised the U.S. flag above the front of the building and posted a detail to guard the building. The Marines, under the command of Navy captain Henry H. Bell, Farragut's chief of staff, then marched through the crowd two blocks to St. Charles Street, where it turned a column left and proceeded up St. Charles Street to Lafayette Square, opposite city hall. There Bell formed the Marines into two lines and positioned the two menacing howitzers to command the street below and above city hall, keeping the crowd at a distance. Leading a small detail, Bell then entered city hall, confronted the mayor and told him that he, Bell, had come to haul down the state flag from the building, to which the mayor submitted. At 12:45 p.m. the flag of Louisiana came down, but no U.S. flag replaced it. The Marines then were ordered to form a column and were marched, with the two artillery pieces, back to the riverfront, where they boarded small boats and returned to the waiting ships. The Marine guard at the custom house also withdrew to their ship, leaving the custom house locked behind them.

U.S. custom house on Canal Street in New Orleans, which was occupied by Butler's troops as their base of operations (Library of Congress).

General Butler, meanwhile, on his way to New Orleans to talk to Farragut about the next move to be made, had learned about Mumford and his comrades cutting down the U.S. flag from the mint and dragging it through the mud before ripping it to pieces. Butler read an account in a New Orleans newspaper that was brought aboard the *Wissahickon* as it neared the city. Having read it, he handed the paper to one of his officers and told him, "I will hang that fellow whenever I catch him."[88] Butler reached New Orleans on Monday, April 28, and conferred with Farragut, who briefed him on the events of the past three days, giving Butler an idea of the problems he would be facing.[89] Having no troops then to move into the city, Butler returned down the river. On April 30 he boarded the transport *Mississippi*, which, with other transports, was taking his wife and 1,400 of his troops to New Orleans.[90]

At noon on Thursday, May 1, the *Mississippi* tied up at a wharf in New Orleans. Butler met again with Farragut and told him that he was about to disembark his troops, whereupon Farragut sent a message to Mayor Monroe notifying him that the U.S. troops under the command of General Butler were being landed and he, Farragut, would have no further communication with the authorities of New Orleans. He told Monroe that General Butler would now be in charge. When Butler's conference with Farragut ended, Butler returned to the *Mississippi* and immediately began disembarking his troops. It was then nearly 4:00 p.m.

First ashore was a company of the Thirty-first Massachusetts Infantry Regiment, the men making their way onto the timbered platform of the wharf. They quickly formed a tight line and at bayonet point forced back the taunting crowd to make room for the rest of the troops to come off the ship. When the rest of the Thirty-first had come ashore and marched from the wharf to the levee, the Fourth Wisconsin Infantry Regiment disembarked and joined the Thirty-first to form a long column and then marched off. Leading the procession was Lieutenant Henry Weigel, Butler's engineering aide, who was familiar with the streets of New Orleans. Behind Weigel came the drum corps of the Thirty-first, followed by Butler and his staff, who were flanked by a file of troops of the Thirty-first on each side as they marched. Then came a battery of artillery, then the Fourth Wisconsin's regimental band, then Brigadier General Thomas Williams, the brigade commander, and his staff, followed by the men of the Fourth Wisconsin.

Butler had issued strict orders to his troops. They were to march in silence, ignoring the shouted taunts and threats from the crowd. If they were fired on from a house, they were to halt, arrest those inside the house and destroy the house. If they were fired on from the crowd, they were to arrest the person who had fired, if possible. They were not to fire into the crowd unless absolutely necessary to defend themselves and were to wait for an order to do so.[91]

At five o'clock the band blared out "The Star-Spangled Banner," and the long column of blue-uniformed soldiers moved out, members of the crowd yelling at them, shouting at them to go home, screaming cheers for their hometown hero, Major General P.G.T. Beauregard. All along the street the crowd surged and pushed to see the marchers and to spot Butler if they could, shouting out, "Where is he?" and then when they saw him, "There he goes! God damn him!" Butler, showing no sign of being affected by the crowd, seemed more concerned with trying to stay in step with the band.

From the wharf where they had come ashore the marchers proceeded along the levee to Poydras Street, turned up Poydras and continued on to St. Charles Street, where they made a column right and marched down St. Charles five blocks to Canal Street, turned right and headed for the custom house, which they quickly reached and surrounded. The door of the massive stone building had to be forced open, since Captain Bell, Farragut's chief of staff, had locked it and kept the key. By 6:00 p.m. the building was occupied by the men of the Thirty-first Massachusetts, who, after posting guards around the building, turned the second floor into a barracks. Butler and his staff then returned to the *Mississippi* to spend the night. Keeping watch over that vessel and the rest of the moored fleet was the Twelfth Connecticut, its men bivouacked on the levee under the stars on a warm May evening. The crowd melted away, and the city became, as Butler's earliest biographer put it, "as still as a country hamlet."[92]

At dawn the next day, Friday, May 2, the landing and distribution of the troops were resumed. The Twelfth Connecticut was moved to Lafayette Square, in front of city hall. Other regiments were posted around the downtown area. One was sent across the river to occupy Algiers and to seize the railroad station and trains there. General Phelps made a reconnaissance of the outskirts of the city and selected a site for a camp. Butler drew up a lengthy proclamation to be printed and distributed as handbills, but ran into difficulty when the owner of the newspaper Butler had chosen to print the proclamation, the *True Delta*, refused to do so. The officers whom Butler had sent to have the proclamation printed told the newspaper's owner they would seize the newspaper's office and use the *True Delta*'s equipment to set the type and print copies of the proclamation. "I cannot resist the seizure of the office," the owner told them, "but under no circumstances shall it be used for the purpose designated with my approval or consent."

The officers bowed politely and left. Two hours later they returned. With them came a detail of armed soldiers who marched up to the newspaper building and stood in formation in front of it. Six of them then entered the building, brushed aside the owner's objections and went about the task of setting type and printing several copies of the proclamation. In the next day's edition the owner told of the seizure and grandly stated, "We will promise this much, and we will perform it, namely, to suspend our publication, even if our last crust be sacrificed by the act, rather than molt one feather of that independence which, in the presence of every discouragement and danger, we have ever made our honest boast."[93] Butler promptly responded to the owner's editorial bravado by shutting down the paper, "suspending" it until further notice. Even more promptly the owner reversed himself and promised to honor General Butler's requisition for the use of the *True Delta*'s facilities. Butler gave him permission to resume publication the next day, and the *True Delta* published Butler's proclamation.

More resistance came on the morning of May 2 when Butler decided to make his headquarters at the posh St. Charles Hotel, where Confederate general Lovell had established his headquarters but which had been closed since Lovell and his troops left town. Butler dispatched a party of his officers to make the arrangements. When they arrived at the hotel and spoke with the son of one of the hotel's owners, he told them the owners were unavailable and that he couldn't turn over the hotel to General Butler without being shot by the hostile crowd. Furthermore, he said, the waiters would not wait on the Union officers, the cooks would not cook for them, and the porters would not carry for them. Major George Strong of Butler's staff replied that the owner's son need not worry about giving the hotel over to the U.S. Army, that they would simply take it. Food would not be a problem either, for they could continue to maintain themselves on Army provisions and what was more, they didn't need waiters; they were soldiers and could wait on themselves. And so Butler's army took over the St. Charles without a fight. Butler came to the hotel later that morning and installed himself and his office in the ladies' parlor, in a corner of the building on the first floor, turning the fashionable hotel into a military command center.

From the St. Charles Hotel the party of Butler's officers walked up the street to city hall to see Mayor Monroe. After keeping them waiting for a time, Monroe allowed them an audience. They told him that General Butler had established his office at the St. Charles Hotel and would be pleased to see the mayor and the members of the city council there at two o'clock that afternoon. Mayor Monroe replied that *his* place of business was at city hall and any gentleman who had business with him could see him there during office hours. Colonel Jonas French of Butler's staff suggested that the mayor's reply was not an answer likely to satisfy the commander of the U.S. Army's Department of the Gulf and said he hoped the mayor would not complicate what already was for the mayor an embarrassing situation by raising questions of protocol. Mayor Monroe decided he could make it to the St. Charles after all.

Butler Handles the Troublemakers

At 2:00 p.m. the mayor and a group of his associates, including Pierre Soule, whom Butler knew from having attended Democratic political conventions before the war, showed up at Butler's office. Outside the hotel a boisterous, threatening throng had gathered, held at bay by a regiment under the command of Brigadier General Thomas Williams and standing guard with an artillery piece at each corner of the hotel. Butler's meeting with the city officials had just begun when it was interrupted by an aide to General Williams, the aide's uniform torn by the crowd. "General Williams's compliments," the officer said to Butler, "and he bids me say to the general commanding that the mob is getting unruly, and asks for orders as to what shall be done with them."

Seemingly unaffected by the report, Butler calmly replied to the officer, "Give my compliments to General Williams and tell him to clear the streets at once with his artillery." Mayor Monroe and the others rose from their chairs. "Don't, general!" the mayor protested. "Don't give such an order as that." Butler, the veteran courtroom actor, responded, "Why this emotion, gentlemen? The cannon are not going to shoot our way. And I have borne this noise and confusion as long as I choose to." "Wait awhile, general," Monroe urged. "Wait awhile. We will go out and speak to the people and advise them to go away, and they will disperse." "Very well," Butler told him. "So they disperse, I do not care as to the means. Go out and try your hand at it."

The mayor stepped out onto a balcony and addressed the crowd while Butler stood behind a window where he could see the crowd, but they could not see him. The mayor's remarks had little calming effect on the crowd, and it was only temporary at that. As Butler observed the individuals in the crowd, he noticed a man on the sidewalk with a piece of a U.S. flag in the buttonhole of his coat, as if wearing the flag fragment as a boutonniere. Butler turned to ask the others standing around him if anyone knew who the man was, and someone said he was the man who had cut down the flag at the mint. Butler turned to his orderly and told him to take a good look at the man so that he would know him if he saw him again.[94]

Suddenly a rumbling noise sounded from the street, quickly growing louder. The Sixth Maine Artillery Battery, with six field pieces and commanded by a Captain Thompson, had been encamped in Tivoli Circle (later renamed Lee Circle), and it was now speeding down St. Charles Street, which was paved with foot-square granite blocks set unevenly on the street's surface. Thompson was leading his battery down the street as if it were empty, the horses pulling the field pieces and caissons being driven at all the speed they could manage and bugles sounding the charge. "No one who has not seen such a charge can imagine the terrible noise and clamor it makes," Butler remarked, "the cannoneers clinging to their seats, and the wheels of the guns bounding up inches as they thunder over the uneven stones."[95] The crowd fell silent in terror, then quickly scattered. The street was suddenly cleared.

After more interruptions, Butler adjourned the meeting with the city fathers until that evening. In the meantime, in the late afternoon, his aides having managed to procure a carriage, Butler was driven to the waterfront and went on board the *Mississippi* to have Mrs. Butler and her maid prepare to go ashore. Mrs. Butler's baggage was hauled off the ship and placed in the carriage, and she and her maid and the general were then driven to the St. Charles without being molested or even shouted at. The general and Mrs. Butler would take temporary accommodations in the St. Charles, but later moved their residence and the general's office into a large, confiscated house near the mint.

The Butlers and several members of the general's staff took dinner in the hotel's vast, ornate dining room, where they gathered at a table at one end of the room, the only diners there. Butler entertained the group by reading aloud excerpts from some of the letters he had received during the day. "We'll get the better of you yet, old cock-eye," one of the anonymous writers told him. Another told him that in another month or two yellow fever would make him a victim. Another warned about his food being poisoned. By the time their dinner was coming to an end, an army band had assembled on a balcony at the front of the hotel and it struck up "The Star-Spangled Banner," filling the cavernous dining room with the loud, insistent strains of the national anthem. The band continued to play throughout the evening, the re-formed crowd standing or sitting quietly, as if pacified by the music.

The dinner over, the time for resumption of the meeting arrived. The ladies' parlor, which was now Butler's office, was described as "spacious, lofty and elegant."[96] On one side of the room sat the mayor, members of the city council, some other leading citizens and Pierre Soule, all of whom arranged themselves in a large semicircle. On the opposite side of the room, also in a semicircle, sat General Butler and members of his staff, all in their dress uniforms.

Butler began the session by saying that the purpose of the meeting was to set forth the principles upon which he intended to govern the army department that he had been assigned to command, the Department of the Gulf, and to learn from city officials how much cooperation he could expect from them. He told the assembly that he had written a proclamation that detailed his intentions in the execution of his responsibilities, a copy of which he then produced and began to read to them:

> The city of New Orleans and its environs, with all its interior and exterior defenses, having surrendered to the combined naval and land forces of the United States, and being now in the occupation of the forces of the United States, who have come to restore order, maintain public tranquility, and enforce peace and quiet, under the laws and constitution of the United States, the major-general commanding hereby proclaims the object and purposes of the government of the United States in thus taking possession of New Orleans and the state of Louisiana, and the rules and regulations by which the laws of the United States will be for the present, and during the state of war, enforced and maintained, for the plain guidance of all good citizens of the United States, as well as others who may have heretofore been in rebellion against their authority.[97]

The proclamation announced that the city would be subject to martial law, that all persons in arms against the United States were required to surrender themselves and their weapons and equipment, that no flags or other emblems except those of the U.S. could be exhibited, that all persons who renewed their oath of allegiance to the U.S. would be protected by the army, but all persons still holding allegiance to the Confederacy would be deemed and treated as enemies of the U.S., that no publication of inflammatory material against the U.S. would be permitted, that all gatherings of persons in the streets were forbidden. Those and other prohibitions were included.

"The sum and substance of the whole," Butler told the group, "is this: I wish to leave the municipal authority in the full exercise of its accustomed functions. I do not desire to interfere with the collection of taxes, the government of the police, the lighting and cleaning of the streets, the sanitary laws, or the administration of justice. I desire only to govern the military forces of the department, and to take cognizance only of offenses committed by or against them. Representing here the United States, it is my wish to confine myself solely to the business of sustaining the government of the United States against its enemies."

Soule, offering himself as spokesman for the city fathers, was quick to reply. He told Butler he didn't believe tranquility could be maintained in the city so long as Butler's troops remained there. He urged Butler to move his men to the outskirts of the city, where they would not be constantly obvious to the people of New Orleans. "I know the feelings of the people so well," he stated, "that I am sure your soldiers can have no peace while they remain in our midst. Withdraw your troops, general, and leave the city government to manage its own affairs. If the troops remain, there will certainly be trouble." The people of New Orleans, he told Butler, would never submit. They were not a conquered people, he asserted, and could not be expected to behave as conquered people. They were a sensitive and high-spirited people, he said, and the hourly sight of Butler's troops would irritate them.[98]

Soule had a reputation for being a silver-tongued orator. Butler did not. His first biographer, James Parton, who spent a lot of time with him, said Butler was slow of speech and that it was in "only the heat and tempest of contention that he acquires the perfect use of the parts of speech."[99] What Butler had in his favor, though, was conviction, passion, an indomitable will—and several thousand United States Army troops at his command. At this moment he also had enough eloquence to answer Soule cogently. "I did not expect to hear from Mister Soule a threat on this occasion," Butler told the group. "I have been long accustomed to hear threats from Southern gentlemen in political conventions, but let me assure gentlemen present that the time for tactics of that nature has passed, never to return. New Orleans *is* a conquered city. If not, why are we here? How did we get here? Have you opened your arms and bid us welcome? Are we here by your consent? Would you or would you not expel us if you could?

"New Orleans has been conquered by the forces of the United States," Butler declared, "and by the laws of all nations, lies subject to the will of the conquerors. Nevertheless, I have proposed to leave the municipal government to the free exercise of all its powers. And I am answered by a threat."[100] Soule hastily denied he had intended a threat, claiming he merely meant to give his opinion of what would happen if the troops remained in the city. Butler rejoined:

> Gladly will I take every man out of New Orleans the very day, the very hour it is demonstrated to me that the city government can protect me from insult or danger if I choose to ride alone from one end of the city to the other, or accompanied by one gentleman of my staff. Your inability to govern the insulting, irreligious, unwashed mob in your midst has been clearly proved by the insults of your rowdies toward my officers and men this very afternoon, and by the fact that General Lovell was obliged to proclaim martial law while his army occupied your city, to protect the law abiding citizens from the rowdies. I do not proclaim martial law against the respectable citizens of this place, but against the same class that obliged General Wilkinson, General Jackson, and General Lovell to declare it.
>
> I have means of knowing more about your city than you think, and I am aware at this hour there is an organization here established for the purpose of assassinating my men by detail. But I warn you that if a shot is fired from any house, that house will never

again cover a mortal's head. And if I can discover the perpetrator of the deed, the place that now knows him shall know him no more forever.

I have the power to suppress this unruly element in your midst, and I mean so to use it that in a very short period I shall be able to ride through the entire city, free from insult and danger, or else this metropolis of the South shall be a desert, from the Plains of Chalmette to the outskirts of Carrollton.[101]

Soule then, with no weapon but his tongue and no armor but his pride, stood to reply. "It was," biographer Parton reported, "in part, a defense and eulogy of New Orleans, and, in part, a secession speech of the usual tenor, illumined by the rhetoric of an accomplished speaker."[102] Butler then turned the discussion to the subject of provisions needed to feed the city's population, particularly the poor, to whom, Butler promised, he would devote his immediate attention. He said he would allow their Confederate currency to continue to be accepted since they had nothing else to use for payment.

Mayor Monroe, his irritation over Butler's domination apparently rising and in a fit of obvious petulance, abruptly announced that effective immediately he was shutting down the operations of the city government and that General Butler could do whatever he wanted with the city. A member of the city council quickly jumped up and told the group that the functioning of the city government was too important a matter to be summarily ended and that the matter should be considered and acted upon by the city council. With both the mayor and General Butler assenting, the group then agreed to have the council meet and take up the matter the next morning, then report their decision to the general later the same day. At that, the evening's meeting concluded. By then the crowd outside had gone home, and the city fathers went their separate ways without harassment.

The next morning, Saturday, May 3, while the city council was meeting, Butler's proclamation, printed as a handbill, was being distributed around the city, handed out to anyone who would take it. Also that morning Butler announced his appointment of Major Bell to be provost judge and Colonel French to be provost marshal. They would become his two chief officials in his administration of the occupied city of New Orleans. As one of his first acts on receiving the assignment, French issued a handbill of his own, emphasizing the prohibitions set forth in Butler's proclamation and particularly calling the public's attention to the problem of harassment. "The soldiers of this command are subject, upon the part of some low-minded persons, to insult," the handbill read. "This must stop. Repetition will lead to instant arrest and punishment."[103]

When the special meeting of the city council concluded, Butler was visited by a delegation that notified him that the council had accepted his proposal concerning the operation of the city government. It did, however, have an important request to make of him. The council asked him to withdraw the troops that were posted at city hall, to avoid the appearance that city hall was functioning under the direction of the U.S. Army. Butler granted the request to move the troops. The camps in the city's squares were dismantled, and the troops were relocated, some sent to Baton Rouge with Farragut, some to a new permanent camp in Carrollton on the northwestern outskirts of the city, some to the various forts on Lake Pontchartrain, Lake Borgne and Lake Maurepas. Others were shifted to spots in the city that were less objectionable than the park-like public squares.

Within days of the imposition of General Butler's style of martial law, the effects became evident. In an editorial published May 8, 1862, the *New Orleans Bee* remarked: "The federal

soldiers do not seem to interfere with the private property of the citizens, and have done nothing that we are aware of to provoke difficulty. The usual nightly reports of arrests for vagrancy, assaults, wounding and killing have unquestionably been diminished. The city is as tranquil and peaceable as in the most quiet times."[104] Five days after the *Bee*'s good report, on May 13, Butler issued his General Order 27, indicating that the spirit of rebellion was still being stoked and that he was determined to stamp it out: "It having come to the knowledge of the commanding general that Friday next is proposed to be observed as a day of fasting and prayer, in obedience to some supposed proclamation of one Jefferson Davis, in the several churches of this city, it is ordered that no such observance be had. Churches and religious houses are to be kept open as in time of profound peace, but no religious exercises are to be had upon the supposed authority above mentioned."[105]

Furthermore, although disturbances by rowdies, ruffians and other troublemakers had noticeably decreased, harassing behavior had not stopped among the city's finer folk. On May 28 Butler issued this order, which vaguely states the problem and orders a measure meant to solve it: "As the officers and soldiers of the United States have been subject to repeated insults from the women (calling themselves ladies) of New Orleans, in return for the most scrupulous non-interference and courtesy on our part, it is ordered that hereafter when any female shall, by word, gesture or movement, insult or show contempt for any officer or soldier of the United States, she shall be regarded and held liable to be treated as a woman of the town plying her occupation."[106] Butler offered some examples of the sort of abuse he meant to stop. A boy about ten years old, walking down Canal Street with his mother, the wife of one of the city's leading lawyers, left her side to spit on a colonel of the Thirty-first Massachusetts Infantry Regiment. A woman standing on a balcony emptied the contents of a chamber pot on Colonel H.C. Deming and Flag Officer Farragut as they were walking together to dinner. Another of Butler's officers was on his way to church on a Sunday, carrying his prayerbook in his hand, when he met two well-dressed women walking side by side, coming toward him. When he stepped aside to yield the sidewalk to them, one stepped in front of the other and spat in the officer's face.

The order drew a swift and vehement reaction from Mayor Monroe, who wrote a letter to Butler saying, among other things, that he, Monroe, would "never undertake to be responsible for the peace of New Orleans while such an edict, which infuriates our citizens, remains in force."[107] Butler fired back with a note and gave it to the provost marshal to deliver to the mayor:

> HEAD-QUARTERS, DEPARTMENT OF THE GULF, NEW ORLEANS, *May 16, 1862.* John T. Monroe, late mayor of the city of New Orleans, is relieved from all responsibility for the peace of the city, and is suspended from the exercise of any official functions, and committed to Fort Jackson until farther orders. B.F. Butler, *Major General Commanding.*[108]

Monroe hurried to see Butler to dissuade the general from jailing him. He apologized to Butler, then withdrew the apology. After three visits to Butler's office, on the third of which Monroe was accompanied by a group of his supporters, Butler reinstated the order to jail

Opposite: Cartoon portraying Butler as Blue Beard of New Orleans following the issuance of his so-called woman order, which stipulated that any woman who assaulted or insulted U.S. troops was "to be treated as a woman of the town plying her occupation" (Library of Congress).

Monroe—and not only Monroe but the chief of police and two others. Monroe was later transferred from Fort Jackson to Fort Pickens, near Pensacola, to be held in custody there. He was promised release if he would take the oath of allegiance to the United States, but after saying he would, he refused. Pierre Soule, the insistent voice of rebellion in New Orleans, his protestations and speeches having finally exhausted Butler's tolerance, was also shipped out of the city into confinement. He was held in custody at Fort Warren, at the entrance to Boston harbor.

What Butler meant in what became known as "the woman order," according to the most sympathetic interpretation, was that a woman who committed such offensive behavior would be liable to be arrested, confined in jail overnight, required to appear before a magistrate the next morning and fined five dollars. One of his staff members saw there were other possible interpretations and warned the general that an enormous scandal would result if only one man should act upon the order in the wrong way. Butler seemed unconcerned about any such happening. "Let us then have one case of aggression on our side," he told the staff member. "I shall know how to deal with that case, so that it will never be repeated. So far, all the aggression has been against us.... I do not fear the troops; but if aggression must be, let it not be all against us."[109]

The order had its intended effect. Although the ladies of New Orleans did not all discontinue unladylike behavior toward Butler's soldiers, what they did or said was limited to slighter offenses. "The outrageous demonstrations ceased," biographer Parton reported. "No more insulting words were uttered; and all the affectations of disgust were such as could be easily and properly borne by officers and men. Gradually even these were discontinued.... [and] in no instance was the order misunderstood on the part of the troops."[110] No arrests were ever made because of the order. "All the ladies in New Orleans forbore to insult our troops because they didn't want to be deemed common women," Butler remarked, "and all the common women forbore to insult our troops because they wanted to be deemed ladies."[111]

Butler of course received an avalanche of criticism for the order, particularly from some, such as Jefferson Davis, General Beauregard and the governor of Louisiana, who clamored against it and against Butler in efforts to arouse Southerners in support of the war effort. To Southerners, especially New Orleanians, Butler then became known as the "Beast." Criticism also came from abroad. In England's House of Commons Butler was denounced by the British prime minister, Henry John Temple, Viscount Palmerston. "An Englishman must blush," he orated, "to think that such an act has been committed by one belonging to the Anglo-Saxon race."[112] France, which, like England, continued to flirt with the Confederacy just in case it might succeed, also weighed in on the matter, condemning Butler and the order. Neither President Lincoln nor Secretary of State William Seward, however, made any move to interfere.

Help for the Needy

Taking up the matter of hunger in New Orleans, Butler on May 9 issued his General Order No. 25:

> The deplorable state of destitution and hunger of the mechanics and working classes of this city has been brought to the knowledge of the commanding general.

> He has yielded to every suggestion made by the city government, and ordered every method of furnishing food to the people of New Orleans that government desired. No relief by those officials has yet been afforded. This hunger does not pinch the wealthy and influential, the leaders of the rebellion, who have gotten up this war, and are now endeavoring to prosecute it, without regard to the starving poor, the workingman, his wife and child. Unmindful of their suffering fellow-citizens at home, they have caused or suffered provisions to be carried out of the city for Confederate service since the occupation by the United States forces....
>
> Ready only for war, we had not prepared ourselves to feed the hungry and relieve the distressed with provisions. But to the extent possible within the power of the commanding general, it shall be done.
>
> He has captured a quantity of beef and sugar intended for the rebels in the field. A thousand barrels of these stores will be distributed among the deserving poor of this city, from whom the rebels had plundered it....
>
> Capt. John Clark, Acting Chief Commissary of Subsistence, will be charged with the execution of this order, and will give public notice of the place and manner of distribution."[113]

Under that order, Butler wrote, 32,400 men, women and children received the provisions he promised, distributed daily. "My supplies for the army having arrived from New York," he reported, "I directed my commissary to 'sell to families for consumption, in small quantities, until further orders, flour and salt meats, viz.: pork, beef, ham, and bacon, from the stores of the army, at seven and a half cents per pound for flour and ten cents for meats, city bank notes, gold, silver, or treasury notes to be taken in payment.... [F]or those who had means to purchase, starvation was not possible."[114] The problem of feeding those without means to purchase, however, remained. How they were to be consistently fed—and at whose cost—were questions Butler struggled to answer.

Butler also struggled to find a way to protect the city—and his troops—from deadly yellow fever, for which New Orleans was notorious. In 1862 there was no known way to do so. Like many others at the time, he mistakenly believed it to be caused by unsanitary living conditions and to be spread by contagion.[115] He ordered a strict quarantine on ships coming to the city and a massive cleanup of the city's streets and gutters and the canals that led from the river to Lake Pontchartrain, giving employment to a great number of unemployed and poor. The cleansing of private homes and even of wagons was also ordered.

To finance the cleanup of the city and his food distribution to the poor Butler summarily ordered the corporations, businesses and individuals that had contributed to the Committee of Public Safety some $1,250,000 to finance the defense of the city against U.S. forces to cough up $312,716 to pay for the employment of the poor and for food to feed them. At the same time, he assessed the cotton brokers who had attempted "to induce foreign intervention in behalf of the rebellion" $29,200. He assessed three other individuals $500 each because they had advised planters not to send produce to New Orleans while the city was under the occupation of the U.S. Army.

New Orleans newspapers chafed under Butler's strict censorship, which allowed not even a hint of support for the rebellion. Violations resulted in the suspension of publication. One newspaper editor, William J. Seymour of the *Commercial Bulletin*, while protesting the censorship rules, so inflamed Butler with his protestation that Butler, according to Seymour—who later became an officer in the Confederate army—"pounded his desk and roared,

'I am the military governor of this state, the supreme power. You cannot disregard my order, sir. By God, he that sins against me, sins against the Holy Ghost!"[116]

When Butler perceived a growing threat to his occupation of New Orleans, arising from the presence of Confederate forces north of the city, he appealed to the War Department for reinforcements. When told there were none to be had, he recruited and organized three regiments of free blacks, a move that drew opposition not only from secessionist whites but from many white Union supporters as well, including many, if not most, of Butler's officers.[117]

To cope with the huge influx of freed and escaped slaves into the city, as well as into Fort Jackson and Fort St. Philip, he put them to work on plantations that had been abandoned by their owners and had been confiscated by Butler under the Confiscation Act of the U.S. Congress's. The workers' wages were paid by the U.S. government, which the government would recoup by the sale of confiscated crops. He also, on behalf of the government, sent displaced and unemployed blacks and whites to work in the fields of the plantations of owners loyal to the Union, issuing the following directive dated October 18, 1862:

> Whereas, many of the persons held to service and labor have left their masters and claimants, and have come to the city of New Orleans, and to the camps of the army of the gulf, and are claiming to be emancipated and free,
>
> And whereas, these men and women are in a destitute condition;
>
> And whereas, it is clearly the duty, by law, as well as in humanity, of the United States to provide them with food and clothing, and to employ them in some useful occupation;
>
> And whereas, it is necessary that the crop of cane and cereals now growing and approaching maturity in said parishes [Plaquemines and St. Bernard, the parishes below New Orleans] shall be preserved, and the levees repaired and strengthened against floods.... It is agreed and determined that the United States will employ all the persons heretofore held to labor on the several plantations [of loyal owners in Plaquemines and St. Bernard parishes].[118]

The workers' pay was fixed at ten dollars a month—a month consisting of twenty-six ten-hour workdays. "Planters shall furnish suitable and proper food," Butler further instructed, "for each of these laborers, and take care of them, and furnish proper medicines in case of sickness." The planters were also to suitably provide for members of the workers' families, "parent, child or wife," who were "incapacitated by sickness or age from labor."[119]

The Second Confiscation Act, approved by Congress on July 17, 1862, authorized the seizure of "all the estate and property, moneys, stocks, credits, and effects" of those who were in armed rebellion against the U.S. government or who were aiding the rebellion, sixty days after the president's public warning that they renew their allegiance to the United States or suffer the confiscations. Butler and his older brother, Colonel Andrew Jackson Butler, who served as Butler's aide and often as his hatchet man, used the Confiscation Act to seize whatever suited the general's public purposes—and in some cases whatever suited the colonel's personal purposes.

Butler's Justice for William Mumford

Butler never forgot his vow to make William Mumford pay for cutting down and desecrating the U.S. flag. Mumford showed up one too many times in public protests of the U.S.

troops' occupation of the city, protests in which he often took a conspicuous part. Butler had him arrested and put him on trial by a military commission. After hearing the testimony of witnesses to the flag incident, the commission found him guilty and pronounced its sentence upon him. On June 5, 1862, Butler issued Special Order No. 10, confirming the commission's verdict and sentence:

> William B. Mumford, a citizen of New Orleans, having been convicted before the military commission of treason and an overt act thereof, in tearing down the United States flag from a public building of the United States, for the purpose of inciting other evil-minded persons to farther resistance to the laws and arms of the United States, after said flag was placed there by Commodore Farragut, of the United States navy,
>
> It is ordered that he be executed, according to the sentence of the said military commission, on Saturday, June 7th instant, between the hours of 8 a.m. and 12 m., under the direction of the provost-marshal of the district of New Orleans; and for so doing this shall be his sufficient warrant.[120]

Mumford, described by Butler as "a fine-looking man, tall, black-bearded" (which a surviving photograph confirms), was a forty-two-year-old professional gambler from North Carolina and a veteran of the Mexican War. He had a wife and three children. Calling him "a man of considerable education, some property, and much influence with the lower class," Butler claimed that Mumford was "the head of the gamblers of New Orleans."[121] Mumford had become a hero to those who took to the streets to vent their hostility toward the United States. "The blacklegs and blackguards," Butler reported, "assembled in large number and voted that he should not be executed, and that if he were executed, Butler should die the death by any and every possible means." Butler received, he said, "forty or fifty" anonymous, threatening letters, enough, he admitted, to frighten him. "I was sensible," he wrote in his memoirs, "that I should be subjected probably to every kind of machination and intrigue for my death if I did my duty."[122] Not all who asked mercy for Mumford were blackguards. The eighty-year-old president of the Bank of Louisiana, Dr. William N. Mercer, whom Butler described as "one of the best gentlemen in the city," with tears coursing down his cheeks pleaded for Butler to spare Mumford. Butler refused. "The question is now to be settled," he told Mercer, "whether law and order or a mob shall govern."[123]

Many in the city, however, believed that Butler would not allow Mumford to be executed but would remit the death sentence in the last hour, which was what he had recently done in the case of six Confederate soldiers who had been captured at Fort Jackson and Fort St. Philip and had been paroled. They had violated the parole by later forming a group to arm themselves and break out of New Orleans to join General Beauregard's rebel army. The men had protested that paroling was for officers and gentlemen and they were not gentlemen, which to Butler seemed obvious. Butler decided they were truly ignorant of the seriousness of their offense and remitted their death sentences to long prison terms at hard labor. But convinced that his lifting the death sentence for Mumford would be interpreted as a sign of weakness, especially in light of the recent case of the six paroled soldiers, Butler was determined that Mumford must die.

Not even the dramatically emotional pleas of Mumford's wife and children could make him change his mind. "She wept bitterly," Butler recalled, "as did the children, who fell about my knees.... I told her that I had given it every thought and had considered it in every aspect;

that while this scene was very painful to me, yet it could not alter my determination." He told her that if in the future he could alleviate any harm that might come to her because of her husband's death, she would find him a source of help. He then told her he had heard that Mumford refused to believe he would be executed, and that he, Butler, wished her to go to the jail and convince him that he was mistaken, that he would indeed be executed. "Whether I live or die," Butler told Mrs. Mumford, "he will die. And let him in the few hours he has to live look to his God for pardon."[124]

Butler ordered a gallows erected in front of the mint, as close to the scene of the crime as possible, and ordered that Mumford be hanged "with the flag of the United States, the companion of which he had desecrated, floating over him."[125] On the morning of June 7, 1862, after Mumford was allowed to make a long speech to the huge crowd that filled Esplanade Avenue, the scaffold's hinged door beneath his feet was sprung open and Mumford dropped to his death.

The execution swiftly set off waves of outrage across the seceded states. The Confederacy's president, Jefferson Davis, promptly issued a proclamation calling for retribution against Butler and Butler's officers. He declared Butler "to be a felon deserving capital punishment. I do order that he be no longer considered or treated simply as a public enemy of the Confederate States of America but as an outlaw and common enemy of mankind, and that in the event of his capture the officer in command of the capturing force do cause him to be immediately executed by hanging." Davis further ordered that "all commissioned officers in the command of said Benjamin F. Butler be declared not entitled to be considered as soldiers engaged in honorable warfare but as robbers and criminals deserving death, and that they and each of them be whenever captured reserved for execution."[126] (Years later, in 1869, when the war was over and Butler was a congressman from Massachusetts, he made good on his promise to help Mary Mumford if ever she needed help. Through an acquaintance of Mrs. Mumford he learned she was living in Virginia and was in dire financial straits. He saved her house from being sold to satisfy a lien and he arranged to have her employed as a clerk in the offices of the U.S. commissioner of internal revenue. When she lost that job in a change of political administrations, he got her a clerk's job in the Post Office Department.)

Butler's zeal for the Union's cause finally got him into trouble with the only people who could control his power—the movers and shakers in Washington, D.C. Butler had gone after the foreign consuls in New Orleans, who protected not only the interests of their home countries but of the Confederacy. So eager were they to cooperate with the Confederate government and rebel businesses and so confident were they that the Confederate states would win their war against the United States they did all they could to thwart Butler and his military rule of the city and its affairs. Their complaints about Butler and his policies went to their governments and then to the U.S. government. The complaints began to pile up on the desk of the U.S. secretary of state, William Seward, who sent an investigator, Reverdy Johnson, to New Orleans to assay the doings of General Butler and to report on them to Seward.

Butler's nineteenth-century biographer, James Parton, assayed Reverdy Johnson, who was a Maryland lawyer and political figure. "His heart and mind, his friends and habits, were southern," Parton wrote. "In New Orleans he associated almost exclusively with secessionists—who felt, who avowed, who boasted that he was their friend.... Nor can we doubt that he was sent to New Orleans, and knew that he was sent, to comply with the demands of foreign powers, if it could be done without concessions too palpably humiliating."[127] Parton also assayed the personalities and contrasting mindsets of Secretary Seward and General Butler:

> The two men are moral antipodes. Mr. Seward has too little, General Butler has *enough*, of the spirit of warfare. Mr. Seward, by the constitution of his mind and the habits of thirty years, is a conciliator, one who shrinks from the final ordeal, who is reluctant to face the last consequences, skillful to postpone, explain away, and "make things pleasant." General Butler, on the contrary, rejoices in a clear issue, goes straight to the point, uses language that bears but one meaning, and "takes the responsibility as naturally as he takes his breakfast...." Mr. Seward, as the head of the foreign department, felt that all his duties were subordinate to the one cardinal, central object of his policy, the maintenance of peace with foreign nations while the rebellion showed front.... Hence we find that when the foreign ministers brought their complaints to the department of state, Mr. Seward generally, and at once, took it for granted that General Butler was wrong.[128]

Seward, Parton concluded, was "chiefly concerned to keep the peace with foreign powers, to deprive them not merely of all cause of complaint, but of all pretext." Parton would not say that Seward was wrong in so doing. "'One at a time,'" Parton conceded, "is a good rule, when a nation has a war on its hands. His [Seward's] course may have been justified by necessity."[129]

A Change of Command

Having heard rumors, and read them in New Orleans newspapers, that he was to be relieved of command of the Department of the Gulf, Butler wrote to the new general in chief, Major General Henry W. Halleck, on September 1, 1862, asking him if the rumors were true. Halleck on September 14 wrote back saying, "The rumor in regard to your removal from the command is a mere newspaper story, without foundation."[130] Nevertheless, on December 14 Major General Nathaniel Banks, another of Lincoln's political generals, arrived in New Orleans, promptly called on Butler and delivered to him the order relieving him[131]:

> WAR DEPARTMENT, ADJUTANT-GENERAL'S OFFICE,
> WASHINGTON, *NOVEMBER* 9, 1862
>
> GENERAL ORDER NO.184,
> By direction of the President of the United States, Major-General Banks is assigned to the command of the Department of the Gulf, including the State of Texas.
> By order of the Secretary of War:
>
> H.W. HALLECK,
> *General-in-Chief.*
> E.D. TOWNSEND, *Assistant Adjutant-General.*

From New Orleans Butler traveled to New York and when he arrived there, he found a letter from President Lincoln inviting him to Washington, an invitation he promptly accepted. In Washington he was warmly received by officials of every sort, including the president. In his meeting with Lincoln, Butler, ever going straight to the point, asked, "Mister President, will you please tell me for what acts of mine I am recalled from New Orleans?"

Lincoln put him off, saying, "I am not at liberty to tell you, but you may ask Mister Stanton."

Butler swiftly accepted that invitation as well. Stanton, Butler reported, received him with great cordiality, and as soon as the greetings and pleasantries were exchanged, Butler asked Stanton the same question he had put to the president. "The reason," Stanton answered, "was one which does not imply, on the part of the government, any want of confidence in your honor as a man, or in your ability as a commander." "Well," Butler responded, "you have told me what I was *not* recalled for. I now ask you to tell me what I *was* recalled for." That drew a laugh from Stanton. He then told Butler, "You and I are both lawyers, and it is of no use your filing a bill of discovery upon me, for I sha'n't tell you."[132]

From Stanton Butler then went to see Secretary of State Seward, who, characteristically, received him politely—"very" politely, Butler remembered—and even invited Butler to have dinner with him that evening, which Butler agreed to do. He then put the question to Seward, in less direct language: "I have asked the president why I was relieved from command, and he declines giving me the reasons, and I have come to you, believing that you can give them if you will." Seward replied, according to Butler: "General, things have changed somewhat since you went away. We were then somewhat new in administration, and we interfered sometimes with each other's departments; but now we confine ourselves more closely to our own business. I do not know what you were recalled for, I assure you, but Halleck knows all about it. He is the general-in-chief, and had everything to do with it." Butler then went to see General Halleck. When Butler asked him the reasons for his being relieved, Halleck told him, "I do not know, general. No reasons were ever given me. It was done solely under the direction of the secretary of state."[133] On December 15 Secretary Seward issued a notice to the foreign ministers with whom he had dealings: "We are inaugurating a system of administration in New Orleans, under General Banks, which will relieve the condition there of much of the uneasiness which it is supposed affected the disposition of foreign powers."[134]

It wasn't until early November 1863 that Butler was given a new assignment. During the intervening ten and a half months he basked in his new fame as a vigorous defender of the Union, a general who had given the rebels what they had coming. He accepted invitations to make speeches, was a spectator at parades staged in his honor, attended banquets given for him, made repeated visits to Washington and, among other things, granted biographer Parton many days of his time, opening his house in Lowell to Parton to facilitate Parton's interviews with him and Parton's writing of the resulting biography, *General Butler in New Orleans*, a prodigious work of more than 600 pages first published in 1864.

During that time, Butler turned down an offer, made by President Lincoln over dinner at the White House, of a new command that would have Butler return to New Orleans once Vicksburg and Port Hudson, the two remaining Confederate strongholds on the Mississippi River, had been captured with Banks's help and General Banks could be eased into a new assignment. Butler declined, apparently believing it was a sop—offered, perhaps, because a politically astute president had become aware of the huge swell of popular support for the heroic general whom Lincoln had ousted, Lincoln now hoping to repair whatever political damage the ouster had caused. In fact, in the North there was so much popular support for Butler that he was now being considered by some people of influence and others as a likely presidential candidate in the election coming up in 1864.

In making the offer to Butler, Lincoln told him, according to Butler, "I want to give you a command quite equal in extent and importance to the one which you won for yourself at New Orleans. In it you can do great good to the country. The question of abolition is now settled. I want you to go down on the Mississippi River, take command there, and enlist, arm, and organize as many negro troops as can be had. I know of no one who can do this as well as yourself."[135] Butler evidently saw that little speech as soft soap and took some offense at it. "I am infinitely obliged to you for your good opinion," he replied to Lincoln, "but I could have enlisted several thousands if you had given me this full power when I was in New Orleans." He then let Lincoln see the umbrage he had taken at the president's offer. "Sending Banks to command in my place and then sending me down on the Mississippi to enlist troops, would be simply saying that I was not fit to command troops, but only fit for a recruiting sergeant."[136]

When Lincoln tried to recover from that, offering him Grant's command on the Mississippi, according to Butler, Butler refused again. He said he saw no reason for Grant to be relieved and that he did not want to be a party to the same sort of injustice that he had suffered. He then countered Lincoln's proposal with one of his own. "Why not do this?" he said he told Lincoln. "Send me back to take my old command and I will go up the Mississippi rolling up troops like a snowball in the soft snow." Lincoln walked back and forth, as if pondering the suggestion, Butler reported, then turned back to Butler and told him, "But I cannot recall Banks." Butler then offered to resign his commission, but Lincoln refused to accept it, and Butler left and returned to Lowell.[137]

On November 2, 1863—"without solicitation," he pointed out[138]—Butler was ordered to take command of the army's Department of Virginia and North Carolina, which placed him in command of the Army of the James, with headquarters at Fort Monroe. Union forces at that time occupied the peninsula between the York River and the James River as far as Williamsburg. They also held Norfolk and Portsmouth, as well as the North Carolina coastal cities of Plymouth, Washington, New Bern, Morehead City and Beaufort and with the support of the navy's gunboats controlled virtually all the sounds and bays between Norfolk and Beaufort. The first four months of his new command brought only relatively minor action, including an attack on New Bern and Beaufort by Major General George Pickett on February 1, 1864, which was repulsed by the troops of Brigadier General Innis Palmer. In March 1864, however, the war took a dramatic turn that forced new demands on General Butler's military ability.

In a White House ceremony on March 9, 1864, President Lincoln commissioned Ulysses S. Grant a lieutenant general, only the third person to hold that rank since the founding of the country, and appointed him general in chief of the United States Army. Grant immediately prepared to commence all-out war against the Confederates. Using the Union's hugely superior numbers, 533,000 troops in twenty-one corps, he engaged the rebels on all fronts simultaneously, allowing neither Robert E. Lee nor Joseph Johnston nor any other of the South's remaining eminent generals to shift their strength to withstand limited-front Union assaults. In Grant's plan the Army of the Potomac, commanded by Major General George Meade, would be at the center of the vast Union front, opposing General Lee's Army of Northern Virginia. To the west as far as Memphis would be Grant's right wing, commanded by Sherman. To the east would be the Army of the James, commanded by Butler.

Under Grant's Command

After conferring with Meade in the field near Brandy Station, Virginia, and with Sherman in Nashville, and going over his plan with them, Grant on April 1 went to see Butler at Fort Monroe. There the two men met each other for the first time. Brigadier General Adam Badeau, a member of Grant's staff and the semiofficial historian of Grant's command, in his chronicle reported Grant's feelings about Butler:

> It is true ... that if the general-in-chief had been allowed his choice, Butler would not have commanded the army of the James. Grant left the West, fully intending and prepared to remove that officer, whom he knew only by reputation, as one who had stepped into the highest grade in the army at the beginning of the war, without experience in a subordinate position. Want of this experience Grant did not believe proper preparation for high command.
>
> In his first interview with the President and the Secretary of War, he expressed this view, in which he was supported by Halleck, the retiring general-in-chief; but he was informed that political considerations of the highest character made it undesirable to displace Butler: the administration needed all its strength, and could not afford to provoke the hostility of so important a personage; and Grant was obliged to yield.
>
> He next proposed to leave Butler in command of the Department of Virginia and North Carolina, but to put W.F. Smith at the head of the column in the field. The President and the Secretary acquiesced in this suggestion, but Butler was too shrewd to allow it to be carried into effect. He had a right to command his own troops, and he made it understood without delay, that he intended to lead them in the field. There was no way to prevent this but to relieve him entirely from command, and thus provoke the very opposition which the administration thought it indispensable to avoid. Grant, therefore, was obliged to work with the tools put into his hands.[139]

In his meeting with Butler at Fort Monroe, before getting into the specifics of his plan, which called for Butler to advance his troops toward Richmond, Grant tactfully solicited Butler's opinion on how a drive on the Confederate capital should be conducted from Butler's position. There were but two feasible routes that Butler's army could take. One was on the north side of the James River, the other on the south side. The one on the north side ran up the peninsula formed by the York and James rivers. It was the route taken by McClellan in his failed campaign of 1862. That route would enable Butler to communicate more easily with Meade, but it offered no other major advantage. The route on the south side, on the other hand, would allow Butler to threaten Lee's communications with rebel-held territory to the south and west, supply links vital to the maintenance of Lee's army. Grant favored the route on the south side, since he intended to have Meade's army cross the James and oppose Lee from the south side, but he waited to hear what Butler had to say before stating his preference.

Butler told Grant that he preferred the south-side route. Doubtless feeling some relief over not having to differ with Butler, he later wrote to Butler to let him know how pleased he was with Butler's choice: "I went to Fortress Monroe for the express purpose of seeing you, and telling you it was my plan to have the forces under you act directly in concert with the Army of the Potomac, and as far as possible towards the same point. My mind was entirely made up what instructions to give, and I was very much pleased to find your previously conceived views exactly coincided."[140] Before leaving Butler, Grant wrote out his instructions for him:

> You will collect all the forces from your command that can be spared from garrison duty,—I should say not less than twenty thousand men—to operate on the south side of James River, Richmond being your objective point. To the force you already have will be added about ten thousand men from South Carolina under Major-General Gillmore, who will command them in person. Maj.-Gen. W.F. Smith is ordered to report to you, to command the troops sent into the field from your own department.
>
> General Gillmore will be ordered to report to you at Fortress Monroe, with all the troops on transports, by the 18th instant, or as soon thereafter as practicable. Should you not receive notice by that time to move, you will make such disposition of them and your other forces as you may deem best calculated to deceive the enemy as to the real move to be made.
>
> When you are notified to move, take City Point with as much force as possible. Fortify, or, rather, intrench at once, and concentrate all your troops for the field there as rapidly as you can. From City Point directions cannot be given at this time for your farther movements.
>
> The fact that has already been stated—that is, that Richmond is to be your objective point, and that there is to be co-operation between your force and the Army of the Potomac—must be your guide. This indicates the necessity of your holding close to the south bank of the James River as you advance. Then, should the enemy be forced into his intrenchments in Richmond, the Army of the Potomac would follow, and by means of transports the two armies would become a unit.
>
> All the minor details of your advance are left entirely to your direction....[141]

Within the next two and a half weeks Grant twice more wrote to Butler. On April 18 he wrote, "I shall aim to fight Lee between here and Richmond, if he will stand. Should Lee, however, fall back into Richmond, I will follow up and make a junction with your army on the James river.... I would say, therefore, use every exertion to secure a footing as far up the south side of the river as you can, and as soon as possible."[142]

On May 5 Butler and his force of 40,000 troops voyaged up the James River in a motley fleet of river steamers, ferry boats, schooners, barges, tugs and canal boats. By sunset the first brigade was ashore in the area of the town of Bermuda Hundred, at the edge of the confluence of the Appomattox and James rivers, southeast of Richmond. By nine o'clock the next morning, both of Butler's two corps, the Tenth and the Eighteenth, had been landed at City Point and Bermuda Hundred and had begun entrenching a line some three and a half miles long, with Richmond on the right across the James about twenty miles distant, and Petersburg on the left about ten miles distant. The two cities were connected by a turnpike, which from the center of Butler's line was about two miles away. Three days later Butler made his first aggressive move. Major General William F. Smith, the officer Grant had vainly tried to have as field commander of the Army of the James, reported that action:

> On the 9th of May the two corps were ordered out in the direction of Petersburg. The enemy were easily driven back to Swift Creek, a distance of four and a half miles, and the railroad and turnpike bridges were reached. The stream was very narrow and with steep banks, and no crossing was possible except by a bridge. Both bridges were guarded by [Confederate] artillery and infantry.... After several hours spent in ineffectual efforts

to find a crossing place which offered a fair prospect of forcing a passage, General Gillmore, commanding the Tenth Corps, and myself met for a consultation, and united in a letter advising General Butler that if Petersburg was to be taken, the proper way was to throw a bridge across the Appomattox behind our lines and, crossing there, to assault the works at Petersburg from the east.[143]

Butler received the advice with less than grace and forcefully rejected it. "His spoken criticism was of such a character as to check voluntary advice during the remainder of the campaign," Smith reported. "He said he was not going to build a bridge for West Point men to retreat over. After that we offered no advice."[144] Both Smith and Gillmore were West Point graduates.

Butler's next big move was to order an advance on Richmond, the move to be made along the turnpike, commencing at daybreak on Thursday, May 12. Smith summarized the order: "The two white divisions of the Eighteenth Corps [Smith's corps], with the exception of the force necessary to leave in the lines, reinforced by a division of the Tenth Corps, were to move out on the turnpike. General Gillmore, with the remainder of his command [the Tenth Corps] was to hold the road from Petersburg. As soon as the Eighteenth Corps had passed Chester Station on the railroad [to Richmond], [Major] General [August] Kautz was to move with his cavalry on the Danville [rail] road, destroying as much as possible of it. The colored division under [Major] General [Edward] Hinks was to move up from City Point to Point of Rocks on the right bank of the Appomattox."[145]

As the James River narrows in its ascent, it makes a sharp turn to the north before entering Richmond, which was about eight miles above the turn. At that point, known as Drewry's Bluff, the Confederates had erected a formidable earthworks fortification, called Fort Darling, on the west side of the river, and in May 1862 its powerful guns had turned back a Union fleet attempting to capture the Confederate capital. Now it stood in the way of Butler's army. To reach Richmond, Butler's army would have to maneuver past it and past or through whatever Confederate force that would come out to meet it. That Confederate force had grown while Butler had inexplicably delayed for nearly a week after arriving at City Point and Bermuda Hundred. General Pickett, then commanding the defense of Richmond and receiving daily intelligence on the movements of Butler's army, had been frantically issuing calls for help, and reinforcements had swiftly poured in from distant points, as far away as Florida, to swell the Confederate numbers from what had been only a meager force estimated at 5,000 troops to an estimated 18,000. And General Beauregard had been rushed from Charleston to take command of the city's defense.

In a dense fog early on the morning of May 16 Beauregard launched a massive attack on the advancing Union force, stopping it in its tracks and inflicting heavy losses on it. Badeau described the situation and the results:

> On that day, Butler's lines ran east and west, reaching from a point near the James river to the Petersburg railroad, a distance of three miles. Smith had the right, towards the river, and Gillmore the left, covering the railroad, and holding a prong of the rebel works, which his troops had carried without hard fighting, three days before. Beauregard disposed his force with great ability. His plan was to advance with three divisions; then, hurling his own left wing on Butler's right, to double it up on the centre, and separate the national column at once from the river and its base at Bermuda Hundred; at the same time, the rebel right was to engage the national left, and finally, a

fourth division from Petersburg to come up in the rear and complete the destruction of Butler's army.

The [Confederate] attack was made in the early morning, and, favored by a heavy fog, was at first completely successful. Nearly one entire brigade of Smith's command was captured, and the whole national right was endangered. Smith, however, was able to re-form his line, and though obliged to fall back, he succeeded in checking the rebel onset. Moreover, the enemy's advance against the left was not well supported, and the attack by the Petersburg division did not occur at all. Later in the day, a second assault was made upon Smith, which seriously threatened his communications, and he was again obliged to give ground.

Again, however, an advance upon the national left was resisted, and Butler might now have redeemed the day, had he moved Gillmore up against the disordered troops of the enemy; but instead of this, alarmed by the danger to Smith's command, he directed the whole line to fall back within the fortifications of Bermuda Hundred, Gillmore not having fired a shot. The enemy made no attempt to interfere, and Butler leisurely retired.

The national returns show thirty-five hundred killed, wounded, and missing, on the 16th of May, and the rebels admit a loss of three thousand, but all the advantage was with Beauregard.... [H]e had absolutely put an end to Butler's campaign; he had re-opened the avenues to Richmond from the South and West, driven thirty thousand men into a position where they could be of no use to Grant, released at least half that number to reinforce Lee, relieved the rebel capital from its most imminent danger, and gained the prestige of a victory.[146]

General Smith saw Butler's week-long delay as having defeated what might have been. "Had the instructions of April 2d of General Grant been strictly carried out," he wrote in his account of the battle, "and had Petersburg been promptly attacked on the 6th of May, it would doubtless have fallen, and the Southern lines of communication would have been at the mercy of General Butler. He could then have waited patiently to be attacked, and the plum he so longed for might have dropped into his mouth."[147]

Even before the disaster of May 16, which came to be known as the Second Battle of Drewry's Bluff, or the Battle of Proctor's Creek, Smith had formed a gloomy opinion of Butler's generalship. When Major General Philip Sheridan visited Smith at Smith's headquarters on May 14, Smith gave Sheridan his evaluation of Butler: "I pointed out to him my exposed right flank, and gave him a history of the campaign made by the Army of the James to that date, expressed my anxiety as to the future, and requested him on his return to the headquarters of General Grant to say to him for me that, in my opinion, the interests of the country would be best forwarded by withdrawing General Butler's army within its strong lines—leaving with him sufficient force to defend himself, and sending the remainder of the command to reinforce the Army of the Potomac."[148]

On May 22, after learning of the disaster of May 16, Grant took Smith's suggestion. Grant's aide, Horace Porter, then a lieutenant colonel on Grant's staff, reported that Grant "said that Butler was not detaining 10,000 men in Richmond, and not even keeping the [rail] roads south of that city broken, and he considered it advisable to have the greater part of Butler's troops join in the campaign of the Army of the Potomac. On May 25 he telegraphed orders to Halleck, saying: 'Send Butler's forces to White House [Virginia], to land on the north side, and march up to join this army. The James River should be held to City Point, but leave nothing more than is absolutely necessary to hold it, acting purely on the defensive.'"[149] True to form, Butler attempted to go over Grant's head when he received the order. He wrote to Secretary Stanton in a transparent appeal, telling him, "I had already got my best troops into a movable column for the purpose of offensive operations.... I found that the rebels had uncovered Petersburg, and its importance as a depot to them cannot be overrated. I had prepared to attack the place this morning with every prospect of success, but the imperative orders transmitted through Major-General Halleck, and the arrival of the transportation rendered necessary a change of orders. General Smith embarked last night.... I regret extremely the loss of this opportunity upon Petersburg."[150]

Determined to show he was a field general, Butler refused to accept a purely administrative role. On June 9,[151] Badeau reported, Butler sent Gillmore with 2,000 infantry and Kautz with a cavalry force of 1,500 toward Petersburg. "They were to destroy the bridges across the Appomattox river," Badeau reported, "and, if possible, capture the town. Gillmore returned, reporting the works in his front too strong to assault, but Kautz carried the fortifications on the southern side, and entered Petersburg, driving before him about 1,400 rebels, mostly militia; being, however, unsupported [by infantry], he also was obliged to retire. The bridges were not destroyed."[152] Butler made Gillmore the scapegoat in that failure and immediately relieved him from his command. Badeau, perhaps reflecting Grant's feelings, put the blame on Butler. "Had a sufficient force been sent against the isolated and almost defenseless town," he wrote, "it could not only have been taken, but held, and months of weary toil and thousands of precious lives would have been saved. But a force of only thirty-five hundred men was sent, and these returned, after having absolutely been in possession of the prize."[153] Not only had the attack failed but it had alerted the Confederates to Petersburg's vulnerability. Beauregard moved quickly to reinforce the city's defenders to the number of 10,000, requiring Grant, after repeated attempts to storm the city, to lay siege to it.

By now Grant had despaired of curtailing Butler. Instead, he now tried to have him transferred away from the heart of the action. On July 1 he wrote to Stanton:

> Whilst I have no difficulty with General Butler, finding him always clear in his conception of orders, and prompt to obey, yet there is a want of knowledge how to execute, and particularly a prejudice against him as a commander that operates against his usefulness.... As an administrative officer, General Butler has no superior. In taking charge of a department where there are no great battles to be fought, but a dissatisfied element to control, no one could manage it better than he. If a command could be cut out, such as Mr. Dana [the assistant secretary of war] proposed, namely: Kentucky, Illinois, and Indiana; or if the Department of Missouri, Kansas, and the states of Illinois and Indiana could be merged together, and General Butler put over it, I think the good of the service would be subserved.
>
> I regret the necessity of asking for a change in commanders here, but General Butler, not being a soldier by education or experience, is in the hands of his subordinates, in the execution of all orders military. I should feel stronger with Smith, Franklin, or J.J. Reynolds commanding the right wing of this army....
>
> I would not ... be willing to recommend his retirement.[154]

No action followed that proposal, and Butler, with his heart set on glory in the field, retained his position as commander of the Department of Virginia and North Carolina.

The Fort Fisher Disaster

As the two opposing armies lay stalemated outside Richmond and around Petersburg, the U.S. Navy issued a call for action elsewhere. Since the winter of 1862 the secretary of the navy, Gideon Welles, had been trying to have the War Department cooperate with the navy in a combined attack on Fort Fisher, the daunting Confederate fortification at the mouth of the Cape Fear River in North Carolina, which protected blockade runners supplying the Confederacy with a wide array of military and civilian goods brought by stealth to the port of Wilmington. Secretary of war Stanton had kept putting Welles off, on the grounds that the army was needed more elsewhere and troops couldn't be spared for a Fort Fisher mission.

In September 1864, though, Welles finally got a show of support. To a new request for army cooperation, he received an encouraging response from General Grant. Wilmington, Grant explained, "was of immense importance to the Confederates, because it formed their principal inlet for blockade runners by means of which they brought in from abroad such supplies and munitions of war as they could not produce at home. It was equally important to us to get possession of it [Fort Fisher], not only because it was desirable to cut off their supplies so as to insure a speedy termination of the war, but also because foreign governments, particularly the British Government, were constantly threatening that unless ours could maintain the blockade of that coast they should cease to recognize any blockade."[155] For those reasons, Grant stated, he decided to send an expedition to capture Fort Fisher.

Rear Admiral David Dixon Porter, commanding the U.S. Navy's North Atlantic squadron, would command the naval force during the operation. The army would have to name a commander of the troops that would participate in it. Porter and the assistant secretary of the navy, Gustavus Fox, went to City Point to confer with Grant about the operation. In his monumental work, *The Naval History of the Civil War*, Porter reported on that meeting. He said he asked for 8,000 troops, and Grant agreed to that number. "The next thing," Porter said, "was to select a General to command, who would act in harmony with the Navy. There were plenty of able commanders, but the trouble was whom could General Grant best spare. Admiral Porter merely suggested one thing—namely, that General Butler should not go in command."[156]

Grant, however, was obliged to appoint Butler because Butler commanded the army department that embraced Fort Fisher as well as other points along the North Carolina coast. Grant wanted Major General Godfrey Weitzel of the Army of the James to be the actual leader of the expedition's troops, and he thought army protocol would be satisfied by having Weitzel receive his orders through Butler, who, Grant intended, would serve merely as the nominal commander. Butler would not permit that arrangement. He would keep every power, privilege and perquisite that was his as the department commander. Furthermore, as if to assert his authority, Butler delayed assembling the army force that was to participate in the expedition, causing Secretary Welles to seek President Lincoln's assistance in getting things moving. Welles wrote imploringly to the president:

> The vessels are concentrated at Hampton Roads and Beaufort, where they remain, an immense force, lying idle, awaiting the movements of the army. The detention of so many vessels from blockade and cruising duty is a most serious injury to the public service, and, if the expedition cannot go forward for want of troops, I desire to be notified so that the ships may be relieved and dispersed for other service....

Ships of the Fort Fisher expedition leave Chesapeake Bay to begin their mission. Among the 60 vessels was the obsolete gunboat that became Butler's bomb boat, with which he thought he could blow up the Confederates' Fort Fisher at the mouth of the Cape Fear River below Wilmington, North Carolina (Library of Congress).

[T]he autumn weather so favorable for such an expedition is passing away. The public expect this attack, and the country will be distressed if it is not made. To procrastinate much longer will be to peril its success. Of the obstacles which delay, or prevent military operations at once, I cannot judge; but the delay is becoming exceedingly embarrassing to this department, and the importance of having the military authorities impressed with the necessity of speedy action has prompted this communication to you.[157]

Butler's orders from Grant concerning the Fort Fisher expedition had been given him early in October, according to Admiral Porter's account, but it wasn't until late November that he showed any sign of participating in the mission. He offered to Porter what he thought was a better idea. "Accompanied by General Weitzel and his personal staff, General Butler went on board the flag-ship 'Malvern' at Hampton Roads," Porter recounted, "and communicated to Rear-Admiral Porter a plan for the destruction of Fort Fisher."[158] Inspired by reports of a massive, devastating accidental explosion of gunpowder at Erith, England, on October 1, 1864, Butler proposed an unusual element as a key part of the planned assault. "I believed," Butler wrote in his memoir, "that possibly, by bringing within four or five hundred yards of Fort Fisher a large mass of explosives, and firing the whole in every part at the same moment ... the garrison would at least be so far paralyzed as to enable, by a prompt landing of men, a seizure of the fort." He managed to present his idea to Lincoln and others in Washington and, he said, "found that the idea had received so much favor at Washington that it was determined it should be tried."[159]

Porter registered his response to the idea: "Any expedient that would get the expedition off was hailed with delight by the Rear-Admiral commanding [Porter himself], who agreed to Butler's proposition, notwithstanding he had little faith in the project."[160] The Navy Department had already gone along with the idea, although Porter wasn't sure whether the department saw a chance of success or was simply afraid to buck Butler. "[A]s the General was then a power in the land," Porter wrote, "it [the Navy Department] would, perhaps, have favored ideas still more absurd emanating from that quarter. An officer who could disobey the orders of his immediate commander-in-chief for months, delay a large fleet assembled at infinite cost and pains to deal a final blow to the Confederacy, and finally assume command of an expedition assigned to another General, all without rebuke from headquarters, must have had immense influence. All men seemed afraid of Butler's political power: it was even potential with the President and Secretary of War."[161] Butler was actually hoping for bigger results than the destruction of Fort Fisher, imagining that "if it should prove a success the whole system of offensive warfare by naval procedure would be changed, for no forts near harbors would be safe if a small vessel loaded with gun-powder and run ashore under a fort and exploded would destroy the people in it, and no garrison would ever remain in a fort when such a vessel was seen approaching."[162]

In early December a fleet of nearly 60 vessels was assembled in Hampton Roads for the assault on Fort Fisher. Included among them was the obsolete gunboat *Louisiana*, which would be loaded with 235 tons of gunpowder and would become the bomb boat. As the fleet made ready to sail, Butler let it be known that he was going to sail with it and take charge of the mission. "I was to go in its command," he wrote, "for a reason which was agreed upon between us [Butler and Grant] in the consultation. The reason was this, that General Weitzel, while a very able general, was quite a young man, and I was very anxious to see this powder expedition go on and succeed, for it was a very grave one."[163] Butler had conferred with Grant at City Point while the arrangements were being made and had told Grant, "I think I had better go with the expedition so as to take the responsibility off General Weitzel, as I am an older officer." To that proposal, Butler wrote, Grant assented.[164] Weitzel was in fact twenty-nine years old, the same age as Fort Fisher's commander. Unlike Butler, he was a professional soldier, a graduate of West Point, ranked second in his class of thirty-four cadets, and in two and a half years had risen from lieutenant to the rank of major general through merit and had become a corps commander.

Grant was highly doubtful about Butler's big-bang idea. "I had no confidence in the success of the scheme," he confessed, "and so expressed myself; but no serious harm could come of the experiment, and the authorities in Washington seemed desirous to have it tried, I permitted it."[165] Grant narrated the event:

> The steamer [*Louisiana*] was sent to Beaufort, North Carolina, and was there loaded with powder and prepared for the part she was to play in the reduction of Fort Fisher.
> General Butler chose to go in command of the expedition himself, and was all ready to sail by the 9th of December (1864). Very heavy storms prevailed, however, at that time along that part of the sea-coast, and prevented him from getting off until the 13th or 14th. His advance arrived off Fort Fisher on the 15th. The naval force had been already assembled, or was assembling, but they were obliged to run into Beaufort for munitions, coal, etc.; then, too the powder-boat was not yet fully prepared. The fleet was ready to proceed on the 18th, but Butler, who had remained outside from the 15th

Interior of Fort Fisher. After landing his troops for the planned assault on the fort, Butler became fearful of being attacked by a rebel force and, disobeying orders from General Grant, withdrew from his beachhead, reboarded his troops on their transports and fled back to Hampton Roads (Library of Congress).

up to that time, now found himself out of coal, fresh water, etc., and had to put into Beaufort to replenish. Another storm overtook him, and several days more were lost before the army and navy were both ready at the same time to co-operate.

On the night of the 23rd the powder-boat was towed in by a gunboat as near to the fort as it was safe to run. She was then propelled by her own machinery to within about five hundred yards of the shore. There the clockwork, which was to explode her within a certain length of time, was set and she was abandoned. Everybody left, and even the vessels put out to sea to prevent the effect of the explosion upon them.

At two o'clock in the morning the explosion took place—and produced no more effect on the fort, or anything else on land, than the bursting of a boiler anywhere on the Atlantic Ocean would have done. Indeed when the troops in Fort Fisher heard the explosion they supposed it was the bursting of a boiler in one of the Yankee gunboats.[166]

Blown up along with the *Louisiana* was Butler's plan to take Fort Fisher without a fight and to change the nature of coastal warfare. What was more, Butler wasn't even there to witness his explosive spectacle, having been delayed at Beaufort. In his memoir he made no further mention of his big idea.

The expedition's attention now turned to Butler's assault force, brought to the scene on army transports. Following a horrific bombardment of the fort on December 24, during which Admiral Porter's fleet fired 115 shells per minute into the fortification, the troops landed north of Fort Fisher, out of range of its guns, on Christmas day, their landing covered by protective U.S. Navy gunboats. The fort was built on the southern tip of a long, narrow sandy strip of land called Federal Point, which forms a peninsula between the Atlantic Ocean and the Cape Fear River. The fort commanded not only the channel through which every vessel entering the river from the ocean must pass, but Federal Point was so narrow that the fort also commanded the lower end of the river. Shaped like a figure 7, the long leg facing the ocean, the fort consisted of sand parapets as high as twenty feet, one parapet, about 500 yards long, facing north and the other, 1,300 yards long, facing the ocean, both with ditches and loop-holed palisades in front of them. There was a bastion at the angle where the two parapets met at the northeast corner and another bastion at the south end of the ocean-facing parapet. Two field pieces at the entrance in the north-facing parapet gave a flanking fire upon the ditch and assisted the guns in the bastion. That front of the fort was armed with 21 heavy guns and three mortars. The ocean-facing front was armed with 24 guns. Manning those guns and protecting the works was Fort Fisher's garrison, which numbered fewer than 1,500 officers and men in December 1864. It was commanded by Colonel William Lamb, a twenty-nine-year-old former newspaper editor from Norfolk, Virginia, who had assumed command on July 4, 1862, and had been building and strengthening the fort ever since. The Christmas Day assault by Butler and his troops was described by General Grant:

> They [the U.S. troops] formed a line across the peninsula and advanced, part going north, and part toward the fort, covering themselves as they did so. [Brigadier General Newton Martin] Curtis pushed forward and came near to Fort Fisher, capturing the small garrison at what was called the Flag Pond Battery. Weitzel accompanied him to within a half a mile of the works. Here he saw that the fort had not been injured [by the naval bombardment], and so reported to Butler, advising against an assault. [Major General Adelbert] Ames, who had gone north in his advance, captured 228 of the reserves. These prisoners reported to Butler that sixteen hundred of [Confederate Major General Robert] Hoke's division of six thousand from Richmond had already arrived and the rest would soon be in his rear.
> Upon these reports Butler determined to withdraw his troops from the peninsula and return to the fleet. At that time there had not been a man on our side injured except by one of the shells from the fleet. Curtis had got within a few yards of the works.... At night Butler informed Porter of his withdrawal, giving the reasons above stated, and announced his purpose as soon as his men could embark to start for Hampton Roads. Porter represented to him that he had sent to Beaufort for more ammunition. He could fire much faster than he had been doing, and would keep the enemy from showing himself until our men were within twenty yards of the fort....
> Butler was unchangeable. He got all his troops aboard, except Curtis's brigade, and started back.[167]

General Grant was unequivocal in his denunciation of Butler's actions. "My instructions to him, or to the officer who went in command of the expedition," Grant wrote, "were explicit in the statement that to effect a landing would be of itself a great victory, and if one should be effected, the foothold must not be relinquished; on the contrary, a regular siege of the fort must be commenced.... But General Butler seems to have lost sight of this part of his instructions, and was back at Fort Monroe on the 28th."[168] Still careful about criticizing Lincoln's political generals, Grant wired a nonaccusatory telegram to the president to report the mission's failure: "The Wilmington expedition has proven a gross and culpable failure. Many of the troops are back here [in Virginia]. Delays and free talk of the object of the expedition enabled the enemy to move troops to Wilmington to defeat it. After the expedition sailed from Fort Monroe, three days of fine weather were squandered, during which the enemy was without a force to protect himself. Who is to blame will, I hope, be known."[169]

A congressional investigation to determine culpability was held soon after the Fort Fisher affair became a national scandal and the bomb boat—called "Butler's powder boat" in the press—became a national joke. Butler, the lawyer and politician, made an eloquent defense of himself, shifting blame to Admiral Porter for not being at the rendezvous point when he should have been. There was no getting around Butler's failure to follow Grant's orders, though. Grant testified that "General Butler came away from Fort Fisher in violation of the instructions which I gave him."[170] The instructions were to entrench if the fort did not quickly fall and stay in place and cooperate with the navy until the fort did fall. Butler obviously knew the orders, for he included them in his memoir: "The object of the expedition will be gained on effecting a landing on the mainland between Cape Fear River and the Atlantic, north of the north entrance to the river. Should such landing be effected, whether the enemy hold Fort Fisher or the batteries guarding the river there, the troops should intrench themselves, and by co-operation with the navy effect the reduction and capture of those places."[171] Butler had once again deemed obedience to orders to be, for him, optional.

Grant requested permission to remove Butler from command. On January 4, 1865, Grant wrote to Secretary Stanton: "I am constrained to request the removal of General Butler from the command of the Department of Virginia and North Carolina. I do this with reluctance, but the good of the service requires it. In my absence General Butler necessarily commands, and there is a lack of confidence felt in his military ability, making him an unsafe commander for a large army. His administration of his department is also objectionable."[172] When he found that Stanton had gone to see Sherman in Savannah, Grant then wired President Lincoln on January 6, asking for prompt action. Lincoln, with political considerations a thing of the past, his reelection having been accomplished two months earlier, responded with the promptness Grant requested. Grant received the president's okay the next day, and on January 8 he sent two of his aides, Lieutenant Colonel O.E. Babcock and Lieutenant Colonel Horace Porter, to Butler's headquarters to deliver the written order relieving him of his duties and his command.

In a final public rationalization of his insubordinate conduct Butler stood before his massed troops in review and told them, "I have refused to order the useless sacrifice of the lives of such soldiers and I am relieved of your command. The wasted blood of my men does not stain my garments. For my action I am responsible to God and my country."[173] He then bade the troops farewell and was escorted to the steamer that would take him home. His military career was ended, as were his chances to succeed Lincoln in the White House, believed by many to have been his longtime, motivating ambition.

As for Fort Fisher, a new assault was soon launched, with other troops and another commander, thirty-seven-year-old Brigadier General Alfred Howe Terry. Terry's 8,000 troops stormed ashore from landing boats on January 13, covered by an intense bombardment from

Porter's warships, and after two days of heavy fighting they overwhelmed the garrison and forced the surrender of the fort on the evening of Sunday, January 15, 1865. The 6,000 rebel troops, the threat of which had so spooked Butler that he ran for safety, proved to be no help to the beleaguered fort. Their commander, Major General Robert F. Hoke, had them make a demonstration against a segment of Terry's line, but when that part of the line was reinforced a light skirmish followed, and Hoke withdrew without further action.

The fall of Fort Fisher came at an awkward time for Butler. The news reached Washington, D.C., on Monday, January 16, just as Butler was defending himself in the congressional investigation. He was telling the joint committee of investigators that he had been relieved for his failure to take Fort Fisher, but, he maintained, Fort Fisher was impregnable, impossible to take, and he had done the right thing in abandoning the mission. Just then cheers erupted in the street, and newsboys with copies of newspaper extras were shouting the news that the fort had been captured, giving an instantaneous and dramatic rebuttal to Butler's protestations. The room where the congressional hearing was being held immediately filled with raucous laughter while Butler exclaimed, "Impossible! It's a mistake!" When he at last realized he had lost his case as well as his military career, he raised his hand and called for silence, then declared, "Thank God for victory."[174]

Shifting his party affiliation from Democrat to Republican, Butler went on to serve as a member of the U.S. House of Representatives from 1867 to 1875. He was elected governor of Massachusetts in 1882 and served in that office from January 1883 to January 1884, Massachusetts then having one-year terms for its governors. He died while in court in Washington, D.C., on January 11, 1893, at age 74.

2

Major General Nathaniel Prentice Banks

Before the War: Born January 30, 1816, in Waltham, Massachusetts. Attended public schools until age 14. Dropped out of school to help support his family. Worked at a textile mill, replacing bobbins as they became full of thread, later apprenticed as a mechanic. Was self-taught from library books and public lectures. Became an actor. Developed skill as a public speaker in a debate club. Opened a dance school. Served as editor of two political newspapers. Worked as a clerk at the Boston customhouse. Married Mary Theodosia Palmer, a mill worker, on April 11, 1847. Four children. Political affiliation: Democrat, later Republican. Elected to the Massachusetts legislature in November 1848, served as a representative from 1849 to 1853. Served as Massachusetts speaker of the house in 1851, 1852. Elected to the U.S. House of Representatives in 1853. Elected speaker of the U.S. House of Representatives in 1856. Served until 1857. Governor of Massachusetts, 1858 to 1860. Sought Republican nomination for U.S. president in 1860. Became resident director of the Illinois Central Railroad in Chicago, 1861. Military experience: None.

Forty-five-year-old Nathaniel Prentice Banks was a longtime successful and influential politician who lived off his words—"born for a talker," one observer said of him[1]—along with his shiftiness on public issues and his ability to make helpful alliances. Banks had the idea that the newly elected president, Abraham Lincoln, would, or might, appoint him to a Cabinet post. Lincoln, however, decided that the plum Banks should get was a major general's commission in the U.S. Army, even though he was without military experience or military education. And so on May 16, 1861, thirty-five days after the assault on Fort Sumter, he became the fourth-highest ranking officer in the United States Army, just below the general in chief, seventy-four-year-old Lieutenant General Winfield Scott, and Major General John Frémont and Major General George McClellan.

He looked good in his new, tailored general's uniform. "Dapper" was probably the word that best described him. In his dark-blue frock coat with two vertical rows of 12 brass buttons cascading down his chest, he was, according to one beholder, "one of the finest appearing and best looking officers in the army." He wore his hair thickly mounded atop his head, it seeming to be brushed only with his hand, and had a bushy, walrus mustache that hid most of his mouth. Nevertheless, a newspaper correspondent wrote that Banks was "the most impressive man, in countenance, language and demeanor, whom I have seen since the war commenced."[2] He stood five feet eight inches, with a compact build and pleasant gray eyes that tended to fasten onto the face of the person he was speaking to. One of his biographers, James Hollandsworth, Jr., wrote that Banks "strove to combine the image of a born aristocrat with the impression of personal charm"—the image and impression that another commentator called "pretentious humbug."[3]

General Banks's first assignment was to take over the army's Department of Annapolis, which had been created to accommodate Banks's fellow political general Benjamin Butler. Butler had been superseded as department commander by Major General George Cadwalader on May 15, 1861. Now Banks superseded Cadwalader a month later, on June 11. It was a job for which Banks, an experienced administrator, was suited well enough. His management style, however, far different from Butler's effective heavy-handedness, proved problematic. His attempts to win friends and influence Baltimoreans did win him some friends, but his leniency and tolerance were seen by others as weakness, and they soon took advantage of him and became dangerously troublesome.

Maj. Gen. Nathaniel Banks, despite having had no military experience or military training, was appointed a major general by President Lincoln in May 1861, making him the fourth-highest-ranking officer in the U.S. Army (Library of Congress).

Made aware of the growing menace of secessionists in Baltimore—and apparently dissatisfied with Banks's handling of them—General Scott on June 24 ordered Banks to crack down on their leaders, issuing him the following instructions:

> Sir: Mr. Snethen,[4] of Baltimore, a gentleman of standing, will deliver to you this communication. He has just given to the Secretary of War and myself many important facts touching the subject of [the] Union in that city. It is confirmed by him that, among the citizens, the secessionists, if not the most numerous, are by far more active and effective than the supporters of the Federal Government.
>
> It is the opinion of the Secretary of War, and I need not add my own, that the blow should be early struck, to carry consternation into the ranks of our numerous enemies about you. Accordingly, it seems desirable that you should take measures quietly to seize at once and securely hold the four members of the Baltimore police board, viz: Charles Howard, Wm. H. Gatchell, J.W. Davis, and C.D. Hinks, esqrs., together with the chief

of the police, G.P. Kane. It is further suggested that you appoint a provost-marshal to superintend and cause to be executed the police law provided by the legislature of Maryland for Baltimore.

Your discretion and firmness are equally relied upon for the due execution of the foregoing views.[5]

Once prodded, Banks took action. A week later, on July 1, he dashed off a brief note to Scott: "The board of police was arrested this morning at 4 o'clock. Troops have been stationed at the principal squares of the city. All is perfectly quiet. We greatly need cavalry for patrol duty."[6] Later that day, from his headquarters at Fort McHenry, Banks wrote a detailed report to Scott and concluded by saying, "I have the gratification to inform you that all the arrests have been made without disturbance, and that the city is now and has been since the arrest of the chief of police more quiet and orderly than for any time for many months previous."[7]

Scott was evidently satisfied with Banks's prompt and effectual action, so satisfied that he gave him a tougher assignment. On July 22, 1861, Scott ordered Banks to Harpers Ferry to take command of the Department of the Shenandoah, relieving Irish-born, sixty-nine-year-old Major General Robert Patterson, who had lost Scott's confidence. Banks arrived at Harpers Ferry on July 25 and assumed command. His first major act came on September 17 when, on orders from secretary of war Simon Cameron, he arrested several members of the Maryland legislature, then meeting in Frederick, to prevent passage of a Maryland secession bill.

Banks's troops spent most of the summer on the banks of the Potomac River and it wasn't until mid–February that they crossed the river and moved into Virginia. The move was made to coincide with the campaign launched by General McClellan, who would advance up the Virginia peninsula, between the James and York rivers, in an attempt to capture Richmond. Banks's movements in the Shenandoah Valley were aimed at keeping the Confederates from shifting troops from western Virginia to reinforce General Joseph E. Johnston in his defense of Richmond. At the same time, Banks's troops could protect Washington when McClellan removed the bulk of his force from the Washington area and sent it to Fort Monroe to commence the march up the peninsula.

Amid all that activity, President Lincoln decided to reorganize the army in which he was most interested. On March 8, 1862, he issued an order that divided the Army of the Potomac into five corps, specifying how many divisions would be in each corps. He also named the generals who would command each of the five corps. Named to command the Army of the Potomac's new Fifth Corps was Major General Nathaniel Banks, whose experience as a soldier now reached back all of ten months and whose combat experience remained nil, a situation that was about to change.[8]

On March 13 Lincoln, through his new secretary of war, Edwin Stanton, issued additional instructions for the Army of the Potomac's commander, General McClellan:

1. Leave such force at Manassas Junction as shall make it entirely certain that the enemy shall not repossess himself of that position and line of communication.
2. Leave Washington entirely secure.
3. Move the remainder of the force down the Potomac, choosing a new base at Fortress Monroe, or anywhere between here and there, or, at all events, move such remainder of the army at once in pursuit of the enemy by some route.[9]

Battle of Winchester, Virginia. By President Lincoln's order, Banks became commander of the Fifth Corps of the Army of the Potomac, which Lincoln ordered to guard the nation's capital. In his first action Banks withstood an attack by Gen. Thomas "Stonewall" Jackson near Winchester on March 23, 1862. Brig. Gen. James Shields, one of Banks's brigade commanders, pictured here, was severely wounded during the battle (Library of Congress).

Responding to the president's instructions, McClellan wrote orders to Banks, whose corps had been selected for the task of keeping Washington safe:

> You will post your command in the vicinity of Manassas, intrench yourself strongly, and throw cavalry pickets well out to the front. Your first care will be the rebuilding of the railway from Washington to Manassas and to Strasburg, in order to open your communications with the valley of the Shenandoah. As soon as the Manassas Gap Railway is in running order, intrench a brigade of infantry, say four regiments, with two batteries, at or near the point where the railway crosses the Shenandoah. Something like two regiments of cavalry should be left in that vicinity to occupy Winchester and thoroughly scour the country south of the railway and up the Shenandoah Valley.[10]

On March 13 the bulk of Banks's corps was concentrated in the vicinity of Winchester. Positioned just below Strasburg was a small Confederate force under the command of General Thomas (Stonewall) Jackson, who had recently evacuated Winchester and moved south in the face of the advancing, larger U.S. force. On March 19 troops under the command of U.S. Brigadier General James Shields, one of Banks's brigade commanders, moved into Strasburg, causing Jackson to fall back farther, to Mount Jackson, some fifty-five miles south of Winchester.

On March 20, in compliance with McClellan's instructions, the first division of Banks's corps, led by Banks, turned east and headed for Manassas, and the units at Strasburg began to fall back toward Winchester. When Jackson discovered that a large part of Banks's army had pulled away, he decided the Union force that remained in the valley was of a size he could handle and he sent out skirmishers to probe the Union line. In a fight with Jackson's skirmishers on March 22 General Shields, commanding the force that Banks had left behind, was wounded and he removed himself to Winchester for treatment, turning his command over to Colonel Nathan Kimball, a thirty-eight-year-old physician who had served as an infantry captain in the Mexican War.

On the cold Sunday morning of March 23, 1862, moving across ground spattered with patches of snow, Jackson struck Kimball's force at the Pritchard farm at Kernstown, several miles south of Winchester, and quickly discovered that the force Banks had left in the valley was a full division, more than 6,000 men, three times the size of Jackson's force. The Union troops formed a line that spread across the valley turnpike, on which it had been moving northward. Sixteen pieces of the division's artillery were emplaced on Pritchard's Hill, commanding the turnpike and valley floor, and they began taking a heavy toll on the advancing Confederates, forcing them to shift westward and move into the relative shelter of the woods on a ridge about a half mile away. As more of Jackson's troops arrived, coming up from the south, they, too, moved toward the ridge.

Seeing the growing concentration of Confederates, Kimball rushed his infantry to face them from behind a line of stone fences that dipped and rose across the rolling fields. Jackson's men delivered a blistering fire as Kimball's troops hurried to take positions behind the fences, but as the afternoon turned into evening, Kimball's superior numbers checked the Confederate advance and forced the attackers from the field. Darkness and quiet then settled over the bloodied hills. Jackson's casualties were put at eighty killed, 375 wounded and 263 captured or missing. Union casualties amounted to 118 killed, 450 wounded and twenty-two captured or missing.[11] In recognition of his victory Colonel Kimball, on April 16, was promoted to brigadier general.

In the good news of Jackson's advance having been blunted, however, President Lincoln saw the bad news of Jackson's continuing threat to the nation's capital. He decided to keep Major General Irvin McDowell's 30,000 troops where they were in northern Virginia, as a protection to Washington, instead of sending them to reinforce McClellan on the peninsula. And he called Banks back from *his* march to join McClellan, ordering him to reunite his corps and chase Stonewall Jackson out of the Shenandoah Valley.

In an effort to comply, Banks, with superior numbers, slowly forced Jackson back, pushing him southward past Strasburg, past New Market, past Harrisonburg, down as far as Staunton and beyond, so far that in late April Banks decided his mission had been accomplished. From his headquarters in Harrisonburg he wrote to Secretary Stanton on April 28: "Our force is entirely secure here. The enemy is in no condition for offensive movements.... Our supplies have not been in so good condition nor my command in so good spirits since we left Winchester.... You need have no apprehensions for our safety. I think we are now just in condition to do all you can desire of us in this valley—clear the enemy out permanently."[12]

Later that same day Banks wrote again to Stanton: "If Jackson retreats from his present position there is no reason for our remaining longer in this valley. If he does not, we can compel his retreat or destroy him. Then a small force, two or three regiments, will safely hold all that is important to the Government in this valley."[13] On April 30 he wrote again

Banks's drive against Stonewall Jackson at Strasburg, Virginia. In April 1862 Banks's forces pushed Jackson's greatly outnumbered army through Strasburg and as far south as Staunton in a campaign to rid the Shenandoah Valley of Confederate troops (Library of Congress).

to Stanton: "Further reflection and full consultations with all leading officers confirm opinion express[ed] in my dispatch of 29th instant. There is nothing more to be done by us in the valley. Nothing this side of Strasburg requires our presence."[14] Having read Banks's sunny report, Stanton issued new orders for him on May 1: "The President directs that you fall back with the force under your immediate command to Strasburg, or such other point near there as will be convenient for supplies and enable you to hold the passage along the valley of the Shenandoah. General Shields will receive orders within a day or two to pass with his division into the Department of the Rappahannock."[15]

Giving half of Banks's corps to General McDowell while keeping Banks tied down at Strasburg wasn't what Banks had in mind. He had been angling for reassignment to where the main event, the drive on Richmond, was going on. That was where the potential glory lay. He wrote back to Stanton with a mild protest on May 3: "I do not think it possible to divide our force at this time with safety. The enemy is largely re-enforced by Ewell's division."[16] Then, apparently having second thoughts about his objection, he wrote again to Stanton later that day: "Your dispatch as to the disposition of troops of the Fifth Corps received, and measures will be taken in accordance therewith. I shall grieve not to be included in the active operations of this summer...."[17] He would soon have more to grieve about. From New

Market on May 7 he wrote to Stanton that his cavalry had reported that Jackson's troops had moved into Harrisonburg, about 25 miles south of Banks's position at New Market. "This refers probably to Ewell's division," he wrote. "Deserters east of mountains confirm report of Jackson's movement in this direction."[18] The next day, May 8, he received a warning from Secretary Stanton: "It is believed at Fort Monroe that a considerable rebel force has been sent toward the Rappahannock and Shenandoah to move on Washington. Jackson is reinforced strongly.... Keep a sharp lookout, and report frequently."[19]

Trouble was mounting. Lieutenant General Richard Ewell was adding some 8,000 troops to Jackson's army, and Major General Edward Johnson, whose division had also been sent to Jackson, was adding another 4,000 or so. Banks, with 9,000 men, would now have to face a formidable enemy commanding 20,000 rebel troops. He began thinking defense. While doing so, he received more orders from Stanton, issued on May 9: "It has become necessary, in the present state of things, to remind you of the orders of the 1st instant, for yourself to take position at Strasburg or its vicinity. New Market seems somewhat distant to fall within the meaning of the order, and might find you out of position should circumstances make it necessary for you to move to the support of McDowell."[20] In a separate communication written that same day Stanton told Banks that he should find out if the enemy was in force in front of him. If the enemy is not in force, Stanton instructed, General Shields should march as fast as possible to support McDowell in protecting Washington, which was Stanton's overriding concern. "The probabilities at present," he told Banks, "point to a possible attempt upon Washington while the Shenandoah army is amused with demonstrations. Washington is the only object now worth a desperate throw."[21]

Banks now decided to establish a defensive line at Strasburg to face Jackson's northward approach on the turnpike. The ridges would protect his right flank, and to guard his left he sent a 1,000-man force under Colonel John Kenly to Front Royal, about ten miles to the east, on the Manassas Gap Railroad. Banks's troops dug in and awaited the approach of Jackson's army, which Banks expected to come straight up the turnpike. Jackson, though, had other plans. From New Market he advanced a short distance on the turnpike, then turned eastward, passed through a gap in Massanutten Mountain, and did a column left at Luray. Here he would be joined by Ewell, then he would march up the road to Front Royal that paralleled the turnpike.

Banks received reports that the Confederates were on the Luray-Front Royal road, but dismissed them, certain that Jackson was still at New Market. On Friday, May 23, the full force of Jackson's army, advancing on the Luray-Front Royal road, fell on Colonel Kenly's troops. Kenly bravely but vainly made a stand in an effort to give Banks time to prepare for an assault from the east instead of the south. Jackson's troops quickly overcame Kenly's resistance and took over Front Royal, inflicting heavy losses on Kenly. Despite the warning that Jackson was at Front Royal, received by a courier from Kenly who managed to slip through Jackson's lines, Banks clung to the idea that Jackson's main force was below Strasburg and would advance up the turnpike. Rejecting the suggestion of a quick withdrawal to Winchester, made at a meeting with his brigade commanders, he revealed his concern over how a retreat would be seen by the public, telling Colonel George H. Gordon, "We have more to fear from the opinions of our friends than from the bayonets of our enemies."[22]

During the night, however, with more information about the size of Jackson's army on his left flank, with the road from Front Royal to Strasburg open to Jackson, as well as the road from Front Royal to Winchester, fearing a huge flanking move by Jackson on the Union left and possibly being surrounded if Jackson made a forced march to Winchester, Banks decided he should make some adjustments to his plan to remain entrenched at Strasburg. About three o'clock Saturday morning, May 24, he ordered his sick and wounded and some of his supply wagons moved northward, and they started rolling about 4:30 a.m. About mid-morning on Saturday Banks finally got the main body of his army moving out of Strasburg, headed for Winchester, twenty miles to the north. It arrived there about five o'clock Saturday afternoon, the impedimenta of his troops left behind them, personal effects and equipment strewn along the sides of the road like so much highway litter, along with abandoned army wagons.

Fearful of Criticism

Still more fearful of a public-relations beating than a defeat at the hands of the rebel army, Banks again resisted Colonel Gordon's advice to continue the northward march past Winchester to avoid a battle with his fewer than 6,000 men against Jackson's estimated 15,000. Banks wired Washington that he had arrived at Winchester and then retired to his room in his commandeered headquarters and took a bath while his troops began to dig in. To Banks's second in command, Brigadier General Alpheus S. Williams, a Michigan lawyer who had served as a lieutenant colonel during the Mexican War but had seen no action, was left the job of laying out Banks's line of defense, which Williams did without making an effort to discover the positions of Jackson's army. Working in darkness, Williams positioned Banks's troops. He put Gordon's brigade on the Union right with its left flank on the turnpike, supported by a battery of artillery. The brigade of Colonel Dudley Donnelly, also supported by a battery of artillery, was placed in a crescent-shaped formation on the left, in a position to cover the road from Front Royal. In the center of the line Williams placed the cavalry brigade commanded by Brigadier General John Hatch, supported by two artillery pieces.

At the crack of dawn on Sunday, May 25, Jackson's skirmishers advanced in force and immediately drove in Banks's pickets. Shortly thereafter, three of General Ewell's four rebel brigades advanced on the valley turnpike to assault Banks's center while the fourth brigade struck Banks's left, advancing on the road from Front Royal. Although hindered by artillery fire and fusillades of musket fire, Jackson's troops swarmed over the outnumbered Union force, overwhelming it and putting it to flight. A courageous cavalry charge made on the rapidly advancing rebels proved futile. Union soldiers dashed through the streets of Winchester in a wild rush to escape capture, leaving behind the wounded and tons of supplies, many of the fleeing soldiers tossing away their weapons to speed their race to safety. Seeing the enemy routed and the streets of Winchester emptied, Jackson's march-weary men slowed their advance and let the fleeing Union troops go, too exhausted to pursue them as they hurried for the Potomac River.

From Martinsburg, West Virginia, some twenty miles above Winchester, on the way to the Potomac, General Banks filed a report to Secretary Stanton at 2:40 that afternoon. It summarized the battle of Winchester:

> The rebels attacked us this morning at daybreak in great force. Their number was estimated at 15,000, consisting of Ewell's and Jackson's divisions. The fire of pickets

began with light; was followed by the artillery, until the lines were fully under fire on both sides. The left wing stood firmly, holding the ground well, and the right did the same for a time, when two regiments broke the line under the fire of the enemy. The right wing fell back. They were ordered to withdraw, and the troops pressed through the town in considerable confusion. They were quickly reformed on the other side, and continued their march in good order to Martinsburg, where they arrived at 2:40 p.m. a distance of 22 miles.... Our loss is considerable, as was that of the enemy, but cannot now be stated.[23]

Banks's losses were eventually put at 62 killed, 243 wounded and 1,714 captured or missing, a total of 2,019. Jackson's losses were put at 400, counting killed, wounded and missing.[24] Comforting himself, Banks three days later wrote to his wife, Mary: "Whatever may be said of our recent movement, I can assure you that it is one of the most remarkable that has occurred or will occur during the war. It is miraculous almost that my entire command and its train should escape without harm the long matured plans of an enemy five times our number."[25] In fact, Jackson's force was about two and a half times larger than Banks's, 16,000 to 6,500. Banks also lost an abundance of wagons, horses, mules, sheep and cattle, tons of food, 9,000 small arms, two artillery pieces and "more medical stores than you ever heard of," as Jackson's quartermaster described the bounty.

By the morning of the 26th Banks's retreating army had reached the banks of the Potomac, and sometime before 9:00 a.m. Banks sent Secretary Stanton a report on his progress: "We believe that our whole force, trains and all, will cross in safety. The men are in fine spirits and crossing in good order. The labor of last night was fearful. The enemy followed us last night on the march, but has not made his appearance this morning."[26] That afternoon, Banks reported to Stanton from Williamsport, Maryland: "I have the honor to report ... the passage of the Fifth Corps across the river to-day with comparatively little loss." At 8:20 that evening he reported, "Everything quiet. Enemy alarmed; has withdrawn, I think."[27] To that report Stanton responded with instructions for Banks to prepare to return to his former lines at Strasburg, telling him reinforcements were on the way and urging him to recross the Potomac and occupy Martinsburg "at once." Banks began slowly, carefully creeping back up the route along which he had so recently fled and from which Jackson was withdrawing to join General Robert E. Lee, who had replaced the wounded General Joseph Johnston as commander of the Confederate forces defending Richmond.

About the same time, President Lincoln was making more changes in the U.S. Army. On June 26 he appointed Major General John Pope to command a reorganized force designated the Army of Virginia. Banks's former Fifth Corps of the Army of the Potomac became the Second Corps of the Army of Virginia. Named to command the new army's two other corps were Major General John Frémont, commanding the First Corps, and General McDowell, commanding the Third Corps. Frémont, however, who like both Banks and McDowell outranked Pope, refused the command in protest and was replaced by Major General Franz Sigel. Determinedly standing his ground after McClellan's peninsula campaign had been thwarted, Pope deployed his army in an arc across northern Virginia, placing its left flank, held by McDowell, near Fredericksburg and its right flank, held by Sigel, at Sperryville, in Rappahannock County. Its center was in Culpeper County and was held by Banks, who had finally got his wish and been moved out of the Shenandoah Valley, closer to the main action. To that daunting array of U.S. forces now a menace to Richmond from the north, General

Lee, commanding Confederate forces in Virginia, quickly turned his attention. On July 13 he moved Stonewall Jackson's 14,000-man army to Gordonsville, just south of Banks's position, and on July 27 he reinforced Jackson with the 10,000-man division of Major General A.P. Hill. Then, with much help and initiative from Stonewall Jackson, he set out to remove the menace. The official reports of generals Lee, Jackson and Pope tell the story of Banks's next big test on the battlefield, confronting Jackson again. Lee wrote:

> General Jackson, now re-enforced by A.P. Hill, determined to assume the offensive against General Pope, whose army, still superior in numbers, lay north of the Rapidan.... Learning that only a portion of General Pope's army was at Culpeper Court-House, General Jackson resolved to attack it before the arrival of the remainder, and on August 7 moved from Gordonsville for that purpose....
>
> The next day the Federal cavalry on the north side of the Rapidan was driven back by General Robertson, and on the 9th Jackson's command arrived within 8 miles of Culpeper Court-House, when the enemy was found near Cedar Run, a short distance northwest of Slaughter Mountain. [also known as Cedar Mountain]. Early's brigade, of Ewell's division, was thrown forward on the road to Culpeper Court-House; the remaining two brigades ... diverging to the right, to position on the western slope of Slaughter Mountain. Jackson's own division, under Brigadier General Winder, was placed on the left of the road....
>
> The battle opened with a fierce fire of artillery, which continued for about two hours, during which Brig. Gen. Charles S. Winder received a wound from the effects of which he expired in a few hours....
>
> The enemy's infantry advanced about 5 p.m. and attacked General Early in front, while another body, concealed by the irregularity of the ground, moved upon his right. Thomas's brigade, of A.P. Hill's division, which had now arrived, was sent to his support, and the contest soon became animated.[28]

In his report, General Jackson stated the following:

> While the attack upon Early was in progress, the main body of the Federal infantry moved down from the wood through the corn and wheat fields, and fell with great vigor upon our extreme left, and by the force of superior numbers, bearing down all opposition, turned it and poured a destructive fire into its rear. Campbell's brigade fell back in disorder. The enemy pushing forward, and the left flank of Taliaferro's brigade being by these movements exposed to a flank fire, fell back, as did also the left of Early's line, the remainder of his command holding its position with great firmness.... At this critical moment Branch's brigade, of Hill's division, with Winder's brigade, farther to the left, met the Federal forces, flushed with their temporary triumph, and drove them back with terrible slaughter through the wood.... Archer and Pender coming up, a general charge was made, which drove the enemy across the field into the opposite wood, strewing the narrow valley with their dead....
>
> Thus repulsed from our left and center, and now pressed by our right, center, and left, the Federal force fell back at every point of their line, and commenced retreating, leaving their dead and wounded on the field of battle.[29]

General Pope, the U.S. forces' over-all commander, who arrived on the battlefield as the action was drawing to a close, summarized the results:

> The action lasted about an hour and a half, and during that time our forces suffered heavy loss, and were gradually driven back to their former position.... The enemy

> followed Banks as he retired with great caution, and emerging from the woods, which had sheltered him all day, attempted to push forward to the open ground in front of our new line. A sharp artillery engagement immediately commenced, when the enemy was driven back to the woods....
>
> The artillery firing was kept up until near midnight of the 9th. Finding that Banks' corps had been severely cut up and was much fatigued I drew it back to the rear and pushed forward the corps of Sigel, which had begun to arrive, to occupy the woods on the left of the road, with a wide space of open ground in his front.... Banks's corps, reduced to about 5,000 men, was so cut up and worn down with fatigue that I did not consider it capable of rendering any efficient service for several days....
>
> In consequence of the vigorous resistance of the night previous, and the severe loss of the enemy in attempting to advance, before daylight of the 10th Jackson drew back his forces toward Cedar Mountain, about 2 miles from our front. Our pickets were immediately pushed forward, supported by Milroy's brigade, and occupied the ground.[30]

Pope found fault with Banks, first in the substantial discrepancy in Banks's reports of his troop strength. "The consolidated report of General Banks' corps, received some days previously [to the battle] exhibited an effective force of something over 14,000 men," Pope wrote. But after the battle, Banks stated to Pope that the force he had led to the front totaled no more than 8,000 men. "That discrepancy," Pope complained, "has never been explained, and I do not yet understand how General Banks could have been so greatly mistaken as to the forces under his immediate command."[31] Second, Pope pointed out, Banks failed to follow Pope's instructions and made some poor choices.

> I desired General Banks merely to keep the enemy in check by occupying a strong position in his front until the whole of the disposable forces under my command should be concentrated in the neighborhood. General Roberts [a member of Pope's staff] reported to me that he had conferred freely with General Banks and urgently represented to him my purposes, but that General Banks, contrary to his suggestions and to my wishes, had left the strong position which he had taken up and had advanced at least a mile to assault the enemy, believing they were not in considerable force, and that he would be able to crush their advance before their main body could come up from the direction of the Rapidan. He accordingly threw forward his whole corps into action, against superior forces of the enemy strongly posted and sheltered by woods and ridges. His advance led him over the open ground, which was everywhere swept by the fire of the enemy, concealed in the woods and ravines beyond.[32]

Pope did manage to find something good to say about Banks's conduct during the battle: "Although I regret that General Banks thought it expedient to depart from my instructions, it gives me pleasure to bear testimony to his gallant and intrepid conduct throughout that action. He exposed himself as freely as any one under his command, and his example went far to secure that gallant and noble conduct which has made his corps famous."[33]

U.S. losses in the Battle of Cedar Mountain amounted to 314 killed, 1,445 wounded and 622 captured or missing, a total of 2,381. Confederate losses were put at 241 killed, 1,120 wounded and four missing, a total of 1,365.[34] Banks himself became a sort of casualty of the battle when he and Pope and several other ranking officers of Pope's command were sitting on the ground in bright moonlight after the battle, reviewing the day's events. Suddenly they heard the sound of approaching horses. A Confederate cavalry detail patrolling behind the Union lines was coming toward them, about forty yards away. They all immediately sprang to their feet and dashed for their horses. The Confederates opened fire on them, mortally wounding an orderly and hitting the orderly's horse as well. The horse reared when it was hit and struck Banks on the left hip with its hoof. Banks was knocked to the ground but managed to get up and mount his horse and escape with the others.

Jackson held his position until August 12, when, upon learning that Pope's entire army had assembled at Culpeper Court House, he fell back to Gordonsville. Banks's battered corps was pulled back to be refreshed and reorganized. Pope held it at Fayetteville, West Virginia. In a series of conflicts Lee and Jackson resumed the campaign to drive Pope's army from northern Virginia, and after Pope's loss to Lee at the Second Battle of Manassas (or Bull Run), fought August 28 to 30, Banks was placed in command of U.S. troops in Washington and ordered to organize the city's defenses. By early November, Lincoln had decided to give him a new assignment. General Butler was to be relieved of command of the Department of the Gulf, which was headquartered in New Orleans, and Banks was selected as his successor.

Ordered to New Orleans

Dated November 9, 1862, the order read: "By direction of the President of the United States Maj. Gen. N.P. Banks is assigned to the command of the Department of the Gulf, including the State of Texas. By order of the Secretary of War."[35] With a force of new enlistees from New York state and New England he had recruited, Banks sailed from New York in a fleet of fifty transports on December 4. Gathering with his top officers in his ship's saloon, he raised a glass and toasted the new venture. "We go to uphold the flag of the Union and sustain the constitution," he declared grandly, "and may God grant that we may be successful."[36] The officers cheered him and his toast, and the fleet sailed off into the evening.

Butler knew Banks was coming to relieve him. Rumors had been circulating in New Orleans for weeks. "I had such complete knowledge of Banks' movements," Butler wrote in his memoir, "that I telegraphed to Forts Jackson and St. Philip to salute Major-General Banks on his steamer with the number of guns appropriate to the commander of the department. When his steamer came to the wharf at the city, I had a battery of artillery to fire a proper salute, and my carriage was in readiness to take him to my house to be entertained."[37] It was at Butler's house that Banks, on December 12, presented the order appointing him to supersede Butler.

Butler was well acquainted with Banks, having known him from their associations in Massachusetts politics, and on December 16 he introduced him to the officers and men of the department, commending him, Butler said, "to their kindest regard." Banks assumed command that same day, and Butler turned over to him and his officers all the public property that Butler and his officers held in their possession, amounting, Butler said, to nearly a million dollars. Then, since he had not received any new orders and had time to spend with Banks, Butler spent the next several days giving Banks "all the information I possessed concerning the military situation of the department and the details of my plans for an immediate attack on Port Hudson."[38]

The responsibility that the president had given Banks was only partly military, but that part was Job No. 1. He became the commander of some 40,000 troops (some of whom were stationed at Pensacola). The army's new general in chief, Major General Henry W. Halleck, told him, "The first military operations which will engage your attention on your arrival at New Orleans will be the opening of the Mississippi River and the reduction of Fort Morgan or Mobile City.... The President regards the opening of the Mississippi River as the first and most important of all our military and naval operations, and it is hoped that you will not lose a moment in accomplishing it.... [T]he opening of the Mississippi River is now the great and primary object of your expedition."[39]

General Banks had other concerns, however. One of them was the impression he wished to make on the people of New Orleans. According to one account, he quickly made his presence felt in New Orleans society as well as in the city's business and civil affairs. "The Bankses," that account related, "with their fashionable clothes, bodyguards, servants, and stylish airs, were comparable to royalty. Mrs. Banks had her weekly receptions at the St. Charles [Hotel] and all the 'best ladies appeared there in lace and diamonds.'"[40]

The problems that came with the job soon became evident. "I find ... on arriving here," Banks wrote to Halleck, "an immense military government, embracing every form of civil administration, the assessment of taxes, fines, punishments, charities, trade, regulation of churches, confiscation of estates, and the working of plantations, in addition to the ordinary affairs of a military department."[41] He also quickly discovered the corruption for which Butler's regime had become infamous. "Everybody connected with the government has been employed in stealing other people's property," he wrote in a letter to his wife soon after arriving. "Sugar, silver plate, horses, carriages, everything they could lay their hands on."[42]

Banks (seated at center) and his staff. In December 1862 Banks was ordered to replace General Butler in New Orleans and became commander of some 40,000 troops, apparently requiring a large staff to assist him (Library of Congress).

Although he decried such abuses, Banks was not above allowing his officers to skim some profits themselves. Butler criticized a practice that he would not allow, but which Banks did allow. "I had always held my army to be deemed in the *field*," Butler wrote. "Then, if they were to have quarters, it would cost the government nothing, for they could occupy houses deserted by those who were serving in the Confederate army. But Banks' officers were inclined to consider themselves in *garrison*, for that would enable them to draw pay for quarters, according to regulations, at a somewhat extravagant rate per month, according to their rank. Then they could hire as cheaply as possible what they desired to occupy, and pocket the difference."[43]

Banks eased or eliminated many of the restrictions Butler had placed on consulates, businesses, planters and churches, but he continued Butler's programs of feeding the poor and finding jobs for the unemployed. He also restored to the owners many of the properties that had been seized. Although such actions won him some friends, to others they gave an impression of weakness. Public displays of scorn and rebellion that Butler had quashed began reappearing, and in a fit of exasperation Banks curtailed publication of several newspapers.[44]

Within a month of his arrival in New Orleans Banks began explaining to General Halleck why he wasn't immediately taking the military action he had been instructed to take, regretting, as he said, that his attention to civil concerns "interfered with matters purely military," but insisting that the civil concerns were of first importance. Besides, he told Halleck, "The troops that accompany my expedition are not in condition for immediate service. They are all new troops, most of them never having handled a musket until their arrival here. The artillery is light, not adapted to such service as is necessary to a successful assault upon the fortifications of the enemy on the river.... I have only four or five very weak companies of cavalry. It is impossible to obtain timely information of the movements of the enemy under such circumstances." But, he assured Halleck, "every possible effort is making to remedy these defects in the military organization."[45] Two months later he was still complaining. In a lengthy report to Halleck on March 21, 1863 he wrote, "I cannot close this dispatch without again referring to the total insufficiency of the forces and material within my reach for the work that is expected of me in this department."[46] Butler found in Banks's delays an opportunity for criticism of Banks's failure to follow up on Butler's plans for Port Hudson. "I may remark here," he commented in his memoir, "that no movement was made upon Port Hudson for many months,—not until the enemy had time to fortify it fully, and to reinforce it."[47]

Altogether, Banks's troops, many of whom were the raw recruits he said they were, comprised the U.S. Nineteenth Army Corps, also known as the Army of the Gulf, which was divided into four divisions. The first division was commanded by Brigadier General Cuvier Grover, the second by Brigadier General William Hensley Emory, the third by Major General Christopher Columbus Augur, and the fourth by Brigadier General Thomas West Sherman (no relation to Major General William Tecumseh Sherman). All four division commanders were West Point graduates. Each division was composed of three brigades of infantry and three field artillery batteries. Also included in his command were six troops of cavalry, numbering about 700 effectives, and a regiment of heavy artillery.

Banks made at least one quick military move in his new command. He had barely arrived in New Orleans when Admiral David Farragut, having returned to New Orleans from blockade duty, urged Banks to provide troops to occupy and hold Baton Rouge, pointing out that Baton Rouge was only twelve or so miles from Port Hudson and would make a good base of operations for an attack against Port Hudson. Banks speedily acceded to Farragut's request. On December 17, 1862, following a brief naval bombardment that drove off the 500 or so Confederates who were garrisoning the city, General Grover and the troops of Banks's first division disembarked from their transport steamers and marched into the wasted and woebegone Louisiana capital. And there they remained.

Port Hudson and Vicksburg were the two remaining Confederate fortresses denying free passage on the Mississippi, the nation's greatest thoroughfare. Gaining control of the Mississippi would not only unstop bottled-up commerce and communication it would also cleave the Confederacy and hasten the end of the war. Above Vicksburg and below Port Hudson the forces of the United States controlled the river, but passage on the 200 or so river miles between those two points was prohibited by the two forbidding fortifications. President Lincoln desperately desired their capture so that the mighty river could once again, as he put it, "flow unvexed to the sea." He kept pressing Grant, above Vicksburg, and Banks, below Port Hudson, to make it happen.

Banks's assistant adjutant general, Lieutenant Colonel Richard B. Irwin, set forth Banks's three options in attempting to carry out his orders. He could choose "to carry by assault a strong line of works [at Port Hudson], three miles long, impregnable on either flank and defended by 16,000 good troops; [or] to lay siege to the place, with the certainty that it would be relieved from Mississippi and the prospect of losing his siege train in that venture; [or] to leave Port Hudson in his rear and go against Vicksburg, thus sacrificing his communications, putting New Orleans in peril, and courting irreparable disaster as the price of the remote chance of achieving a great success."[48]

Shortly after arriving in New Orleans Banks had been informed that Port Hudson was garrisoned by 12,000 men, a strength that tempted him, but then, on December 18, 1862, he heard that reinforcements had increased that number to 23,000 and that more reinforcements were on the way. On December 31, 1862, Banks had 31,253 officers and men present for duty, about 10,000 of whom were occupying Baton Rouge.[49] Believing his force insufficient in numbers and in preparation, he ruled out the first option.

He then decided to try a variant of option number three and he developed a plan to implement it. The idea for the operation he proposed had come from Brigadier General Godfrey Weitzel, commander of the U.S. brigade posted at Brashear City (now Morgan City), Louisiana, about 70 miles southwest of New Orleans, on the east bank of the Atchafalaya River. From his position Weitzel could see how Port Hudson could be bypassed. The plan called for Banks to take his troops across the Mississippi at New Orleans, proceed west by rail to the Atchafalaya, cross it, then march up beside Bayou Teche, paralleling the Atchafalaya, all the way to the Red River at Alexandria, Louisiana. Then, assuming steamers could be obtained one way or another, he could move down the Red River to its mouth on the Mississippi, between Port Hudson and Vicksburg. He could then either turn upstream to join Grant at Vicksburg or downstream to attack Port Hudson.

It seemed to Banks a good plan and it temporarily satisfied Washington, which was pushing him to move on Vicksburg. At the same time, it would delay a confrontation at Port Hudson. On January 15, 1863 Banks wrote to Halleck to inform him and to justify the move, telling Halleck the operation would give Banks's army "control of the water communications and approaches to the Red River, which will become of great importance to us as soon as we are prepared to move against Port Hudson."[50]

At the same time, Admiral Farragut came up with his own plan for defeating the menace at Port Hudson. Two U.S. gunboats, the *Queen of the West* and the *Indianola*, had managed to forge past the guns at Vicksburg and had been patrolling the Mississippi between Vicksburg and Port Hudson, paying special attention to the mouth of the Red River, where Confederate vessels were entering the Mississippi to supply Port Hudson. Both gunboats had been lost, however, one by capture and the other by sinking in a battle with four Confederate gunboats. Their removal had allowed the Confederates to regain free access to the Mississippi for supply boats descending the Red River into the Mississippi. Although Commander (later Admiral) David D. Porter commanded the navy's Mississippi River fleet, Farragut had been given the responsibility for bottling up rebel shipping on the Red River. On October 2, 1862, navy secretary Welles had issued to Farragut the following orders: "While the Mississippi River continues to be blockaded at Vicksburg, and until you learn from Commander D.D. Porter, who will be in command of the Mississippi squadron, that he has, in conjunction with the army, opened the river, it will be necessary for you to guard the lower part of that river, especially where it is joined by the Red River, the source of many of the supplies of the enemy."[51]

Banks Fails to Cooperate with Farragut

Farragut, who had boldly blasted his way past the guns of Fort Jackson and Fort St. Philip to capture New Orleans in April 1862, now determined to force his way past the guns of Port Hudson and asked Banks to help him. Banks was to cooperate by having a force make a demonstration on the land side of the fortifications, drawing the attention and fire of Port Hudson's gunners away from the river while Farragut's vessels attempted to steal past under cover of darkness. Banks agreed to do so. He saw the possibility that Farragut's choking off supplies to Port Hudson could lead to its surrender, gaining for Banks a bloodless victory and an open door to Vicksburg. He and Farragut set the date and time for the demonstration by Banks's troops.

On March 12, 1863, the seven warships that Farragut had selected for the mission had come up from New Orleans and were at Baton Rouge. Two days later they anchored at Profit Island, several miles below Port Hudson, where they were arranged for their perilous run past the rebel guns. All but one of the seven vessels were screw propelled, three of them large warships, heavily armed, the others smaller vessels. Farragut had them lashed together in pairs—one large, one small, the small vessels protected by the large vessels at their starboard sides and also serving as auxiliary engines in the event the large vessels were disabled by rebel fire. Farragut's flagship, the USS *Hartford*, was paired with the USS *Albatross* and would lead the file of vessels as they steamed up the river. In the rear of the file would come the frigate *Mississippi*, alone, the only side-wheeler, its wheel housings and guards making pairing impractical. Supporting the seven vessels with suppressing fire would be the gunboats *Essex* and *Sachem*, positioned along the east bank of the river just below the fortification.

Farragut's flotilla waited at Profit Island for several hours, till darkness covered them, then shortly before 10:00 p.m. the vessels shoved off, heading into the night, stealthily making their way toward the rebel fortification. Farragut's nineteenth-century biographer, Captain A.T. Mahan, described the unimaginable event that came next:

Just as they were fairly starting, a steamer was seen approaching from down the river, flaring lights and making the loud puffing of the high-pressure engines. The flag-ship slowed down, and the new arrival came alongside with a message from the general [Banks] that the army was then encamped about five miles in rear of the Port Hudson batteries. Irritated by a delay which served only to attract the enemy's attention and to assure himself that no diversion was to be expected from the army, the admiral was heard to mutter: "He [Banks] had as well be in New Orleans or at Baton Rouge for all the good he is doing us." At the same moment the east bank of the river was lit up, and on the opposite point huge bonfires kindled to illumine the scene.[52]

General Banks's messenger boat had given away the flotilla's approach as clearly as if it had sounded an alarm for the Confederate gunners. And it had done so to deliver a worthless message. General Banks and 12,000 of his troops, on whom Farragut was depending for a diversion that would perhaps save ships and lives, would not be participating after all. They had taken too long to march the two dozen miles from Baton Rouge and had missed their crucial appointment. And so they had simply bedded down for the night, far from the action, leaving Farragut on his own.

The attempt at passage was a disaster. Farragut's vessels ran the Confederate gantlet of heavy guns for a mile and a half, and only two of the seven—the *Hartford* and its partner, the *Albatross*—made it to the other end. One pair turned back after being struck and losing power in one of the vessels. Another pair lost power and drifted downstream, with six of the crew killed and twenty-one wounded, and the *Mississippi*, at the rear of the line of ships, ran aground and was set on fire and abandoned, many of the crew escaping to the west bank of the river in lifeboats. The ship burned until three o'clock the next morning, then floated free and exploded. Its losses included twenty-five killed, thirty-nine missing and thirty-seven taken prisoner. Altogether, Farragut's flotilla lost some seventy-five men killed or wounded.

Although a disaster in its losses of ships and men, Farragut's run past Port Hudson would prove a success in hindering the Confederacy's war effort. The *Hartford* and *Albatross* would not be able to patrol and command the entire 200-mile stretch of river between Port Hudson and Vicksburg, as Farragut had intended, but they would substantially hamper the Confederates' use of the Red River to supply Vicksburg and Port Hudson. On March 20, a week after Farragut's passage, Lieutenant General John C. Pemberton, commanding Confederate forces at Vicksburg, reported to his superiors in Richmond: "The Mississippi is again cut off. Neither subsistence nor ordnance can come or go."[53]

Farragut's two successful vessels proceeded to Vicksburg and anchored below the fortification to allow Farragut to communicate with General Grant. Then, accompanied by a gunboat that had run past Vicksburg's guns to join Farragut's little flotilla, Farragut headed back toward the Red River. On April 1 the three vessels dropped anchor near the mouth of the Red River. Shortly afterward Farragut sent a message to General Banks, still below Port Hudson, via a courier aboard a skiff camouflaged as a tree, which floated past the rebel guns unmolested. The message was that Grant planned to send Major General James B. McPherson's Seventeenth Corps from Lake Providence, Louisiana, on the west bank of the Mississippi, down to Bayou Sara, Louisiana, also on the west bank, just above Port Hudson. From that position McPherson would be able to cooperate with Banks in a campaign against Port Hudson.

Banks doubtlessly welcomed the news, but, hounded by General Halleck to move against Port Hudson promptly, he was desperate to take some sort of action immediately.

"Nothing but absolute necessity will excuse any further delay on your part," Halleck told him, and then warned him that there was "much dissatisfaction here at the delay" in attacking Port Hudson. President Lincoln apparently was expressing to Halleck his growing displeasure over the lame efforts of his political general. And so Banks acted, launching his campaign into the heart of Louisiana as General Weitzel had suggested. As March ended, he ferried two divisions—General Grover's and General Emory's—across to the west side of the Mississippi at and above New Orleans, leaving behind General Thomas Sherman's division and a contingent of General Augur's division to defend New Orleans and Baton Rouge. Grover's and Emory's divisions, moving southwestward, converged on Brashear City. The entire force, numbering some 16,000 men, including Weitzel's brigade, with Banks himself in command, crossed the Atchafalaya River on April 11 and prepared to turn northwestward on the west bank of Bayou Teche, an ancient former course of the Mississippi, which was as muddy brown as the big river itself, lined with gnarled, Spanish moss-draped oaks as it flowed southeastward through Cajun country to the Atchafalaya.

Contesting Banks's advance was a 3,000-man force commanded by a Louisianan, Major General Richard Taylor, the son of former U.S. president Zachary Taylor. Hearing of Banks's approach, Taylor raised a line of mud breastworks, named Fort Bisland, that extended on both sides of the Teche about four miles north of Pattersonville (now Patterson), west of Brashear City. Banks overwhelmed the outnumbered Confederates, attacking with Emory's artillery on their front beginning April 12 while sending Grover's division around Taylor's left flank, using transport steamers to carry Grover's troops across Grand Lake, a broad, lakelike expanse of the river, east of Bayou Teche. Once he learned the enemy was in his rear, Taylor abandoned Fort Bisland in the middle of the night and hastily withdrew northwestward, his retreating troops on April 14 desperately fighting their way past Grover's force at a bow in Bayou Teche called Irish Bend. Each side suffered some 600 casualties in the April 12–14 engagements.

Taylor continued to retreat to the northwest along the west side of the Teche, and Banks stayed right behind him, skirmishers from the two forces intermittently engaging each other and Taylor's army gradually losing strength as deserters dropped out of the march and headed for home intending to defend their families from the Yankee invaders. On April 17 Banks's army reached Vermillionville (now Lafayette) and on April 20 it arrived at Opelousas, from which Louisiana's government officials had recently fled to seek new refuge in Shreveport.

At Opelousas the pursuit abruptly halted, Banks leaving his troops for two weeks while he hurried back to New Orleans and tended to some mysteriously urgent business there. He rejoined his army on May 4, and it resumed its march toward Alexandria. Seeing the U.S. Army rushing toward them and unable to stop it, the Confederates evacuated Alexandria. Taylor's diminishing force retreated toward Shreveport, and the troops of Major General Edmund Kirby Smith, which had occupied Alexandria, hurriedly moved west to Texas, many civilians fleeing with the rebel troops, the slaveholders among them taking their slaves with them to avoid their confiscation. General Banks and his army marched triumphantly into Alexandria, on the banks of the Red River, on May 7. Well pleased with himself for having registered his first successful military campaign, Banks wrote to his wife: "Our success has been splendid. All say it is the cleanest, the best conceived and best executed campaign of the war."[54] He didn't say who the "all" were.

On entering Alexandria, Banks discovered Admiral Porter's ironclad gunboats tied up in the Red River, with Porter aboard his flagship, awaiting Banks's arrival. Porter had brought not only congratulations to Banks but also disappointing news. Grant and his army, including the troops of General McPherson, which Grant had promised would help Banks attack Port Hudson, had crossed to the east side of the Mississippi on the night of April 30 and were now marching on Vicksburg from the east. McPherson, one of the Union's most able and most promising young generals, would not be coming to Banks's aid after all. The conquest of Port Hudson, if there was to be one, would be for Banks alone to manage.

Having considered his options after learning of Grant's crossing to the east side of the Mississippi below Vicksburg, Banks decided he could not catch up with Grant's army outside Vicksburg. "It is out of human power to do this," he wrote to Washington, "and I am left to move against Port Hudson."[55] In search of reinforcements for his Army of the Gulf, which casualties, sickness, service term expirations and other losses had reduced to about 10,000 men, Banks took a steamer to New Orleans via the Atchafalaya River. After arriving, he learned that the garrison at Port Hudson had also diminished. The Port Hudson commander, Major General Franklin Gardner, had been ordered by the Vicksburg commander, General Pemberton, to send three brigades, about 5,000 men, to join the forces of General Joseph Johnston at Jackson, Mississippi. On May 19, with orders to hold Port Hudson to the last, Gardner had fewer than 6,000 troops manning the fortifications there.

To make matters worse for Gardner, Johnston, contrary to President Davis's wishes and General Pemberton's orders, on May 19 ordered Gardner to "evacuate Port Hudson forthwith."[56] Gardner received Johnston's order on May 21. By then events had overtaken the order. Gardner fired back a message to Johnston, letting him know that evacuation was not feasible and telling him "a large force ... is moving down to cross [the Mississippi River] at Bayou Sara against this place. His whole force from Baton Rouge is in my front. I am very weak and should be rapidly re-enforced."[57]

Banks's drive against the rebel stronghold had finally begun. On May 14, his Army of the Gulf had begun a march from Alexandria southeast to Simmesport, had crossed the Atchafalaya River and continued on to Bayou Sara on the west bank of the Mississippi. During the night of May 23 Banks's troops crossed the Mississippi and moved to the rear of Port Hudson. There they had linked up with two brigades commanded by General Augur that had come up from Baton Rouge and two brigades from New Orleans that were commanded by General Thomas Sherman. Augur's troops had been forced to fight their way up to their position, overcoming a Confederate force in what became known as the Battle of Plains Store, fought on May 21 near a two-story building at a crossroads east of Port Hudson.

Altogether, Banks now had a force estimated at about 25,000 men. Morale was high among his troops, who had so recently marched through central Louisiana with a succession of victories in the Bayou Teche campaign, and they were eager to take on the rebels again at Port Hudson. Banks was also eager to get on with the confrontation. By May 26 his troops had fully invested the Confederate fortifications, and he chafed at the thought they would have to remain there for a prolonged siege before the garrison was starved out. He worried about the possibility of a rebel attack on New Orleans, now occupied by a shrunken Union force, and about the oncoming summer that would bring yellow fever and malaria, and about the imminent end of his nine-month volunteers' term of service, which could cut his army in half. On the day the investment was completed, May 26, he called his commanders together

Assault on rebel fortification at Port Hudson, Louisiana. On May 27, 1863, supported by a naval bombardment, Banks attempted to storm the rebel stronghold but was repulsed with heavy losses, including 293 killed and 1,545 wounded (Library of Congress).

for a council of war and proposed to them an immediate, all-out assault on the Confederate defenses. Not all of his commanders thought it was a good idea, but Banks was insistent and ordered a general assault to be made the next morning.

General Gardner was braced and prepared for the coming assault. He placed one of his brigades, about 2,000 men from Alabama, Arkansas and Mississippi commanded by Colonel Isaiah Steedman, on the left of his line, facing north and northwest. On the right side of the line, facing southeast, he placed some 1,100 Louisiana troops commanded by Colonel William Miles, and in the center of his line, facing east and northeast, he put the 2,300 men, mostly from Arkansas, of Brigadier General William N.B. Beall's command. The rest of the garrison was assigned to the big guns facing the Mississippi River on the west side of the fortification. Lieutenant Colonel Irwin, Banks's assistant adjutant general, described the battlefield and the opening action:

> Early in the morning [General] Weitzel, who commanded the right wing on this day, moved to the attack in two lines, [Brigadier General William] Dwight at first leading, and steadily drove the Confederates in his front into their works. Thus unmasked, the Confederate artillery opened with grape and cannister, but our batteries, following the infantry as closely as possible, soon took commanding positions within 200 and 300 yards of the [Confederate] works that enabled them to keep down the enemy's fire. The whole fight took place in a dense forest of magnolias, mostly amid a thick undergrowth,

and among ravines choked with felled or fallen timber, so that it was difficult not only to move but even to see.... Soon after Weitzel's movement began [Brigadier General Cuvier] Grover, on his left, moved to the attack at two points, but only succeeded in gaining and holding commanding positions within about two hundred yards of the works. This accomplished, and no sound of battle coming from his left, Grover determined to wait for further orders, and Weitzel conformed his action to Grover's.[58]

The uncertainty and hesitation of Grover and Weitzel were the results of Banks's slipshod planning. In his haste to launch the assault Banks had neglected to coordinate the movements of his forces, leaving commanders to move on their own as they saw fit. One of them, Thomas Sherman, who had opposed making the assault and who commanded on the far left of the Union line, had not moved at all. When Banks rode over to Sherman's position to find out why, he found Sherman in his tent, lounging over a late breakfast or early lunch—and perhaps a few drinks. Convinced the assault would fail, Sherman had decided not to participate. Banks relieved him of his command on the spot, but Sherman dashed away, sprang up on his horse and led his troops on an advance across an open area called Slaughter's Field, on the southeast section of the Confederate line.

The consequences of his charge against the rebel works were as bad as he had expected. As his troops neared the rebel line, advancing across the open field, they were struck by intense artillery and rifle fire and took heavy losses. Several hundred of his men managed to make it to the ditch that ran in front of the Confederate works, but they were quickly felled by gunfire or driven back. Sherman himself became one of the casualties, suffering a severe wound that forced him out of the action and sent him to New Orleans to recover. Brigadier General Neal Dow, one of Sherman's brigade commanders, was also wounded.

Elsewhere along the Union line the results were not much better. Weitzel's and Grover's troops were driven back from the Confederates' left side and forced to dig in to hold their line. Augur's advance against the Confederates' center was likewise repulsed. General Banks's insistence that Port Hudson be taken that day had gone for naught but disaster. He summed up the battle in a message to General Grant: "The fight was very bitter and our losses severe."[59] Banks's army had suffered nearly 2,000 casualties—293 killed, 1,545 wounded (including 90 officers) and 157 missing—and all that his troops had to show for their efforts was a new line somewhat closer to the Confederate works. In contrast to the Union losses, Gardner's rebel garrison had lost an estimated 235 men, including killed, wounded and missing. Among the U.S. units that had braved the fierce rebel fusillades that day were the First Louisiana Native Guards and the Third Louisiana Native Guards, two regiments of black troops, the First composed of free Negroes from New Orleans and the Third composed of recently freed slaves.

Gardner's vastly outnumbered garrison, with pluck, determination and a botched Union attempt, had withstood and turned back Banks's army, and now Banks decided he would resort to a siege after all. Soldiers and free blacks who were hired for the task began digging rifle pits, gun emplacements, breastworks and zigzag approaches to the rebel line, while Union artillery relentlessly pounded Port Hudson. Porter's fleet lying in the river joined the intense bombardment, his mortar boats showering the rebel positions with shells by night, his gunboats blasting them by day.

At the same time, Gardner was strengthening his works and trying to keep ahead of the damage done by Union guns. His artillery, though, was mostly silent, saving its ammunition for a new U.S. infantry assault. A shortage of ammunition was only one of the problems within the Confederate lines. The situation was slowly deteriorating, the food supply running out and sickness plaguing the beleaguered garrison as it suffered alternating periods of scorching heat and drenching rains. Tons of food were destroyed in a blaze set off by Union shells that hit a storehouse, and Gardner's troops began butchering their horses and mules to feed themselves. Desertions began to increase, the desperately hungry soldiers stealing away during the night. Gardner, defiant in the face of disaster, had told his troops, "The enemy are coming, but mark you, many a one will get to hell before he does to Port Hudson."[60]

For more than two weeks Banks's army dug and waited, dug and waited. Banks finally lost patience and decided to try another assault. He summoned his commanders to meet with him on the evening of June 13 and at the meeting he laid out a new plan of attack, providing more details this time. The plan called for his forces to concentrate their assault on two points believed to be vulnerable. One was called the Priest's Cap, a salient on the left center of the rebel line. The other was called the Citadel, a redoubt the rebels had built on the far right of their earthworks near their line of heavy guns that overlooked the river.

The attack was scheduled for early morning on the next day, June 14, 1863, allowing officers and men little time to prepare themselves. Union artillery opened up on the rebel line before the infantry was to rush the rebel positions, and when it did, the rebel soldiers took quick refuge in their gopher holes. As soon as the bombardment stopped, they hurried out of their holes and took their places on the parapets and delivered merciless volleys into the advancing Union ranks. The leading regiments—the Fourth Wisconsin, Eighth New Hampshire and Twenty-fifth Connecticut—of Brigadier General Halbert Paine's division suffered heavy losses in their attack on the east side of the salient. Paine himself was severely wounded, but some of his troops managed to force their way across the Priest's Cap parapet. All who did, however, were soon killed or captured by the defenders, members of the Forty-ninth Alabama and First Mississippi infantry regiments. More than half of Paine's men, with their nine-month enlistments about to expire, balked at making the charge and stood idly by.

The planned simultaneous attack on the north side of the Priest's Cap by General Grover's troops, after getting off to a late start and emerging from their narrow sap into a forbidding abatis, also failed. Their tardiness in launching their attack had allowed the rebel regiments to shift from the east side, where they had just turned back Paine's regiments, to the north side in time to repulse Grover's men. At the Citadel the only achievement of the attack by the division commanded by Brigadier General William Dwight, who had replaced the wounded General Sherman, was to capture a high, flat piece of land that became the site of an artillery emplacement from which Union guns could more effectively hammer the Confederate positions.

For the second time, Banks's attempt to take Port Hudson by storm had failed. This time his army had lost 1,792 men—203 killed, 1,401 wounded and 188 missing. The Confederates lost twenty-two killed and twenty-one wounded. Celebrating their victory, the rebel soldiers, accompanied by bugles and drums, loudly sang "Bonnie Blue Flag" as the Union troops pulled back from the Confederate works.

For three days after the assault the bodies of the U.S. dead and wounded lay where they had fallen, the odor of corpses rotting in the Southern summer sun so strong that the Confederates at last asked for a truce to allow them to take the bodies to the Union lines. Banks agreed, and details of rebel soldiers went out to the bloodied field, picked up the bodies and delivered them into Union hands for burial. Meanwhile, Banks's demoralized troops resumed digging the saps that stretched toward the rebel line. Before the saps had been extended very much, Banks issued a call for 1,000 volunteers to make a third assault on the rebel line—which proved a futile effort when only about 300 men answered his call for volunteers.

While the Union soldiers dug, the Confederates kept busy repairing and strengthening their works and dealing with growing hunger and thirst. By the first of July they had run out of meat, the corn supply was nearly exhausted, and cowpeas, difficult to digest, were taking the place of corn, resulting in widespread stomach ailments. Molasses and sugar remained in adequate supply, and the troops used them to brew a sort of beer, which they found easier to drink than the only water that was available to them, putrid as it was. They also came up with substitutes for coffee—parched rye, parched meal, parched sweet potatoes—that lasted as long as the ingredients could be scrounged. When the supply of tobacco ran out, the men chewed or smoked leaves or pieces of bark.

On July 4 the U.S. troops took the day off from their digging and other toils to observe Independence Day. The observance included a public reading of the Declaration of Independence, the firing of blank artillery salutes, patriotic speeches and the distribution of rounds of wine and whiskey—and an occasional rifle shot at the Confederate line. Three days later, the ram *General Price*, captured by the U.S. Navy from the rebels' River Defense Fleet at Memphis, pulled into shore above Port Hudson to deliver a dispatch from General Grant. Colonel Irwin, Banks's assistant adjutant general, narrated the climactic events that followed:

> At last on the 7th of July, when the sap-head was within 16 feet of the priest-cap, and a storming party of 1000 volunteers had been organized, led by the intrepid [brigade commander Colonel Henry] Birge, and all preparations had been made for springing two heavily charged mines, word came from Grant that Vicksburg had surrendered. Instantly an aide was sent to the "general-of-the-trenches" bearing duplicates in "flimsy" of a note from the adjutant-general announcing the good news. One of these he was directed to toss into the Confederate lines. Some one acknowledged the receipt by calling back, "That's another damned Yankee lie!"
>
> Once more the cheers of our men rang out as the word passed, and again the forest echoed with the strains of the "Star-Spangled Banner" from the long-silent bands. Firing died away, the men began to mingle in spite of everything, and about 2 o'clock next morning came the long, gray envelope that meant *surrender*.
>
> Formalities alone remained.[61]

With the noise of celebration resounding in their ears, the Confederate soldiers at last accepted the truth of the message from Vicksburg. Soon hundreds of them clambered over their parapets to join the joyful U.S. soldiers, grasping their hands to shake, joking and laughing with them, the relief strikingly obvious on both sides. It was not till after midnight that General Gardner made a formal effort to receive the news himself. He dispatched a party of officers to Banks asking for a copy of the message Banks had received from Grant. Banks sent it to him. Satisfied, Gardner then wrote to Banks to arrange a discussion of surrender terms.

Surrender of Port Hudson. On July 8, 1863, four days after the fall of Vicksburg, Confederate major general Franklin Gardner, commanding at Port Hudson, gave up his defense and surrendered the rebels' last fortification on the Mississippi River. Banks telegraphed his good news to General Grant, proclaiming, "The Mississippi is opened" (Library of Congress).

The Surrender of Port Hudson

At 9:00 a.m. on July 8 Gardner sent three of his senior officers—Colonel I.G.W. Steedman, Colonel W.R. Miles and Lieutenant Colonel Marshall J. Smith—to meet with three of Banks's senior officers, Brigadier General Charles Stone (a member of Banks's staff), General Dwight and Colonel Birge. In the shade of a cluster of magnolia trees, the two sets of officers calmly and cordially discussed the surrender arrangements while sipping from glasses of Bordeaux wine. The surrender was to be unconditional. Gardner would turn over Port Hudson and its garrison and all weapons, materiel and military equipment to Banks. The Confederate officers and men would become prisoners of war, the officers to be held until they could be exchanged and the men to be paroled after they had been processed. The sick and wounded would receive care from U.S. medical personnel. Personal property could be kept by its owners. The troops were to line up for the formal surrender ceremony at 7:00 a.m. the next day, July 9.

At seven o'clock on the morning of the ninth, Brigadier General George L. Andrews rode into Port Hudson leading a procession of regiments selected from each of Banks's divisions and military bands playing "Yankee Doodle." At the head of his troops General Gardner stood waiting. The order "ground arms" was shouted, and the Confederate soldiers abandoned their weapons in stacks before them. General Gardner then unbuckled his sword and held it out for General Andrews to accept as the ultimate symbol of surrender. Andrews told Gardner to keep it.

The Confederate flag was then lowered and the Stars and Stripes raised to replace it as the Union bands again started to play and Union artillery boomed in triumphant salute. General Gardner, still a favorite of his troops, made a short farewell speech, and after his men had cheered his announcement of their imminent parole, the ceremonies concluded. The rebel officers, including Gardner, would be shipped off to New Orleans or Memphis or a camp in the North to be interned until they could be exchanged. The enlisted men, once they had gone through the records-keeping process, would be free to go home. The total number of Confederates surrendered by General Gardner that day was put at 6,340—405 officers and 5,935 enlisted men. The fight for Port Hudson was over. After relentless bombardment, repeated assaults and more than six grueling weeks of siege, the last Confederate stronghold on the Mississippi River had fallen. In a terse sentence General Banks announced the historic good news to General Grant: "The Mississippi is opened."[62]

His Port Hudson mission having been accomplished, Banks now expected to be sent on a campaign to capture Mobile, which the general in chief had earlier implied was second in importance only to the opening of the Mississippi. Mobile was an objective urged by both General Grant and Admiral Farragut. After the surrender of Port Hudson, Banks went to Vicksburg to confer with Grant, and Grant later went to New Orleans for another meeting with Banks. Grant furthermore, in apparent anticipation of Banks's being assigned a Mobile mission, sent the Thirteenth Corps, commanded by Major General Edward Ord, plus another division, to reinforce Banks's army.[63]

Nevertheless, "for reasons avowedly political rather than military," Banks's assistant adjutant general, Lieutenant Colonel Irwin, asserted in his report on Port Hudson, "the government ordered, instead, an attempt to 'plant the flag at some point in Texas.'"[64] "The government" was President Lincoln, who worried about the presence of French troops in Mexico. They had taken over Mexico City in June, allowing France to set up a puppet government headed by Austrian Archduke Maximilian, a relative of France's emperor, Louis Napoleon. Lincoln feared that Louis Napoleon intended to expand his new Mexican empire into Texas, and so he had had General Halleck order Banks to Texas.

At first, Halleck told Banks it didn't matter where the flag was to be planted, at Galveston or Indianola or "any other point you may deem preferable." What really mattered, he said in a memo dated August 6, 1863, was that it be done "as prompt as possible."[65] Then, in a lengthier note dated August 10, he expressed second thoughts: "In my opinion, neither Indianola nor Galveston is the proper point of attack. If it be necessary, as urged by Mr. Seward, that the flag be restored to some one point in Texas, that can be best and most safely effected by a combined military and naval movement up Red River to Alexandria, Natchitoches, or Shreveport, and the military occupation of Northern Texas. This would be merely carrying out the plans proposed by you at the beginning of the campaign, and, in my opinion, far superior in its military character to the occupation of Galveston or Indianola. Nevertheless, your choice is left unrestricted.... I write this simply as a suggestion and not as a military instruction."[66]

Banks had become acquainted with the water route through Louisiana that Halleck suggested. The Red River was best navigable for navy vessels, which were needed to transport and support the army, during the spring. Even then the water level varied and presented a serious risk for anything but shallow-draft vessels. It was now August. Banks decided that attacking Houston by way of Sabine Pass, where the Sabine River empties into the Gulf of Mexico, was a better plan for establishing a U.S. position in Texas.

It was to be a joint army-navy operation. On August 31, 1863, Banks ordered Major General William B. Franklin, a forty-year-old West Pointer, to embark a brigade from General Weitzel's division onto 18 transport steamers and, supported by navy gunboats, land them at Sabine Pass as the commencement of a drive on Houston. The expedition arrived at Sabine Pass on September 7, and after a naval reconnaissance of the pass and its protecting fort, a plan of battle was drawn. Three of four gunboats were to bombard the rebels' little fort, Fort Griffin, while the fourth gunboat covered the landing of a 500-man advance unit from a transport named the *General Banks*. At the "all ready" signal, given about 4:00 p.m. on September 8, the gunboats steamed slowly ahead toward the rebel fortification.

The gunboats blasted away at the fortification, pouring broadside after broadside onto it and into it, while the forty-six-man rebel garrison, manning six heavy guns, held its fire until the U.S. vessels came in closer. When they did, the rebel guns opened on the *Arizona* and the *Sachem*, then on the *Clifton*. The *Sachem* had almost made it out of the rebel guns' range when a shell hit it amidships, smashing in its sides. "An instant more, and she was enveloped in the scalding vapor of escaping steam," the *New York Herald*'s correspondent reported, "and lay a helpless wreck at the mercy of the enemy. The flag was lowered [in surrender], and the enemy, ceasing their fire on her, now turned their entire attention to the *Clifton*, probably aware of the fact that the draught of the *Arizona* [the largest of the gunboats] would not permit her to advance near enough to become a very formidable antagonist."[67]

In the end, the expedition lost two gunboats, had an estimated thirty men killed or wounded and 200 sailors captured before General Franklin ordered the attack halted. Although he might have landed his 5,000 troops and flanked the little fort and overwhelmed its garrison, he chose not to try it, and the mission went unaccomplished. The vessels withdrew and steamed back to New Orleans, humiliatingly defeated by a tiny force of Confederate defenders commanded by a gallant young lieutenant, Richard Dowling, who became a celebrity as a result of the heroic rebel stand against the U.S. Navy and U.S. Army.

On September 13 Banks took up his pen to write to Halleck an excuse for the failure:

> General, it is with regret that I am obliged to report that the effort to effect at landing at Sabine Pass was without success. The immediate cause of the failure was the misapprehension of the naval authorities of the real strength of the enemy's position, and the insufficient naval force with which the attempt was made.
> It represented, however, the entire naval power that the department affords for an enterprise of this character. No vessel drawing over 6 feet of water can pass the bar at the mouth of the Sabine. This reduced the number of boats able to enter to four.... These were all old boats of decayed frames and weak machinery, constantly out of repair, even when engaged in the ordinary service of the river.
> The naval authorities most familiar with the Sabine, which has been constantly under blockade, believed that this force would be sufficient. They supposed the battery at the Pass to mount but two guns.... It proved, however, that the battery mounted six heavy guns.... To these were added a light battery and two gunboats.
> The attack would have been successful as it was had the boats been adapted to the waters in which they engaged.[68]

Apparently Halleck's interpretation of the events did not coincide with the spin that Banks put on the disaster, and lest President Lincoln get the wrong impression about Banks's competence Banks wrote a special explanation to the president on September 22, placing all the blame for failure on the Navy:

> Sir, Dispatches from the General-in-Chief impress me with the belief that my plan of action in the movement to the Sabine Pass is not perfectly understood by the Government. It was not intended for the occupation of Sabine City, nor was it, indeed, the purpose to land at that point except it could be done without serious resistance. The landing contemplated and referred to in the orders given to General Franklin, as an alternative for that of Sabine Pass, was upon the coast, 10 or 12 miles below. Had the landing been accomplished either at the Pass or below, a movement would have been immediately made for Beaumont from the Pass, or for Liberty if the landing had been made below, and thence directly to Houston, where fortifications would have been thrown up, and our line of communication and supplies immediately established at the mouth of Brazos River, west of Houston, until we could have gained possession of Galveston Island and City.... Houston would have given us ultimately the possession of the State....
>
> The movement to the Sabine was made upon the reports furnished by the naval officers, who were perfectly confident of their success in being able to destroy the enemy's guns. The grounding of two boats, and the withdrawal of the other two boats, caused the failure to effect a landing and the return of the army. In my judgment, the army should not have returned, but should have continued to the point indicated for landing upon the coast, as contemplated in the instructions. This would have been done but for the withdrawal of the two boats that were free after the loss of the Sachem and Clifton.[69]

Banks then determined to have another shot at giving the president the Texas toehold he had ordered. He sent General Franklin's force to Berwick with instructions to move along Bayou Teche toward Alexandria, and if he got an opportunity to move into Texas to take it. Franklin and his army got as far as Washington, Louisiana, about five miles north of Opelousas, and Franklin decided his supplies were running too low and his supply line had become too attenuated. Banks had given him vague instructions that in effect told him to do what he thought best, and so he turned around and retreated down past New Iberia to Franklin, Louisiana, less than twenty miles from where he had started, and there he and his troops settled down for a long winter's rest. Another failed mission.

The Texas Expedition

Meanwhile, Banks himself was leading a new expedition to plant the U.S. flag on Texas soil. This time the planting attempt would be made along the Gulf Coast, starting at Brownsville. With a force of some 6,000 troops from Major General Napoleon Dana's corps Banks sailed from New Orleans on October 26, 1863, his transports convoyed by three navy warships, the *Monongahela*, *Owasco* and *Virginia*. "After encountering a severe 'norther' on the 30th, from which the men, animals and transport suffered greatly," Lieutenant Colonel Irwin, Banks's assistant adjutant general, reported, "on the 2d of November [General] Dana landed on Brazos Island, drove off the small Confederate force on the mainland on the 3d, and on the 6th occupied Brownsville, thirty miles up the river."[70] Having finally won one, Banks promptly reported to General Halleck, "We have raised our flag in Texas again."[71]

Brownsville, which had become an important port for receiving supplies for the Confederates and for shipping Texas cotton, was taken without a fight. General Hamilton Bee, the Confederate commander in Brownsville, immediately ordered the evacuation of the town and abandoned its fortification, Fort Brown. The rebel troops burned their supplies as well as parts of the town and fled. Not staying long, Banks left a contingent of troops to occupy the town. Then, feeling triumphant about having captured an abandoned town and fort, he prepared to move eastward along the Texas coast to plant more flags. He re-embarked the remainder of his army onto the transports and sailed off to his next objective on November 16, 1863. He landed at Corpus Christi and occupied Mustang Island, crossed Aransas Pass, then went on to Pass Cavallo and on December 30 captured a rebel fortification called Fort Esperanza, which commanded the entrance to Matagorda Bay, its garrison hastily withdrawing to the mainland.[72]

Feeling exultant, Banks wrote to Mary, his wife: "I have always known that there was a protecting Hand above us but I never *felt* it till now. I have experienced the sensation of deliverance. I may say[,] for the first time in my life, I believe our success to have [been] one of great importance to the Country."[73] Actually, it wasn't. Galveston was still untouched, as was Houston; the Sabine River also was still under rebel control, and Banks's proposed move up the Rio Grande to link up with U.S. forces in New Mexico never happened. His vision of establishing a U.S. presence along the Texas coast having produced only results of small consequence—with the possible exception of the occupation of Brownsville—Banks's attention was abruptly turned back to Halleck's favorite plan, the penetration of Louisiana culminating in the capture of Shreveport and from Shreveport a march into east Texas.

The Disastrous Red River Campaign

Reporting the turn of events, Banks's assistant adjutant general wrote, "General Halleck on the 4th of January [1864] renewed his instructions of the previous summer for the naval and military operation on the Red River."[74] This time, Colonel Irwin pointed out, the proposed operation was to be on a larger scale, with troops under Major General Frederick Steele coming down from Arkansas to participate in the campaign, along with as many troops as could be spared from Major General William T. Sherman's command, the Department of the Tennessee, a unit of General Grant's Military Division of the Mississippi.

On March 2, 1864, Sherman traveled by steamer from Vicksburg to New Orleans to confer with Banks about the plans for the Red River campaign. In his memoir, Sherman gave details of the meeting:

> I found General Banks, with his wife and daughter, living in a good house, and he explained to me fully the position and strength of his troops, and his plans of action for the approaching campaign.... The bulk of General Banks's army was about Opelousas, under command of General Franklin, ready to move on Alexandria. General Banks seemed to be all ready, but intended to delay his departure a few days to assist in the inauguration of a civil government for Louisiana, under Governor Hahn.... General Banks urged me to remain over the 4th of March, to participate in the ceremonies, which he explained would include the performance of the "Anvil Chorus" by all the bands of his army, and during the performance the church-bells were to be rung, and

cannons were to be fired by electricity. I regarded all such ceremonies as out of place at a time when it seemed to me every hour and every minute were due to the war.

General Banks's movement ... contemplated my sending a force of ten thousand men in boats up Red River from Vicksburg, and that a junction should occur at Alexandria by March 17th. I therefore had no time to wait for the grand pageant of the 4th of March, but took my departure in the [steamer] Diana the evening of March 3d.[75]

The plans had originated in Washington and involved a whole set of objectives. One, like Banks's efforts on the Texas coast, was to show a military presence that would quash any plot against Texas or the United States that might be in the mind of the emperor of France, whose troops were already in Mexico. Another of the objectives was to secure areas of Texas for the U.S. and provide encouragement to U.S. loyalists in Texas, in hopes that Confederate control could be overcome and the state promptly returned to the Union.

President Lincoln's own political considerations were a big part of the plans. A presidential election was coming up in November, and its outcome was far from certain. Restoring Texas to the Union would allow Texas to cast votes in the electoral college, and those votes could be expected to go for President Lincoln. Louisiana, of course, was being groomed for a similar role, and Banks, who was Louisiana's military governor, had been instructed by Lincoln to replace Louisiana's secessionist government with one that was loyal to the U.S., a task for which the political general Banks was well qualified and at which he succeeded by having Michael Hahn, the loyalist candidate, elected civil governor on February 22. Once the new governor and a new legislature were in place and a new state constitution adopted, Louisiana would be back in the Union, with its electoral college vote restored and expected to go to Lincoln.

And then there was cotton, probably the most important objective of the planned Red River campaign. It was for good reason called *King* Cotton, for it was America's leading export, a commodity vital not only to the economy of the United States but also to the economy of much of Europe. The huge textile industry of Great Britain alone processed some 400,000 tons of cotton annually, and 77 percent of that cotton came from the American South. The wartime blockade that had virtually shut off shipments of cotton from the South had idled a third of Britain's cotton mills, throwing a half million people out of work. Cotton-mill operators everywhere were hard-pressed to keep their businesses running. Many mills in the American Northeast had closed. The government in Washington was feeling intense pressure to do something to relieve the painful shortage, while cotton prices had shot up from around ten cents a pound before the war to as much as $1.89 a pound by 1864.

For those who could get their hands on it—and ship it out to the open market—the potential profits were dizzying. The entire Mississippi River valley, according to one account, "seethed with cotton speculation." Civilians and members of the military alike tried ways legal and illegal to obtain and sell whatever cotton they could find. Some army and navy officials, on both sides of the conflict, confiscated all the cotton they could discover for their own enrichment. Characterizing cotton speculators, Admiral Porter, commander of U.S. naval forces on the Mississippi and soon to become part of the Red River campaign, claimed that "a greater pack of villains never went unhung"—although he was not one to pass up an opportunity to acquire cotton himself.

Banks had received reports—perhaps merely rumors—that tens of thousands of bales of cotton were stockpiled in the western parts of Louisiana, some piled up on the banks of the Red River awaiting steamers to carry them off, and that they could be seized or purchased cheaply. That information was helping Banks change his mind about taking an expedition up the Red River, a mission he had earlier opposed. Sherman, too, had become interested. Four weeks before going to New Orleans to meet with Banks, Sherman wrote to him and told him, "I will be most happy to take part in the proposed expedition, and hope, before you have made your final dispositions, that I will have the necessary permission."[76] Sherman never received the necessary permission, which had to come from Grant and which Grant declined to give, and by the time Sherman left for New Orleans he knew he would not take part in the expedition.

Grant had opposed the Red River expedition, but, he said, he had "acquiesced because it was the order of my superior at the time."[77] His acquiescence meant the loan of those 10,000 men from Sherman's corps, troops he expected to get back within thirty days, on successful completion of the Red River mission, so that they—and Banks—could be used in Grant's overall plan, which included the capture of Mobile, turning it from a Confederate base of supply into a Union base for Deep South operations.

Propelled by the president's desires, by Halleck's orders and by Banks's newfound enthusiasm, the Red River expedition got under way. The expedition's plan called for the convergence in Shreveport, in the northwest corner of Louisiana, of four different forces: 17,000 troops from Banks's command, who would move up along Bayou Teche, headed for Alexandria; 15,000 men from Major General Frederick Steele's Department of Arkansas, who would march from Little Rock down into Louisiana, headed first for Monroe, then for Shreveport; the 10,000 men from Sherman's command, headed for a rendezvous with Banks's force in Alexandria; and a navy fleet composed of thirteen ironclads and seven lightly armored, shallow-draft gunboats called tinclads, including the *Black Hawk*, then the flagship of Admiral Porter, who was commanding the naval part of the operation.

Banks's units started from Berwick Bay, near Morgan City (then known as Brashear City), on March 7, 1864, running days behind schedule for the planned March 17 rendezvous in Alexandria. They soon ran into more delays, caused by heavy rains that turned muddy roads into quagmires. On March 9 Banks, still in New Orleans working on forming a new state government, sent word that he would be further delayed in joining his troops, who were under the command of General Franklin.

On March 10 Sherman's troops, commanded by Brigadier General Andrew Jackson (A.J.) Smith, boarded transports that carried them down the Mississippi from Vicksburg and on March 12 turned up the Red River to take them as far as Simmesport, where they disembarked under the protection of the fleet's guns and began their overland march to Alexandria, pressing back whatever Confederate troops they encountered as they moved northward. By then Smith had received a wire from Banks informing him that because of the delays Banks's troops would not be able to reach Alexandria before March 21. In Arkansas, General Steele, for his own reasons, was not moving at all, but he sent word to Sherman that when he got around to participating in the expedition he could send only 7,000 troops, not the 15,000 Banks was expecting. The combined armies of Banks and A.J. Smith alone, Steele told Sherman, would be enough to drive the Confederates into the Gulf of Mexico.[78]

While four of the gunboats proceeded up the Red River to clear away obstructions known to have been planted in the river, Smith's troops marched up beside the river without significant opposition, scattering rebel defenders as they went. Their first objective was the rebels' Fort DeRussy, a formidable earthworks fortification that stood beside the river about thirty miles northwest of Simmesport and about twenty-five miles below Alexandria, presenting a threat to U.S. vessels moving up the river. Reaching the fort on the morning of March 14 and drawing the fire of its guns, Smith instructed Brigadier General Joseph Mower to have his division assault it while the remainder of Smith's force fended off a possible rebel attack on its left flank. A valiant leader who had served in the Mexican War as a private, Mower had been commissioned and had risen rapidly in grade by virtue of his fighting ability. He now ordered his men to charge the works. Two brigades dashed forward under covering fire from Mower's skirmishers that forced the rebel defenders to keep their heads down. The Union troops swiftly swarmed over the fort's parapets, confronted the heavily outnumbered 350-man garrison and forced its surrender. Mower's casualties were three killed and thirty-five wounded. Confederate casualties totaled five killed, four wounded and most of the rest of the garrison taken prisoner. Captured, too, were the fort's four guns. The battle had lasted about twenty minutes.

The way to Alexandria, by river and by land, was now clear. Once the obstructions were removed from the river below Fort DeRussy, Admiral Porter's vessels steamed up to the fort, where the transports on the evening of March 15 took most of A.J. Smith's troops aboard to carry them to Alexandria, leaving behind the command of Brigadier General Thomas Kilby Smith to destroy the fort. Mower's troops entered Alexandria and relieved the 180 U.S. sailors who, under the command of Lieutenant Commander (later Captain) Thomas O. Selfridge, captain of the ironclad *Osage*, on the morning of March 16 had moved into the town, recently abandoned by the Confederates, and occupied it, awaiting the arrival of the army.

Banks's troops, originally scheduled to rendezvous with A.J. Smith's force at Alexandria on March 17, did not start arriving until March 19, when Banks's cavalry showed up. It was not until March 26 that Banks's entire force assembled in Alexandria. Banks himself had arrived on the 24th and had set up a headquarters in Alexandria. On March 27, when General Grant's orders dated March 15 caught up with him, Banks learned the intentions that Grant, now a lieutenant general and the army's general in chief, had for Banks's army and the Red River expedition. A.J. Smith's troops were to rejoin Sherman's army for the campaign against Atlanta, and Banks's army was to take Mobile. The Red River expedition was to complete its task as soon as possible and was not to hinder the planned campaigns against Atlanta and Mobile. If Shreveport was not taken by April 25, A.J. Smith and his men were to pull out of the expedition and return to Vicksburg—even, Grant's orders stated, if doing so "should lead to the abandonment of the expedition."[79] Grant also instructed Banks to turn over the defense of the Red River to General Steele and the navy. Banks was to abandon all of Texas except the Rio Grande, which he was to hold with not more than 4,000 men.[80]

With those orders in his hands, Banks faced a big decision. He had less than a month to capture Shreveport before his army would be split apart, and even if he took Shreveport by then its use as a base for operations in Texas, a large part of the rationale for going to the trouble of taking Shreveport, had been foreclosed by Grant's order. Except for the cotton, Banks might have wondered, what was the point of continuing the expedition? Why not abort it now? The cotton, however, mattered a great deal, and Banks decided to continue on toward Shreveport.

Lieutenant Commander Selfridge's gunboat, the *Osage*, was one of the vessels that were ordered to proceed up the Red River above Alexandria to support the movements of the troops on their march toward Shreveport. Selfridge described that action:

> On March 29th fourteen of the squadron left Alexandria for the upper river, the *Eastport* and the *Osage* being in the advance; thus fourteen days of precious time had been lost [from the time the gunboats and transports had first reached Alexandria], allowing the Confederates to concentrate their forces for the defense of Shreveport, our objective point.
>
> As we advanced[,] the enemy's scouts set fire to all the cotton within ten miles of the river-bank. Millions of dollars worth of it were destroyed, and so dense was the smoke that the sun was obscured, and appeared as though seen through a smoked glass....
>
> Our supply of coals having given out, we were dependent upon fence rails for fuel. Two hours before sunset the fleet and transports would tie up to the bank, and whole crews and companies of soldiers would range over the country, each man loading himself with two rails, and in an incredibly short time the country would be denuded of fences as far as the eye could see. So dependent were we upon these rails for fuel that it was a saying among the Confederates that they should have destroyed the fences and not the cotton.[81]

On April 7 Admiral Porter left Grand Ecore, about halfway between Alexandria and Shreveport, on the tinclad *Cricket*, bound for Shreveport. Along with one other tinclad and four ironclads, he was convoying the twenty transports bearing the 1,700 troops of Kilby Smith's division to Springfield Landing, where they were to rendezvous with the troops moving toward Shreveport by land. The river at that time, Selfridge reported, was "at a lower stage than usual at this season, and there was barely water to float the gun-boats."[82] On April 10 the fleet of gunboats and transports arrived at Springfield Landing, "about 30 miles, as the crow flies, from its destination [Shreveport], meeting with no obstructions beyond the usual bushwhacking," Selfridge reported. At Springfield Landing, though, the river was blocked by a large steamboat that had been scuttled and sunk. The convoy was forced to halt. While there, Admiral Porter received a message by courier from General Banks. Banks and his army had turned around and were headed back toward Alexandria.

The Confederate troops that had repeatedly fallen back before the advance of Banks's army as it moved up the west side of the river had been reinforced and under the command of Major General Richard Taylor had formed a battle line at Sabine Crossroads, just below Mansfield, Louisiana, some thirty miles below Shreveport. There they had awaited the approach of Banks's force. Banks's troops had arrived at mid-morning on Friday, April 8, and had begun forming a line of battle. About four o'clock in the afternoon, after a series of exchanges between skirmishers of both sides, Taylor, although outnumbered, had launched an attack on both flanks of the Union front. Two of Banks's divisions were rolled up, and the whole Union line was driven back.

By nightfall that attack had been beaten off, but at 2:00 a.m. the next day, Saturday, April 9, 1864, strengthened by newly arrived reinforcements, Taylor had put his troops in motion to catch Banks's hastily retreating army in hopes of demolishing it. Late that afternoon the Confederates caught up with it at Pleasant Hill, where A.J. Smith's troops had been left. About 5:00 p.m. the rebels attacked, Brigadier General Thomas J. Churchill's troops hitting the Union left flank, the weakest part of the line, scattering it and threatening to set off a chain reaction along the extent of the Union position. Smith promptly ordered

Battle of Pleasant Hill. As Banks's army retreated through north Louisiana it was pursued by the force commanded by Maj. Gen. Richard Taylor, which caught up with the Union army at Pleasant Hill and attempted to smash it. Taking command of the situation, Maj. Gen. A.J. Smith ordered a counterattack and routed the Confederates (Library of Congress).

his veteran warriors to charge the entire Confederate line, Mower's division leading the way. Under that onslaught the Confederates gave way and began falling back in confusion, their formation broken, their retreat taking them back as far as six miles from the front, a lone brigade of cavalry covering their speedy withdrawal. The Battle of Pleasant Hill thus ended. U.S. casualties in the two days of fighting totaled some 4,000, killed or wounded. Confederate losses totaled about 3,500.

After A.J. Smith and his troops had won a battle for him, Banks thought about resuming the advance toward Shreveport, but during the night, apparently having had enough fighting, he decided to continue the retreat to Grand Ecore, where his army reunited on April 11. He had his troops entrench, then had a pontoon bridge laid across the river and positioned a strong detachment on the north side of the river. He then asked for reinforcements from New Orleans and Texas. Meanwhile, Porter's fleet was fighting its way back down the river. Selfridge narrated the perilous retreat:

> The Confederates, being relieved by the falling back of the army, were now free to attack us at any point of the river. There were but half-a-dozen gun-boats to defend the long line, two of which were light-draughts, known as "tin-clads," from the lightness of their armor, which was only bullet-proof. The river was falling; its narrowness and its

high banks afforded the best possible opportunities for harassing attacks, and the bends of the river were so short that it was with the greatest difficulty they were rounded by vessels of the *Osage* type. Steaming with the current, the *Osage* was almost unmanageable, and on the morning of April 12th the transport *Black Hawk* was lashed to her starboard quarter, and thus the descent was successfully made till about 2 p.m. when the *Osage* ran hard aground opposite Blair's Plantation, or Pleasant Hill Landing, the bows down stream and the starboard broadside bearing on the right bank.

While endeavoring to float her, the pilot of the *Black Hawk* reported a large force gathering in the woods some three miles off dressed in Federal uniforms. I ascended to the pilot-house, and scanning them carefully made sure they were Confederates, and at the same time directed Lieutenant Bache of the *Lexington* to go below and open an enfilading fire upon them.... The [Confederate] battery unlimbered near the *Lexington*, but a caisson being blown up they quickly withdrew. The enemy came up in column of regiments, and, protected by the high and almost perpendicular banks, opened a terrific musketry fire, and at a distance not exceeding one hundred yards. Shell-firing under the circumstances was almost useless. The great guns of the *Osage* were loaded with grape and canister, and when these were exhausted, with shrapnel having fuses cut to one second. Our fire was reserved till the heads of the enemy were seen just above the bank, when both guns were fired.... This unequal contest could not continue long, and after an hour and half the enemy retreated with a loss of over four hundred killed and wounded, as afterward ascertained.... The *Osage* sustained a loss of seven wounded.[83]

By April 15 the gunboats and transports were back at Grand Ecore. The worst, though, was yet to come. On the way from Grand Ecore to Alexandria the ironclad *Eastport* struck a torpedo (or mine) eight miles below Grand Ecore and sank. With a lot of difficult work and the help of two steam-pump boats, the *Eastport* was repaired and refloated, but twice grounded when its voyage was resumed, and under the threat of rebels along the river bank was ordered blown up to avoid capture. The tinclads *Cricket, Juliet* and *Ford Hindman* had gone about twenty miles below Grand Ecore when the rebels opened on them with twenty pieces of artillery. "Nineteen shells went crashing through the *Cricket*," Selfridge reported, "and during the five minutes she was under fire she was struck thirty-eight times and lost twelve killed and nineteen wounded out of a crew of fifty, one third whom were negroes. The escape of the *Cricket* [the flagship] was almost miraculous, and was largely owing to the coolness and skill of the admiral. The remainder of the squadron turned up stream [to escape the artillery fire], except the two pump-boats, *Champion No. 3* and *No. 5*, which being unarmed [unarmored] were destroyed."[84] The next day the boats got up a head of steam and ran past the Confederate guns despite their heavy fire. The *Juliet* suffered the loss of fifteen killed and wounded, and the *Fort Hindman* lost seven, killed or wounded.

By April 27 the fleet had reassembled at Alexandria, except for twelve of the gunboats that were stalled by the low water at the rocky falls just above Alexandria. Colonel Irwin, the assistant adjutant general, explained the problem: "In the month that had elapsed since the fleet had, even then with some difficulty, ascended the rapids, the river had fallen more than six feet; for a mile and a quarter the rocks were now bare; there were but three feet four inches of water, the gunboats needing at least seven feet; and in some places the channel, shallow as it was, was narrowed to a mere thread."[85] An unthinkable disaster loomed.

Then someone proposed a possible solution. "From this danger the navy," Irwin stated, "from this reproach the army, from this irreparable disaster the country was saved by the

Crisis on the Red River. A fall in the level of water in the river threatened to strand the U.S. Navy gunboats that were supporting the Banks expedition. Disaster was averted when Lt. Col. Joseph Bailey devised wing dams to deepen the water and provide a channel through which the gunboats could pass (Library of Congress).

genius and skill of Lieutenant Colonel Joseph Bailey, of the 4th Wisconsin regiment, then serving on General Franklin's staff as chief engineer."[86] Bailey's idea was to build a pair of wing dams, one on each side of the river, leaving a gap between them for the vessels to shoot through once the water level was raised by the dams. "From the north bank," Irwin reported, "a wing dam was constructed of large trees, the butts tied by cross-logs, the tops toward the current, and kept in place by weighting with stone, brick, and brush. From the cultivated south bank, where large trees were scarce, a crib was made of logs and timbers, filled in with stone and with bricks and heavy pieces of machinery taken from the neighboring sugar-houses and cotton-gins."[87]

The current was rushing through the gap between the two dams at a rate of nine miles an hour while still another foot of depth was needed to float the larger boats. To close the 150-foot gap and stop, or hinder, the flow of water through it, two of the navy's loaded coal barges were maneuvered into the gap, secured by lines from the river banks. Work on the dams had begun on April 30, and by May 8 the water level had been raised five feet, four inches. "On the morning of the 9th," Irwin wrote in his report, "the tremendous pressure of the pent-up waters drove out ... the barges, making a gap sixty-six feet wide, and swung them against the rocks below. Through the gap the river rushed in a torrent. The admiral [Porter] at once galloped round to the upper fall and order the *Lexington* to run the rapids. With a full head of steam she made the plunge, watched in breathless silence of suspense by the army and the fleet, and greeted with a mighty cheer as she rode in safety below."[88] The rest of the fleet followed, and by May 13, after an additional set of wing dams were built, all the surviving vessels of the fleet were back at Alexandria. Lost were the *Eastport*, the two pump boats and two small gunboats, *Covington* and *Signal*. Also lost were the more than 200 men who had been aboard the two pump boats, and an estimated 120 other navy casualties, including killed, wounded and missing.[89]

The fleet having passed its crisis, Banks's defeated army began moving out of Alexandria on the morning of May 13, pillaging and burning the houses of Alexandria as they pulled out, leaving the city in flames and ruins. Repeated attacks on the retreating column were beaten off, a fight at Yellow Bayou claiming 267 casualties among the army's rear guard, which inflicted 452 casualties on the attacking rebels. The troops of the thwarted expedition reached Simmesport on May 16. Colonel Bailey, who had saved the Union fleet with his wing dams, fashioned a bridge out of steamboats for Banks's army to cross the Atchafalaya River, and by May 19 the entire surviving force had safely crossed over. General A.J. Smith's troops, those men who had been borrowed from Sherman's army, embarked on transports bound for Vicksburg shortly thereafter. When the expedition's cost in men was added up, U.S. Army losses in the debacle amounted to 454 killed, 2,191 wounded and 2,600 captured or missing. Confederate losses totaled 3,976 killed, wounded or missing. "On the 21st of May, the squadron and transports reached the Mississippi," Captain Selfridge wrote, concluding his account. "And thus ended the Red River expedition, one of the most humiliating and disastrous that had to be recorded during the war."

All of the expedition's strategic missions having failed, only the acquisition of cotton remained as an accomplished objective. According to one account, Admiral Porter and General Banks competed with each other in securing that objective. While the fleet waited in Alexandria for Banks's arrival Porter had sent his sailors out into the countryside in search of cotton, and they had seized whatever they found. An estimated 3,000 bales had been seized by the time Banks arrived. Unable to stop Porter, Banks responded by ordering his troops to take wagons into the countryside and grab whatever cotton they could before Porter's sailors found it. Thousands of bales were reportedly seized by the army. Without wagons of their own, navy personnel allegedly stole army wagons and mules, painted over the wagons' army designations, rebranded the mules and expanded their quest, roving deeper into the Louisiana countryside.

Rumors inevitably arose that both Porter and Banks had connections to cotton traders and were allowing speculators to join the expedition. Colonel Irwin vigorously defended Banks from such rumors and charges of corruption and rebutted similar charges against the navy. He claimed that the speculators "who certainly went with the army as far as Alexandria had for the most part passes from Washington; the policy under which they were permitted to go was avowedly encouraged by the Government, for reasons of state.... All the cotton gathered by the army was turned over first to the chief quartermaster, and by him to the special agent of the Treasury Department designated to receive it. All the cotton seized by the navy was sent to Cairo, was adjudged 'lawful prize of war,' and its proceeds distributed as prescribed by the statute."[90]

When all was said and done, the Red River expedition's one signal success was the dispossession of Louisiana's cotton from its growers and owners. Among the men in the ranks cotton was believed to be the whole reason the expedition was conducted. "Whatever its merits," a soldier in the Forty-seventh Illinois Regiment wrote, "the Red River campaign was viewed ... as a veritable cotton raid for the enrichment of speculators, and was, therefore, extremely repugnant and entered upon ... with ill grace."[91]

The defeat at Mansfield and his craven retreat proved to be the final nails in the coffin of Banks's military career. On April 22, less than two weeks after the humiliating defeat, Grant asked that Banks be removed from command. On April 26 General Halleck, now the army's chief of staff under the arrangements that followed Grant's promotion, wired Grant at Grant's headquarters in Culpeper, Virginia, to tell him "your telegram of the 22d, asking for the removal of General Banks was submitted to the President, who replied that he must await further information before he could act in the matter."[92]

On April 29 Grant suggested a reorganization that would exclude Banks. "I think," he wrote to Halleck, "it will be better to put the whole of that territory [west of the Mississippi River] into one military division, under some good officer, and let him work out the present difficulties without reference to previous instructions."[93] Grant suggested that Banks be replaced by Major General Joseph J. Reynolds, a forty-two-year-old West Pointer who commanded the troops occupying New Orleans.[94] Halleck's response to that wire spelled out some of the problems in superseding Banks. "I think the President will consent to the order," Halleck wrote on April 29, "if you insist upon General Banks' removal as a military necessity, but he will do so very reluctantly, as it would give offense to many of his friends, and would probably be opposed by a portion of his Cabinet. Moreover, what could be done with Banks? He has many political friends who would probably demand for him a command equal to the one he now has.... Before submitting the matter to the President, the Secretary of War wishes to have in definite form precisely the order you wish issued."[95] Then, on May 3, Halleck again wrote to Grant, this time in a communication marked "Confidential." He told Grant that his (Grant's) previous telegrams concerning superseding Banks had been passed along to Secretary Stanton and had been read by Lincoln:

> General Banks is a personal friend of the President and has strong political supporters in and out of Congress. There will undoubtedly be a very strong opposition to his being removed or superseded, and I think the President will hesitate to act unless he has a definite request from you to do so, as a military necessity, you designating his superior or superior in command.
>
> On receiving such a formal request (not a mere suggestion), I believe, as I wrote you some days ago, he would act immediately. I have no authority for saying this, but give it simply as my own opinion, formed from the last two years' experience, and the reason, I think, is very obvious. To do an act which will give offense to a large number of his political friends the President will require some evidence in a positive form to show the military necessity of that act. In other words, he must have something in a definite shape to fall back upon as his justification.... The administration would be immediately attacked for his removal.[96]

By May 7, 1864 President Lincoln had decided that winning the war was more important than keeping friends in high places and critical positions. On that day, May 7, 1864, the following order was issued from the office of the army's adjutant general: "General Orders, No. 192. By direction of the President, Maj. Gen. E.R.S. Canby, U.S. Volunteers, is assigned to the command of the Military Division of West Mississippi, which will include the Departments of Arkansas and of the Gulf. By order of the Secretary of War."[97]

Edward Richard Sprigg Canby was a forty-six-year-old West Point graduate and career soldier, a Kentuckian. He would command the new division that Grant had proposed, and Banks, still in nominal command of the Department of the Gulf, would serve under him. Issuing Canby instructions, also on May 7, General Halleck tersely described the plan that the Red River expedition was meant to carry out, then informed Canby as follows:

The failure to carry out this plan has, it is believed, resulted from General Banks' delay to co-operate in time with the movements of Generals Steele and A.J. Smith, and his meeting and fighting the enemy by detachments instead of his whole force in mass. You will perceive by Lieutenant-General Grant's dispatches that he has no confidence in General Banks' military capacity, and has consequently directed him to turn over the command of his troops to the senior officer in the field and return to New Orleans. General Grant at one time ordered a part of the troops of the Department of the Gulf to New Orleans to operate against Mobile, but this project has been given up, and all troops in your division will be retained for duty west of the Mississippi.... You are therefore invested with all the power and authority which the President can confer upon you, and you will act in all things as in your opinion may be best to secure the object in view, the restoration of the authority of the United States west of the Mississippi.[98]

Canby now had been apprised of Banks's standing and could feel free to resist any or all suggestions or advice that Banks might offer, knowing that Banks had no official support or credibility in military matters. The army rug had been completely pulled out from under General Banks. He got the message when Canby showed up to assume command at Simmesport on May 19. Perhaps sensing that he was about to lose his job, Banks had written a distressed letter to his wife on May 13, telling her, "I have nobody to talk to, nobody to embrace. I am alone."[99] Banks returned to New Orleans and to the administrative and political work that he was good at, guiding Louisianans to write a new constitution and moving the state into the Reconstruction period. He was mustered out of the army in August 1865, and despite being urged by some in New Orleans to stay and reside in the city, he returned to Massachusetts and, professional politician that he was, ran for a congressional seat. He was elected to the U.S. House of Representatives from Massachusetts' Sixth Congressional District, where he served from December 1865 to March 1873 (and was succeeded by Benjamin Butler). He was then elected the U.S. representative from the Massachusetts Fifth Congressional District and served from March 1875 to March 1879, then served again from March 1889 to March 1891.

He died in his hometown of Waltham, Massachusetts, on September 1, 1894, at age 78.

3

Major General Franz Sigel

Before the War: Born November 18, 1824, in Sinsheim, Baden, Germany. Graduated from Karlsruhe Military Academy in 1843. Commissioned a lieutenant in the Baden army. Resigned commission in 1847 and studied law at the University of Heidelberg. Joined the German revolutionary movement. Was wounded in a skirmish and fled to Switzerland after the collapse of the revolution. Took temporary refuge in England and in 1852 immigrated to the U.S. Became a tutor, gave fencing lessons, played the piano at German-American clubs in New York. Operated a cigar store with his brother. Became a professor in the private school operated by his father-in-law and became deeply involved in the German community in New York. Became an instructor and a major in the Fifth New York militia regiment, composed largely of German-Americans. Active in politics. Wrote editorials and essays for German publications. In 1857 he became a professor at the German Institute in St. Louis and grew to be influential in the German community in St. Louis. Was appointed superintendent of the St. Louis public school system in 1860. Became a U.S. citizen. Married Elise Dulon in 1854, daughter of a German revolutionary refugee. Three children. Political affiliation: Republican. Military experience: Received a military school education. Joined the German revolutionary movement and became a colonel in the revolutionary militia that he recruited in Baden. Led a siege of the city of Freiburg and suffered a crushing defeat in April 1848. Commander of the army of the revolutionary government of Baden in 1849.

  Franz Sigel had the credentials: A military education, experience as a leader of troops, a battlefield record, albeit a losing one. He had the look: Five-foot-seven, about 150 pounds, straight-backed, grim-faced, like a bird of prey, prominent cheekbones, piercing dark eyes, smoothed-down coal-black hair, mustached and goateed, uniformed in a brass-buttoned frock coat and plumed Hardee hat, caparisoned with a three-foot sword and bright scabbard, mounted on a tall, black stallion. He had the attitude: Assertive, self-assured, arrogant. He also had a following: German-Americans who loved their new country but who were still attached to the culture of their old one. Through his writings and speeches and his heroic though futile efforts in the German revolution, Sigel had become their champion. They loved him.

As war became more imminent, loyalists in Missouri—particularly in St. Louis, where there was a large and loyal German-American population—began forming militia groups, called the Home Guard, to defend the Union. Captain John Schofield, a West Point physics professor then serving as a visiting professor at Washington University in St. Louis, was instructed by the War Department to recruit Home Guard members into the ranks of the U.S. volunteer army and to appoint officers for the new volunteer units. Sigel was recruited and received an appointment as colonel in command of the U.S. Third Missouri Volunteer Infantry Regiment. He resigned as school superintendent and resumed the military career he had begun in Germany.

Missouri soon had its own civil war going on. The governor, Claiborne Jackson, a secessionist sympathizer, commanded the Missouri militia and turned it into an auxiliary of the Confederate army. In early May 1861, two weeks after the outbreak of war, he ordered a militia brigade into a threatening position on the hills overlooking the U.S. arsenal, its twenty or so buildings sprawled on a bluff above the Mississippi River just outside of what was then St. Louis, near Jefferson Barracks, a U.S. Army post. Governor Jackson assured the arsenal's commandant, U.S. Army captain Nathaniel Lyon, that he had no hostile intent in placing the troops there, claiming they were there only for maneuvers. Lyon suspected otherwise, believing a raid on the arsenal's supply of weapons and munitions was what Jackson had in mind. Rebels had already overrun the U.S. arsenal at Liberty, Missouri, and made off with a thousand muskets and rifles. On the morning of May 10, 1861, a combined force of the St. Louis arsenal's garrison and regular army units posted at Jefferson Barracks, some 6,000 men with Lyon in command, marched south from the arsenal and surrounded the rebel militia as it lay encamped at what had become known as Camp Jackson. Sigel and his troops, with six field pieces, marched from St. Louis to reinforce Lyon. Lyon sent a note to the rebel commander, General Daniel Frost, demanding his capitulation, and after conferring with his senior officers, Frost, outnumbered nearly ten to one, agreed to an unconditional surrender.

Maj. Gen. Franz Sigel, who had fled Germany after participating in a failed revolution, was valued for his popularity and leadership among German-Americans (Library of Congress).

On the march of the surrendered rebels from Camp Jackson to the arsenal, through the streets of St. Louis, a riot broke out among onlookers sympathetic to the rebels, and U.S. troops opened fire on the crowd. In the confused melee that followed, twenty-eight persons were killed, including Captain Constantin Blandowski of the Third Missouri Volunteer

Regiment, Sigel's outfit, and fifty or more were wounded. Seven more were killed as the rioting continued through the night.

In reaction to the action by the U.S. troops, the Missouri general assembly, meeting in Jefferson City, the Missouri capital, on May 11 passed legislation creating a Missouri State Guard to oppose Union forces and appointed fifty-one-year-old Sterling Price, a former Missouri governor who had served as a U.S. brigadier general during the Mexican-American War, as the State Guard's commander, giving him the rank of major general. Not long after that action by the legislature, Governor Jackson appealed to Confederate President Jefferson Davis for troops to assist the Missouri State Guard in driving U.S. troops out of Missouri.

On May 17 Lyon, a forty-two-year-old West Pointer who had served in the Seminole Indian wars and the Mexican-American War, was appointed a brigadier general and placed in command of all U.S. troops in Missouri. He and Governor Jackson met on June 11 in St. Louis to work out an arrangement to assure U.S. troops access to the interior of Missouri, but the meeting failed in its purpose, Jackson having no intention of allowing such access. Instead, he insisted U.S. troops be restricted to St. Louis and its environs and that the pro–Union Home Guard be disbanded. Determined to assert U.S. authority, Lyon rejected Jackson's demands, and the meeting ended with Lyon announcing that Jackson's demand for restrictions on the federal authority would mean war.

Once Jackson and General Price had been escorted out of St. Louis they headed for Jefferson City, ordering the railroad bridges burned behind them. Days later, pursuing the rebels, Lyon boarded 2,000 of his troops on steamboats and steamed up the Missouri River to capture Jefferson City, which he took without a fight. From Jefferson City Lyon pursued the fleeing rebels to Boonville, northwest of Jefferson City, where he routed the State Guard in a battle on June 17. Jackson and his rebel troops then fled south, toward Springfield, and Lyon followed them, continuing the pursuit.

Sigel, meanwhile, had been promoted to brigade commander and was ordered to move his regiments, some 3,000 men, southwestward from St. Louis. His mission was to prevent the army of Confederate brigadier general Benjamin McCulloch from marching up from Arkansas to reinforce the Missouri rebels and, at the same time, to intercept Jackson's army if it withdrew toward Arkansas. On the day that Lyon defeated the State Guard at Boonville, Sigel and his troops reached Rolla by train. There Sigel learned of the Boonville battle and received reports that the retreating rebels were headed south. Sigel then headed for Springfield. At Springfield he received intelligence that a rebel force was headed toward the town of Lamar, about sixty miles northwest of Springfield and that another rebel army was at Neosho, about sixty-five miles southwest of Springfield. Determined to prevent those two rebel armies from uniting, Sigel on June 25 marched his troops about thirty miles westward from Springfield to Mount Vernon; from there he turned toward Neosho. By the time he got to Neosho, though, the rebel force had already passed through the town and linked up with the southbound rebel force near Lamar.

From spies that had been in Sigel's camp Governor Jackson, having taken command of the united rebel armies, learned Sigel's position and prepared to meet Sigel. Jackson had about 6,000 men, but a third of them were unarmed. Sigel had about 1,100 men, armed and better trained and supported by eight field pieces. Advancing on Sigel's position at Carthage, Jackson reached the Union line on the morning of July 5. Sigel had his troops deployed along Dry Fork Creek, about six miles north of Carthage. Jackson, advancing from

Battle of Carthage, Missouri. Outnumbered by the rebel army of Missouri governor Claiborne Jackson, Sigel's force was driven from the field after an hours-long struggle on July 5, 1861 (Library of Congress).

the northwest, positioned his rebels on the hills above the creek, poised for an assault on the Union line.

About 11:00 a.m. Sigel ordered his artillery to open fire on Jackson's right wing, and Jackson replied with volleys of his artillery as well as furious musket fire. After an hours-long, back-and-forth battle, seeing he had underestimated the strength of the rebel force Sigel decided to withdraw southeastward to Sarcoxie. The rebels pursued, but Sigel's strong rear guard held them off, and as darkness covered the field, Jackson gave up the chase, and Sigel encamped at Sarcoxie. Jackson's army had suffered more casualties than Sigel's, an estimated 200 killed, wounded or missing. Sigel had lost forty-four killed, wounded or missing. Even so, the rebels considered the Battle of Carthage (or the Battle of Dry Fork) a notable victory, and indeed it was. Sigel's little Union army that had been driven from the field by a superior force. Sigel withdrew to Springfield, where he was later joined by Lyon's army. By late July Lyon had gathered an army of some 6,000 men at Springfield. He organized his force into four brigades, commanded by Major Samuel Sturgis, Lieutenant Colonel George Andrews, Colonel George Dietzler and Colonel Sigel.

On August 1 Lyon received intelligence that a rebel force commanded by General Price was advancing toward Wilson's Creek, on the west side of Springfield. Lyon quickly responded by marching out to meet it. The vanguards of the two armies clashed at Dug Springs, three miles southwest of Clever, Missouri, late in the afternoon of the next day, August 2, and the morning of August 3. Lyon learned that the rebel force, which had been reinforced by McCulloch's troops and by the Arkansas state militia under Brigadier General Bart Pierce, amounted to 12,000 or more men and outnumbered him more than two to one.

Fearful that he was being drawn into a trap, he withdrew and fell back to Springfield to ponder his next move. Lyon received repeated reports that the rebels were preparing to move against him at Springfield. He held onto his position, having established a line of defense on the edge of town, and hoped his requested reinforcements would arrive in time. On August 9 he learned there would be no reinforcements. He was on his own and would have to do the best he could.

His plan, to which his senior officers had agreed, had been to set his troops in motion on the night of August 8 and to attack the rebel front with his full force at Wilson's Creek at daylight on the 9th. That plan was postponed for twenty-four hours to allow the men to receive the new supplies that had just arrived from Rolla. The plan, with later changes, was described by Brigadier General William Wherry, Lyon's aide-de-camp: "During the morning [of August 9] Colonel Sigel visited Lyon's headquarters, and had a prolonged conference, the result of which was that Colonel Sigel was ordered to detach his brigade, the 3d and 5th Missouri, one six-gun battery, one company of the 2d Dragoons, under Lieutenant Charles E. Farrand, for an attack upon the enemy from the south, while Lyon with the remainder of his available force should attack on the north."[1] Sigel had figured out a more prominent role for himself in the plan. Lyon would launch the bulk of his army against the rebel front, and Sigel, after slipping around the rebels' right flank, would simultaneously strike the rebel line in its rear. The battle was on. General Wherry narrated the action:

> Lyon put his troops in motion at early dawn on the 10th, and about 4 o'clock struck [Confederate Brigadier General James] Rains's most advanced picket, which escaped and gave warning of the attack, of which General Price was informed just as he was about to breakfast.[2]
>
> Advancing a mile and a half and crossing a brook tributary to the creek, the Union skirmishers met and pushed the Confederate skirmishers up the slope. This disclosed a considerable force of the enemy, along a ridge perpendicular to the line of march and to the valley of the creek, which was attacked by the 1st Missouri and the 1st Kansas, assisted by [Captain James] Totten's battery, who drove back the Confederates on the right to the foot of the slope beyond.

Fierce exchanges between the two sides were followed by a temporary lull in the fighting, which, Wherry reported, "enabled the enemy to re-adjust his lines and bring up fresh troops, having accomplished which, Price made a determined advance along nearly the whole of Lyon's front.... Every available man of Lyon's was now brought into action and the battle raged with redoubled energy on both sides."[3]

About nine o'clock that morning, Wherry wrote,

> great anxiety began to be felt for the fate of Sigel's command. Shortly after Lyon's attack the sound of battle had been heard in the rear of the enemy's line. It continued but a short time, and was renewed shortly afterward for a very brief period only, when it ceased altogether. Sigel had proceeded to within a mile of the [rebel] camps, and his cavalry had cut off the enemy's small parties and thus suppressed information of his coming. He then advanced his infantry.... At about 5:30 a.m., hearing the musketry on Lyon's front, he opened fire with his guns, pushing his infantry across the creek and into the [rebels'] lower camp, whence they had fled, overwhelmed by the suddenness of the attack.
>
> Sigel crossed his guns and pushed with infantry and artillery forward a short distance

in pursuit, meeting with slight resistance. He advanced from his first position near the creek, by a road west of the deserted camp, and formed line of battle in a field between the road and the camp. Afterward he advanced to Sharp's house.... McCulloch called upon a battalion of mounted Missourians and upon a part of the Louisiana regiment which had been confronting [Brigadier General Joseph] Plummer in the corn-field, and with these attacked Sigel's men, who were in line at Sharp's farm, and drove them from the field. When the attack by the Confederates, from the direction of Lyon's front, was made, the confusion of Sigel's men was brought about ... by the belief that the infantry in their front were friends.

Sigel went back the way he came with a part of his command.... All but the cavalry, who were ahead, were ambuscaded and, for the most part, killed or captured; Sigel narrowly escaped capture.... Thus by 10 o'clock Sigel was out of the fight, and the enemy could turn his whole force upon Lyon.[4]

Sigel himself described his flight from the battlefield:

In this chase the greater part of our men were killed, wounded, or made prisoners, among the latter Lieutenant-Colonel Albert and my orderly, who were with me in the last moment of the affray. I was not taken, probably because I wore a blue woolen blanket over my uniform and a yellowish slouch-hat, giving me the appearance of a Texas Ranger.[5] I halted on horseback, prepared for defense, in a small strip of corn-field on the west side of the creek, while the hostile cavalrymen swarmed around and several times passed close by me. When we had resumed our way toward the north-east, we were immediately recognized as enemies, and pursued by a few horsemen, whose number increased rapidly. It was a pretty lively race for about six miles, when our pursuers gave up the chase. We reached Springfield at 4:30 in the afternoon, in advance of Sturgis, who with Lyon's troops was retreating from the battle-field, and who arrived at Springfield ... at 5 o'clock.[6]

Death of General Lyon

Command of Lyon's army devolved upon Major Samuel Sturgis following the death of Lyon, who was struck by a musket ball in the left breast while leading a column forward in the fight. He dismounted after being hit and fell into the arms of his devoted orderly, telling him, "Lehmann, I am killed." Lyon died seconds later, the first Union general to lose his life in the war. Colonel Robert B. Mitchell of the Second Kansas Regiment, the ranking Regular Army officer, would have succeeded Lyon, but he was severely wounded about the same time that Lyon was shot. General Wherry described the conclusion of the battle:

The flash and roar were incessant, and the determined Southrons repeatedly advanced nearly to the muzzles of the pieces of their foes, only to be hurled back before the withering fire as from the blast of a furnace and to charge again with a like result. At a moment when the contest seemed evenly balanced, except for the overwhelming numbers of the Confederates on the field, Captain Gordon Granger, noted for his daring and intrepidity, rushed to the rear and brought up the supports of DuBois's battery, hurling them upon the enemy's right flank, into which they poured a murderous, deadly volley, which created a perfect rout along the whole front. Our troops continued to send a galling fire into the disorganized masses as they fled, until they disappeared, and the battle was ended.[7]

Major Sturgis then ordered the troops to withdraw, and Lieutenant John DuBois's artillery was moved to a commanding hill and ridge in the rear to cover the withdrawal. Wherry reported:

> Before the withdrawal of the main body took place, Captain [John] Granger [of the Third U.S. Cavalry] and others urged remaining on the ground, but Sturgis had received information of Sigel's rout, and in view of the depleted, worn-out forces and exhausted ammunition, [he] persisted in a return to Springfield....
>
> On reaching Springfield, Sturgis found that Sigel had arrived there half an hour earlier. Regarding him as the senior, the command was given over to him. On the following morning [August 11, 1861] the army withdrew.

So ended the Battle of Wilson's Creek, one of the most fiercely fought of the war. The results were inconclusive, but victory was claimed by the rebels, since the U.S. force had quit the field and retreated. The Union losses, as officially reported, were 223 killed, 721 wounded, and 291 missing, a total of 1,235 men lost. The rebel losses, as officially reported, were 265 killed, 800 wounded, and thirty missing, a total of 1,095 lost.[8] Other estimates of the casualties put the losses of both sides slightly higher.

From Springfield the battered U.S. force turned northeast toward Rolla, about halfway back to St. Louis. At a council of war on the evening of August 10, Sigel's senior officers had

Battle of Wilson's Creek, Missouri. Sigel's force was virtually wiped out by the rebels on August 10, 1861. Narrowly escaping capture, Sigel raced to safety in Springfield, arriving ahead of the retreating Union army (Library of Congress).

agreed to start moving out on the road to Rolla at 3:00 a.m. on August 11. However, the march wasn't begun until several hours past three because Sigel failed to have his brigade ready to move at that time. Sigel's troops caused more delays en route to Rolla as they took time out to prepare meals. His disgusted officers then forced Sigel to turn command back over to Sturgis.[9]

The rebels didn't follow the retreating U.S. troops. Price wanted to pursue, but McCulloch, commanding the Confederate and Arkansas troops and worried about overextending his line of supply from Arkansas, demurred and took his men back to Arkansas. Price then led his Missouri troops into northern Missouri.

Despite Sigel's poor showing on the battlefield at Wilson's Creek and his other displays of ineptness, his army career suffered no serious ill effects. President Lincoln, with an eye on Sigel's German-immigrant following, had promoted him to brigadier general on August 7, his commission to date from May 17, 1861, for purposes of seniority. Sigel returned to St. Louis to accept the new commission and while he was there, he tended to some administrative and recruiting assignments. On September 23 his new superior, Major General John C. Frémont, whom Lincoln had sent to Missouri in July to take command of the army's Department of the West, gave Sigel command of that army's Third Division. Sigel traveled by rail to Sedalia, midway between Jefferson City and Kansas City, to establish a headquarters for himself and a base for his troops. Weeks later, in mid–October, Frémont ordered Sigel to join his troops to Frémont's own force, together comprising some 30,000 men. Frémont's plan was to oust the rebels from Springfield and to cut off Price's rebel force, which had penetrated northward into the state as far as Lexington, on the Missouri River just east of Kansas City. Price's rebels, with vastly superior numbers, had overwhelmed the U.S. garrison defending Lexington and had captured the city on September 20 in the First Battle of Lexington.

Frémont's plan went awry when he was relieved of command of the department, President Lincoln having decided Frémont, with his freelance way of doing things, was in danger of driving Missouri out of the Union rather than holding it in the Union, as he was expected to do. Further frustrating the plan was that Sigel came down with a severe case of flu. By then Sigel was in Rolla and he took a leave of absence to return to St. Louis to recover. While he was in St. Louis, the U.S. War Department again shuffled the deck. On November 9 it reorganized the army's Department of the West into two departments, one the Department of Kansas, to be commanded by Major General David Hunter, and the other, the Department of the Missouri, to be commanded by Major General Henry Halleck. Halleck soon set about to impose discipline on the idle troops positioned at Rolla, whose lack of that quality had become a problem. Sigel being unavailable, Halleck put Brigadier General Samuel Curtis, a fifty-seven-year-old West Pointer, in command of them.

By December 22 Sigel had decided he was ready to return to action, and Halleck sent him back to Rolla. Sigel later gave his account of the events:

> Toward the end of December, '61, when not fully recovered from a severe illness, I was directed by General Halleck ... to proceed to Rolla, to take command of the troops encamped there, including my own division (the Third, afterward the First) and General Asboth's (the Fourth, afterward the Second), and to prepare them for active service in the field. I arrived at Rolla on the 23d of December, and on the 27th, when the organization [of Halleck's command] was completed, I was superseded by General Samuel R. Curtis, who had been appointed by Halleck to the command of the District

of South-west Missouri, including the troops at Rolla.... I was doubtful about my personal relations to General Curtis, which had been somewhat troubled by his sudden appearance at Rolla and the differences in regard to our relative rank and position, but the fairness he showed in the assignments of the commands ... and his frankness and courtesy toward me, dispelled all apprehensions on my part, and with a light heart and full confidence in the new commander, I entered into the earnest business now before us.[10]

Writing for public consumption, Sigel had put the best face on the awkward situation. On December 29 Curtis had reported to Halleck's office about his first meeting with Sigel:

I arrived here [at Rolla] 8 p.m. Thursday night [December 26] and immediately rode to the camp of Brigadier-General Sigel, about 3 miles from town. I communicated to him the wishes of the major-general [Halleck] in regard to moving the cavalry forthwith, and requested him to order immediate preparations for the movements. The general not having received the order placing me in command of the district and I not having assumed command (wishing to treat the general with all possible courtesy by conferring with him before-hand), it was with some expression of doubt as to my rank and authority that he finally issued the order to the cavalry to report when they should move. Yesterday morning [December 28] your telegraphic copy of Order 92 was received by General Sigel, and at his request I gave him the date of my commission and showed him our relative position in the Army Registers.[11]

Halleck's order to Sigel had let Sigel assume he was to command the southward thrust that was about to commence. In a terse message on December 24 Halleck had told Sigel, "You will assume command of all the troops at Rolla and vicinity, including the Fourth Division."[12] But on December 25 Halleck had issued Order No. 92, stating, "Brig. Gen. S.R. Curtis is assigned to the command of the South-western District of Missouri, including the country south of the Osage and west of the Meramec River."[13]

On December 31 Sigel, affronted, submitted a letter resigning his commission. He also wrote a letter to Curtis, saying he did not blame Curtis for the situation but letting Curtis know he was much put out about being superseded by an officer of equal rank. The letter of resignation got as far as Halleck, and Halleck refused to accept it. He wrote Sigel a letter saying Sigel had erred in assuming that he would command all troops in the coming campaign and moreover that it was the War Department's ranking, not Halleck's, that made Curtis senior to Sigel. He said he was confident of Sigel's ability and he hoped Sigel would withdraw his resignation. In response, Sigel aired a long list of grievances, especially including his claim that German soldiers like him were victims of discrimination. In the end, however, he got over his wounded feelings and told Halleck he would stay on the job.

Not all were as confident of Sigel's ability as Halleck claimed to be. By mid–February of 1862 some officers had become so distrustful of Sigel as a commander that they took the bold step of writing letters of complaint to Halleck. On February 13 John Schofield, the former West Point physics professor who had appointed Sigel a colonel in the fledgling army of Missouri volunteers and who was now a brigadier general, wrote this illuminating and damning letter to Halleck:

General: The question of the merits of Brig. Gen. Franz Sigel, as a commander, having assumed such shape as to deeply involve the interests of the service, I deem it my duty to make a statement of facts which came to my knowledge during the campaign of last summer in the Southwest, ending in the death of General Lyon and the retreat of his army from Springfield.

Soon after the capture of Camp Jackson, in May, General Lyon sent Colonel Sigel, with his two regiments of infantry and two batteries of artillery, to the southwestern part of the State, by way of Rolla, to cut off the retreat of Price's force, which he (Lyon) was about to drive from Booneville. Colonel Sigel passed beyond Springfield, reaching a point not far from the Kansas line, and on the main road used by Price's men in their movement south to join him. Here he [Sigel] left a single company of infantry in a small town, with no apparent object, unless that it might fall into the hands of the enemy, which it did the next day (5th of July). Sigel met Price the next day and fought the celebrated "battle of Carthage." Sigel had about two regiments of infantry, well armed and equipped, most of the men old German soldiers, and two good batteries of artillery. Price had about twice Sigel's number of men, but most of them mounted, armed with shot-guns and common rifles, and entirely without organization and discipline, and a few pieces of almost worthless artillery. Sigel retreated all day before this miserable rabble, contenting himself with repelling their irregular attacks, which he did with perfect ease whenever they ventured to make them. The loss on either side was quite insignificant. Price and McCulloch were thus permitted to join each other absolutely without opposition; Sigel, who had been sent there to prevent their junction, making a "masterful retreat."

Several days before the battle of Wilson's Creek it was ascertained beyond a doubt that the enemy's strength was about 22,000 men, with at least twenty pieces of artillery, while our force was only about 5,000. About the 7th of August the main body of the enemy reached Wilson's Creek, and General Lyon decided to attack him. The plan of attack was freely discussed between General Lyon, the members of his staff, Colonel Sigel, and several officers of the Regular Army. Colonel Sigel, apparently anxious for a separate command, advocated the plan of a divided attack. All others, I believe, opposed it.

On the 8th of August the plan of a single attack was adopted, to be carried out on the 9th. This had to be postponed on account of the exhaustion of a part of our troops. During the morning of the 9th, Colonel Sigel had a long interview with General Lyon, and prevailed upon him to adopt his plan, which led to the mixture of glory, disgrace, and disaster of the ever-memorable 10th of August. Sigel, in attempting to perform the part assigned to himself, lost his artillery, lost his infantry, and fled alone, or nearly so, to Springfield, arriving there long before the battle was ended. Yet he had almost nobody killed or wounded. One piece of his artillery and five or six hundred infantry were picked up and brought in by a company of regular cavalry. No effort was made by Sigel or any of his officers to rally their men and join Lyon's division, although the battle raged furiously for hours after Sigel's rout, and most of his men in their retreat *passed in rear of Lyon's line of battle.*

On our return to Springfield, at about 5 o'clock p.m., Major Sturgis yielded the command to Colonel Sigel, and the latter, after consultation with many of the officers of the army, decided to retreat toward Rolla; starting at 2 o'clock a.m., in order that the column might be in favorable position for defense before daylight. At the hour appointed for the troops to move I found Colonel Sigel asleep in bed, and his own brigade, which was to be the advance guard, making preparations to cook their breakfast. It was 4 o'clock before I could get them started. Sigel remained in command three days, kept his two regiments in front all the time, made little more than ordinary days' marches, but yet did not get in camp till 10 and one occasion 12 o'clock at night.

On the second day he kept the main column waiting, exposed to the sun on a dry prairie, while his own men killed beef and cooked their breakfast. They finished their breakfast at about noon, and then began their day's march.

The fatigue and annoyance to the troops soon became so intolerable that discipline was impossible. The officers, therefore, almost unanimously demanded a change. Major Sturgis, in compliance with the demand, assumed the command.

My position as General Lyon's principal staff officer gave me very favorable opportunities for judging of General Sigel's merits as an officer, and hence I appreciate his good as well as his bad qualities more accurately than most of those who presume to judge him. General Sigel, in point of theoretical education, is far above the average of commanders in this country. He has studied with great care the science of strategy, and seems thoroughly conversant with the campaigns of all the great captains, so far as covers their main strategic features, and also seems familiar with the duties of the staff, but in tactics, great and small logistics, and discipline he is greatly deficient. These defects are so apparent as to make it absolutely impossible for him to gain the confidence of American officers and men, and entirely unfit him for a high command in the Army. While I do not condemn General Sigel in the unmeasured terms so common among many, but on the contrary see in him many fine qualities, I would do less than my duty did I not enter my protest against the appointment to a high command in the Army of a man who, whatever may be his merits, I *know* cannot have the confidence of the troops he is to command.

I am, general, very respectfully, your obedient servant.[14]

Four days later, on February 17, nine other officers wrote to Halleck, telling him, "The undersigned officers of the Army of the United States, who have been constantly more or less connected with the service since the present trouble commenced in Missouri, entirely agree with the facts, strictures, and sentiments expressed in the annexed communication of Brigadier-General Schofield, and concurring as we do with these thoroughly, we sincerely pray that such steps and precautions may be taken by the proper authorities as will insure care at least in the future in the selection of those who are to command our armies." The letter was signed by Major John V. DuBois, Lieutenant Colonel James Totten, Assistant Adjutant General G. Granger, Surgeon Florence M. Cornyn, Major W.L. Lothrop, Captain P.E. Burke, First Lieutenant George O. Sokalski, Lieutenant and Quartermaster John L Woods Jr., and First Lieutenant Lucien J. Barnes.[15]

Meanwhile, a major battle was looming. Within two weeks after assuming command of all U.S. forces in southwestern Missouri, some 10,250 men, General Curtis had organized his army into four divisions of two brigades each, plus a reserve unit. On February 10, in a storm of swirling snow, Curtis put his troops in motion, headed for Springfield, where Price's 7,000-man rebel army lay encamped. On February 13 the Union troops marched into Springfield and found it empty. Price had picked up and fled toward Arkansas. Curtis then split his army into two columns to speed his pursuit of the fleeing rebel army. Curtis would command one column, the left wing, composed of the Third and Fourth divisions, which would march down the Fayetteville road. Sigel would command the right wing, the First and Second divisions, which would proceed down the road toward Little York. At or near Cassville, Missouri, about fifteen miles from the Arkansas line, the two columns would merge.

Price and his army of Missourians were hurrying to unite with McCulloch's army of assorted Confederate troops from Arkansas, Missouri, Texas and Louisiana, as well as 800

Indians from Indian Territory (now Oklahoma). Together, the two rebel forces would form an army estimated at 16,500 men. That army would be commanded by forty-one-year-old Major General Earl Van Dorn, a West Point graduate who had been appointed by President Jefferson Davis on January 10 to command the Confederate army's Trans-Mississippi Department. Van Dorn was a man of big ambitions far beyond his means to attain them. On February 14, the day U.S. troops entered Springfield and found it abandoned by Price, Van Dorn wrote Price a letter detailing Van Dorn's plan to capture St. Louis and take the war into Illinois.

The two pursuing columns of Curtis's army came together near Cassville and from there, marching down muddy Telegraph (or Wire) Road, splotched with snow and ice, continued their move south. On February 17 the U.S. troops entered Arkansas, stepping lively to the rhythm of "The Arkansas Traveler" and other tunes played by army bands as the cheering troops crossed the state line. Curtis congratulated the men and sent a message back to General Halleck in St. Louis, exclaiming triumphantly, "The flag of our Union again floats in Arkansas."

Curtis's troops were one day behind Price's army, which had crossed into Arkansas on the 16th. As the Union column continued south, across Pea Ridge, past the inn called Elkhorn Tavern and slightly past Little Sugar Creek, near the present town of Avoca, they ran into a line of rebel infantry and cavalry supported by artillery. Curtis immediately had his artillery unlimber and return the rebel fire, beginning a fierce exchange that lasted till nearly dark. The rebels, under General Price, then withdrew down Telegraph Road to Cross Hollows, about twelve miles south, where McCulloch's Confederate army was encamped. The skirmish below Little Sugar Creek had cost Curtis thirteen killed and about twenty wounded. Rebel losses were put at more than twenty killed.

With Price's army having cleared out of the area, Curtis encamped in the valley of Little Sugar Creek and the next day, February 18, 1862, sent Brigadier General Alexander Asboth, of Sigel's command, with a brigade of cavalry to reconnoiter down Little Sugar Creek, moving west toward Bentonville, in hopes of finding a way to flank the rebel position at Cross Hollows. Asboth came back reporting that the area west of Cross Hollows, rolling terrain, was clear of rebels, and Curtis decided to move toward that area. McCulloch, however, on the approach of the Union force, decided to fall back farther south, and on February 19 he had his troops burn the shelters and other buildings at Cross Hollows, where they were spending the winter, and evacuate the site, making their way through miserable wintry weather to Fayetteville, which they ransacked, and then on into the Boston Mountains, where they encamped along the Illinois River. Price and his army encamped just to the west of McCulloch's position.

In the meantime, General Van Dorn, the newly appointed commander of the two rebel armies and who had set up his headquarters at Pocahontas, Arkansas, in the northeast corner of the state, finally learned what was going on with his army. He quickly set out to take command. On the way, hurrying on horseback, he fell into a frigid stream, suffering some ill effects but continuing as fast he could, carried in an ambulance, taking nine cold and wearing days to reach the site in the Boston Mountains where his forces waited. He arrived on March 2.

Curtis now had his army encamped at two separate sites, apparently for better foraging, Sigel's two divisions to the west, and the two other divisions to the east. Briefed on the situation and the position of the Union forces, Van Dorn planned an immediate attack. His plan was to have his army, some 16,000 men and sixty-five pieces of artillery, move out of the mountains on March 4 to begin a drive that would plunge the rebels into the gap between the two sites of the Union army. He would then turn his full force on one site, overrun it and then turn on the other site.

On March 5, however, a loyalist resident of the area reported to Curtis that the rebels were moving out toward Curtis's two positions. Curtis instantly ordered his troops, the entire force, to withdraw northward, climb the slope of the bluff on the north side of Little Sugar Creek, entrench and fortify their position overlooking the creek. By the morning of Thursday, March 6, nearly all of Curtis's army was in its new defensive position atop the bluff overlooking Little Sugar Creek. A 600-man detachment serving as the rear guard for Sigel's divisions as they withdrew was nearly cut off by the advancing rebels while Sigel dallied over breakfast at a Bentonville hotel. Sigel's men managed to fight off the rebels in a running battle, and after four miles, the rebels gave up the chase. Sigel then joined Curtis at Little Sugar Creek.

Van Dorn reached Bentonville later that day and soon learned he was facing a changed situation. The Union force was dug in and fortified in a practically impregnable position. Besides that, Van Dorn's troops were hungry, their meager rations having been consumed, and they were cold and worn out from three days of marching in horrible winter conditions. Nevertheless, Van Dorn was reluctant to give up on an attack.

The Road Around Curtis's Right Flank

That evening McCulloch, who was well acquainted with the area, told Van Dorn there was a route around Curtis's right flank, a road called the Bentonville Detour, which intersected Telegraph Road near the state line, behind Curtis's stout line of defense. If the rebels could slip around the rear of the Union line and reach Telegraph Road, Curtis's army would be cut off and would be forced to surrender. Despite pleas by both McCulloch and Price to let the men sleep before taking on the Union army, Van Dorn insisted on moving out immediately. The march through the cold over a route obstructed by trees felled by Curtis's troops, through frigid streams, the men feeling their way through the darkness, was a nightmare. Many of the men, perhaps a thousand or more, weakened by hunger, fatigue and the biting cold, simply fell out of the line of march and collapsed along the way. At daybreak on March 7 the head of the rebel column reached Telegraph Road, while the rearmost units had just made their way across Little Sugar Creek below the Union position.

Now Van Dorn had a new idea. He sent Price's troops down Telegraph Road on the east side of a rocky hill called Big Mountain and sent McCulloch's men down Ford Road on the east side of Big Mountain. The plan was to have the two parts of Van Dorn's army reunite at Elkhorn Tavern about noon on Friday, March 7. The combined force would then deploy into a line of battle and attack the unsuspecting Union line, which would be facing south while the rebels struck from the north.

Union patrols, however, had discovered the rebels' move early in the morning of the 7th and had reported it to General Curtis, who ordered his troops to face about, holding their positions but expecting an attack from the north instead of from across Little Sugar

Creek below them to the south. Sigel's two divisions—the First commanded by Colonel Peter Osterhaus, the Second by General Asboth—which had been on the right side of the line but now, as the line faced north, held the left side. Curtis's two divisions, commanded by Colonel Eugene Carr and Colonel Jefferson C. Davis, made up the new right side of the Union line. Carr's troops were posted at and around Elkhorn Tavern, on the east side of the line.

Not waiting for the rebel attack, Curtis launched an attack of his own, sending a detachment to intercept Van Dorn's columns moving down the sides of Big Mountain. Osterhaus met and took on McCulloch's troops near the community of Leetown. McCulloch turned his 3,000 cavalrymen on Osterhaus and overwhelmed the Union force. Just west of that encounter the Cherokees under Confederate brigadier general Albert Pike slipped through the woods and struck two isolated companies of U.S. cavalry, killing some and wounding others, some of whom they scalped. Survivors of the two rebel attacks quickly fell back through a densely wooded area and across a large cornfield on the farm of Samuel Oberson. On the south side of the cornfield they joined the rest of Osterhaus's division and formed a defensive line as Osterhaus's artillery opened on McCulloch's position, scattering the Cherokees, who fled as the shells burst overhead.

McCulloch now turned his full attention on Osterhaus's force in Samuel Oberson's field, diverting his troops from their march past Big Mountain. As he was used to doing, McCulloch rode ahead to scout out the enemy's position, making his way through the woods on horseback. As he emerged from the woods he was spotted by skirmishers from the Thirty-sixth Illinois Infantry Regiment, who turned their rifles on him, fired a volley and dropped him from his saddle, shot dead in the heart. Confederate brigadier general James M. McIntosh took over command of McCulloch's troops and reacted to the death of the beloved McCulloch by leading the Second Arkansas Mounted Rifles Regiment, now dismounted, through the woods to attack the Union line. His charge was met by fierce fire, and McIntosh, too, was shot from his saddle, killed by a bullet in his heart.

Command of McCulloch's army then devolved upon Colonel Louis Hebert, who was leading a furious assault on the Union line on the right side of the spot where McIntosh had fallen. The Confederates, with superior numbers, were pushing the U.S. troops back for a time, but with reinforcements from Colonel Davis's Third Division, Osterhaus's men halted the rebels and drove them back into the woods, capturing Colonel Hebert in the process. The leaderless troops of the late General McCulloch gave up the attack, drifting away in the dense fog of gunsmoke that filled the woods.

While that half of Van Dorn's rebel army was engaged near Leetown, the other half, with Van Dorn himself commanding, had moved off Telegraph Road and was battling Colonel Eugene Carr's Fourth Division on the far right side of the Union line, near Elkhorn Tavern. The fight had started around noon on the 7th; and when Van Dorn had deployed and advanced on the Union line, Carr, a tough Regular Army officer and West Point graduate, counterattacked with a ferocity that blunted the rebel attack. A long artillery exchange followed, each side hammering away at the other.

When Van Dorn at last realized he outnumbered Carr's troops, he ordered Price to stretch out the rebel line beyond the flanks of Carr's line, and by late afternoon the line had been extended from a point near Elkhorn Tavern to high ground about a mile east of the tavern. Van Dorn then ordered a massive assault along the entire Union line. With no more than an hour of daylight remaining, the rebels struck, coming on with "a yell and a fury," as one Iowa soldier in Carr's line put it. The center of the Union line caved in and pulled back, allowing the rebels to capture Elkhorn Tavern. East of the tavern about a quarter mile a U.S. brigade commanded by Colonel Grenville Dodge, fighting from behind a breastwork of felled trees, repulsed repeated rebel assaults but finally fell back when superior numbers threatened to overwhelm the brigade. Carr's entire division then withdrew as darkness grew deeper, falling back to a cornfield where the units regrouped.

While the cold night came on, Van Dorn launched one last effort of the day to smash the Union army, his rebels streaming across farmer Benjamin Ruddick's cornfield, their cheers and yells rising above the roar of artillery, as one survivor described the charge. Curtis's relentless artillery spewed out barrage after barrage of canister, slicing down the onrushing attackers like scythes in a wheat field. At last the surviving rebels quit the bloody field and withdrew toward Elkhorn Tavern, their force, like the daylight, completely spent.

Around midnight, Curtis and his commanders held a council of war in Curtis's headquarters tent, where he rested on a bed of straw and blankets. Sigel was the first to speak up. He advocated what he had shown he was good at—retreat. The army was cut off from Missouri, he argued, and it had to pick an escape route and force its way through Van Dorn's line in the morning. Osterhaus and Carr, whose divisions had done most of the fighting, agreed with Sigel. Davis, taciturn as ever, offered no suggestion. Curtis, the oldest soldier among them, heard his commanders out, then said what he thought. He said he believed they had already taken the rebels' best shot and now that the Union left had thrown back and scattered the rebel right, he could turn his entire left eastward onto the rebel left as his right struck the rebels from the south. It was no time for retreat, Curtis declared. He didn't know it at the time, but there was another factor in his favor. Fearing his supply wagons might be captured, and eager to have his flanking army move as fast as possible, Van Dorn had left his supply train in the rear of his original front. Now, bearing needed provisions for his men and ammunition for his guns, it was out of reach.

Early on the morning of Saturday, March 8, Sigel sent Colonel Osterhaus to scout out the area into which Sigel's troops would be moving, and Osterhaus came back reporting that he had found a knoll that would provide an excellent position for Sigel's artillery. By 8:00 a.m. Asboth's division was in place on the far left of the Union line. Next to it was Osterhaus's division; then came Davis's and Carr's divisions. On the knoll that Osterhaus had suggested, to the west of Elkhorn Tavern, Sigel massed twenty-one field pieces. As they opened fire, Sigel rode out among the guns, occasionally dismounting to sight guns himself, then with the gun adjusted, he would pat the guns' breech, as if to the tell gun crews, many of whom were German, "Okay, fellows, continue firing," then he would step back out of the way of the gunners, and firing would resume. Battery after battery of rebel guns were smashed by the extraordinarily accurate and devastating fire of Sigel's guns. The gun crews, as well as the infantrymen poised for the charge, cheered Sigel as the rebel artillery was blown apart and surviving rebel gunners hastily fled the twisted wreckage. Once the rebel guns were silenced, Sigel ordered his artillery to fire into the woods where the rebel infantry lay in wait. The storm of huge, jagged splinters from shattered trees and shrapnel-like fragments blasted from the rocks drove a brigade of Price's Missourians from their position beside the base of Big Mountain. It was about this time that Van Dorn realized his ammunition wagons were out of reach and beyond recall. All the while, Sigel's infantry was creeping forward, swinging

3. *Major General Franz Sigel* 117

Battle of Pea Ridge, Arkansas. In the U.S. Army's first major victory of the war, Sigel and his troops played a heroic role. Sigel, on horseback, led the charge of nearly 10,000 Union soldiers and routed the army of Maj. Gen. Earl Van Dorn on March 8, 1862 (Library of Congress).

the left side of the Union line toward the north. By 9:30 a.m. Sigel's troops had executed their wheel to the right and now faced east, toward Elkhorn Tavern.

About 10:00 a.m. Curtis ordered the general advance to begin. Cantering toward the long line of infantrymen, Sigel raised his saber as he approached, then signaled the charge, and the entire Union line moved out, nearly 10,000 U.S. soldiers sweeping across the top of Pea Ridge, through the fields, through the woods, an awesome tidal wave of blue-coated warriors moving toward Elkhorn Tavern from the west and from the south. A witness reported the sight and the sounds of the advancing army: "With banners streaming, with drums beating, and our long line of blue coats advancing upon the double quick, with their deadly bayonets gleaming in the sunlight, and every man and officer yelling at the top of his lungs."[16]

Seeing the situation was hopeless, Van Dorn ordered a general withdrawal and joined in the rapid retreat, his units disintegrating as they rushed from the front, turning the withdrawal into a rout, madly dashing in all directions. Van Dorn himself hurried eastward down the Huntsville Road, away from the ridge and Elkhorn Tavern. Around noon the two scissor-like arms of Curtis's army, Sigel's troops on the left and Davis's troops on the right, came together at the tavern. Curtis, exultant, rode among his triumphant troops, waving his hat and shouting, "Victory! Victory!"

The United States Army had just won its first major victory of the war. First claim on the credit belonged to General Curtis, who had stood his ground when others advised retreat, but a considerable share of credit rightfully went to Sigel, whose generalship in the field on that day was characterized by one observer as "stellar." Two weeks later, on March 21, he was rewarded by being promoted to major general. His enjoyment of his newfound glory, however, was dampened by the onset of illnesses that left him too weak to function in his command. Curtis issued him a leave of absence on April 4, and on April 10 he returned to St. Louis to recuperate. He then soon developed a severe case of the flu. His leave was extended, and he suffered the sickness through the entire month of April, so seriously ill that it seemed he might never return to duty. By early May, however, he had begun recovering and by mid-May he was well enough to be considered for a new assignment.

In another reshuffle of the army the War Department created a new Army of Virginia, and on June 26 Major General John Pope was placed in command of it. In protest of Pope's appointment, General Frémont, who, like Sigel, was a recent transfer to the eastern theater of operations from Missouri, resigned his command and his commission and quit the army. Sigel was then appointed to command the First Corps of the Army of Virginia, replacing Frémont. The two other corps of the Army of Virginia were commanded by Major General Nathaniel Banks, commanding the Second Corps, and Major General Irvin McDowell, commanding the Third Corps. Sigel's corps totaled some 11,500 men and was posted in the lower Shenandoah Valley.

Pope's mission, as he described it, was to "cover the city of Washington from any attacks from the direction of Richmond, make such dispositions as were necessary to assure the safety of the valley of the Shenandoah, and at the same time so operate upon the enemy's lines of communication in the direction of Gordonsville and Charlottesville as to draw off, if possible, a considerable force of the enemy from Richmond, and thus relieve the operations against that city of the Army of the Potomac."[17] Pope decided to shift his troops and place them not in the Shenandoah Valley but at points from which they could swiftly move to intercept any Confederate force's move into the valley, checking its advance and cutting off its retreat. "I accordingly sent orders," Pope reported, "to Major General Sigel, commanding the First Corps, to move forward from Middletown, cross the Shenandoah at Front Royal, and, pursuing the west side of the Blue Ridge, to take post at Sperryville."[18] Late in the afternoon of August 7, 1862, Pope received reports that the rebels were crossing the Rapidan River at several points, moving north, advancing toward Pope's positions. From the reports it was hard to tell whether the Confederates were headed for Madison Court House or Culpeper, but Pope decided to concentrate his force at Culpeper. On the morning of August 8 he sent orders to Sigel to march at once from Sperryville to Culpeper Court House, a distance of some twenty-five miles. "To my surprise," Pope reported, "I received after night on the 8th a note from General Sigel, dated at Sperryville at 6:30 that afternoon, asking me by what road he should march to Culpeper Court-House. As there was but one road between those two points, and that a broad stone turnpike, I was at a loss to understand how General Sigel could entertain any doubt as to the road by which he should march. "This doubt, however," Pope reported, "delayed the arrival of his corps at Culpeper Court-House several hours, and rendered it impracticable for that corps to be pushed to the front, as I had designed, on the afternoon of the next day."[19]

When Sigel's troops finally did arrive at Culpeper, they were not ready to go into action. "I had given orders a number of days previously," Pope related, "that all the troops belonging to the Army of Virginia should be ready to march at the shortest notice and should habitually keep two days' cooked rations in their haversacks. Notwithstanding this order, General Sigel's corps arrived in Culpeper without any rations and was unable to move forward until provisions could be procured from McDowell's train and cooked at Culpeper Court-House."[20]

What followed was the Battle of Cedar Mountain, which began with an exchange of artillery fire on August 9. The rebel force facing Pope was the army of Stonewall Jackson reinforced by that of Major General A.P. Hill, a combined force of about 24,000 men. Jackson had learned that Pope's army, which outnumbered Jackson's nearly two to one, had not yet concentrated and he decided to strike it before it did, moving up from Gordonsville and driving back Pope's cavalry on the north side of the Rapidan and engaging Banks's corps in the center of the Union line. There Jackson ran into a tough fight but rallied and counterattacked. By 7:00 p.m. the Union line was in full retreat, and by 10:00 p.m. the fighting had ended. Jackson halted and held his position for two days, expecting Pope to try another assault, but it never came. Jackson pulled back to a better defensive position below the Rapidan River around Gordonsville. Pope fell back to Culpeper. Banks having precipitated the engagement, his corps took the brunt of the beating. Pope moved Sigel's corps forward to relieve Banks, but Sigel had no significant role in the outcome, which was a Confederate victory.

Sigel's next action was in the Second Battle of Bull Run (Second Manassas), during which he suffered a wound in his left hand. Fought on August 28 through August 30, 1862, it was another Union defeat at the hands of Stonewall Jackson and one in which Sigel and his men, although heavily engaged in the fighting, played no major part in the result. General Pope, who lost his job after the Bull Run defeat, in paying his respects to his commanders in his final official report on his disastrous northern Virginia campaign seemed to damn Sigel with faint praise: "General Sigel rendered useful service in reorganizing and putting in condition the First Army Corps of the Army of Virginia, and made many valuable and highly important reconnaissances during the operations of the campaign."[21]

On orders from General Halleck, now the army's general in chief, Pope's Army of Virginia withdrew toward Washington. In mid–September the War Department enlarged Sigel's corps to 15,000 men, redesignated it the Eleventh Corps of the Army of the Potomac and assigned it to the defense of Washington, with its troops based around Fairfax Court House, Virginia, just outside Washington. By mid–December Sigel had moved southward toward Fredericksburg and had set up his headquarters at Stafford Court House, Virginia. He spent much of the winter either agitating for more troops and asking favors or requesting and taking leave when he didn't get them. On leave, he visited New York, refreshing himself in the adulation of the German-American community there and eventually buying a house that became his permanent residence.

In early March of 1863, his disgruntlement with the War Department having become chronic, Sigel wrote to Secretary Stanton asking that he either be relieved from his command or that his resignation from the army be accepted. Stanton relieved him of his command. By late April 1863 Sigel had changed his mind and asked to be returned to the command of the Eleventh Corps. Halleck turned him down, but under political pressure gave him another job, assigning him to the Department of the Susquehanna, headquartered in Harrisburg, Pennsylvania. Throughout the summer and fall of 1863 Sigel repeatedly took leave to return to New York or travel elsewhere, making public appearances and delivering speeches.

When winter came, Sigel renewed his importuning of Washington to give him a more important command. Now facing an election mere months away, President Lincoln, with his eye on the German-American vote, in March 1864 instructed secretary of war Stanton to put Sigel in command of the army's newly formed Department of West Virginia. Also in March, on the 9th, Lincoln promoted Ulysses S. Grant to lieutenant general and made him general in chief of the entire U.S. Army. Now Grant would have to deal with Sigel, for whom he had an important part in his action-on-all-fronts campaign to win and end the war.

On March 29 Sigel received his first orders from Grant in a letter delivered to him at his headquarters in Cumberland, Virginia, by Major General Edward Ord. The letter, as Sigel reported it, said that he "should immediately assemble 8000 infantry, 1500 cavalry ('picked men'), besides artillery, provided with ten days' rations, at Beverly [West Virginia], for the purpose of marching by Covington to Staunton; the troops to be under the command of General Ord."[22] Sigel said he took "the most energetic measures" to get the troops and their supplies to Beverly but was hampered by days of rain that made it impossible to move even empty wagons over the soggy roads. Only 6,500 men could be assembled for the intended expedition, he informed Grant. Amid the delays and the problems, which General Ord observed while spending days in Sigel's headquarters, Ord decided he had endured enough of Sigel and asked Grant to relieve him, which Grant did, replacing him with Brigadier General William W. Averell.

Grant's plan was for Sigel to march southwest through the Shenandoah Valley from Winchester to Staunton, where he would link up with the columns of Averell and Brigadier General George Crook, which would also march southwestward, to the west of Sigel's column. Crook's objectives were the Virginia & Tennessee Railroad and the railroad bridge over the New River near Dublin, Virginia. Averell's objectives were the lead mines and saltworks at Wytheville and Saltville, Virginia.

From the link-up at Staunton the three columns would proceed eastward to join Major General George Meade and the Army of the Potomac, which Meade now commanded, In the meantime, they would have ripped up and disrupted the Confederates' railway supply line, deprived the rebels of two crucial necessities—lead and salt—and cut a wide swath of devastation and destruction through an area of Virginia that was vital to keeping General Lee's rebel army fed. Grant had little confidence that Sigel himself would accomplish much, saying so when he wrote to General Sherman and told him, "From the expedition from the Department of West Virginia I do not calculate on very great results; but it is the only way I can take troops from there."[23]

Sigel and his infantry reached Winchester on Sunday, May 1, 1864, while his cavalry units advanced as far as Cedar Creek and Strasburg. "From our position at Winchester and Cedar Creek," Sigel related, "we learned that there was no hostile force in the Shenandoah Valley, except General Imboden's cavalry and mounted infantry, reported to be about 3000 strong. It seemed to me, therefore, necessary to advance farther south toward Staunton, in order to induce [Confederate Major General John] Breckinridge to send a part of his forces against us, and thereby facilitate the operations of Crook and Averell."[24]

Brigadier General John D. Imboden, commanding the Confederate force that Sigel had learned was alone in defending the length of the Shenandoah Valley, was a forty-one-year-old lawyer, a former teacher at a school for the deaf, dumb and blind, and a former member of the House of Delegates in the Virginia legislature, where he had served two terms. He was born and grew up in Staunton. In November 1859 he was given a commission as captain in the Staunton military unit of the Virginia State Militia, a unit he had helped organize. He commanded that unit when it participated in the capture of Harpers Ferry and commanded an artillery battery at the First Battle of Bull Run (First Manassas). Deafened in one ear by the firing of an artillery piece, Imboden gave up the artillery in September 1862 and recruited a battalion of partisan rangers that became the 62nd Virginia Mounted Infantry and fought under Jeb Stuart in the Gettysburg campaign. On July 21, 1863, General Lee, commanding all Confederate operations in Virginia, assigned Imboden as commander of the Valley District, comprising the area west of the Blue Ridge Mountains as far south as the James River.

"By the month of April, 1864," Imboden related, "information reached us that General Sigel had established himself at Winchester, and was preparing for a forward movement with over eight thousand infantry, twenty-five hundred cavalry, and three or four field-batteries. On the 2d of May I broke camp at Mount Crawford, in Rockingham County, something over seventy miles from Winchester, and moved to meet Sigel and find out as far as possible his strength and designs and report the facts to General Lee."[25] Included in Imboden's command were the 62nd Mounted Infantry Brigade, the 23rd Virginia Cavalry, the 18th Virginia Cavalry, a cavalry battalion from Maryland, part of another Maryland cavalry battalion, a unit of partisan rangers, a horse artillery unit with six field guns, and the signal corps of the Valley District.

By this stage of the war, the Confederates, including General Imboden, desperate for manpower, were looking for help wherever it could be found, including those too young or too old for conscription. Imboden reported the following:

> [I] ordered General William H. Harman at Staunton to notify the "reserves" (militia) of Rockingham and Augusta Counties, consisting of men over forty-five and boys between sixteen and eighteen years of age, and all detailed men on duty in shops, at furnaces, etc., to be ready to move at a moment's notice. A similar notification was sent to General Francis H. Smith, Commandant of the Virginia Military Institute at Lexington, where there were about three hundred cadets under eighteen years of age at school. My veteran troops "effective present," numbered but 1492 men when we left Mount Crawford on the 2d of May, to which should be added about 100 men scouting either in front of or behind Sigel. Harman's "reserves" did not amount to one thousand men, and these were undisciplined and armed mostly with hunting-rifles and shot-guns. This was the total scattered and incongruous force in front of Sigel in the valley the first week in May.[26]

On May 5 Imboden's motley army reached Woodstock, Virginia, about twelve miles below Sigel's position at Strasburg. Intelligence from Imboden's scouts and residents of the area gave Imboden a clear idea of the force he was facing. "About eleven thousand men were reported in my front," he reported. "The Signal Corps in the mountains west of us reported a force of 7000 men at Lewisburg, only a little over 100 miles from Staunton, apparently awaiting Sigel's movements to cooperate with him."[27] Imboden swiftly relayed that information to Lee and made, as he said, the most earnest appeals to him, asking Lee to send more troops to the valley immediately. Lee responded that he was too sorely pressed by Grant to be able to spare any men to aid the defense of the Shenandoah Valley. Imboden would have to do the best he could with what he had. Although he had offered no help, Lee ordered Imboden to retard Sigel's advance in every way he could and to be careful to avoid being surrounded and captured.

Imboden set out to do his best. From atop Massanutten Mountain, overlooking Strasburg, his signalmen on May 8 spotted two cavalry reconnaissance parties that Sigel had sent out, one moving westward on the road to Moorefield, West Virginia, and one moving eastward through Front Royal, Virginia. "These facts," Imboden wrote, "convinced me that Sigel, before venturing to advance, meant to ascertain whether he had enemies in dangerous force within striking distance on either flank, an investigation that would consume several days. As there were no troops, except my little band, nearer than General Lee's army, it was manifestly important to attack these detachments as far from Strasburg as possible and delay their return as long as possible."[28]

Imboden turned first to Sigel's reconnaissance detail moving on Imboden's left. Leaving Colonel George H. Smith in charge at his Woodstock headquarters, Imboden himself led the attack force, composed of the 18th Virginia Cavalry Regiment—commanded by Colonel George Imboden, the general's brother—the partisan rangers commanded by Captain John N. McNeill, and two field pieces from the battery commanded by Captain J.H. McClanahan. The plan was to take the attack force that night through a mountain pass called the Devil's Hole and intercept the reconnaissance detail on the Moorefield road some twenty miles from Strasburg. Imboden's account of the incident was vague, but Sigel supplied details. "Before leaving Winchester," he reported, "a force of 500 cavalry, under Colonel Jacob Higgins, was sent toward Wardensville to protect our right flank, and Colonel William H. Boyd, with 300 select horsemen, into the Luray Valley to cover our left flank, especially from [Colonel John S.] Mosby; but Colonel Higgins was attacked and beaten by a detachment of Imboden's brigade between Wardensville and Moorefield on the 9th of May, and pursued north toward Romney."[29]

Sigel's reconnaissance detail on his left flank fared even worse. Imboden received intelligence that that detail, commanded by Colonel Boyd, was on its way to New Market, Virginia, and was expecting to join Sigel's main force there by the middle of the week. "Upon this information," Imboden reported, "we laid a trap for Colonel Boyd, and on Wednesday [May 11, 1864], we captured 464 men, nearly all of this force."[30] Sigel claimed that Boyd's force had but 300 men in it and that "Colonel Boyd was ambuscaded on his way from the Luray Valley to New Market on the 13th and defeated, suffering a loss of 125 men and 200 horses."[31] Sigel was wrong about the date. The ambush actually occurred on May 11, and perhaps he was wrong about the losses as well. "To gain more detailed information," he wrote, "two regiments of infantry, under Colonel August Moore, assisted by five hundred of the 1st New York (Lincoln) Cavalry, under Major Timothy Quinn, were sent forward on the 13th."[32]

"This force," Sigel continued in his account, "met a part of Imboden's troops near Mount Jackson on the 14th, forced them across the Shenandoah, took possession of the bridge, and, animated by this success, followed them as far as New Market, seven miles beyond Mount Jackson, or nineteen miles from the position of our forces at Woodstock."[33] When he learned that Moore's men were unopposed at Mount Jackson, Sigel decided to move his whole army there, believing Mount Jackson would provide a better defensive position in a confrontation with the combined forces of Breckinridge and Imboden. On the night of May 14 Sigel ordered his troops to move out at five o'clock the next morning. They arrived at Mount Jackson about 10:00 a.m. on the 15th. Not long after their arrival, Sigel received a note from a member of his staff saying that the troops were in a good position and eager for a fight.

On Thursday, May 12, Breckinridge had wired Imboden to tell him he had arrived in Staunton and was on his way to reinforce Imboden. Thursday and Friday, Imboden reported, were spent "in perfect quiet at New Market, awaiting Sigel from the north-east and Breckinridge from the south-west, being well informed of the movements of each" as both moved toward New Market.

The Battle at New Market

New Market was a town of about 1,000 souls, situated in what was reputed to be the most beautiful site in the Shenandoah Valley, with the north fork of the river running beside a range of hills on the southwest side of the town. The hills were cleared and cultivated on the side facing the town, and beside the base of the hills ran the valley turnpike, which was New Market's main street.

Imboden received reports that Sigel's advance was so cautious and slow that he would not be able to proceed past Rude's Hill, about four miles north of New Market, by the end of the day on Saturday, May 14. Imboden then took time to ride to Lacey Springs, ten miles south of New Market, where he met up with Breckinridge and had dinner with him. During dinner a courier came to Imboden with a message from Colonel Smith, commanding during Imboden's absence, saying that Sigel's cavalry, 2,500 strong, had reached Rude's Hill, and that the Confederate 18th Cavalry, vigorously pressed, was falling back and that Smith had formed a line of battle just west of New Market to cover his retreat. Imboden immediately left to join his troops and as he was leaving, Breckinridge, taking charge, ordered Imboden to hold New Market "at all hazards" until dark and then fall back four miles to a previously prepared position.

When he arrived back in New Market, Imboden saw that his line of battle extended from halfway up the hillside west of the town, across the valley turnpike toward Smith's Creek, about a mile southeast of the town, and terminated at a spot concealed by woodlands. McClanahan's artillery was posted on the extreme left of the line, up the hillside, giving it the advantage of plunging fire across the town and down on Sigel's guns. "From what I saw," Imboden wrote, "I felt no apprehension of any attempt to dislodge us that evening."[34] And Sigel made no attempt.

At daylight Breckinridge's troops arrived at New Market, and after looking over the ground, Breckinridge established his line of battle. Imboden recounted the following:

> He had brought with him two small infantry brigades, commanded respectively by Brigadier-Generals John Echols and Gabriel C. Wharton.... He also had Major William McLaughlin's artillery—six guns—and a section of the cadet battery from the Virginia Military Institute, temporarily attached to McLaughlin. He had also ordered out the full corps of cadets—boys from 16 to 18 years old—and they were present to the number of 225, under command of Colonel Ship[p], one of their professors, and an excellent soldier in every sense. The "reserves" from Augusta and Rockingham Counties

had also been ordered out, but had not had time to assemble from their scattered homes, and were not up. The entire force, above enumerated and present, of all arms, did not exceed three thousand men. My whole effective force, then present, did not exceed 1600 additional men.[35]

The total Confederate force facing Sigel, then, did not exceed 4,600 men, according to Imboden. Breckinridge, though, was satisfied. Having studied the ground and the Confederates' formation, he told Imboden, "We can attack and whip them here, and I'll do it."[36]

Breckinridge issued orders at once for all the troops to advance as rapidly as possible, and for Major McLaughlin not to wait for the infantry but to bring up his guns immediately. "I was ordered," Imboden related, "as soon as the artillery and infantry came up, to concentrate all my cavalry and with McClanahan's battery take position on our extreme right next to Smith's Creek, to cover that flank. Within little more than an hour these dispositions were all made and McLaughlin 'opened the ball.'"[37] Colonel George D. Wells of the 34th Massachusetts Infantry Regiment described the action:

> The rebels advanced in three lines of battle, each, I think, as heavy as ours, with masses on the right and left. The ground was perfectly open, not a tree or shrub to obstruct the view. Nothing could be finer than their advance. Their yelling grew steadily nearer; our skirmishers and infantry in front came back on the double-quick, some of them running through and over my lines.
>
> The air was filled with bullets and bursting shells, and my men began to fall. I was ordered to deploy one company across my front as skirmishers, and Captain Leach, with Company G, went forward, and his groups halted and deployed in the tumult about 200 yards in advance, each man taking his exact interval and dressing to the right as steadily as on drill. The officers in the line were giving their orders in low tones, and every man stood, his gun at the ready, his finger on the trigger waiting to see the face of his foe. It was a marvel to me then and is now how men who almost never before had heard the rebel yell and the terrible din of the battle-field could be so entirely calm and self-possessed.
>
> Soon our men in front were, by the confusion, cleared away, the rebel lines were plainly seen, and the battle began. Our front fire was heavy, and the artillery had an enfilading fire, under which their [the Confederates'] first line went down. They staggered, went back, and their whole advance halted. Their fire ceased to be effective. A cheer ran along our line, and the first success was ours. I gave the order to "cease firing." Just then Colonel Thoburn, brigade commander, rode along the lines telling the men to "prepare to charge." He rode by me shouting some order I could not catch, and went to the regiment on my left, which immediately charged. I supposed this to be his order to me, and I commanded to fix bayonets and charge. The men fairly sprang forward. As we neared the crest of the hill we met the entire rebel force advancing and firing. The regiment on my left, which first met the fire, turned and went back, leaving the Thirty-fourth rushing alone into the enemy's line.... I was able to look about the field, and saw, to my surprise, that the artillery had limbered up and was moving off the field, and that the infantry had gone, save one regiment, which was gallantly holding its ground far to the left. The rebel line advanced until I could see, above the smoke, two battle-flags on the hill in front of the position where the artillery had been posted. I ordered a retreat.... But the rebels were coming on at the double-quick and concentrating their whole fire upon us. I told the men to run and get out of fire as quickly as possible, and rally behind the first cavalry line found to the rear.[38]

Sigel gave his own account of the action:

I personally directed and superintended this arrangement of the right wing, [describing the placement of his units] and was about to proceed to the left to see whether all the troops were in their proper positions, when my attention was directed to the approach of the enemy, whose lines appeared on the crest of the hills opposite our front, northwest of New Market.

Our skirmishers began to fall back, and fire was opened by Snow's battery on our right. I ordered the 34th Massachusetts to kneel down and deliver their fire by file as soon as the enemy came near enough to make it effective. A very severe conflict now followed at short range, the enemy charging repeatedly and with great determination against our line of infantry and the batteries, and being repulsed by the coolness and bravery of the 34th Massachusetts, 1st West Virginia, and 54th Pennsylvania, and the batteries.

The smoke from the infantry fire on the left and the batteries on the right became so dense that I could not distinguish friend from foe. During the battle rain fell in torrents and the wind drove clouds of smoke from our own and the enemy's lines against us, giving the latter the advantage in distinguishing our position and rendering his fire more effective, thus accounting in part for the greater number of killed on our side. There was an interruption of a few minutes when the enemy's lines recoiled, and our men cheered; then the fire began again and lasted about thirty minutes; the enemy again charged, this time especially against our batteries; he came so near that Lieutenant Ephraim Chalfont of Carlin's battery rode up to me and said that he could not hold his position. I immediately ordered two companies of the 12th West Virginia to advance and protect the pieces, but to my surprise there was no disposition to advance; in fact, in spite of entreaties and reproaches, the men could not be moved an inch!

...I determined to make a counter-charge of the whole right wing.... Bayonets were fixed and the charge was made in splendid style, but the enemy rallied, received our line with a destructive fire, and forced it back to its position. Before the charge was made, our extreme left wing had given way; two pieces of Von Kleiser's battery fell into the enemy's hands.... When Thoborn's regiments [which had made the countercharge] came back, strewing the ground with their dead and wounded, the enemy, close on their heels, now again turned against the batteries on the right, filling the air with their high-pitched yells. I saw that the battery would be lost, as men and horses were falling.

I therefore reluctantly gave orders to Captain Carlin, through Lieutenant Chalfont, who was nearest to me, to withdraw his pieces successively, by sections from the right, and take a position on an eminence, a short distance in the rear. Suddenly Carlin, who acted as chief-of-artillery, galloped back in hot haste, and his whole command followed him immediately. As some of the horses of two pieces had been killed, the guns were abandoned. Our whole position now became untenable, and the infantry retreated, pursued for a short distance by the enemy....

There was some confusion and scattering of our retreating forces, but very soon order was restored. They rallied again and formed a line opposite the Dunker Church, and west of the turnpike leading to Mount Jackson, about three-quarters of a mile from the battle-field. Here we could see a dark line on Rude's Hill, and discovered it was the line of the 28th and 116th Ohio, the two regiments that were unfortunately not with us during the battle....

I met with [Brigadier] General [Jeremiah] Sullivan, and after some consultation we came to the conclusion not to await another attack, for the reason that our losses were severe; that the regiments that had sustained the brunt of the fight were nearly out of ammunition and would have no time to receive it from the train, which was in the rear, beyond the bridge; that our position was not a good one, being commanded by the enemy's guns posted on the hill in front of our left; and that in case of defeat we could not cross the swollen river, except by the bridge.... I therefore directed the troops to Mount Jackson, which was done slowly and in perfect order.... We would have remained at that place [to which they had withdrawn], but since the cavalry on our flank, under Colonels Boyd and Higgins respectively, had been beaten, flanks and rear were unprotected.... It was therefore thought best to bring our little army back to Cedar Creek.[39]

At 8:00 p.m. on the day of the battle, May 15, from his headquarters near Strasburg, Sigel wired this telegram to the U.S. Army's adjutant general in Washington:

A severe battle was fought to-day at New Market between our forces and those of Echols and Imboden, under Breckinridge. Our troops were overpowered by superior numbers. I, therefore, withdrew them gradually from the battle-field, and recrossed the Shenandoah at about 7 p.m. Under the circumstances prevailing I find it necessary to retire to Cedar Creek. The battle was fought on our side by 5,500 in all against 8,000 to 9,000 of the enemy. We lost about 600 killed and wounded, and 50 prisoners.

The next day, May 16, he wired the adjutant general a second report:

After the battle of yesterday I retired gradually to Strasburg and Cedar Creek, bringing all my train and all the wounded that could be transported from the battle-field with me. In consequence of the long line and the trains which had to be guarded I could not bring more than six regiments into the fight, besides the artillery and cavalry. The enemy have about 7,000 infantry, besides the other arms. Our losses are about 600 killed and wounded, and 50 prisoners. Five pieces of artillery had to be left on the field after being disabled or the horses shot. The retrograde movement to Strasburg was effected in perfect order, without any loss of material or men. The troops are in very good spirits, and will fight another battle if the enemy should advance against us. I will forward the full report, with list of casualties, by letter.

General Grant, hoping to hear good news from the campaign in the Shenandoah valley, instead got the bad news in a wire from General Halleck, now his chief of staff in Washington: "Sigel is in full retreat on Strasburg. He will do nothing but run; never did anything else."[40] Grant immediately asked Halleck to relieve Sigel and put in his place Major General David Hunter. On Saturday, May 21, Sigel was told he had been relieved of command of the Department of West Virginia. The message was brought to him by General Hunter.

Hunter's cousin, Colonel David Hunter Strother, who was a member of Sigel's staff and held a low opinion of him as a general, was satisfied that the Battle of New Market, though lost, had achieved a worthwhile result. "We can afford to lose such a battle as New Market," he remarked, "to get rid of such a mistake as Major General Sigel."[41] The army, however, was not quite rid of him. Believing Sigel could still be useful, General Hunter offered him a job, letting him choose between commanding the Department of West Virginia's infantry or its cavalry or its reserve division based at Harpers Ferry. Sigel chose the reserve division and assumed the responsibility of keeping Hunter's troops provided with reinforcements, supplies and ammunition and, with some 10,000 troops, protecting the Baltimore & Ohio rail line. After Sigel's failing to halt attacks on the B&O and failing to impede Confederate Lieutenant General Jubal Early's march on Washington, Grant decided the army could do without General Sigel, and the War Department on July 8, 1864, notified Sigel he was relieved. A month later he was granted a leave of absence, and he spent the rest of the war without a command. He resigned his commission on May 4, 1865, at the end of the war.

After the war he was an editor on German-American newspapers in Baltimore and New York, ran for public office and was defeated, held a variety of political-appointment jobs in New York, later became publisher of a German publication and editor of another, the *New York Monthly*, wrote articles about his war experiences and involved himself in the affairs of the German-American community, to whom he remained a beloved figure, in New York and elsewhere.

He died on August 22, 1902, at age 77, survived by a son, Franz Sigel, Jr., a New York lawyer, and was buried in Woodlawn Cemetery in the Bronx in New York.

4

Major General John Charles Frémont

Before the War: Born January 21, 1813, in Savannah, Georgia. Attended Charleston College from 1829 to 1831, when he was expelled. Served as a mathematics instructor aboard the USS *Natchez* from 1833 to 1835. Served as a civil engineering assistant and second lieutenant in the army's corps of topographical engineers, exploring and mapping the area between the Missouri River and the Canadian border, 1838 to 1839. Participated in expedition to seek and survey a route from the Mississippi River to the Pacific coast, 1842. Settled in California. Married Jessie Benton, daughter of Missouri senator Thomas Hart Benton, in 1841. Political affiliation: Republican. Elected to a one-year term as senator from California and served from September 1850 to March 1851. Was the Republican party's first candidate for president, losing to Democrat James Buchanan in the 1856 election. Military experience: Second lieutenant, army corps of topographical engineers; major of a California volunteers battalion, 1846. Court-martialed for mutiny and insubordination and found guilty. Pardoned by President James Polk; resigned from the army on March 15, 1848.

John Frémont was in England when he heard about Fort Sumter. Ever restless, he hurried back to New York and Washington, eager to get in on the action. Already a prominent political and public figure, renowned as the "Pathfinder of the West," Frémont seemed to President Lincoln to be a well-suited commander of men. He was forty-eight years old but seemed younger. Slim and muscular, not tall, his mass of dark hair and thick dark beard showing only touches of gray, he was graceful in his movements and dramatic in his manner. At the urging of some of Frémont's influential friends, the president appointed him a major general in the army that would defend the nation now threatened by organized, armed rebellion. Frémont of course was interested in the West, and Lincoln wanted someone to take charge in the West. He decided to put Frémont in command of the army's Department of the West, with headquarters in St. Louis, in the strife-plagued state of Missouri. He was to succeed Major General William Harney and would command U.S. military operations in Missouri and all other states between the Mississippi River and the Rocky Mountains, and Illinois as well.

4. Major General John Charles Frémont

His mission was to keep Missouri, which was teetering on the brink of secession, in the Union, and to launch a campaign to take back the Mississippi River from the rebels. The president himself outlined the mission to Frémont, stopping short, however, of providing details or directions. "The President," Frémont related in his memoirs, "had gone carefully over with me the subject of my intended campaign, and this with the single desire to find out what was best to do and how to do it.... When I took leave of him, he accompanied me down the stairs, coming out to the steps of the portico at the White House; I asked him then, if there was anything further in the way of instruction that he wished to say to me. 'No,' he replied, 'I have given you *carte blanche;* you must use your own judgment and do the best you can....'"[1]

With that purpose—and that blank check—in mind, Frémont set out for St. Louis, arriving there on the morning of July 25, 1861. He moved into a three-story mansion that he had rented from a relative of his wife, at a cost to the government of $6,000 a year. It was commodious enough to house his entire administrative staff and himself. Either out of fear of unruly secessionists or love of ostentation he had the place practically surrounded by guards and he turned a nearby building into a barracks where he posted a regiment of troops.

Maj. Gen. John Frémont, a former army lieutenant who had been court-martialed and found guilty of mutiny and insubordination, was appointed a major general by President Lincoln at the urging of Frémont's influential friends and placed in command of the army's Department of the West, which included all the troops in the states between the Mississippi River and the Rocky Mountains, plus Illinois (Library of Congress).

The abundance of guards had the main effect of making an interview with Frémont almost impossible to get. Major General William T. Sherman tried to see Frémont after being warned of the difficulty. He was told that Frémont kept senators, governors and other important persons waiting for days, even weeks, before granting an audience. Sherman, known for his determination, was undeterred. When he arrived at the mansion's front gate about sunrise, "a sentinel with drawn sabre," Sherman recounted, "paraded up and down in front of the house. I had on my undress uniform indicating my rank, and I inquired of the sentinel, 'Is General Frémont up?' He answered, 'I don't know.' Seeing that he was a soldier by his bearing, I spoke in a sharp, emphatic voice, 'Then find out.'" The sentinel called for the corporal of the guard, to whom Sherman spoke the same words in the same tone, which resulted in the front door of the mansion being opened about fifteen minutes later and Sherman being ushered into a large parlor where after about ten minutes, Frémont showed up and received him, "very politely," according to Sherman.[2] Few others were able to do what Sherman had done.

As for fear, there was good reason for extreme caution if not fear. St. Louis was a city in turmoil when Frémont arrived. Its population of 160,000 seemed more sympathetic to secession than to the Union, with far more rebel flags than Stars and Stripes flying from houses and other buildings. In one building recruits for the Confederate army were openly solicited and enlisted. At night, gangs of secessionists brazenly and boisterously marched through the streets shouting cheers and support for the Confederacy and its president. U.S. Army personnel stayed close to their billets to avoid the gangs. In areas outside the city the situation seemed even more threatening, so that Frémont decided the city needed to be defended against an onslaught by secessionists. He ordered the construction of a line of redoubts that would encircle the city to stave off attackers and would be built not by troops—which, he determined, needed to be engaged in drill, not construction—but by civilian labor, thereby giving work to the city's large number of unemployed and restive inhabitants. He also began construction of fortifications at Jefferson City, Rolla, Ironton and Cape Girardeau.

While work proceeded on the earthworks redoubts in St. Louis—which were never finished and never manned and were believed by at least some army professionals to be useless anyway—Frémont busied himself with work, putting in long days that stretched from sunup to midnight, immersing himself in every possible aspect of his responsibilities as he saw them. In a desperate-sounding letter to President Lincoln dated July 30, 1861, he spelled out some of his problems, doubtless hoping for help, or at least understanding, from on high:

> *My dear sir:* You were kind enough to say that as occasions of sufficient gravity arose I might send you a private note.
>
> I have found this command in disorder, nearly every county in an insurrectionary condition, and the enemy advancing in force by different points on the southern frontier. Within a circle of 50 miles around General Prentiss there are about 12,000 of the Confederate forces, and 5,000 Tennesseans and Arkansas men, under Hardee, well armed with rifles, are advancing upon Ironton.... I have already re-enforced it with one regiment; sent on another this morning and fortified it. I am holding the railroad to Ironton and that to Rolla, so securing our connections with the South....
>
> I have ordered General Pope back to North Missouri, of which he is now in command. I am sorely pressed for want of arms.... Our troops have not been paid, and some regiments are in a state of mutiny, and the men whose terms of service have expired generally refuse to enlist. I lost a fine regiment last night from inability to pay them a portion of the money due. This regiment had been intended to move on a critical post last night. The Treasurer of the United States has here $300,000 entirely unappropriated. I applied to him yesterday for $100,000 for my pay-master, General Andrews, but was refused. We have not an hour for delay....
>
> I have infused energy and activity into the departments, and there is a thorough good spirit in officers and men. This morning I will order the treasurer to deliver the money in his possession to General Andrews, and will send a force to the treasury to take the money, and will direct such payments as the exigency requires. I will hazard everything for the defense of the department you have confided to me, and I trust to you for support.
>
> With respect and regard, I am, yours, truly,
>
> J.C. FRÉMONT
Major-General, Commanding.[3]

Trouble was everywhere, as Frémont reported in a postwar account:

> In addition to the bodies of armed men that swarmed over the State, a Confederate force of nearly 50,000 men was already on the Southern frontier: Pillow, with 12,000,

advancing upon Cairo; Thompson, with 5000, upon Girardeau; Hardee, with 5000, upon Ironton; and Price, with an estimated force of 25,000, upon Lyon, at Springfield. Their movement was intended to overrun Missouri, and, supported by a friendly population of over a million, to seize upon St. Louis and make that city a center of operations for the invasion of the loyal States.

To meet this advancing force I had 23,000 men of all arms. Of this only some 15,000 were available, the remainder being three-fourths men whose term of service was expiring. General John Pope was fully occupied in North Missouri with nearly all my disposable force, which was required to hold in check rebellion in that quarter. For the defense of Cairo B.M. Prentiss had 8 regiments, but 6 were three-months men, at the end of their term, unpaid, and unwilling to reenlist. At Springfield General Lyon had about 6000 men, unpaid and badly fed, and in need of clothing. In this condition he was in hourly expectation of being attacked by the enemy, who was advancing in three times his nominal strength. This was the situation to be met at the outset.[4]

In a fit of frustration over the lawlessness and rebel threat in Missouri—the state he was frantically attempting to hold for the Union as ordered—on August 31, 1861, Frémont issued a proclamation decreeing that "all persons who shall be taken with arms in their hands within these lines [the area of the U.S. Army's occupation of Missouri] shall be tried by court martial, and if found guilty will be shot. Real and personal property of those who take up arms against the United States, or who shall be directly proven to have taken an active part with their enemies in the field, is declared confiscated to public use and their slaves, if any they have, are hereby declared free men."[5]

Frémont had the proclamation printed and distributed to the public. He also sent a copy of it to Washington, D.C., where it swiftly came to the attention of President Lincoln. Thinking both practically and politically, Lincoln instantly foresaw the effects of the proclamation and pointed them out to Frémont in a tactful letter, explaining that he was writing to the general "in a spirit of caution and not of censure." The two troublesome points to which Lincoln objected were:

> First. Should you shoot a man, according to the Proclamation, the Confederates would very certainly shoot our best men in their hands in retaliation; and so, man for man, indefinitely. It is, therefore, my order that you allow no man to be shot under the proclamation without first having my approbation and consent.
>
> Second. I think there is a great danger that the closing paragraph, in relation to the confiscation of property and the liberating [of] slaves of traitorous owners, will alarm our Southern Union friends and turn them against us; perhaps ruin our rather fair prospect for Kentucky. Allow me, therefore, to ask that you will, as of your own motion, modify that paragraph so as to conform to the first and fourth sections of the Act of Congress entitled "An act to confiscate property used for insurrectionary purposes," approved August 6, 1861, a copy of which I herewith send you.[6]

Frémont refused to rescind his order voluntarily. He wrote to the president that he had issued the proclamation when he found himself "between the Rebel armies, the Provisional Government [of Missouri], and home traitors" and that it was "as much a movement in the war as a battle."[7] Returning Lincoln's tact with bluntness, he told the president, "If your better judgment decides that I was wrong in the article respecting the liberation of slaves, I have to ask that you will openly direct me to make the correction. The implied censure will be received as a soldier always should receive the reprimand of his chief. If I were to retract on my own accord it would imply that I myself thought it wrong, and that I had acted without the reflection which the gravity of the point demanded. But I did not. I acted with full deliberation, and the certain conviction that it was a measure right and necessary, and I still think so."[8]

In further defiance, Frémont dispatched his wife, Jessie, to carry the letter to Washington and to argue his case to President Lincoln in person. It was all to no effect except to anger the president, stiffen his resistance and draw from him a statement of the principle that he, as a lawyer, believed was involved. A general could rightfully seize and temporarily hold property for strictly military purposes, he wrote in explaining himself to Senator Orville Browning of Illinois, an old friend, but a general could not rightfully determine permanent possession of the property. "That," Lincoln wrote, "must be settled according to the laws made by law-makers, and not by military proclamations." Allowing no further protest, the president gave Jessie Frémont a cold shoulder and promptly and publicly ordered General Frémont to modify the proclamation's statement regarding the liberation of slaves.

In the field, things were not going well for Frémont either. The two regiments that he sent to reinforce Brigadier General Nathaniel Lyon—the Seventh Missouri Regiment and a Kansas regiment—never reached him, and Lyon found himself outside Springfield confronting a rebel force that outnumbered him more than two to one. In a desperate move, Lyon ordered his force to attack the rebel position. In the ensuing fight, the Battle of Wilson's Creek, waged about ten miles south of Springfield on August 10, 1861, both sides nearly exhausted themselves in combat, each losing more than 200 men killed. Among the 1,300 total Union casualties—killed, wounded and missing—was General Lyon, who was wounded in the head and then shot through the heart. Upon his death, the assault ended, and the battered Union troops disengaged and withdrew to Springfield. Fortunately for them, the equally battered rebels, who suffered some 1,200 total casualties, did not pursue them.

After that, Frémont began bombarding Washington with entreaties for men, equipment, supplies and money. He also urged the governors of the loyal western states to rush to his aid all the troops they could raise. Not taking time to respond to Lincoln's replies, Frémont managed to exhaust the usually inexhaustible patience of the president, who with obvious irritation on August 15 sent Frémont a wire saying, "Been answering your messages since day before yesterday. Do you receive the answers? The War Department has notified all Governors you designate to forward all available force. So telegraphed you. Have you received these messages? Answer immediately."[9]

None of the help Frémont received saved him from the next disaster in the field. The Chicago Irish Brigade, which included some other Illinois troops and some Missouri troops and was commanded by Colonel James A. Mulligan, was posted at Lexington, Missouri, a critical location on the Missouri River about thirty-five miles east of Kansas City. The brigade arrived there on September 9 and immediately began to entrench. Not long after they had dug in, an overwhelmingly superior rebel force commanded by Major General Sterling Price began moving toward Mulligan's position, and Mulligan instantly wired St. Louis for reinforcements to be rushed to him, which could have been done by steamer on the Missouri River. No help came. The brigade held out from September 18 to 21, when Mulligan was forced to surrender. That battle cost Frémont's forces a hundred casualties and the loss of about 2,700 troops who became prisoners of war. The defeat in a loyal state was so humiliating that it drew reaction directly from U.S. Army's grand old general in chief, Winfield Scott. President Lincoln, Scott informed Frémont, "expects you to repair the disaster at Lexington without loss of time."[10]

Unlike those political generals who sought glory—and notoriety—on the field of battle, Frémont was disposed to mastermind the part of the war that had been assigned him and do so from a distance. In an oversized room on the second floor of his headquarters mansion, along with the desks of his two secretaries and several of his staff officers, were large tables across which maps were spread and on which diagrams, memoranda and sheets of data sat for ready reference. As he pored over the maps, and with the reports he received, he determined which were the most critical trouble spots in his jurisdiction. Cairo, Illinois, he decided, was the place that demanded immediate attention, not Springfield, Missouri. General Lyon, he reasoned, could withdraw from Springfield, but Cairo could not be given up. "Among the various points threatened," he wrote in his account of his operations, "Cairo was the key to the success of my operations. The waterways and the district around Cairo were of first importance. Upon the possession of this district depended the descent and control of the Mississippi Valley by the Union armies, or the inroad by the Confederate forces into the loyal States."[11] So it was Cairo that had gotten the reinforcements:

> Five days after my arrival, hearing that [Confederate Brigadier General Gideon] Pillow was moving upon Cairo, I left St. Louis for that place, with all my available force, 3800 men. I distributed my command over a transport fleet of eight large steamboats, in order to create in the enemy an impression of greater strength than I possessed....
>
> The sudden relief of Cairo and the exaggerated form in which the news of it reached Pillow had the intended effect, He [Pillow] abandoned his proposed attack, and gave time to put it effectively beyond the reach of the enemy, and eventually to secure a firm hold on the whole of that important district.[12]

Frémont Chooses Grant

Frémont made another, even one more important and more significant, decision regarding Cairo. He was looking for someone to succeed the officer commanding there and he called into his headquarters office a thirty-nine-year-old West Pointer who only days earlier had been appointed a brigadier general after serving briefly as a colonel and regimental commander under Brigadier General John Pope. During the interview Frémont saw something he liked in the new general. What he saw, as he later wrote, were traits "of unassuming character not given to self elation, of dogged persistence, of iron will."[13] And so, in a decision of immeasurable historic importance, Frémont in August 1861 chose not the likeliest prospect for the job—blustering John Pope—but this new general. His name was Ulysses S. Grant. The command that Frémont gave him was the District of Southeast Missouri, comprising all of Missouri south of St. Louis and southern Illinois as well. For Grant and for the nation the door to destiny had been opened.

Nevertheless, Frémont's days as commander in the West were numbered. He had made too many enemies, including some who had been friends, such as the politically powerful Blairs. Montgomery Blair was the U.S. postmaster-general and a member of President Lincoln's cabinet. His brother, Frank, was a political boss in Missouri and the most prominent of pro–Union leaders in the state. Both were severely irked at Frémont's declaration of martial law in Missouri and his proclamation that freed the slaves of secessionists who supported the rebels. Frémont had other problems as well. His headquarters had become a morass of confusion, cronyism and corruption.

Ruffled by Jessie Frémont's presumption during her meeting with him and in light of rumors of graft concerning Frémont, plus Lincoln's general dissatisfaction with the way the war in the West was going, President Lincoln sent his long-time friend, the manager of his 1860 presidential campaign, David Davis, to St. Louis with a commission to discover what he could about Frémont's conduct and competence.

At the same time, secretary of war Simon Cameron, assisted by army adjutant-general Lorenzo Thomas, launched his own investigation. Thomas's report to Cameron, following the investigation of Frémont's administration, was the first to come to light and included these allegations, as stated in the report:

- Col. Andrews, Chief Paymaster, called and presented irregularities in the Pay Department, and desired instructions from the Secretary for his government, stating that he was required to make payments and transfers of money contrary to law and regulations. Once, upon objecting to what he conceived an improper payment, he was threatened with confinement by a file of soldiers.
- Maj. Allen, Principal Quartermaster, had recently taken charge of St. Louis, but reported great irregularities in his Department, and requested special instructions.... He gave the indebtedness of the Quartermaster's Department in St. Louis to be $4,506,309.73.
- Captain Edward M. Davis, a member of his [Frémont's] staff, received a contract by the direct order of Gen. Frémont for blankets.... The blankets were found to be made of cotton and were rotten and worthless. Notwithstanding this decision they were purchased and given to the sick and wounded soldiers in hospitals.
- One week after the receipt of the President's order modifying Gen. Frémont's proclamation relative to emancipation of slaves, Gen. Frémont, by note to Capt. McKeever, required him to have 200 copies of the original proclamation and address to the army, of same date, printed and sent immediately to Ironton, for the use of Maj. Gavitt, Indiana Cavalry, for distribution through the country. Capt. McKeever had the copies printed and delivered. The order is as follows: "Adjutant-General will have 200 copies of proclamation of Commanding General, date Aug. 30th, together with the address to the army of the same date, sent immediately to Ironton, for the use of Maj. Gavitt, Indiana Cavalry. Maj. Gavitt will distribute it through the country. J.C.F., Commanding General, Sept. 23rd, 1861."
- Gen. Hunter stated that he had just received a written report from one of his Colonels, informing him that but 20 out of 100 of his [artillery] guns would go off. These were the guns procured by Gen. Frémont in Europe.... Gen. Frémont wrote to some friend in San Francisco that his share of the profit of the purchase of these guns was $30,000.[14]

Brigadier General Samuel Curtis, one of the investigators, declared that Frémont lacked "the intelligence, the experience, and the sagacity necessary to his command."[15] The other investigators, the secretary of war and the president all reached the same conclusion.

Lincoln now could see that Frémont had to be removed. That sight, however, was more than Frémont could see. Determined to take possession of the Mississippi River valley—for the glory and whatever other benefits might follow—he did not intend, insiders warned

Lincoln, to relinquish his command at the president's order. Jessie Frémont, in a burst of temper during her meeting with Lincoln, had hinted that Frémont would oppose being relieved and she had threateningly told the president that her husband was no ordinary soldier, that in a test of political strength, Lincoln would find him a worthy adversary.

Aware of the storm brewing behind him, Frémont decided to take action to forestall it. The rebel army that had overwhelmed Colonel Mulligan's Irishmen at Lexington shrank as thousands of Missouri militia soldiers returned to their homes after the Lexington victory and General Price began falling back to the southwest corner of the state. Anxious for a victory to save his job, Frémont emerged from his St. Louis mansion and placed himself at the head of an impressive force comprising five divisions—some 38,000 men—and began a march to confront the now weakened Price. To let his superiors know of his intended heroics, Frémont fired off a telegram to Washington: "I am taking the field myself.... Please notify the President immediately."[16]

In Washington, however, General Frémont's decisive action was coming too late. On October 28 Lincoln sent General Curtis two messages to be delivered to Frémont. One notified Frémont that he was relieved of his command. The other notified him that his replacement was Major General David Hunter, who was on his way to St. Louis to take over. Curtis, in turn, then gave to a captain the task of delivering the president's orders to Frémont. By then news of the orders had found its way to the press and had been published, and so Frémont, encamped with his troops outside Springfield, learned from newspaper reports what was coming.

Pretending to be a farmer who had valuable information for the general, and disguised to fit the part, the captain bearing the president's orders managed to get past Frémont's line of pickets about five o'clock in the morning on November 1 and arrived at the Frémont's command post. When told he could not see the general then but that his information would be passed on to the general, the captain replied that he would rather wait until he could give the general the information himself. After many hours of waiting, he finally was taken to see Frémont. The captain removed from inside the lining of his coat the president's orders and handed them to Frémont, who read them with mounting anger. Frémont ordered the captain placed under arrest and then roused his troops to ready them for a massive assault on General Price's shrunken army, which at last report lay not far in front of the Union camp. A huge victory over the rebel army that had taken Lexington would, Frémont believed, vindicate him and force President Lincoln to back down and rescind his orders. In the excitement of Frémont's troops preparing for the attack, the arrested captain managed to slip out of custody and, having overheard the password of the day, passed quickly through the camp's perimeter guard and fled.

With his army now marshaled to fall mightily upon the enemy and ready to move out, Frémont was soon struck by another stark disappointment. Price's entire army had vanished, having stealthily decamped and stolen away without its being noticed. There would be no battle, no huge victory for General Frémont, no vindication, no recision of the president's orders. Having finally resigned himself to his situation, Frémont the next morning addressed his troops and bade them farewell, then turned away and began his dismal return to St. Louis.

He was passing from the scene of the campaign to recapture the Mississippi River, but behind him he was leaving important elements of it, to be useful in the future. Included in the $15,000,000 of expenditures that he had ordered while in command of the Department of the West were two steamboats that he had ordered to be converted into gunboats in preparation for the planned drive down the Mississippi. He had also ordered a flotilla of mortar boats that were planned to assail Confederate fortifications on the river. Moreover, he had dispatched spies into enemy territory to make maps and collect intelligence that would prove highly important.

News of Frémont's dismissal set off a tidal wave of public protest that was reflected in newspaper editorials, in Congress and in the hearings conducted by Congress's Committee on the Conduct of the War. In early 1862 Frémont was called before the committee, and following his appearance reports of his testimony gave the public the impression that Frémont had refuted every accusation made against him. Seeing Frémont's popularity undiminished and responding to pressure from Frémont's friends, President Lincoln decided to give Frémont a new command—the army's newly created Mountain Department, which included western Virginia, eastern Kentucky and eastern Tennessee as far west as Knoxville.

In March 1862 Frémont traveled with Jessie and their two children to Wheeling, West Virginia, and on March 29 he assumed command of the new department, setting up a temporary headquarters at the McLure Hotel in Wheeling. Showing that he had learned at least a little from his experience in St. Louis, he restricted himself to military operations as commander of a force of some 25,000 troops, putting civil matters in the hands of his judge-advocate or leaving them to West Virginia's governor, Francis Pierpont. Jessie took over the task formerly performed by the legion of guards that had kept Frémont isolated in his St. Louis headquarters, fending off virtually all callers.

Frémont's new theater of operations was not an ideal location for success at waging war. In his contemporary account Major General Jacob Cox described the problems Frémont faced:

> There was a little too much sentiment and too little practical war in the construction of a department out of five hundred miles of mountain ranges, and the appointment of the "path-finder" to command it was consistent with the romantic character of the whole. The mountains formed an admirable barrier at which comparatively small bodies of troops could cover and protect the Ohio Valley behind them, but extensive military operations across and beyond the Alleghanies from west to east were impracticable, because a wilderness a hundred miles wide, crossed by few and most difficult roads, rendered it impossible to supply troops from depots on either side. The country was so wild that not even forage for mules could be found in it, and the teams could hardly haul their own provender for the double trip. Quick "raids" were therefore all that ever proved feasible.[17]

The President's Plan

Yet, President Lincoln thought it was feasible to march an army across the mountains, from western Virginia into eastern Tennessee, and then to seize the railroad at Knoxville and to protect the loyalists in that area. Frémont was put into the position of having to try it. To carry out the president's wishes, Frémont formed a campaign plan, General Cox related, "which consisted in starting with Blenker's division (which had been taken from the Army of the Potomac and given to him) from Romney [Virginia] in the valley the south branch of the Potomac, ascending this valley toward the south, picking up Schenck's and Milroy's brigades in turn, the latter joining the column at Monterey.... From Monterey Frémont intended to move upon Staunton and thence, following the south-western trend of the valleys, to the New River near Christiansburg. Here he would come into communication with me, whose task it would have been to advance from Gauley Bridge on two lines.... The plan looked to continuing the march to the south-west with the whole column till Knoxville should be reached."[18]

The plan—and Frémont—it turned out, would have more than geography to contend with. Stonewall Jackson, with a heavily reinforced army that now amounted to at least 15,000 men, was lurking in the upper Shenandoah Valley. When he saw how the Union forces were separated from one another in the valley, he decided to attack, moving on General Banks's army in an effort to drive it from the valley. To begin, he would make a swift, forced march to Staunton, overwhelm Brigadier General Robert Milroy's brigade, of Frémont's army, which was in a threatening position at McDowell, Virginia, just west of Staunton, and then continue the advance on Banks, positioned above Strasburg. General Cox related the following in his account:

> Moving with great celerity, he [Jackson] attacked Milroy at McDowell on the 8th [of May 1862], and the latter calling upon Frémont for help, [Major General Robert] Schenck was sent forward to support him, who reached McDowell, having marched 34 miles in 24 hours. Jackson had not fully concentrated his forces, and the Union generals held their ground and delivered a sharp combat, in which their casualties of all kinds numbered 256, while the Confederate loss was 498.... Schenck as senior assumed the command, and on the 9th began his retreat to Franklin, abandoning the Cheat Mountain road. Franklin was reached on the 11th, but Jackson approached cautiously and did not reach there till the 12th, when, finding that Frémont had concentrated his forces, he did not attack, but returned to McDowell, whence he took the direct road to Harrisonburg, and marched to attack [Banks] at Strasburg, Ewell meeting and joining him in this movement.[19]

What followed then was the Battle of Winchester on May 25, where Banks was routed and driven north, across the Potomac and into Maryland. "Frémont resumed preparations for his original campaign," Cox reported, "but Banks's defeat deranged all plans, and those of the Mountain Department were abandoned."[20]

Having chased off Banks, Jackson now prepared to fall back to a more secure position farther south. Frémont turned his attention then to Jackson's move southward. "On the 25th of May," Confederate Brigadier General John Imboden reported in his account of the action, "as soon as Frémont learned of Banks's defeat and retreat to the Potomac, he put his army of about 14,000 in motion from Franklin to cut off Jackson's retreat up the valley." In anticipation of Frémont's move, Imboden had posted a fifty-man detail on the heights overlooking the pass through which he expected Frémont to move toward Harrisonburg, where Frémont could try to block Jackson's retreat. As Frémont's column entered the pass, Imboden's men let it get well into the pass's narrow gorge, then opened fire. "They poured a deadly volley into the close column," Imboden reported. "The attack being unexpected, and coming from a foe of unknown strength, the Federal column halted and hesitated to advance. Another volley and the 'rebel yell' from the cliffs turned them back, never to appear again."[21]

Frémont then turned northeastward, his whole army thwarted by fifty Confederates.

He took the road to Moorefield, from which he could turn east and march on Strasburg, although he had been ordered by Lincoln to proceed directly to Harrisonburg, more than fifty miles below Strasburg.[22] Two miles west of Strasburg Frémont's advance encountered Jackson's rear guard, and a sharp skirmish took place as Jackson continued his march southward toward Harrisonburg, Frémont was now in his rear, rather than ahead of him, where Frémont was intended to be, blocking Jackson's retreat.

Meanwhile, Washington was sending Frémont some help. Major General James Shields was ordered to hurry his 10,000 troops from their position east of the Blue Ridge to cooperate in Frémont's pursuit of Jackson:

> Jackson was advised of Shields's approach [Imboden related] and his [Jackson's] aim was to prevent a junction of their forces till he reached a point where he could strike them in quick succession. He therefore sent cavalry detachments along the Shenandoah to burn the bridges as far as Port Republic, and ordered me from Staunton, with a mixed battery and battalion of cavalry, to the bridge over North River near Mount Crawford, to prevent a cavalry force passing to his rear.
>
> At Cross Keys, about six miles from Harrisonburg, he delivered battle to Frémont, on June 8th, and, after a long and bloody conflict, as night closed in he was master of the field.[23]

Frémont formed a line of battle, placing the brigade led by Colonel Gustave Cluseret in the center, with Schenck's brigade on the right, Milroy's brigade on Cluseret's immediate left and Brigadier General Julius Stahel's brigade on the far left. Two other brigades were held in reserve. The plan was to advance the line and wheel to the right to envelop Jackson's position, but as the Union troops moved forward, the rebel units that had been concealed behind the crest of a hill suddenly appeared and delivered a withering fire on the advancing Federals. Stahel's brigade, taking heavy casualties, recoiled and withdrew from the fight. Schenck's brigade attempted to turn the Confederate left flank but was repulsed by heavy fire. Frémont then ordered a withdrawal, supported by artillery. The artillery fire continued for a time, but the fighting had ended. The next day Jackson defeated Shields's troops at Port Republic, a hamlet in Rockingham County, Virginia.

President Lincoln responded to news of the twin defeats by ordering Frémont to call off the chase of Jackson and pursue no farther than Harrisonburg. Much of the blame for the disasters fell on Frémont, who, when he should have been standing athwart the valley turnpike blocking the road in front of Jackson as ordered, had been turned away by a detail of fifty rebels and was miles behind Jackson instead of in front of him.

Lincoln then decided to reshuffle again. He combined all the forces that were posted in northern Virginia and put them into an army designated the Army of Virginia, created to unify the command of the scattered units. The Mountain Department ceased to exist. In the reorganization Frémont would in effect be demoted, reduced from a department commander to the level of a corps commander, his corps to be one of three comprising the new Army of Virginia. The new army's overall commander would be John Pope, whom Lincoln appointed to the position on June 26, 1862. Pope was a general outranked by Frémont (as well as by the new army's two other corps commanders), a general who had served under Frémont in Missouri, a general of whom Frémont thought so little that he had passed over him to appoint Ulysses Grant as commander of the District of Southeast Missouri.

Insulted and outraged, Frémont asked Lincoln to relieve him of his command. Lincoln promptly did so, naming Franz Sigel as his replacement. Temporarily keeping his commission, his staff and his major general's pay, Frémont, in March 1863, withdrew to New York City. On August 12, 1863, facing reality, he resigned his commission. As one of his biographers put it, "He was once more out of the army—this time forever."[24]

In 1864 a band of severely disgruntled radicals, convinced that Lincoln, facing reelection, was so incompetent that he could not be reelected, pulled away from the Republican party and formed a party of their own: the Radical Democracy Party. On May 31 in Cleveland they opened a convention that chose Frémont as their candidate for president, with a platform that appealed to the Republican party's radical, pro-abolition wing. On September 22, however, Frémont issued a statement saying he was no longer a candidate, probably the result of a deal arranged by radical Republicans, whose support Lincoln could not afford to lose. The next day, September 23, 1864, Lincoln removed from his cabinet Montgomery Blair, the postmaster-general and a long-time foe of the radicals and a man hated by Frémont. Frémont then retired from politics.

He went on to involve himself in business failures that wiped out the fortune he had made in California. Appointed by President Rutherford Hayes, he served as governor of the Arizona Territory from 1878 to 1881, at a salary of $2,000 a year. Harassed by complaints of incompetence and conflict of interest, Frémont resigned on October 11, 1881, and headed back to New York, where Jessie was living on Staten Island. Jessie was ecstatic over his return, writing, "He looks young, rested, and as handsome as that day in '41 when I saw him swinging down the avenue in his uniform."[25]

Sick and broke, Frémont was offered help from a wealthy friend and he and Jessie took a train back to California in 1887. Seeking a healthier climate, they settled in a cottage on Oak Street in Los Angeles. In 1889 he returned to New York, on business, he said. While still there in July 1890 he died of peritonitis apparently caused by a ruptured appendix. His death at age seventy-seven came three months after he had been placed on the army's list of retired major generals and Congress voted him an annual $6,000 stipend "in view of the services to his country rendered by John C. Frémont."

He was survived by Jessie and their three children, a daughter, Lily, and sons Charles, a navy officer, and Frank, an army officer. He was buried at Piermont-on-the-Hudson in Rockland County, New York.

5

Major General John Alexander McClernand

Before the War: Born May 30, 1812, near Hardinsburg in Breckinridge County, Kentucky. Grew up in Shawneetown, Illinois. Mostly self-educated. Studied law and was admitted to the bar in Illinois in 1832. Founded and served as editor of the *Shawneetown Democrat.* Married Sarah Dunlap of Jacksonville, Illinois, a friend of Mary Todd Lincoln, the president's wife, in November 1842. Married Minerva Dunlap, Sarah's sister, in December 1862, following Sarah's death from tuberculosis. Political affiliation: Democrat. Served in the Illinois House of Representatives, 1836 and 1840 to 1843. Served in the U.S. House of Representatives, 1843 to 1851 and 1859 to 1861. Defeated in attempt to become speaker of the House in 1860. Military experience: Served as an army private in the Black Hawk War in Illinois in 1832.

The Illinois congressional delegation was certain that Illinois deserved more generals and so they—the state's representatives and its two senators—met in the Washington office of Senator Lyman Trumbull in early July, three months after the attack on Fort Sumter, and came up with the names of seven men that they offered to President Lincoln for appointment as brigadier generals. Lincoln went through the list and picked three: Ulysses Simpson Grant, a West Pointer who was already serving as a colonel and regimental commander; Benjamin Mayberry Prentiss, a lawyer, ropemaker, failed candidate for a seat in Congress and a militia officer who had served in the Mexican War; and John Alexander McClernand, a lawyer, politician and U.S. representative.

On August 7, 1861, McClernand, who represented a congressional district in southern Illinois and was considered one of the state's most influential politicians, received his commission from Lincoln—along with an instruction. "Keep Egypt"—as southern Illinois was called—"right side up," Lincoln told him at the conclusion of their meeting. The president had picked a politician he believed could keep southern Illinois, about which there was some doubt, given its Southern-sympathizing citizens, loyal to the Union and supportive of the Union's war effort. McClernand also received authorization to recruit four companies of infantry, four of cavalry and two of artillery.

Quickly assuming his direct ways of getting things done, once he and his brigade were assigned to Frémont's Department of the West, McClernand began writing letters to Frémont for supplies and equipment for his brigade. Frémont let him know that he would have to do the same as any other commander and put in detailed requisitions to the Department of the West's quartermaster. Other army procedures he also ignored, as when he and his troops were ordered to Cairo and, having arrived and encamped there, he neglected to assume command from the colonel, whom he of course outranked, who had been commandant in Cairo. Grant, who by then had become commander in southeastern Missouri and southern Illinois and thus McClernand's commander, had to issue an order directing McClernand to assume command of the post at Cairo.

On September 4, 1861, Grant moved his headquarters from Cape Girardeau, Missouri, to Cairo and had no sooner settled into his chair when he received a report that a Confederate force had occupied Columbus, Kentucky, on the Mississippi River about twenty-five miles below Cairo, and was preparing to move on Paducah, Kentucky, at the confluence of the Ohio and Tennessee rivers, an important strategic point that commanded the Ohio and the mouth of the Tennessee as well. U.S. forces could not afford to have Paducah occupied by the enemy, who could block passage of Union vessels on the Ohio before they reached the Mississippi and prevent passage up the Tennessee.

Maj. Gen. John McClernand. His military experience was negligible, having served as a private in the Black Hawk War in Illinois in 1832, but he was an influential U.S. representative from a southern Illinois congressional district. Lincoln appointed him a brigadier general at the same time he appointed Ulysses Grant brigadier general (Library of Congress).

Grant immediately telegraphed General Frémont to inform him of the report and to tell him that he was planning to leave with force that night so that he could beat the Confederates to Paducah. To speed McClernand's troops the forty-five miles up the Ohio to Paducah, Grant scrambled to hire steamboats idled by the conflict that were tied up at Cairo's wharves. With two regiments of infantry and a battery of artillery he embarked on the hired steamers and, escorted by three U.S. gunboats, around midnight of September 5 he steamed off for Paducah.

The Union force arrived at Paducah early on September 6 as planned, completely surprising the town's citizens, who were expecting the arrival not of U.S. troops but of a Confederate army, which then was but ten to fifteen miles away on its march to Paducah. Grant quickly positioned McClernand's troops on the roads leading into the town, blocking the rebels' entrance. The rebel force approaching Paducah was estimated at nearly 4,000 men, substantially outnumbering the Union force. But expecting to occupy the town unopposed and unwilling to engage the U.S. force, the Confederates, on learning of the Union troops' presence, halted their advance and withdrew back to Columbus.

Once he was satisfied that Paducah was secure, at least for the time being, Grant left an occupation force behind, along with the gunboats that he stationed to guard Paducah's riverfront, and he and the remainder of McClernand's troops returned to Cairo. In his official report on the Paducah expedition Grant tipped his hat to McClernand for his contribution to its success. "I must acknowledge my obligations to General McClernand, commanding this force," Grant wrote, "for the active and efficient co-operation exhibited by him in fitting out the expedition."[1]

On November 5, 1861, it was learned in St. Louis that the Confederates were preparing to send a large force from Columbus down the Mississippi River by steamboat and then up the White River in Arkansas to reinforce the army of Major General Sterling Price in southern Missouri. To forestall that move Grant was ordered to make a feint against Columbus, where the rebels had erected a forbidding fortification on the edge of the river.

Grant promptly responded. He sent a regiment from Bird's Point, Missouri, just below Cairo, to reinforce the troops of Colonel Richard Oglesby, who were already marching south to prevent Price from being reinforced. Grant wired Brigadier General Charles F. Smith, in command at Paducah, to move all the troops he could spare immediately toward Columbus, halt them a few miles outside the town and await further orders. He then, on November 6, embarked on steamers at Cairo some 3,000 troops—including two brigades of infantry and cavalry and artillery units. One infantry brigade was commanded by McClernand, the other by Colonel Henry Dougherty. McClernand's brigade comprised three regiments, the Twenty-seventh Illinois, the Thirtieth Illinois and the Thirty-first Illinois. Doughety's brigade comprised two infantry regiments, the Seventh Iowa and the Twenty-second Illinois. Escorting the transports that carried the troops were two timberclad gunboats, the *Tyler* and the *Lexington*. The convoy steamed down the Mississippi to a spot on the Kentucky side about six miles above Columbus, where Grant sent ashore a detail to set up a line of pickets that would make contact with the troops coming from Paducah.

Although Grant had no thoughts of attacking the Confederate position at Columbus, it being strongly fortified, armed with more than a hundred pieces of artillery and manned by a garrison estimated at as many as 40,000 men, he, aboard one of the transports as it steamed toward Columbus, noticed the elation of his officers and men at the prospect of at last confronting the rebels and realized that he would have to make some sort of move against the enemy. "I did not see how I could maintain discipline," he related, "or retain the confidence of my command, if we should return to Cairo without an effort to do something."[2]

Early the next day, Thursday, November 7, at about two o'clock in the morning, Grant learned that Confederate troops from Columbus were crossing the Mississippi and he assumed they were on their way to intercept Colonel Oglesby's column. He quickly decided to hit the rebels' rear, diverting their attention from Oglesby. He hastily planned a lightning assault on the camp the Confederates had established at Belmont, Missouri, a boat landing and collection of shacks across the river from Columbus. At Belmont, Confederate Major General Leonidas Polk had established an outpost manned by an infantry regiment, a squadron of cavalry and a battery of artillery. Grant's intention was to overwhelm and destroy the outpost, then reboard his transports and head back to Cairo.

5. Major General John Alexander McClernand

While the convoy still lay off the Kentucky shore, Grant began retrieving the pickets he had posted outside Columbus and sent the two gunboats down the river to engage the Confederate batteries at Columbus to draw their attention from the landing site near Belmont. The gunboats, however, ran into heavy fog before reaching Columbus and had to turn around and return to the spot where they had started. They waited until 6:00 a.m., then moved out from the Kentucky shore in the early daylight, taking the lead as the convoy of troop-carrying transports steamed down the river.

About an hour later the troop-carrying transports pulled up to the river's west bank, out of range of the Confederate guns at Columbus. There, at Hunter's Landing, about three miles above Belmont, the U.S. force began disembarking from the transports, the eager troops surging ashore under the protection of the gunboats, forming up beside a cornfield, one of the few clearings between the landing site and Belmont. As the troops filed ashore, the two gunboats opened fire on the Columbus fortification, keeping up a diversionary assault as they steamed in circles in the broad expanse of the river.

While the troops were still streaming off the transports, Grant led one regiment down along the river and positioned the men in a hollow in the woods below a clearing. Along with the gunboats they would guard the transports and prevent the main body of troops from being taken by surprise by the rebels below them. By now the steamers disgorging the troops had been observed from Columbus. But facing a possible threat from the force that had arrived from Paducah, the Confederates at Columbus made no immediate response to the Union troop movements on the west bank of the river.

McClernand went along with the reconnaissance detail to scout out the area, which was mostly woods and marshes, then came back and prepared to advance. The force went westward through the woods, intending to flank the rebel encampment. After about a mile and a half, the troops halted in a marshy, densely wooded area, then faced to the left. Grant ordered skirmishers to be sent out, and McClernand responded with skirmishers from his brigade, the main body of the brigade following them, advancing across a bayou and into dense woods on the other side of it. As his troops advanced, he rode on horseback among them, keeping the units aligned.

About a hundred yards beyond the bayou, the Twenty-seventh Illinois, commanded by Colonel Napoleon Bonaparte Buford, ran into rebel skirmishers and began an exchange of fire that grew more fierce. McClernand quickly ordered Colonel Philip Fouke, commanding the Thirtieth Illinois, to shift his regiment to support Buford. The advance of the other regiments was slowed by dense underbrush and marshy ground, and seeing the misalignment of the front, McClernand instructed Buford to fall back and realign the Twenty-seventh with the other regiments.

As the fighting grew in intensity, Buford found a way around the rebels' left flank. He led the Twenty-seventh Illinois regiment around a slough, met up with Captain Dollin's cavalry and pushed on around the Confederates' flank and into the rear of their line. The fighting raged for four hours as the rebels were slowly forced back, until they were at last at the clearing where their tents were pitched. At that point they bolted for the riverbank, which rose high and steep from the river and shielded them from the sight and fire of McClernand's pursuing troops, who made their way through the rebels' abatis and overran the campsite.

Instead of forcing the surrender of the Confederate troops, who lay trapped between the steep riverbank and the water's edge, the Union troops, most of them new recruits facing action for the first time, put aside their weapons and went on a wild rampage through the camp, ransacking the rebels' tents, scavenging whatever trophies and souvenirs they thought worth grabbing. "Some of the higher officers," Grant complained in his account of the battle, "were little better than the privates."[3] It's unclear which "higher officers" Grant meant, but McClernand was reported to have joined the celebration by leading the disordered soldiers in three cheers for the Union.

Unable to bring order back to the reveling troops, Grant finally called his staff officers together and ordered them to set fire to the rebel camp. Soon flames and smoke were rising into the air, and the Confederate guns at Columbus for the first time opened fire on the campsite, the rebel gunners realizing the site had fallen into enemy hands. At the same time, transports laden with gray-clad Confederate soldiers were steaming from Columbus and landing below Belmont, rushing troops across the river to reinforce and rescue their trapped comrades, who had formed a line at the water's edge up the river from the campsite and now stood between the rampaging U.S. troops and their transports.

A report that they were then surrounded spread rapidly through the mass of Union soldiers, and suddenly the celebrations stopped. "The guns of the enemy and the report of being surrounded brought officers and men completely under control," Grant related. "At first some of the officers seemed to think that to be surrounded was to be placed in a hopeless position, where there was nothing to do but surrender. But when I announced that we had cut our way in and could cut our way out just as well, it seemed a new revelation to officers and soldiers."[4]

McClernand ordered Captain Taylor, commanding the expedition's artillery unit, to open fire on the Confederates as they were forming up. He ordered Colonel John Logan, commanding the Thirty-first Illinois regiment, to charge the rebel line and break through it. Seemingly heedless of the gunfire around him, McClernand sat mounted while he watched the troops rush forward, a bullet grazing his head and his horse being wounded. The sudden and desperate charge against the rebel line burst it apart, and the U.S. troops rushed through the gap, plunging back into the woods, racing for the transports and gunboats that lay waiting for them upriver.

At the boat landing, the troops streamed onto the waiting transports, the wounded being among the last to be taken aboard. As one contingent of pursuing Confederates drew close to the transports, threatening them, the *Tyler* and the *Lexington* turned their guns on the rebels, firing grapeshot, canister shot and five-inch shells into them, stopping their advance and silencing their guns.

In the confusion of the hasty, headlong retreat, Buford's Twenty-seventh Illinois regiment was separated from the rest of McClernand's brigade and became lost in the dense woods. Looking for a way out of the woods and back to the riverfront, Buford led his men north until they reached the bayou and the road on which they had come that morning. He then marched the regiment up the road and finally reached the river about three miles above the transports' landing site. He arrived just in time to see the transports steaming up the river, headed back toward Cairo. Acting quickly, he managed to find a farmer's horse and sent his adjutant, Lieutenant Henry Rust, mounted on the borrowed horse, galloping along the riverbank in pursuit of the convoy.

Realizing Buford's regiment was missing, McClernand had unsuccessfully tried to find it, whereupon he had asked navy commander Henry Walke, captain of the *Tyler*, to look out for the missing men and then later instructed the captain of the transport *Chancellor* to pull over to shore so that a party could be sent out to find the Twenty-seventh. McClernand and two of his staff officers went ashore, mounted horses and started out on a search. They soon met Lieutenant Rust racing toward them. The Twenty-seventh Illinois was quickly boarded, and the *Chancellor* resumed its voyage upriver. "We went peacefully on our way to Cairo," Grant wrote in his memoir, "every man feeling that Belmont was a great victory and that he had contributed his share to it."[5] By midnight the entire expedition was back in Cairo.

The U.S. casualties in the Battle of Belmont totaled 120 men killed, 104 captured and 383 wounded (including Colonel Dougherty, who was wounded in the leg and had to have it amputated), many of whom fell into enemy hands, including Dougherty. The Confederates, who claimed victory after having driven the Union force from the field, lost 105 killed, 419 wounded and 117 missing.

Although Grant was criticized by Northern newspapers for having waged an unnecessary fight that had no lasting results, he was convinced that it was a worthwhile effort and a success. "The two objects for which the battle of Belmont was fought were fully accomplished. The enemy gave up all idea of detaching troops from Columbus" to attack Colonel Oglesby's force, Grant wrote. He insisted that if the battle had not been fought, "Colonel Oglesby would probably have been captured or destroyed with his three thousand men. Then I should have been culpable indeed." What was more, "the National troops acquired a confidence in themselves at Belmont that did not desert them through the war."[6] The same could probably be said for Grant and McClernand, both of them new generals.

Curiously, while Grant was being criticized for his actions at Belmont, McClernand was being lauded in the press. Newspapers in Illinois claimed McClernand had saved the day after Grant's having bungled the attack. Other newspapers, farther away from the scene of action, also praised McClernand. The *New York Herald* reported that McClernand had set for his troops "an example of heroism by plunging headlong into the rebel ranks and making himself a road of blood."[7]

Being the practiced politician that he was, McClernand was quick to call attention to his deeds at Belmont, delivering his own report to the army's new general in chief, Major General George McClellan, and winning from the president a letter of congratulations, which Lincoln failed to offer Grant. McClernand was also swift to give credit and thanks to his troops, as if to his constituents. "The general commanding the First Brigade of Illinois Volunteers," he instructed his assistant adjutant-general to state in general orders, "takes pleasure in meeting to-day those who conferred honor upon his command by their gallantry and good conduct on yesterday. Few of you had before seen a battle. You were but imperfectly disciplined, and supplied with inferior arms; yet you marched upon a concealed enemy, of superior numbers.... While mourning the dead and offering sympathy to the suffering, the general commanding gratefully acknowledges his gratitude, and offers the thanks of a grateful country and State to the officers and soldiers of Illinois under his command."[8]

Grant himself had good things to say about McClernand's conduct at Belmont. McClernand, Grant wrote in his official report, "was in the midst of danger throughout the engagement, and displayed both coolness and judgment."[9] Grant also mentioned that McClernand's horse had been shot under him, as had Grant's.

Once back in Cairo, McClernand kept his troops busy with drilling and inspections and kept himself busy with administrative matters, especially persisting in efforts to obtain more and better weapons for his men. He also sought to have the army create a new department that would be headquartered in Cairo and would stretch east and south, leaving the west to the new commander of the Department of the Missouri (formerly the Department of the West), Major General Henry Halleck, who had replaced General Frémont. In that proposal McClernand had the concurrence of General Grant.

The Action Shifts Eastward

By early January of 1862 some organizational changes had been made. Grant's military jurisdiction was shifted eastward from southeast Missouri to an area designated the District of Cairo, which included the mouths of the Tennessee and Cumberland rivers. On January 6, with that area now within the scope of his responsibility, Grant was ordered by the army's new general in chief, General McClellan, through General Halleck's headquarters, to make a show of strength in western Kentucky. Brigadier General Don Carlos Buell, commanding the U.S. Army's Department of the Ohio, was expected to engage a large Confederate force at Bowling Green, Kentucky, a Confederate stronghold, and Grant was to make menacing moves to prevent rebel reinforcements from Columbus or Fort Henry or Fort Donelson from reaching Bowling Green.

A study of his maps showed Grant that the Confederates, to protect against U.S. attacks from the north, had established a line of defense that ran through Kentucky from Columbus, where it was anchored on the bluffs above the Mississippi River, eastward to Bowling Green and on to Mill Springs, Kentucky. Each of those three locations had been heavily fortified by the Confederates. The maps also showed the paths of the Tennessee and Cumberland rivers, which streamed toward Cairo. They were veritable highways into the South, twisting through Kentucky and into Tennessee, the two rivers at times running practically parallel, the Cumberland diverging and sweeping across northern Tennessee, the Tennessee plunging through Tennessee and into northern Alabama.

Near the Kentucky-Tennessee state line, west of Clarksville, Tennessee, the two rivers, less than fifteen miles apart at that point, were defended by Confederate fortifications—Fort Heiman and Fort Henry, opposite each other on the Tennessee River, and Fort Donelson on the Cumberland, all three fortifications positioned to forbid passage to Union forces coming up the rivers. Rebel engineers had begun laying them out within a month after the Confederate assault on Fort Sumter. "These positions were of immense importance to the enemy," Grant explained, "and of course correspondingly important for us to possess ourselves of. With Fort Henry in our hands we had a navigable stream open to us up to Muscle Shoals, in Alabama. The Memphis and Charleston Railroad strikes the Tennessee [River] at Eastport, Mississippi, and follows close to the banks of the river up to the shoals. This [rail] road, of vast importance to the enemy, would cease to be of use to them for through traffic the moment Fort Henry became ours.

"Fort Donelson," Grant went on, "was the gate to Nashville—a place of great military and political importance—and to a rich country extending far east into Kentucky. [With] these two points in our possession the enemy would necessarily be thrown back to the Memphis and Charleston [rail] road, or to the boundary of the cotton states, and, as before stated, that road would be lost to them for through communication."[10]

Responding to his instructions, Grant ordered Brigadier General Charles F. Smith to take a force from Paducah up the west bank of the Tennessee River to threaten Fort Heiman and Fort Henry, and he ordered McClernand to march his 6,000-man brigade south from Cairo and then to split into two columns, one heading toward Columbus, the other proceeding up along the Tennessee River. At the same time, Brigadier General Eleazar Paine would march from Bird's Point, Missouri, opposite Cairo, to a position directly across the Mississippi from Columbus.

It was mostly for show. Grant had no orders to actually engage the rebels. Even so, as eager for action as were his men, Grant accompanied McClernand's force, apparently thinking it was the most likely to see combat. Along with the troops, the two generals suffered the bad January weather and difficult roads that had turned into soft, wet mud under the steady rain and snow. After more than a week of slogging through the muddy mush, the McClernand brigade returned to Cairo without having done much, but with Grant satisfied that their mission had been accomplished. "The enemy did not send reinforcements to Bowling Green, and," he wrote, citing an unrelated but important Union victory, "[Brigadier] General George H. Thomas fought and won the battle of Mill Springs before we returned."[11]

McClernand, however, was not so happy with the expedition. Days after his return to Cairo, with no regard for the chain of command, he wrote a complaining letter to President Lincoln. "Our men are disappointed in not being allowed to march upon Columbus," he told Lincoln. "I am tired of delays and inaction. We should fight and push forward, and push forward and fight again.... I feel an assurance that you sympathize with these views."[12]

McClernand's feeling was correct, and his letter was not necessary to move the president. On the day before McClernand wrote his letter, January 27, 1862, Lincoln had issued his General War Order No. 1 that "the 22d day of February, 1862, be the day for a general movement of the land and naval forces of the United States against the insurgent forces. That especially the army at and about Fortress Monroe; the Army of the Potomac; the Army of Western Virginia; the army near Munfordville, Ky.; the army and flotilla at Cairo, and a naval force in the Gulf of Mexico, be ready to move on that day.... That the heads of Departments, and especially the Secretaries of War and of the Navy, with all their subordinates, and the General-in-Chief, with all other commanders and subordinates of land and naval forces, will severally be held to their strict and full responsibilities for prompt execution of this order."[13] Lincoln apparently was thinking of an auspicious celebration of George Washington's birthday.

General Halleck, the forty-seven-year-old sluggish, indecisive warfare scholar whom his classmates at West Point had dubbed "Old Brains" and who now controlled U.S. military action east, west and south of St. Louis, needed that order, needed to be prodded into taking action. General Charles F. Smith, following the January expedition toward Fort Henry, had reported to Grant that from what he had seen of Fort Heiman, which was still under construction, he thought it could be captured. It stood on high ground on the west bank of the Tennessee River, commanding Fort Henry on the east side of the river. Its possession by Union forces would likely ensure the capture of Fort Henry as well. Smith's report confirmed what Grant had already determined. His maps showed that "the true line of operations for us," as he said, "was up the Tennessee and Cumberland rivers. With us there, the enemy would be compelled to fall back on the east and west entirely out of the state of Kentucky."[14]

When he presented his plan to capture Fort Henry to Halleck, though, the meeting did not go well. "I had not uttered many sentences," Grant reported, "before I was cut short as if my plan was preposterous."[15] Flag Officer Andrew Foote, commanding the navy's fleet of gunboats, didn't think it was preposterous. Neither did McClernand, who in his own self-assertive way had suggested in a letter to Halleck a move to occupy the area between Columbus and the Tennessee River.

Having recovered from his rebuff by Halleck, Grant, on January 28—the day of President Lincoln's order—renewed his request for permission to attack Fort Henry, telegraphing Old Brains and telling him that "if permitted, I could take and hold Fort Henry on the Tennessee." On the same day, Flag Officer Foote also wired Halleck: "General Grant and myself are of the opinion that Fort Henry, on the Tennessee River, can be carried with four ironclad gun-boats and troops, and be permanently occupied. Have we your authority to move for that purpose when ready?"[16] The next day, January 29, Grant again wrote to Halleck, this time providing more detail about the proposed expedition. Three days later, on February 1, Grant received, as he said, "full instructions from department headquarters to move upon Fort Henry." Old Brains was in compliance with the president's call for action.

There was no waiting until February 22 to get moving, though. Even before he got the go-ahead from Halleck, Grant had alerted General Smith on January 31 that an expedition was likely. On February 1 Grant organized his forces, some 15,000 to 17,000 men, into divisions. The First Division, composed of two brigades, would be commanded by McClernand. The Second Division would be commanded by Smith. "The troops of your division," Grant told McClernand, "will be held in readiness to move by steamer to-morrow [February 2], taking with them all their camp and garrison equipage, three days' rations and forage." Smith's division would leave the following day, February 3, there being insufficient steamers and crewmen in Cairo to take the entire force up the Tennessee in one convoy, and so it would take two trips to move Grant's entire army. More than half the force would go up and disembark at Paducah, and the steamers would then return to Cairo for the remainder of the force.

With his orders in hand, McClernand called his regimental commanders together for a meeting at his headquarters and briefed them on the planned operation. He told them it was not a demonstration, but an all-out attack. He gave them their embarkation times and detailed instructions on the embarkation procedure, saying which units were going on which steamers.

On Sunday, February 2, 1862, the expedition force started out from Cairo. Leading the convoy were Foote's seven gunboats, including four ironclads, being careful to evade the torpedoes, or mines, that the Confederates had anchored in the river. The transports followed. Onboard a vessel at the rear of the convoy was General Grant. McClernand's troops reached Paducah on Monday afternoon, February 3, and McClernand conferred with Grant there, receiving orders to move up the Tennessee a short distance and disembark his cavalry about thirteen miles from Paducah to screen the main body and then proceed up the river to Pine Bluff, about seven miles above Fort Henry, where he would then disembark the rest of his division. McClernand promptly passed the information on to his brigade commanders and instructed them to immediately establish picket lines once the troops had landed.

Grant wanted to land the troops as close to Fort Henry as possible but still stay beyond the range of its guns. He particularly wanted to put McClernand's men ashore on the fort side of a stream that emptied into the Tennessee north of the fort. Ordinarily, Grant guessed, the stream would be easily fordable, but now, swollen from weeks of rain, it presented a significant obstacle to his troops. To see for himself if putting them ashore where he wanted them was feasible, Grant boarded the gunboat *Essex* to move up the river toward Fort Henry and draw fire from the fort. The fort opened fire with a rifled gun that sent a shot beyond the *Essex* and the stream. Another shot passed close to where Grant and the gunboat's captain were standing, striking the vessel near the stern and passing through the cabin and falling into the river. The *Essex* immediately turned around and hurried back downstream. Having discovered what he needed to know, Grant ordered the troops of McClernand's division to be landed on the side of the stream farthest from the fort, out of the rifled gun's range.

Fort Henry was a strong, five-sided earthwork covering ten acres, with ramparts about twenty feet thick at their base and tapering up to a thickness of ten feet at their top. Its five bastions were four to six feet high, and its artillery embrasures were stoutly framed with sandbags. Its armament consisted of seventeen heavy guns, including one ten-pounder Columbiad, one twenty-four-pounder rifle, twelve thirty-two-pounders, two twelve-pounders and one twenty-four-pounder siege gun. Six of the guns were placed to protect the fort from an assault by land. The eleven others commanded a stretch of the river extending about two miles downriver, toward a fleet advancing from the Ohio River or the Mississippi.

The fort stood in a dogleg of the Tennessee on its east bank in Stewart County, Tennessee, and was connected to Fort Donelson, eleven miles away on the west bank of the Cumberland River, by a road that led also to the town of Dover, about two miles up the Cumberland, or south, from Fort Donelson. Built on low, marshy ground, Fort Henry was subject to flooding when the Tennessee River rose out of its banks, as it had now, engorged by weeks of rain. Part of the ground on which the fort stood was now two feet deep in water. Below the fort, where McClernand's troops would be debarking, the floodwater extended from the river into the woods for a distance of several hundred yards.

Within the fort's walls were barracks and tents to accommodate as many as 15,000 men, although the garrison now numbered only about 3,000, including those men entrenched in rifle pits and outworks that extended some two miles back along the road to Fort Donelson and Dover. In addition, according to Grant's intelligence, a sizeable body of reinforcements from Fort Donelson stood waiting on that road seven miles away. "The plan," Grant explained, "was for the troops and gunboats to start at the same moment. The troops were to invest the garrison and the gunboats to attack the fort at close quarters. General Smith was to land a brigade of his division on the west bank during the night of the 5th and get it in rear of [Fort] Heiman."[17] On February 4, 1862, men of the garrison at Fort Henry looked over the ramparts and beheld a fearsome sight, which was described by Confederate Captain Jesse Taylor, commanding at the fort:

> The Federal fleet of gun-boats, followed by countless transports, appeared below the fort. Far as eye could see, the course of the river could be traced by the dense volumes of smoke issuing from the flotilla—indicating that the long-threatened attempt to break our lines was to be made in earnest. The gun-boats took up a position about three miles below and opened a brisk fire, at the same time shelling the woods on the east bank of the river, thus covering the debarkation of their army.
>
> The 5th [of February] was a day of unwonted animation on the hitherto quiet waters of the Tennessee; all day long the flood-tide of arriving and the ebb of returning

Capture of Fort Henry. McClernand and his troops were to march along the Tennessee River and attack the fort from the rear. But they were delayed by high water in the streams they had to cross, and under bombardment from navy gunboats, the fort surrendered to the commander of the gunboat fleet. Even so, McClernand took credit, claiming in a letter to President Lincoln that the threat of his advancing troops had been as effective as the gunboats' bombardment in forcing the fort's surrender (Library of Congress).

transports continued ceaselessly. Late in the afternoon three of the gun-boats, two on the west side and one on the east at the foot of the island, took position and opened a vigorous and well-directed fire, which was received in silence until the killing of one man and the wounding of three provoked an order to open with the Columbiad and the rifle. Six shots were fired in return—three from each piece,—and with such effect that the gun-boats dropped out of range and ceased firing....

The forenoon of February 6th was spent by both sides in making needful preparations for the approaching struggle. The gun-boats formed line of battle abreast under the cover of the island.... When they were out of cover of the island the gun-boats opened fire, and as they advanced they increased the rapidity of their fire, until as they swung into the main channel above the island they showed one broad and leaping sheet of flame. At this point, the van being a mile distant, the command was given orders to commence firing from the fort....[18]

Meanwhile, on that cold, wet morning the movements of U.S. troops began as planned. McClernand's division advanced up the eastern side of the river to be in position to attack Fort Henry from the rear and to block the flight of the rebel garrison if they attempted to retreat toward Fort Donelson. Two brigades of General Smith's division started moving up the west side of the river to capture Fort Heiman and turn its guns on Fort Henry. The troops on both sides of the river had to march some five miles to reach the forts, and their progress, through mud and water, was slower than expected. The storm had turned every stream into a torrent, repeatedly forcing the troops to halt long enough to build hastily erected bridges for the artillery to cross the raging water. Things were not going well for the Confederates either. Captain Taylor continued his narrative of Fort Henry's fight with the U.S. gunboats:

> The action now became general, and for the next twenty or thirty minutes was, on both sides, as determined, rapid, and accurate as heart could wish, and apparently inclined in favor of the fort.... The fleet seemed to hesitate, when a succession of untoward and unavoidable accidents happened in the fort; thereupon the flotilla continued to advance. First, the rifle gun ... burst, not only with destructive effect to those working it, but with disabling effect on those in its immediate vicinity. Going to the Columbiad as the only really effective gun left,... I found [it] spiked with its own priming wire, completely disabled for the day at least.
>
> The Federal commander, observing the silence of these two heavy guns, renewed his advance with increased precision of fire.... His rifle shot and shell penetrated the earthworks as readily as a ball from a navy Colt would pierce a pine board, and soon so disabled other guns as to leave us but four capable of being served. General Tilghman [the over-all commander at Forts Henry and Heiman] now consulted with Major Gilmer and myself as to the situation, and the decision was that further resistance would only entail a useless loss of life. He therefore ordered me to strike the colors.[19]

When the crewmen aboard the gunboats saw the Confederate flag lowered and a white flag of surrender raised in its place, they broke into loud cheers and wild excitement. It was their victory, the U.S. Navy's victory, stunning in its achievement. The gunboats drew up to Fort Henry and received a deputation from General Tilghman. Flag Officer Foote, commanding the gunboat flotilla, informed the deputation that he would receive Tilghman on the flotilla's flagship. He came on board soon after the Navy crewmen had taken possession of the fort. "I received the general, his staff, and some sixty or seventy men as prisoners," Foote related, "and a hospital ship containing sixty invalids, together with the fort and its effects ... which I turned over to General Grant, commanding the army, on his arrival in an hour after we had made the capture."[20] The remainder of Fort Henry's garrison, some 2,500 rebel troops, had fled the fort when a surrender had become obvious and, with McClernand's troops having arrived too late to block their route, had escaped to Fort Donelson. Also escaped was the garrison of Fort Heiman. When General Smith reached the fort, he discovered it had been abandoned.

In spite of his having had nothing to do with the fort's capture and having failed in his mission to prevent the garrison to escape, McClernand decided to take some credit for the capture and to cut himself a large piece of the glory. He wrote letters to Governor Richard Yates of Illinois and to President Lincoln informing them of his troops' role. He asserted that his advance on the fort had been just as responsible for the fort's capture as the gunboats' bombardment had been. The garrison's "hasty surrender," he wrote in his official report, "without a more protracted struggle can only be accounted for by the terrible cannonade from our gunboats and their apprehension of being cut off from retreat by the rapid advance of our land forces."[21] He also thought it was worth pointing out to Lincoln the insignificant fact that his division—the only U.S. troops on the same side of the river as the fort—"was the first of the land forces to enter the fort."[22] He furthermore presumed to rename the conquered fort. "I have the honor to announce," he wrote in his official report, "the name of Fort Henry has been changed to Fort Foote, by an order formally published by me to that effect"[23]—as if he had any authority to do so or that such an order would have any effect. Grant ignored McClernand's foolish grandstanding. The fort remained Fort Henry.

Grant now turned his attention to Fort Donelson. His reconnaissance had given him a clear picture of the fort and the ground on which it was situated. The fort stood on a tract of about 100 acres. On the east it fronted the Cumberland River. On the north it faced a stream which at that time was deep and wide because the swollen river had backed up into it. On the south was a ravine that opened into the Cumberland. It also was filled with water from the river. The fort, built on a bluff, rose about a hundred feet above the river, which allowed the fort's guns to pour plunging fire onto enemy vessels in the river. The batteries along the riverfront included ten 32-pounder smoothbore guns, a 6.5-inch rifled gun, and a 10-inch Columbiad. A semicircular line of defense, a series of trenches three miles long, curved around the land side of the fort, embracing the town of Dover within its perimeter. The trenches were dug into a commanding ridge and were fronted by a thick abatis.

Unsolicited, McClernand came up with a plan for attacking Fort Donelson and quickly submitted it to Grant. It called for his division to lead the attack. His detailed proposal included a diagram that showed the recommended positions of the brigades and the placement of artillery during the attack. Days later, on February 11, at a meeting that Grant had called to consult with his commanders aboard the steamer *New Uncle Sam*, McClernand read his proposal aloud to the group. "The proceeding smacked of a political caucus," Brigadier General Lew Wallace, one of the meeting's attendees, commented, "and I thought both Grant and [General] Smith grew restive before the paper was finished."[24] The main issue to be decided at the meeting was the timing of the attack on Fort Donelson. Grant wanted to know whether his commanders thought the attack should be held off until reinforcements arrived or it should be commenced immediately. Smith responded, "There is every reason why we should move without the loss of a day." The others, including McClernand, agreed.

The March on Fort Donelson

The march on Fort Donelson's line of defense began on the morning of Wednesday, February 12 (President Lincoln's fifty-third birthday), a day of bright sunshine and springlike warmth. General Wallace recounted in his narration of the battle:

> By 8 o'clock in the morning, the First Division, General McClernand commanding, and the Second, under General Smith, were in full march. The infantry of this command consisted of twenty-five regiments in all, or three less than those of the Confederates. Against their six field-batteries General Grant had seven. In cavalry alone he was materially stronger. The rule in attacking fortifications is five to one; to save the Union commander from a charge of rashness, however, he had also at control a fighting quality ordinarily at home on the sea rather than the land. After receiving the surrender of Fort Henry, Flag-Officer Foote had hastened to Cairo to make preparation for the reduction

of Fort Donelson. With six of his boats, he passed into the Cumberland River; and on the 12th, while the two divisions of the army were marching across to Donelson, he was hurrying, as fast as steam could drive him and his following, to a second trial of iron batteries afloat against earth batteries ashore.[25]

The "second trial" began at 9:05 a.m. on Thursday, February 13, when the gunboat *Carondelet* opened fire, commencing the naval assault on the fort. The return fire soon indicated Fort Donelson would not be another Fort Henry. Foote's gunboats, approaching to within 400 yards of the fort, took a devastating beating from the rebel gunners and were so damaged, their crews so bloodied, that they were forced to withdraw. One of the casualties was Foote himself, who suffered a wound in his foot.

With the supporting action from the navy ended, the army was now on its own. As the failed naval assault began, Grant's forces, numbering some 15,000 men on the morning of the 13th but being rapidly reinforced, stood before the outer works of the fort in a wide semicircle. McClernand's division was positioned on the right side of the Union line, General Smith's on the left. General Wallace, whose talent as a writer was later proved by his hugely popular novel *Ben Hur*, described the opening of the battle:

> The [forward] movement by Smith and McClernand was begun about the same time. A thick wood fairly screened the former. The latter had to cross an open valley under fire of two batteries.... McClernand, following a good road, pushed on rapidly to the high grounds on the right. The appearance of his column in the valley covered by the two Confederate batteries provoked a furious shelling from them. On the double-quick his men passed through it; and when, in the wood beyond, they resumed the route-step and saw that nobody was hurt, they fell to laughing at themselves. The real baptism of fire was yet in store for them.
>
> When McClernand arrived at his appointed place and extended his brigades, it was discovered that the Confederate outworks offered a front too great for him to envelop. To attempt to rest his right opposite their extreme left would necessitate a dangerous attenuation of his line and leave him without reserves. Over on their [the rebels'] left, moreover, ran the road ... passing from Dover on the south to Charlotte and Nashville.... If the road to Charlotte were left to the enemy, they might march out at their pleasure.... [Seeing the problem, Grant responded by calling from Fort Henry and Fort Heiman the infantry brigade and artillery battery that had been left there under Wallace's command and ordering Wallace to take command of a third division, made up of reinforcement regiments arriving by transport steamers. The brigade was assigned to General Smith's division, and Wallace's new division was placed in the center of the Union line, enabling McClernand to extend his line.]
>
> It is now—morning of the 14th—easy to see and understand with something more than approximate exactness the oppositions of the two forces. Smith is on the left ... opposite [Brigadier General Simon] Buckner. My division, in the center, confronts Colonels Heiman, Drake, and Davidson, each with a brigade. McClernand, now well over on the right, keeps the road to Charlotte and Nashville against the major part of [Brigadier General Gideon] Pillow's left wing. The infantry on both sides are in cover behind the crests of hills or in the thick woods, listening to the ragged fusillade which the sharp-shooters and skirmishers maintain against each other almost without intermission. There is little pause in the exchange of shells and round shot. The careful chiefs have required their men to lie down.... In brief, it looks as if each party were inviting the other to begin....

> The night of the 14th of February fell cold and dark, and under the pitiless sky the armies remained in position so near to each other that neither dared light fires. Overpowered with watching, fatigue, and the lassitude of spirits which always follows a strain upon the faculties of men ... thousands on both sides lay down in the ditches and behind logs and whatever else would shelter them from the cutting wind, and tried to sleep. Very few closed their eyes....
>
> That morning [the Confederate commander, Brigadier] General [John B.] Floyd had called a council of his chiefs of brigades and divisions. He expressed the opinion that the post was untenable, except with fifty thousand troops. He called attention to the heavy reinforcements of the Federals, and suggested an immediate attack upon their right wing to reopen land communication with Nashville, by way of Charlotte. The proposal was agreed to unanimously....
>
> In the night the council was recalled, with general and regimental officers in attendance. The situation was again debated, and the same conclusion reached. According to the plan resolved upon, Pillow was to move at dawn with his whole division, and attack the right of the besiegers [McClernand's part of the line]. General Buckner was to be relieved by troops in the forts, and with his command to support Pillow by assailing the right of the enemy's center. If he succeeded, he was to take post outside the intrenchments on the Wynn's Ferry road [the road to Charlotte] to cover the retreat. He was then to act as rear-guard.[26]

During the frigid night of February 14–15 the rebel commanders took some 10,000 or more of their troops—infantry, cavalry and artillery—out of the snow-covered rifle pits and massed them on the Union right, moving so quietly that Union sentries had not detected them. Explaining that failure, General Wallace said, "The pickets of the Federals were struggling for life against the [wintry] blast, and probably did not keep good watch."[27] Wallace then described the Confederates' surprise attack:

> Here and there the musicians were beginning to make the woods ring with reveille, and the numbed soldiers of the line were rising from their icy beds and shaking the snow from their frozen garments. As yet, however, not a company had "fallen in." Suddenly the pickets fired, and with the alarm on their lips rushed back upon their comrades. The woods on the distant became alive.
>
> The regiments formed, officers mounted and took their places; words of command rose loud and eager. By the time Pillow's advance opened fire on [Colonel] Oglesby's right [on McClernand's extreme right], the point first struck, the latter was fairly formed to receive it. A rapid exchange of volleys ensued.... An hour passed, and yet another hour, without cessation of the fire. Meantime the woods rang with a monstrous clangor of musketry, as if a million men were beating empty barrels with iron hammers.
>
> Buckner flung a portion of his division on McClernand's left, and supported the attack with his artillery.... McClernand, watchful and full of resources, sent batteries to meet Buckner's batteries.... The roar never slackened. Men fell by the score, reddening the snow with their blood. The smoke, in pallid white clouds, clung to the underbrush and tree-tops as if to screen the combatants from each other....
>
> The pressure on the front grew stronger. The "rebel yell," afterward a familiar battle-cry on many fields, told of ground being gained.... At last he [Colonel Oglesby] realized that the end was come. His right companies began to give way, and as they retreated, holding up their empty cartridge-boxes, the enemy appeared emboldened, and swept

more fiercely around his flank, until finally they appeared in his rear. He then gave the order to retire the division.[28]

By eleven o'clock that morning, General Pillow held the road to Charlotte, as well as the entire position that General McClernand's division had occupied. The way out of Fort Donelson was now clear for its Confederate defenders.

Meanwhile, General Grant was away from the scene of the action. Early in the morning of the 15th a messenger from Flag Officer Foote had brought Grant a note asking him to come to a meeting on Foote's flagship, the *St. Louis*. Foote explained that he had been wounded and he was unable to come to Grant. Grant rode to the spot on the river where Foote's crippled flotilla lay and was taken by rowboat out to the *St. Louis*, where he met with Foote. Foote suggested that Grant should entrench his troops while the gunboats returned to Mound City, Illinois, for repairs. He told Grant that he believed the repairs could be made within ten days and that he could then resume his bombardment of Fort Donelson to coincide with Grant's land attack. Grant agreed to that suggestion. Just as he was leaving, having been rowed back to shore, Grant was met by Captain W.S. Hillyer, a member of his staff, who reported the surprise Confederate attack and said that McClernand's division had been scattered and was in full retreat.

Hurrying as fast as the ice-glazed roads would allow his mount to move, Grant passed the left side of his line, held by General Smith's division, then passed the center of the line, held by Wallace's division. Along both sections he saw, as he said, "everything favorable." Then at last, during a lull in the battle, he reached the right side of his line. There he found McClernand and Wallace holding a conversation. "Wholly unexcited," Wallace related, "he saluted and received the salutations of his subordinates.... He was then informed of the mishap to the First Division, and that the road to Charlotte was open to the enemy.... His face flushed slightly.... In his ordinary quiet voice he said, addressing himself to both officers, 'Gentlemen, the position on the right must be retaken.'"[29] McClernand started to make an excuse, but Grant cut him off and although clearly angry with McClernand for having lost control of his men,[30] Grant held his temper, gave his simple order, then turned away and galloped off.

Grant discovered that although McClernand's division had broken, only some of the troops had fled. Most of the men, when they found they were not pursued, merely fell back out of range of the rebels' fire. About that time, Colonel Thayer, of Wallace's division, pushed his brigade in between the rebels and the U.S. troops who had run out of ammunition, and the Confederates fell back within their entrenchments. That was where they were when Grant returned. Grant also discovered that although many of McClernand's men had run out of ammunition there were, as Grant said, "tons of it close at hand." Having surveyed the situation, Grant turned to Colonel J.D. Webster, a member of his staff, and told him, "Some of our men are pretty badly demoralized, but the enemy must be more so, for he has attempted to force his way out, but has fallen back. The one who attacks first now will be victorious—and the enemy will have to be in a hurry if he gets ahead of me."[31]

Grant quickly decided he would immediately make an assault on his left, sending General Smith's force against the section of the Confederate line commanded by General Buckner. "It was clear in my mind," Grant recalled, "that the enemy had started to march out with his entire force, except a few pickets, and if our attack could be made on the left before the enemy could redistribute his forces along the line, we would find but little opposition except from the intervening abatis."³² Riding swiftly to General Smith's command post, Grant explained the situation to him and ordered him to charge the rebels' works in front of him with his entire division, telling him that he would find only a thin line to oppose him. Smith almost immediately had his units on the move. General Wallace described the action:

> Taking [Colonel Jacob] Lauman's brigade, General Smith began the advance. They were under fire instantly. The guns in the fort joined in with the infantry who were at the time in the rifle-pits, the great body of the Confederate right wing being with General Buckner.... General Smith, on his horse, took position in the front and center of the line. Occasionally he turned in the saddle to see how the alignment was kept. For the most part, however, his face [was] steadily toward the enemy. The air around him twittered with minie-bullets.... On to the abatis the regiments moved without hesitation, leaving a trail of dead and wounded behind. There the fire seemed to get terribly hot, and there some of the men halted, whereupon General Smith put his cap on the point of his sword, held it aloft, and called out, "No flinching now, my lads! Here, this is the way! Come on!.".. [T]he effect was magical. The men swarmed in after him, and got through [the abatis] in the best order they could.... At the last moment the keepers of the rifle-pits clambered out and fled. The four regiments engaged in the feat—the 25th Indiana, and the 2d, 7th, and 14th Iowa—planted their colors on the breastwork.³³

"[On] the night of the 15th," Grant wrote in his memoir, "General Smith, with much of his division, bivouacked within the lines of the enemy. There was now no doubt but that the Confederates must surrender or be captured the next day."³⁴

While Smith engaged the rebels on the left of the Union line, General Wallace and General McClernand were doing their best to retake the ground lost on the Union's right, which they managed through a ferocious struggle. Wallace's eyewitness account of the fight concluded with his statement: "By sunset the conditions of the morning were all restored."³⁵

The Confederate commanders now convened a desperate meeting at the Dover hotel that was the command's headquarters. They faced their situation. General Pillow at first proposed holding out in the trenches for another day, arguing that by Sunday night—February 16—the steamer transports that had evacuated the Confederates' prisoners and the mounted troops would have returned and could move the rebel army across the river and allow it to escape to Clarksville. Buckner, the professional soldier and realist, resisted that proposal, saying, "Gentlemen, you know the enemy occupy the rifle pits on my right, and can easily turn my position and attack me in the rear or move down on the river battery. I am satisfied he will attack me at daylight, and I cannot hold my position half an hour."³⁶ Pillow and Floyd announced that they refused to surrender. Floyd, who had been the U.S. secretary of war under President James Buchanan, was especially insistent in his refusal, fearing a prison sentence or worse if he was taken prisoner. Buckner said he was satisfied nothing else could be done and that if he were placed in command, he would surrender the fort and its army of defenders and would accept whatever fate awaited them. Floyd immediately responded, "General Buckner, I place you in command. Will you permit me to draw out my brigade?" Buckner answered, "Yes."

When the meeting broke up, Floyd swiftly prepared for his departure. He ordered his brigade assembled, and following the arrival of two steamboats shortly before daylight on

Storming Fort Donelson. At the siege of Fort Donelson, McClernand's section of the Union line was burst apart in a Confederate assault. Under orders from General Grant to regain the lost ground, McClernand, with help from Maj. Gen. Lew Wallace's division, managed to do so in a ferocious fight. Led by Brig. Gen. Charles F. Smith's division, Grant's army stormed through the Confederates' defense line to force the fort's surrender on February 16, 1862 (Library of Congress).

Sunday, February 16, he hurried to the riverfront, embarked his troops, numbering some 3,000 men, and quickly steamed off to Nashville. Pillow procured the assistance of J.W. Smith of Dover, who during Saturday night rowed Pillow and his staff across the Cumberland in a twelve-foot flatboat. He fled to Clarksville and later was reunited with his horse, servant and baggage. From Clarksville he trotted off to Nashville. Also during the night other elements of the Confederate force slipped away, evading the Union line by passing between its right end and the river, slogging across the flooded ravine above the fort and escaping. Among those who escaped were Lieutenant Colonel Nathan Bedford Forrest and an estimated 1,000 of his cavalrymen.

Buckner's message of capitulation was received by Grant shortly before daylight on Sunday, February 16. In it Buckner asked for a ceasefire and the appointment of commissioners to work out terms for surrender. Grant coldly responded: "No terms except an unconditional and immediate surrender can be accepted. I propose to move immediately upon your works."[37] Calling Grant's terms "ungenerous and unchivalrous" in his reply, Buckner, with little choice, accepted them anyway. The number of men surrendered with the fort is uncertain, but estimates put it at 12,000 to 18,000. Confederate casualties were estimated at 327 killed and 1,127 wounded. U.S. losses were put at 507 killed, 1,976 wounded and 208 captured or missing. In his official report McClernand put his division's losses at 307 killed, 1,026 wounded and 169 missing, giving evidence that the First Division had felt the brunt of the battle.

In his official report McClernand also did his best to try to claim credit for the ultimate victory despite his division's having been routed in the Confederates' initial assault on the Union line. "The victory, though complete and signal, cost us a dear and mournful price," he wrote. Then he reported that "our trophies corresponded with the magnitude of the victory; 13,360 prisoners, 20,000 stand of small arms, 69 pieces of cannon, and corresponding proportions of animals, wagons, commissary, and quartermaster's stores fell into our hands,"[38] as if the prizes won by Grant's entire army had been gained by the First Division alone.

He furthermore took credit for having conceived Grant's plan to strike the full extent of the rebel line all at once. "In reply to my suggestion, urging a simultaneous assault at all points," he wrote in his official report, "I was gratified to receive an order to that effect."[39] Falsely claiming credit for success was to become a growing problem with McClernand, but this time Grant made only a small objection, which he included in his remarks that accompanied McClernand's report, forwarded to General Halleck: "I transmit herewith the report of the action of the First Division at the battle of Fort Donelson. I have no special comments to make on it, farther than that the report is a little highly colored as to the conduct of the First Division, and I failed to hear the suggestions spoken of about the propriety of attacking the enemy all around the lines on Saturday. No suggestions were made by General McClernand at the time spoken of."[40]

Grant put McClernand in charge of the captured fort, guarding it and the nearby area, especially the roads between the Tennessee and Cumberland rivers. Far from being content as commander of a garrison and reconnaissance force, McClernand began campaigning for a grander assignment. In a letter to Grant written on February 26 he began his efforts to gain an independent command that would, as he conceived it, capture the Mississippi from the Confederacy. "I have," he wrote in his convoluted prose, "from the breaking out of the rebellion, attentively and carefully studied the immediate valley of the Mississippi as a principal field of military operations. These considerations may occasionally be supposed to afford some assurance of the efficiency of my command if employed in that field."[41]

Other matters were then occupying Grant's mind. Following Halleck's March 1 order to move a force up the Tennessee River on a mission to interrupt the Confederates' rail lines near Eastport and Corinth in Mississippi, and near Jackson and Humboldt in Tennessee, Grant on March 2 ordered McClernand and Smith to prepare two brigades each to make up that expedition. Halleck, in the meantime, supposedly acting on an anonymous complaint, irritatedly wired General McClellan, the army's general in chief, on March 3 and told him, "I have had no communication with General Grant for more than a week. He left his command without my authority, and went to Nashville. His army seems to be as much demoralized by the victory at Fort Donelson as was that of the Potomac by the defeat at Bull Run. It is hard to censure a successful general immediately after a victory, but I think he richly deserves it. I can get no reports, no returns, no information of any kind from him. Satisfied by his victory, he sits down and enjoys it without any regard to the future. I am worn out and tired by this neglect and inefficiency. C.F. Smith is almost the only officer equal to the emergency."[42]

Without waiting for corroboration of the accusations, which included the rumor that Grant had returned to his old drinking habits, McClellan swiftly replied to Halleck the same day, March 3: "The future success of our cause demands that proceedings such as General Grant's should at once be checked. Generals must observe discipline as well as private soldiers. Do not hesitate to arrest him at once if the good of the service requires it, and place

C.F. Smith in command. You are at liberty to regard this as a positive order, if it will smooth your way."⁴³

Grant Is Removed from Command

Halleck immediately removed Grant from command, notifying him in a dispatch dated March 4: "You will place Maj. Gen. C.F. Smith in command of expedition, and remain yourself at Fort Henry. Why do you not obey my orders to report strength and positions of your command?"⁴⁴ On March 6 Grant received another wire from Halleck: "Your going to Nashville without authority, and when your presence with your troops was of the utmost importance, was a matter of very serious complaint at Washington, so much so that I was advised to arrest you on your return."⁴⁵ Grant answered the messages the next day. "Troops will be sent under command of Major-General Smith, as directed," he told Halleck. "I am not aware of ever having disobeyed any order from your headquarters—certainly never intended such a thing. I have reported almost daily the condition of my command, and reported every position occupied."⁴⁶ In his response Grant also asked to be relieved from any further duties under Halleck.

Also on March 6 McClernand learned that Smith had been placed in command of the expedition up the Tennessee River and he fired off a hot letter of complaint to Grant, not knowing that Smith had been nominated for promotion to major general on March 3 and that although his nomination was awaiting Senate confirmation, Halleck had already named him a major general. (All four brigadiers who had seen action at Fort Donelson—Grant, C.F. Smith, McClernand and Lew Wallace—were in the process of being promoted to major general.) "I rank him as a brigadier," McClernand protested, "and cannot recognize his superiority without self-degradation, which no human power can constrain me to do."⁴⁷

The whole flap soon came to naught after President Lincoln entered the controversy over Grant. The army's adjutant general, Major General Lorenzo Thomas, on March 10 wrote to Halleck, telling him, "It has been reported that, soon after the battle of Fort Donelson, Brigadier-General Grant left his command without leave. By direction of the President, the Secretary of War directs you to ascertain and report whether General Grant left his command at any time without proper authority, and if so, for how long; whether he has made to you proper reports and returns of his forces; whether he has committed any acts which were unauthorized or not in accordance with military subordination or propriety, and if so, what?"⁴⁸ Unlike McClellan, President Lincoln wanted specifics. He demanded that Halleck provide details of the charges made against Grant.

Then, in a stunning development the next day, March 11, Lincoln, fed up with McClellan's lethargic pursuit of the war in the East, fired McClellan from his job as general in chief. Halleck, in fearful reaction to that disturbing news, began back-pedaling. On March 13 he telegraphed Grant, telling him, "You cannot be relieved from your command. There is no good reason for it. I am certain that all which the authorities at Washington ask is, that you enforce discipline and punish the disorderly.... Instead of relieving you, I wish you, as soon as your new army is in the field, to assume the immediate command and lead it on to new victories."⁴⁹ When McClernand learned that Grant had been restored to command, he sent Grant a note of congratulations.

McClernand's Second and Third brigades had begun boarding steamers for the expedition on March 5 and by the end of the next day they were ready to shove off from Fort Donelson. His First Brigade was to march overland to Fort Henry, where they were to be posted and would await further instructions. The transports bearing the two other brigades would turn from the Cumberland into the Tennessee River, heading generally southeastwardly up the river. The latest instruction from Halleck was for the troops to establish a camp at Savannah, Tennessee, on the Tennessee River about fifteen miles northeast of another steamboat stop, called Pittsburg Landing.

The transports bearing McClernand's troops started up the Tennessee on March 10, and on the next day McClernand arrived at Savannah. He met with Smith on March 13, shortly before Grant was restored to command, and was instructed to land his men at Savannah and take over the countryside around Savannah. He did so, and promptly sent out reconnaissance details to patrol the area and map it. Grant reassumed command of the expedition on March 17 and made his way to Savannah to join his army immediately upon his rank being restored. He quickly assessed his army's situation. Half of his troops, including McClernand's division, were on the east bank of the Tennessee at Savannah; Lew Wallace's division was at Crump's Landing on the west bank, about four miles above Savannah; and the rest of the force was at Pittsburg Landing, on the west bank, five miles above Crump's Landing. Grant also saw the objective. "The enemy was in force at Corinth [Mississippi]," he wrote in his memoir, "the junction of the two most important railroads in the Mississippi valley—one connecting Memphis and the Mississippi River with the East, and the other leading south to all the cotton states.... If we obtained possession of Corinth, the enemy would have no railroad for the transportation of armies or supplies until that [railroad] running east from Vicksburg was reached. It [Corinth] was the great strategic position at the West between the Tennessee and the Mississippi rivers and between Nashville and Vicksburg."[50]

Knowing the Confederates were massing a force at Corinth, about twenty-five miles southwest of Savannah, Grant began moving his troops from Savannah to Pittsburg Landing, the river port nearest Corinth. Soon the area around the landing was bustling with the continual arrivals of U.S. troops and boatloads of supplies and equipment and wagons and horses, all crowding the waterfront and nearby roads.

In the army's latest reshuffling of commands, the army of General Buell, about 25,000 strong, had been placed under Halleck's command, and Halleck had ordered Buell to cooperate in the Union thrust into the South's heartland. Buell was now on his way from Nashville to join forces with Grant. Grant planned to position Buell's troops at Hamburg Landing, six miles upriver from Pittsburg Landing. He was waiting for their arrival before launching an attack on the Confederate position at Corinth. On March 19 Buell was eighty-five miles away at Columbia, Tennessee. Grant figured that the Confederate commanders, General Albert Sidney Johnston and Johnston's second-in-command, Major General P.G.T. Beauregard, would wait for him to make the first move and he believed that he could take his time to make it. He had no idea, as he related in his memoir, "that the enemy would leave strong intrenchments to take the initiative when he knew he would be attacked where he was if he remained."[51] Guided by that belief, Grant declined to entrench his men or construct fortifications around Pittsburg Landing. His decision was supported by the report from his chief military engineer, who told him that if he were to entrench the troops, the trenches would have to be dug along a line that would move the troops farther back from their present position, closer to the river, farther from the enemy.

Grant's shifting of troops placed four of his six divisions—McClernand's, Brigadier General Stephen Hurlbut's, Sherman's and Smith's—between Pittsburg Landing and the local Methodist log meetinghouse, Shiloh Church, about two miles west of the boat landing. Their placement seemed almost haphazard, forming an irregular line that faced mostly toward the south. McClernand may have been the only commander concerned about the weaknesses in the line, which twisted and turned and had the effect of scattering the brigades of the same division. He suggested to Grant that "the various camps here should be formed upon some general and connected plan. Such a precaution," he wrote, "might be necessary to avoid confusion and self destruction in case of a possible night attack."[52]

Meanwhile, Johnston and Beauregard were planning to attack Grant as soon as expediency would permit. Beauregard drew up the plan of attack, explaining it to the rebel commanders orally in an early-morning conference on April 3, then having detailed written orders issued. The rebel army was to begin moving out later that day, bivouac for the night, then deploy for the advance against the Union position on the morning of April 4.

Flanking Pittsburg Landing were two roughly parallel creeks, streaming toward the Tennessee River about three miles apart, both flowing southwest to northeast. One of them, Owl Creek, ran through a swamp and merged with another stream, Snake Creek, which emptied into the river north of the landing. The other, Lick Creek, joined the river south of the landing. Enclosed by those three creeks was a plateau that rose eighty to a hundred feet above the level of the river and ended at the river in sloughs and ravines and the bluff on which stood Pittsburg Landing. The plateau was mostly wooded, with a dozen or so cleared fields of about eighty acres each that formed giant patches on the expanse of high ground.

The roads in the area were little more than dirt trails, one of which paralleled the river, although a distance away from it to avoid the sloughs. That road connected Pittsburg Landing with Crump's Landing, about five miles to the north, and with Hamburg Landing, about six miles to the southeast. Two roads came to Pittsburg Landing from Corinth. One, called Ridge Road, ran north toward the landing and then curved eastward; the other ran east then turned northward to join Ridge Road about four miles from the landing. On the way to the landing, the easternmost road ran past a hamlet named Monterey, and from Monterey two other small roads, the roads to Savannah and Purdy, ran northward and crossed Ridge Road. At the intersection of the Savannah road and Ridge Road stood a house known as Mickey's, about eight miles from Pittsburg Landing.

Beauregard's plan called for the Confederates to turn the Union left flank and force it away from the river and drive it up into the swamp through which Owl Creek flowed. Driven into that hopeless position, with no good means of escape, Grant's army would be forced to surrender. As Beauregard planned it, the Confederate attack would be equally strong all along the three-mile front, rather than being weighted with more strength on its right side in order to drive back the Union left.

The Confederate advance, however, was soon hampered by all sorts of delays, and Beauregard moved it back one day, to the morning of April 5. Shortly after midnight of the 4th the menacing clouds over the area burst with a heavy rain, which continued past 3:00 a.m., the hour at which the first rebel units were to launch the attack. Slowed by the rain and darkness, those troops were not in position to advance until dawn. Then a whole division was found to be blocked from advancing on the congested road that led to the front. The delays of clearing the road and getting units in the proper order finally forced Beauregard to reconsider the whole operation. He made the case to Johnston that the element of surprise had been completely lost in the delays, that the Union forces were growing stronger in numbers and that, having learned of the Confederates' planned assault, they would be, as he said, "entrenched to the eyes." Johnston disagreed. He said he didn't think their presence was known and even if the enemy did know the Confederates were about to attack, the operation was too far along to cancel it. "We shall fight them tomorrow," he declared, ending the discussion. He then turned and walked off, telling a staff officer as he strode away, "I would fight them if they were a million."[53]

At about five-thirty in the morning of Sunday, April 6, 1862, the Confederates began to advance with Major General William Hardee's corps in front and Major General Braxton Bragg's following 500 yards behind them. Johnston rode up to the front of the advancing troops, and Beauregard, who would be responsible for directing the reserve forces, rode off to the rear of the formations. The men of Hardee's corps pushed their way through two miles of thickets and brush, driving back the scattered Union pickets. As the advancing rebels last came upon the Union lines the musket fire that had been sporadic soon became continuous, punctuated by blasts of artillery fire. The wave of Confederate attackers crashed all along the Union front, striking Grant's surprised army. The Union line had the brigade commanded by Colonel David Stuart on its extreme left, the division commanded by Brigadier General Benjamin Prentiss on Stuart's right, McClernand's division on Prentiss's right and Sherman's division to the right of McClernand. Behind that forward line were the division of Brigadier General Stephen Hurlbut and, positioned on Hurlbut's right, the division commanded by Brigadier General W.H.L. Wallace, who had taken over for the injured and incapacitated General Smith.

"The Confederate assaults were made with such disregard of losses on their own side, that our line of tents soon fell into their hands," Grant recounted. "The ground on which the battle was fought was undulating, heavily timbered, with scattered clearings, the woods giving some protection to the troops on both sides. There was also considerable underbrush. A number of attempts were made to turn our right flank, where Sherman was posted, but every effort was repulsed with heavy loss. But the front attack was kept up so vigorously that, to prevent the success of these attempts to get on our flanks, the National troops were compelled several times to take positions to the rear, nearer Pittsburg Landing."[54]

Sherman's brigade commanders rushed their troops into position to face the onslaught, but the overwhelming Confederate force pushed Sherman's men back from Shiloh church, breaching Sherman's line as it did so. Keeping an eye on Sherman's line, to McClernand's right, McClernand ordered his Third Brigade, commanded by Colonel Julius Raith, to move forward to support Sherman. With furious fusillades of musket fire Raith's brigade managed to temporarily stall the rebel advance, but finally gave way and fell back. McClernand also ordered his First and Second brigades to shift toward Sherman's position, then directed them as they moved into new positions. As Sherman's and McClernand's divisions were pushed back by the unrelenting assault, they formed a new line stretching from Owl Creek to the Corinth road.

About nine o'clock the Confederates smashed into that new line, striking all along

McClernand's front, overwhelming it, forcing McClernand's three brigades and one of Hurlbut's which had come in support to fall back. McClernand ordered another new line to be formed about 200 yards to the rear as Union troops became scattered in their haste to escape the rebel advance. The left side of McClernand's line had been overrun when the Third Brigade had exhausted their ammunition, and Colonel Raith had been mortally wounded. The newest line was formed up around 11:00 a.m., but by noon it, too, had been broken. Gathering up his scattered troops, McClernand launched a counterattack that managed to regain much of the ground that had been lost, but he was unable to hold it as rebel reinforcements arrived. By 2:30 p.m. McClernand's men were back at the ridge from which they had launched the counterattack.

During the thickest part of the fight, McClernand made his presence felt, urging his troops on.[55] He later described the action: "[T]he enemy continued his endeavors to turn the flanks of my line and to cut me off from the landing. To prevent this I ordered my left wing to fall back a short distance and form an obtuse angle with the center, opposing a double front to the enemy's approach. Thus disposed, my left held the enemy in check, while my whole line slowly fell back to my sixth position.... Advancing in heavy columns, led by the Louisiana Zouaves, to break our center, we awaited his approach within sure range and opened a terrific fire upon him. The head of the column was instantly mowed down; the remainder of it swayed to and fro for a few seconds, and turned and fled."[56] Before the day was done, the Confederates made one more desperate attempt to turn the Union left flank but were repulsed. After thirteen hours of fighting, the troops of the two sides were exhausted in both body and spirit. Rebel troops were at last ordered to disengage and pull back a short distance to bivouac for the night, which was fast coming on and bringing more rain.

"When the firing ceased at night," Grant reported, "the National line was all of a mile in rear of the position it had occupied in the morning." His report continued:

> The situation at the close of Sunday was as follows: Along the top of the bluff just south of the log-house which stood at Pittsburg Landing ... [were] twenty or more pieces of artillery facing south, or up the river. This line of artillery was on the crest of a hill overlooking a deep ravine opening into the Tennessee. Hurlbut, with his division intact, was on the right of this artillery, extending west and possibly a little north. McClernand came next in the general line, looking more to the west. His division was complete in its organization and ready for any duty. Sherman came next, his right extending to Snake Creek. His command, like the other two, was complete in its organization and ready, like its chief, for any service.... All three divisions were, as a matter of course, more or less shattered and depleted in numbers from the terrible battle of the day. The division of W.H.L. Wallace ... had lost its organization, and did not occupy a place in the line as a division; Prentiss's command was gone as a division, many of its members having been killed, wounded, or captured. But it had rendered valiant service before its final dispersal, and had contributed a good share to the defense of Shiloh.[57]

The Confederates had also suffered severe casualties, none more critical than the loss of their commander, General Johnston. Around noon he had ridden out to the right side of the rebel line to spur new effort by his troops to hammer the Union left and push it out of its path to the landing, where Grant's transport steamers and two timberclad U.S. gunboats lay, the gunboats pouring deadly broadsides into the rebel ranks. At about 2:30, astride his horse while he observed the battle, suddenly Johnston reeled in his saddle. Tennessee governor Isham Harris, serving as a volunteer aide to the general, saw him sway and galloped over to his side and asked him, "General, are you hurt?" "Yes," Johnston answered. "And I fear seriously." A bullet had severed the femoral artery in his right leg, and he was bleeding profusely. Harris maneuvered his mount beside Johnston's, held Johnston up in the saddle and guided the two horses away from the front and into a ravine, where he lowered Johnston, unconscious, to the ground. Moments later General Johnston was dead. Harris then remounted and sped off to find Beauregard and give him the awful news.

Though the Confederate assault had forced the Union line to yield its positions, it had failed in Beauregard's plan to drive Grant's army into the swamp west of Pittsburg Landing. It had merely pushed the Union line into a more defensible position closer to the landing.

Meanwhile, as Sunday afternoon faded into evening, Grant's army was being reinforced. General Buell arrived during the day, and behind him came the first element of his divisions, the brigade commanded by Colonel Jacob Ammen, which took a position on the left side of the Union line. Lew Wallace's division of Grant's army, which had somehow gone astray before the battle began, at last showed up around 7:00 p.m. As evening passed into night, the rest of Buell's 20,000 troops arrived and were swiftly ferried across the river to join forces with Grant's army, bringing the total Union strength up to some 40,000 effectives, who now faced a Confederate force diminished by heavy losses and numbering no more than 28,000 effectives.

Shortly after sunrise on Monday, April 7, 1862, the action resumed. Moving forward over the ground that the Confederates had won and withdrawn from when the engagement was ended late Sunday afternoon, Sherman's troops soon reached the extreme right of McClernand's former position. There Sherman encountered rebel artillery fire and halted, waiting for sounds of Buell's units coming down Ridge Road to join the battle. Lew Wallace, as ordered, moved west and then south toward the rebels. McClernand also moved forward, and then Hurlbut. McClernand wrote about it in his official report:

> Preceded by skirmishers, my line advanced through my camp obliquely to the southwest, thus retaking it. At the same time Generals Sherman and Wallace were seen advancing in the same general direction. Approaching a hasty and rude breast work of logs formed by the enemy during Sunday night, his skirmishers opened an irregular fire, which caused the Fifty-third Ohio to retire in disorder, breaking my line. My right staggered for a moment, recovered itself, and, under the lead of Colonel Marsh, opened an oblique fire, which immediately dispersed the enemy in that direction, leaving us in possession of my recaptured camp.
>
> About the same time information was brought that the enemy were advancing in strong force to turn the left of my line. To prevent this I ordered my command to move by the left flank, which, being promptly done, confronted the opposing forces. Here one of the severest conflicts ensued that occurred during the two days. We drove the enemy back and pursued him with great vigor to the edge of a field, a half mile east and to the left of my headquarters, where reserves came to his support. Our position at this moment was most critical and a repulse seemed inevitable, but fortunately the Louisville Legion, forming part of General Rousseau's brigade, came up at my request and succored me....
>
> The ... last stand of the enemy was in a wood skirting a field still further south. Here he brought into action a number of guns, which were used with most annoying effect until silenced by McAllister's battery of 24-pounder howitzers. Although the enemy was

Battle of Shiloh. Resisting a Confederate onslaught on Sunday, April 6, 1862, McClernand's division, with Brig. Gen. Benjamin Prentiss's division, prevented the rebels from turning the left flank of the Union line, thwarting General Beauregard's plan to force the U.S. troops into the swamp north of Pittsburg Landing. The next day, with reinforcements that arrived late Sunday afternoon and during the night, Grant's army overwhelmed the exhausted Confederates and drove them back to Corinth, Mississippi (Library of Congress).

further pursued, this artillery engagement actually terminated the conflict, which had passed over a space of some 3 miles, and had been continued from 7 o'clock a.m. to about 4 o'clock p.m. of the second day.[58]

"This day," Grant recalled in his memoir, "everything was favorable to the Union side. We had now become the attacking party. The enemy was driven back all day, as we had been the day before."[59]

Beauregard Withdraws

Sometime after noon, realizing he was facing a superior force and aware that substantial Union reinforcements had arrived, Beauregard began preparations to retire from the field. His 40,000-man army, having suffered enormous casualties, along with desertions, had so shrunk that it now numbered no more than Buell's troops alone. And those troops he still had were worn out. He instructed members of his staff to ride out and tell the generals to retire, slowly and in good order, maintaining an attitude of dignity rather than defeat. He positioned a strong rear guard, including artillery units, near Shiloh Church to cover the withdrawal, and by four o'clock Monday afternoon Beauregard's dispirited army was on the road to Corinth, its victory of April 6, paid for at a high cost, having been seized from its grasp on the morning of April 7.

The Confederates had suffered 10,699 casualties, including 1,728 killed, 8,012 wounded and 959 missing or captured. Union casualties totaled 13,047, including 1,754 killed, 8,408 wounded and 2,885 missing or captured. McClernand reported his casualties at 1,861, including killed and wounded, out of an effective force of 7,028 that he had on the day the battle had begun. "The loss of that portion of the enemy encountered by my command," he claimed with a generous guess, "is doubtless doubly as great."[60]

To call special attention to himself and his command, McClernand wrote to President Lincoln a week after the battle. "My division," he told Lincoln, "as usual, has borne or shared in bearing the brunt." He also wanted Lincoln to know how close he himself had been to the action. "Among the killed," he wrote, "is General A.S. Johnston ... who fell within 30 yards of my tent. Part of a battery belonging to the enemy was taken within 150 yards of my tent, and some 30 or 40 horses were killed within the same distance."[61]

Grant decided not to pursue the retreating rebel army. "After the rain of the night before," he later wrote, "and the frequent and heavy rains for some days previous, the roads were almost impassable. The enemy carrying his artillery and supply trains over them in his retreat, made them still worse for troops following. I wanted to pursue, but had not the heart to order the men who had fought desperately for two days, lying in the mud and rain whenever not fighting, and I did not feel disposed to positively order Buell, or any part of his command, to pursue."[62] In the same self-congratulatory letter that he wrote to President Lincoln McClernand took a swipe at Grant, his commander, for not pursuing. "It was a great mistake," he told the president, "that we did not pursue him [the enemy] Monday night and Tuesday."[63]

Following the battle at Shiloh McClernand was given command of the reserve of the Army of the Tennessee and he relinquished command of his division. The new assignment failed to satisfy McClernand, and he complained to Halleck that it was in effect a demotion, a complaint that Halleck rejected, although he later reinstated McClernand as a division commander. What McClernand continued to angle for was an independent command, something that promised more glory and that would get him out from under Grant and Halleck. On July 11, however, after relieving McClellan of the job, Lincoln appointed Halleck general in chief, raising a major obstacle to McClernand's plan for an independent command.

By late August 1862, with no additional significant service in the field, McClernand had wangled an assignment organizing the recruits that responded to the president's call for 300,000 more volunteers, 26,148 of whom were requested from Illinois. The assignment had come in a political move made by Illinois governor Richard Yates to Secretary of War Stanton at the request of McClernand. McClernand then managed to have Yates provide him entree to the chief movers and shakers in Washington, including treasury secretary Salmon Chase—with whom he conferred in a private meeting held in Yates's Washington hotel room—and Lincoln himself, with whom he conferred in a meeting with General McClellan in the field at Sharpsburg, Maryland. McClernand furthermore importuned Secretary Stanton for help in forming a 20,000-man army (later increased to 24,000 infantry, 1,600 artillery and 300 hundred cavalry), composed of new recruits and independent of Grant's command, that McClernand proposed to lead on a mission to capture Vicksburg, site of the forbidding Confederate fortress that continued to block free passage on the strategically and economically vital Mississippi River. But he soon ran into another obstacle to the realization of his plan. On October 25 Grant was placed in command of the Department of the Tennessee, putting Vicksburg within his area of responsibility. To Vicksburg Grant then immediately turned his complete attention.

McClernand's orders, issued by Secretary Stanton on October 21 and labeled "Confidential," directed him "to proceed to the States of Indiana, Illinois, and Iowa, to organize the troops remaining in those States and to be raised by volunteering or draft, and forward them with all dispatch to Memphis, Cairo, or such other points as may hereafter be designated by the general in chief, to the end that, when a sufficient force not required by the operations of General Grant's command shall be raised, an expedition may be organized under General McClernand's command against Vicksburg and to clear the Mississippi River and open navigation to New Orleans. The forces so organized will remain subject to the designation of the general-in-chief, and be employed according to such exigencies as the service in his judgment may require."[64]

Grant was not immediately informed about McClernand's latest assignment and apparently first learned about it from Rear Admiral David Dixon Porter, commander of U.S. naval forces on the Mississippi River, who was expected to cooperate with McClernand in his campaign to capture Vicksburg. Porter had been in Washington and had met with the president, who, according to Porter, had asked Porter who should be the general to lead the army in a joint army-navy operation to capture Vicksburg. "General Grant, sir," Porter answered. "Vicksburg is within his department, but I presume he will send Sherman there, who is equal to any occasion." Lincoln surprised Porter by replying, "Well, admiral, I have in mind a better general than either of them. That is McClernand, an old and intimate friend of mine." From there the president went on to give McClernand credit for the victory at Shiloh. He then handed Porter a note of introduction to his old friend, who was also then in Washington, and suggested Porter go see him and discuss the Vicksburg operation. Porter did go to see McClernand at his hotel—and, having met him, decided McClernand was a pompous ass.[65]

Alarmed by the prospect of having to cooperate with McClernand, and by the possibility that McClernand might be superseding Grant, Porter wrote to Grant to tell him of Lincoln's plans for McClernand. Grant's reaction to the news was predictable. "At this stage of the campaign against Vicksburg," Grant wrote in his memoir, "I was very much disturbed by newspaper rumors that General McClernand was to have a separate and independent command within mine, to operate against Vicksburg by way of the Mississippi River. Two commanders on the same field are always one too many, and in this case I did not think the general selected had either the experience or the qualifications to fit him for so important a position. I feared for the safety of the troops intrusted to him, especially as he was to raise new levies, raw troops, to execute so important a trust."[66] Halleck agreed. He wasn't keen on McClernand's idea or on McClernand himself, whose military ability Halleck, like Grant, distrusted. Halleck apparently worked the matter out with Lincoln and then wrote Grant to reassure him. "On the 12th [of November]," Grant reported, "I received a dispatch from General Halleck saying that I had command of all the troops sent to my department and authorizing me to fight the enemy where I pleased."[67]

Grant developed a plan that called for him to move down from Jackson, Tennessee, to Holly Springs, Mississippi, on the Mississippi Central Rail Road Line, where he would establish a supply base, then proceed with some 60,000 troops farther south to Grenada, Mississippi, forcing Vicksburg's defenders, led by Lieutenant General John C. Pemberton, to try to stop Grant's army before it reached Vicksburg. That plan would later have to be scrapped when Pemberton's cavalry swept into Holly Springs, Grant's forward supply base, and captured the entire garrison of 1,500 men and destroyed all of Grant's supply of munitions and provisions. About that same time, the rebel cavalry of Brigadier General Nathan Bedford Forrest tore up sections of the railroad between Jackson, Tennessee, and Columbus, Kentucky, cutting off Grant's line of communication with the North. Grant now realized he could not maintain a lengthy, overland communication line deep in enemy territory and he decided he must make the Mississippi River his communication line.

In the meantime, stalled with his troops outside Oxford, Mississippi, south of Holly Springs, as he waited for the broken bridge across the Hatchie River to be repaired, Grant learned that an expedition down the Mississippi was being planned. To make certain a competent general would command it, Grant quickly ordered Sherman to return to Memphis from his position just north of Oxford and upon his arrival in Memphis to "assume command of all the troops there ... and organize them into brigades and divisions in your own army. As soon as possible move with them down the river to the vicinity of Vicksburg, and with the co-operation of the gunboat fleet under command of Flag Officer Porter proceed to the reduction of that place."[68] Grant explained his haste: "My object in sending Sherman back was expedited by a desire to get him in command of the forces separated from my direct supervision. I feared that delay might bring McClernand, who was his senior and who had authority from the President and Secretary of War to exercise that particular command—and independently, I doubted McClernand's fitness."[69]

With swift efficiency Sherman gathered and organized the troops in Memphis, many of them recently recruited. He put them aboard a flotilla of transport steamers and took them down the Mississippi toward Vicksburg. On the day after Christmas 1862, the transports reached the mouth of the Yazoo River above Vicksburg and then proceeded up the Yazoo. His intention was to land a force of 30,000 men southwest of Vicksburg and attack the fortress city from the north. Sherman launched his attack on December 29, but was repulsed with heavy losses and was forced to put his troops back on their transports and withdraw, starting back down the Yazoo on January 2, 1863, the operation a complete failure.

As the convoy got under way, Admiral Porter met with Sherman and informed him that McClernand had arrived at the mouth of the Yazoo aboard the steamer *Tigress* and the scuttlebutt was that he had come to take command of Sherman's army. On that news Sherman promptly boarded a tugboat, left the convoy and sped down the river to find McClernand. Reporting to him, Sherman learned that McClernand carried orders from the War Department, endorsed by President Lincoln, to command the forces on the Mississippi. Sherman had been superseded.

McClernand, who was up to date on the fortunes of Grant's campaign, then informed Sherman that Grant was not coming to Vicksburg, that his supply base at Holly Springs had been overrun, that he had fallen back toward Memphis and that one of his divisions was already at Memphis getting supplies when McClernand stopped there days earlier. Grant had notified Sherman of those events, but his dispatches had been routed to Memphis, and Sherman had not yet received them.

On January 3, 1863, the two Union commanders and their troops rendezvoused at Milliken's Bend, Louisiana, about ten miles up the Mississippi from Vicksburg, while Admiral Porter and his gunboats remained at the Yazoo. On January 4 McClernand issued his general order no. 1, stating that he was assuming command of the Army of the Mississippi (until then that army had been called the right wing of Grant's Thirteenth Army Corps and numbered about 30,000 men) and that his army would be divided into two corps, of two divisions each, one corps to be commanded by Brigadier General G.W. Morgan, the other by Sherman.

While at Milliken's Bend, Sherman learned that two weeks earlier the Union steamer *Blue Wing* had left Memphis carrying arms and ammunition and towing coal barges, bound for the Yazoo, and had been captured by a Confederate vessel that had steamed out of the Arkansas River and fallen on the unescorted vessel. The captured steamer had been taken up the Arkansas to Fort Hindman, a strong, earthworks fortification the Confederates had erected at Arkansas Post, a community built around an Indian trading post that the French had founded nearly two centuries earlier. Sherman was familiar with the fort, which lay about forty miles above the mouth of the Arkansas River. It was held by about 5,000 rebel troops and commanded the river.

Like many politicians, McClernand had a way of speaking in platitudes and generalizations, without offering specifics. "He spoke in general terms of opening navigation of the Mississippi," Sherman wrote in his memoir, "'cutting his way to the sea,' etc., etc., but the *modus operandi* was not so clear."[70] Sherman, on the other hand, had definite ideas about waging the campaign to capture the Mississippi. Believing that as long as Fort Hindman provided a convenient base from which rebel vessels could attack unescorted Union shipping on the Mississippi the fort would remain an impediment to the campaign to take Vicksburg, Sherman decided it would be a good idea to capture the fort and eliminate it as a Confederate haven. He proposed to McClernand that they launch an attack on it with the army they now had aboard their transports. McClernand had objections to an attack, but he eventually agreed to go with Sherman to ask Porter for his opinion.

On the night of January 4, Sherman, on his headquarters boat, the *Forest Queen*, stopped to pick up McClernand from his command vessel, the *Tigress*, and together they called on Admiral Porter aboard his flagship, the *Black Hawk*. "It must have been near midnight," Sherman recounted, "and Admiral Porter was in *dishabille*. We were seated in his cabin and I explained my views about Arkansas Post, and asked his cooperation." During the conversation Sherman noticed that Porter's manner toward McClernand was curt, so much so that Sherman took him to task. "I invited him out into a forward-cabin where he had his charts, and asked him what he meant by it. He said that 'he did not like him.' ... I begged him, for the sake of harmony, to waive that, which he promised to do."[71] They then rejoined McClernand and resumed their discussion. According to his own account of the meeting, Porter refused to have anything to do with the proposed attack on Fort Hindman unless Sherman went as commander. "To this McClernand agreed," Porter reported, "only stipulating that he [McClernand] should accompany the expedition. So the matter was arranged, and the expedition started."[72]

The entire army of more than 30,000 men on their transports, convoyed by a flotilla of Porter's gunboats, including the *Black Hawk*, steamed up the Mississippi to the mouth of the White River, which they reached on January 8. Then they continued up the White to its confluence with the Arkansas and proceeded up the Arkansas to Notrib's farm, a site just below Fort Hindman beyond the range of the fort's big guns, arriving there in the evening of January 9. The troops began disembarking early the next morning.

One column, the division of Brigadier General (formerly Colonel) David Stuart, moved up along the riverbank to within about four miles of the fort, where it encountered the rebels entrenched behind an earthworks line that extended from the river on the rebels' right to the swamp on their left. Behind the line was a dense woods. Sherman had another column, the division commanded by Brigadier General Frederick Steele, march around the Confederates' left, using a road that passed through the swamp and debouched onto firm grounds at the rear of the fort. While Steele's troops were proceeding up that road, they were overtaken by a message from McClernand, both reporting that the Confederates had abandoned their line and had withdrawn toward the fort and ordering Sherman to turn around and march back to where General Stuart's division was now advancing through the woods, continuing toward the fort.

The early darkness of the short winter day came on as the Union troops neared the fort, and after a bright moon rose, Sherman's patrols reconnoitered the approaches to the fort, observing some abandoned huts and discovering that the whole force of defenders had fallen back into and around the fort. At dawn, in the growing daylight, the Union forces could see that the Confederates had erected a new parapet straight across the peninsula formed by the curve of the river. The peninsula was divided into halves by a road, and Sherman's corps had the ground to the right of the road while the corps of General Morgan had the left. "McClernand," Sherman related, "had his quarters still on the *Tigress*, back at Notrib's farm, but moved forward that morning (January 11th) to a place in the woods to our rear, where he had a man up a tree, to observe and report the movements. There was a general understanding with Admiral Porter that he was to attack the fort with his three ironclad gunboats directly by its water-front, while we assaulted by land in the rear."[73]

Porter had begun pounding the fort, seeking to silence its guns, on the day before, January 10. Now, about ten-thirty on the morning of the 11th, while the troops of Sherman and Morgan stood within six hundred yards of the fort, poised to launch their assault, awaiting the sound of the navy's guns, Porter's ironclads opened up on the fort once more. "The battle commenced and soon became very hot," Porter reported. "In a short time all the guns in the works were silenced and the flag-ship 'Black Hawk' was run to the bank alongside the fort to board it with her crew; at the same time a messenger was sent to General Sherman informing him of the condition of affairs, and that if he would send a storming party from the rear, the Navy would board from the water side."[74]

From his vantage point in the field behind the fort Sherman could see the flags of Porter's gunboats wafting above the fort's parapets as the vessels drew up to the fort. Shortly after he noticed them, someone on the rebels' new line suddenly stood up waving a large white flag, and smaller white flags then began popping up all along the line. Sherman immediately shouted, "Cease firing!" and ordered one of his aides to mount his horse and ride straight to the large white flag. Sherman and the rest of his staff followed him.

Sherman ordered the Confederate officer commanding that section of the line, Colonel Garland, to have his men stack their arms and wait for further orders. He asked who was the fort's commander and was told it was Brigadier General Thomas Churchill. He then rode into the fort and found Churchill in a conversation with Porter and General A.J. Smith.

5. Major General John Alexander McClernand 171

Capture of Fort Hindman. The fort was taken in a joint army-navy operation on January 11, 1863. The naval commander, Adm. David Porter, refused to participate unless Maj. Gen. William Sherman, instead of McClernand, commanded the army in the operation (Library of Congress).

The *Black Hawk*'s officers and crewmen had entered the fort from the river side, and Churchill and his officers had come forward to give their swords to Porter and surrender.

Meanwhile, McClernand sent a messenger from his command post with orders for Sherman to leave General Smith in charge of the fort and for Sherman and his troops, who had faced the toughest part of the battle, suffered the heaviest casualties, captured two of the fort's three brigades of defenders and held the ground outside the fort, to withdraw. Miffed by the order, Sherman went to see McClernand. "I found General McClernand on the *Tigress* in high spirits," Sherman recalled. "He said repeatedly: 'Glorious! Glorious! My star is ever in the ascendant!' He spoke complimentarily of the troops, but was extremely jealous of the navy.... He very kindly ordered something [to eat] be brought, and explained to me that by his 'orders' he did not wish to interfere with the actual state of facts; that General A.J. Smith would occupy 'Fort Hindman,' which his troops had first entered, and I could hold the lines outside, and go on securing the prisoners and stores as I had begun."[75]

The next day, January 12, Sherman ordered the Confederate prisoners herded onto transports that would take them to St. Louis, and he then dismantled and leveled the fortifications, destroying or removing the stores. He also went about the grim business of counting casualties. Union losses totaled 1,047, including 134 killed. "The number of rebel dead," he reported, "must have been nearly one hundred and fifty; of prisoners, by actual count, we secured four thousand seven hundred and ninety-one."[76] "General McClernand," Admiral Porter wrote in his account, "assumed all the direction of affairs on the surrender of the fort and the Confederate troops, and wrote the report of this affair, in which he gave fair credit to the Navy; but he actually had nothing to do with the management of the Army.... Sherman was virtually the military commander."[77]

On January 13 the Union troops re-embarked on their transports and steamed down the Arkansas through a heavy snowstorm to the mouth of the river at Napoleon, Arkansas. There Sherman and McClernand could be again in touch with Grant in Memphis. Besides reports of their success at Fort Hindman, Sherman and Porter wired him other, more pressing messages. "I received messages from both Sherman and Admiral Porter," Grant reported, "urging me to come and take command in person, and expressing their distrust of McClernand's ability and fitness for so important and intricate an expedition [as the capture of Vicksburg]."[78]

Heeding their appeal, Grant took a steamer down to Napoleon and visited with McClernand on January 17. Grant then drew his own conclusions: "It was here [at Napoleon] made evident to me that both the army and navy were so distrustful of McClernand's fitness to command that, while they would do all they could to insure success, this distrust was an element of weakness. It would have been criminal to send troops under these circumstances into such danger. By this time I had received authority to relieve McClernand, or to assign any person else to the command of the river expedition, or to assume command in person. I felt great embarrassment about McClernand. He was the senior major-general after myself within the department. It would not do, with his rank and ambition, to assign a junior over him. Nothing was left, therefore, but to assume the command myself. I would have been glad to put Sherman in command, to give him an opportunity to accomplish what he had failed in the December before; but there seemed no other way out of the difficulty, for he was junior to McClernand."[79]

McClernand, true to form, protested his removal to the president. Lincoln put him off, telling him in a note dated January 22, "I have too many family controversies (so to speak) already on my hands, to voluntarily, or so long as I can avoid it, take up another. You are now doing well—well for the country, and well for yourself—much better than you could possibly be, if engaged in open war with Gen. Halleck...."[80] McClernand protested to Grant as well. "His correspondence with me on the subject was more in the nature of reprimand than a protest," Grant recalled. "It was highly insubordinate, but I overlooked it, as I believed, for the good of the service."[81]

On January 20 Grant ordered McClernand and his entire command to Young's Point and Milliken's Bend, neighboring towns in Louisiana on the west bank of the Mississippi above the mouth of the Yazoo. Both were occupied by Union forces and together they provided bases for the army as well as the navy. Returning to his headquarters at Memphis, Grant made preparations for an indefinite absence and placed Major General Stephen A. Hurlbut, another political general and friend of President Lincoln, in charge while he was gone.

On January 29 Grant arrived at Young's Point and took command of the Army of the Mississippi the next day. By now he had seen the hopelessness of attempting to take Vicksburg by an assault from either the north or the west, where the terrain and Confederate arms remained insurmountable, impenetrable barriers. The problem then became, as he said, how to secure a landing on high ground east of the Mississippi. President Lincoln's idea was to dig a canal on the west side of the river to divert the Mississippi's flow and circumvent Vicksburg's guns. "General McClernand," Grant related, "had been, therefore, directed before I went to Young's Point to push the work of widening and deepening the canal. After my arrival the work was diligently pushed with about 4,000 men—as many as could be used to advantage."[82]

Grant had no confidence in the project, believing that even if it were made into a navigable channel, it would not avoid Vicksburg's guns, since it ran almost perpendicular to the bluffs on which the guns stood. "As soon as the enemy discovered what we were doing he established a battery commanding the canal throughout its length. This battery soon drove out our dredges, two in number, which were doing the work of thousands of men."[83] Yet he resumed the work on the canal, knowing that the president favored the idea.

Grant's own idea was to cut a breach in the levee at Lake Providence, which is part of a former course of the Mississippi, in the northeast corner of Louisiana, and divert the Mississippi from there into a chain of connected bayous and rivers, the last of which is the Red River, which joins the Mississippi above Baton Rouge near Port Hudson, about four hundred river miles below Vicksburg. On the day after he arrived at Young's Point, Grant ordered Major General James McPherson, who was positioned with his corps at Lake Providence, to cut the levee there. He then waited to see if that diversion would work. While waiting, Grant pursued another scheme to divert the Mississippi, this one on the east side of the river, and then another one on the west side.

McClernand Begins Grant's Plan

In the end, none of the schemes worked. In early April, Grant ordered McClernand to take his Thirteenth Corps down the west side of the Mississippi, marching southward from Milliken's Bend to New Carthage, Louisiana. Grant by then had decided he must attack Vicksburg from the south, and New Carthage would serve as a staging area for the troops to be boarded on transports and taken across the river to the east side, below Vicksburg.

He had already contacted Admiral Porter about having ironclad gunboats support the proposed crossing and landing, and Porter had agreed to provide them, but he wanted to wait until Grant's troops had established their base at New Carthage before he attempted to run past Vicksburg, so that the boats would have a friendly port to put into once they had withstood Vicksburg's forbidding guns. On April 11, though, Porter received orders from navy secretary Gideon Welles to "occupy," as he said, the Mississippi below Vicksburg, taking over that stretch of the river from Rear Admiral David Farragut so that Farragut could get back to his Gulf blockading assignment.

Porter now would have to make the run past Vicksburg sooner than he had expected or wanted to. He notified Grant of the sudden move and, knowing that Grant was eager to get transport steamers down to New Carthage as soon as possible, Porter asked him if the transports were ready to go and how many would be going. Grant answered that he was ready to go whenever the navy was. The run was then tentatively scheduled for the night of April 14 or 15, but when a windstorm suddenly blew into the area, the run was postponed to the night of the 16th. Three transport steamers, carrying only stores, no passengers, and twelve loaded barges, escorted by seven gunboats, would attempt to pass the rebel batteries. Barges loaded with coal were lashed to the port side of the gunboats, both as protection from the rebel fire and as a future fuel supply. Barges freighted with equipment for the troops were tied to the starboard side of five of the gunboats. The transports were insulated from gunfire by bales of cotton and water-soaked hay stacked around their boilers and decks.

The convoy shoved off from its anchorage on the east side of the Mississippi above the mouth of the Yazoo at 9:15 p.m. skirting the west bank of the river. The plan was to try to avoid drawing the fire of the Confederate guns and slip silently past the fortification, a muffling contrivance having been installed on the steamers to abate the noise of their engines. But if the convoy was detected and fired on, the boats were to shift over to the east side of the river to make it more difficult for the rebel guns to be depressed sufficiently to fire on them. The barge bearing ammunition was cut adrift as the convoy started, allowing it to float downriver on its own, lest it be struck and explode, destroying any vessel that was towing it. Down the river the convoy steamed in single file, Porter's flagship, the *Benton*, in the lead, followed by five of the gunboats, then the transports, then the gunboat *Tuscumbia* in the rear.

The Confederates had posted pickets in yawls in the river off De Soto Point, opposite Vicksburg, and as the convoy approached, at about 11:00 p.m. gliding menacingly through the darkness, the pickets spied it and quickly rowed for shore, the pickets in one yawl heading for the east bank to warn the Confederate gunners, the others rowing hard to the west bank to light up the night by setting fire to tar barrels and a number of buildings in the village of De Soto, opposite the fort's guns.

Fierce fusillades immediately opened, the gunboats returning the fire as they ran before the rebel batteries, billows of smoke from the guns mingling with thick black smoke from the burning buildings and barrels of tar along the shore. A Confederate shell blasted a hole in the coal barge being towed by the gunboat *Lafayette*, and the barge had to be cut loose and set adrift. The tug *General Price*, formerly a Confederate ram, tied to the starboard side of the *Lafayette*, was struck twice and run into by the gunboat *Louisville* in the smoky confusion. The crew then cut it free from the *Lafayette* and sped away on their own. The *Louisville* lost its coal barge when it sideswiped a transport. The *Benton* was hit six times, wounding six crewmen but suffering only minor damage to the boat. The gunboat *Carondelet* was hit twice, wounding four sailors. The *Tuscumbia*, repeatedly hit, ran aground but managed to free itself and take in tow the steamer *Forest Queen*, which had taken a disabling hit. Lost was the steamer *Henry Clay*, which was struck in the stern by a shell that exploded and set the vessel afire. Soon the entire river seemed ablaze as the wrecked steamer and flaming bales of cotton streamed southward down the river. Then suddenly the noise of battle ended. The battered flotilla had passed the mighty guns and survived. By 3:00 a.m. all seven gunboats as well as the tug *Ivy* and the transport *Silver Wave* had anchored near Diamond Island, about twelve miles above New Carthage. All were damaged, but none so severely that they could no longer serve. Twelve crewmen were wounded. Only one transport, the *Henry Clay*, had failed to make it past the rebel guns.

When Grant heard the news, he was eager to do it again. This time the gantlet would be run by six transports and twelve barges, two barges lashed to the sides of each of the transports. No gunboats would escort them. At nine o'clock on the night of April 22 the six transports cast off at Milliken's Bend, assembled at the mouth of the Yazoo and formed a single file, with the *Tigress*, formerly McClernand's headquarters boat, in the lead. By noon of the next day, April 23, all of the transports except the *Tigress*, which had been struck repeatedly and sunk, had arrived at New Carthage, all battered and broken but not beyond repair. Porter estimated that all five of the surviving vessels would be back in service within two days. Six of the twelve barges had also made it past the gantlet, their cargoes intact. The boats' casualties totaled two crewmen mortally wounded and six others slightly wounded.

Grant now had his transports where he wanted them. He could see, though, as more and more of his troops arrived, that New Carthage would not accommodate the embarkation of his army. The torrential rains of the past several days had left too limited an area dry for staging so large an operation. The troops of McClernand's four divisions and two of McPherson's divisions were already crowded in the dry areas, and Sherman's Fifteenth Corps was yet to arrive. On April 19 Grant had McClernand march his troops southward in two parallel columns a short distance apart, moving toward Somerset, Louisiana, a river landing about eight miles below New Carthage. Somerset proved inadequate also. McClernand's men then slogged farther south to Hard Times, Louisiana, the next landing, which McClernand's reconnaissance patrol had discovered, offered enough high, dry ground to marshal Grant's vast army for the crossing.

About thirty land miles below Vicksburg, on the east side of the Mississippi, where the Big Black River flows into the Mississippi, stands the town of Grand Gulf, much of which Farragut's warships had blasted into charred ruins after his vessels were fired on from the town. Unaffected, though, were the roads leading out of Grand Gulf, roads that could provide an invading army access to the interior of Mississippi. Moreover, Grand Gulf was situated nearly opposite Hard Times, which would make the crossing of the river by Grant's troops a short, quick boat ride. Grand Gulf was just the place, Grant decided, to land his army for the attack on Vicksburg.

On the morning of April 29 McClernand embarked all of his troops that the transports and barges could carry, which amounted to some 10,000 men. Once aboard the vessels, the troops waited for the gunboats to shatter Grand Gulf's fortification before disembarking. Shortly before 8:00 a.m. they opened fire on the rebel works, and the Confederates, from a fortification nearly as strong as Vicksburg's, returned the Union fire. Aboard the tug *Ivy* in the middle of the river Grant watched the exchange of fire and decided it was too hazardous to land troops at Grand Gulf. He would try an alternate plan. The assault was halted about midday, the troops were disembarked from the transports and barges, still waiting on the west side of the river, and Porter's gunboats drew back to the west bank to assess their damage and count the dead and wounded.

That evening, at about 7:45, the gunboats shoved off again and resumed their assault on Grand Gulf, this time merely covering the movement of the empty transports as they slipped untouched past the Grand Gulf fortifications in the darkness. Once the transports were gone, the gunboats ceased firing and followed the transports downriver. At the same time, McClernand and McPherson marched their troops down the west bank, and around midnight they reached the Disharoon plantation, about four miles below Grand Gulf, where the transports were waiting for them. Having received intelligence from a cavalry reconnaissance party sent out during the day, Grant had decided on a new landing point, at Bruinsburg, Mississippi, on the east bank about ten miles below Grand Gulf.

By eight o'clock the next morning, April 30, the troops had been loaded aboard the transport steamers, and on a signal from the flagship *Benton*, the little armada of gunboats and transports shoved off from the Disharoon plantation and headed downstream again. At a point opposite Bruinsburg, the flagship signaled "prepare to land" and then slowly rounded to, headed for the riverbank. By noon most of McClernand's Thirteenth Corps—

some 17,000 men—was ashore, and without opposition Bruinsburg had been secured as a Union bridgehead.

The next objective was the capture of Grand Gulf so it could be used as a base for the assault on Vicksburg. To reach that city from Bruinsburg, the troops would have to cross rain-swollen Bayou Pierre, over which the bridge on the Bruinsburg-Grand Gulf road had been burned by the rebels. The nearest other bridge was at Port Gibson, thirteen miles east of Bruinsburg. Grant quickly ordered McClernand to march through the night to Port Gibson and prevent the Confederates from destroying that bridge also. A sergeant in the 99th Illinois regiment, one of McClernand's units, gave a glimpse of the march: "At 9 o'clock ... we start away and climbing the steep hill [behind Bruinsburg] push on toward Port Gibson. As we pass along[,] an old darkey gives us his blessings, but fears there will be few of us ever to return. The moon is shining above us and the road is romantic in the extreme. The artillery wagons rattle forward and the heavy tramp of many men gives a dull but impressive sound."[84]

About five miles west of Port Gibson, McClernand's point unit ran into the rebel defenders. The sixteen-man patrol, backed up by four companies of the Twenty-first Iowa regiment, was passing a clearing when they were fired on from a cluster of trees. In the dim moonlight they instantly turned toward the trees, fired off a volley and then scurried for cover behind trees and a fence. Skirmishers went out to probe the rebel position, and as they advanced, more shots came from the position, prompting return fire from the skirmishers. The sounds of gunfire set off a sudden alarm among McClernand's regiments following the point unit. The artillery units swiftly wheeled into position at the head of the column, unlimbered their guns and blasted away at the shadowy targets to their front as hundreds of infantrymen deployed on both sides of the narrow dirt road. It was not until around three o'clock in the morning that the firing tapered off and then stopped.

At daylight the fight resumed. Grant described the action:

> Near the point selected by [the commander of the Grand Gulf garrison, Confederate Brigadier General John S.] Bowen to defend, the road to Port Gibson divides.... These roads unite just outside the town [Port Gibson]. This made it necessary for McClernand to divide his force. It was not only divided, but it was separated by a deep ravine.... One flank could not reinforce the other except by marching back to the junction of the roads.
>
> McClernand put the divisions of [Major General Alvin] Hovey, [Major General Eugene] Carr and [Major General] A.J. Smith upon the right-hand branch and [Major General Peter] Osterhaus on the left.... On the right the enemy, if not being pressed back, was at least not repulsing our advance. On the left, however, Osterhaus was not faring so well. He had been repulsed with some loss.
>
> As soon as the road could be cleared of McClernand's troops, I ordered McPherson, who was close upon the rear of the 13th [McClernand's] corps, with two brigades of [General] Logan's division. This was about noon. I ordered him to send one brigade (General John E. Smith's was selected) to support Osterhaus, and to move to the left and flank the enemy out of position. This movement carried the brigade over a deep ravine to a third ridge and, when Smith's troops were seen well through the ravine, Osterhaus was directed to renew his front attack. It was successful and unattended by heavy loss. The enemy was sent in full retreat on their right, and their left followed before sunset.... We followed up our victory until night overtook us about two miles from Port Gibson; then the troops went into bivouac for the night.[85]

The Confederates took advantage of the darkness to withdraw to Port Gibson and then back across Bayou Pierre. The Battle of Port Gibson was over. The rebels had abandoned the field. At daylight the next morning, May 2, the Union troops continued to Port Gibson and found the remaining bridge there burned. It was replaced, however, by a hastily constructed temporary bridge that allowed the Union troops to cross Bayou Pierre and proceed back toward Grand Gulf, which they reached the next day, May 3.

Grant's intention had been to detach McClernand's corps and have it assist General Banks in an effort to capture Port Hudson, and after that, Banks, with McClernand's troops, would assist Grant in the campaign to take Vicksburg. Now he learned that Banks had run into trouble in his drive up the Red River toward Shreveport and that he would be delayed. Grant then decided on a new plan.

The new plan relieved Grant's troops of the necessity of struggling northward from Grand Gulf toward Vicksburg, traversing deep ravines thick with underbrush ideal for resistance by an outnumbered but stubborn rebel defensive force and costly in men and time for an attacking force. So instead of crossing the Big Black River above Grand Gulf and trudging up beside the Mississippi for an attack from the south side of Vicksburg, Grant decided to advance his army northeastward toward Jackson, Mississippi, using the Big Black River as a shield against General Pemberton's Confederate force. He planned to capture the Jackson-to-Vicksburg road and rail line, then execute a huge column left and turn westward to launch his assault on Vicksburg from the east. He intended to move quickly, not allowing the Confederates time to receive substantial reinforcements or form strong defensive positions. He also planned on deception, ordering McClernand and McPherson to make reconnaissances that would lead rebel commanders to believe he intended to cross the Big Black and move on Vicksburg immediately. He put McClernand's corps on the left of the massive movement, nearest Pemberton's army, and put McPherson's corps on the right. Sherman's corps was positioned in the center and rear, where it could quickly support either McClernand or McPherson.

By May 11, McClernand, advancing with his left flank skirting the Big Black River, was at Five Mile Creek; Sherman was at Auburn; and McPherson was five miles outside Utica. All three corps were southwest of Jackson and moving. On the morning of May 12, as McPherson's troops marched from Utica toward Jackson they ran into a rebel line about two miles southwest of Raymond. But after an hours-long fight the Confederates hastily withdrew through Raymond, and McPherson continued toward Jackson. McPherson and Sherman reached Jackson on May 14 and found the city empty of rebel troops except for a rear guard manning a number of artillery pieces to hold off the Union advance as long as possible.

Meanwhile, Pemberton's army of Vicksburg defenders was moving out to meet the invaders, several units having crossed over to the Union army's side of the Big Black River on May 13. On May 14 Pemberton received a message from General Joseph Johnston, Pemberton's commander, who was fleeing from Jackson north toward Canton. The message had been written the night of the 13th and had been dispatched to Pemberton by courier, as McPherson's troops, on the way to Jackson, had cut the telegraph line west of Jackson. To ensure the message's delivery to Pemberton, Johnston had sent it in triplicate, one copy carried by each of three couriers. "I have lately arrived," the message read, "and learn that Major-General Sherman is between us with four divisions at Clinton. It is important to establish communication, that you may be reinforced. If practicable, come up in his rear at once. To beat such a detachment would be of immense value. All the troops you can quickly assemble should be brought. Time is all-important."[86]

One of the couriers was a Union loyalist, and instead of delivering his copy of the message to Pemberton he took it to General McPherson, who passed it on to Grant. Grant received it on the 14th and immediately ordered McPherson to move promptly on the morning of the 15th back to Bolton, about twenty miles west of Jackson and the nearest point where Johnston, with reinforcements, could reach the Jackson-Vicksburg road. Grant also sent orders to McClernand, telling him to move all his forces to Bolton immediately using the shortest, quickest route to get there. On the night of May 14, after the capture of Jackson, Johnston sent a new message to Pemberton: "As soon as the reinforcements are all up, they must be united to the rest of the [Pemberton's] army. I am anxious to see a force assembled that may be able to inflict a heavy blow upon the enemy."[87]

Pemberton, however, was anything but eager to meet Grant's army head-on, preferring to defend from a prepared position. He was firmly opposed to the idea of trying to join forces with Johnston at Clinton, which was occupied by McPherson's troops, and then making a major attack against the Union force just west of Jackson. He believed that plan to be extremely hazardous. Instead, he would follow the plan proposed by Major General William Loring, his senior division commander. It would have Pemberton's army move southeastward toward Raymond and interdict what his commanders mistakenly thought was Grant's line of communication. That move, they reasoned, would force Grant to pull back from the Jackson-Vicksburg road and attack Pemberton's army at a place of the rebels' choosing where they would hold the advantage.

Following the alternate plan, on May 15 Pemberton marched south from Edwards Station, but when his troops reached Baker's Creek, which they had to cross, they found the bridges washed away by the swift and swollen waters and the creek too deep to ford. They then turned around and returned to the Jackson-Vicksburg road, on which there was a good bridge at Baker's Creek. There Pemberton received an additional order from Johnston, directing him to join Johnston's force at Clinton, and now he decided to follow Johnston's orders after all.

Early in the morning of May 16 Grant received a report that Pemberton's army of about 25,000 men was moving eastward, toward the Union position. Grant reacted swiftly to that intelligence. He sent orders to Sherman, who was still in Jackson, to move to Bolton on the Jackson-Vicksburg road. Sherman's corps would be positioned on the Union's right as Grant's army did an about-face to confront its enemy on the west instead of the east. Grant ordered Major General Francis Blair, Jr., then near Auburn, to move his division, part of Sherman's Fifteenth Corps, quickly to Edwards Station, also on the Jackson-Vicksburg road west of Bolton. Grant further ordered McPherson to clear his supply wagons from the roads to make way for the advancing Union troops, and he ordered McClernand to begin an advance on the Raymond road, moving toward the rebel position.

By midmorning on the 16th Grant's forces were moving toward what was to Grant a long-sought showdown fight with Pemberton's Vicksburg defenders. Union skirmishers, advancing in front of the forward units, were already exchanging fire with rebel pickets, and Union artillery had already opened up on the rebel positions.

When he learned that a Union column was headed toward him, Pemberton gave up on joining forces with Johnston. Responding to General Loring's urging, he began looking for a likely location where he could establish a line of defense against the rapidly approaching Union forces. About three-fourths of a mile west of Ellison's plantation, Pemberton noticed a ridge, the highest point of which was called Champion Hill. Pemberton ordered the defensive line to be laid there. Grant thought it was a site well selected, "whether taken by accident or design," he commented. "It is one of the highest points in that section, and commanded all the ground in range. On the east side of the ridge, which is quite precipitous, is a ravine running first north, then westerly, terminating at Baker's Creek. It was grown up thickly with large trees and undergrowth, making it difficult to penetrate with troops, even when not defended.... On the west side the slope of the ridge is gradual and is cultivated from near the summit to the creek."[88]

At that ridge Grant hurled his army. He put McPherson in tactical control of the assault, and at ten-thirty in the morning of May 16, McPherson gave the signal that sent the division of General Hovey, of McClernand's corps, and the division of General Logan, of McPherson's corps, some 10,000 men altogether, storming forward, yelling and cheering. By early afternoon, after fierce fighting, the Union troops had swept across the crest of Champion Hill, driving the Confederates before them in disarray.

Facing disaster, Pemberton ordered a counterattack, which struck the surprised Union troops at the crossroads south of Champion Hill and drove them back over the hill. Union reinforcements, however—the divisions of generals Osterhaus and Carr, both of McClernand's corps—struck the flank of the outnumbered Confederates and forced a withdrawal that turned into a rout as rebel soldiers dropped their weapons and ran pell-mell through the woods to escape. Others suffered the storm of Union fire as they dashed back to the crossroads with McClernand's troops at their heels.

Apprised of the desperate situation, Pemberton sent word to his commanders to fall back northwestward to Edwards Station and ordered Brigadier General Lloyd Tilghman to have his brigade hold the Baker's Creek bridge at all costs until the retreating rebel army had crossed it—a mission Tilghman accomplished, but at the cost of his life. In hot pursuit of the retreating Confederates. Grant's troops crossed Baker's Creek late in the afternoon and continued on toward Edwards Station, reaching there about eight o'clock that evening and finding the community blazing with the supplies and equipment the rebels had set afire before swiftly moving farther westward. At Edwards Station Grant called it a day for his worn and weary troops, and they bivouacked for the night.

The Battle of Champion Hill had been fought, Grant affirmed in his official report, "mainly by Hovey's division, of McClernand's corps, and Logan's and Quinby's divisions ... of McPherson's corps."[89] Both sides had paid a stiff price for the results at Champion Hill, especially the Confederates, who from a force of 22,000 men had lost 381 killed, 1,018 wounded and 2,441 missing, a total loss of 3,840 men. From a Union force of 32,000 Grant had lost 410 killed, 1,844 wounded and 187 missing, a total loss of 2,441.

McClernand Leads the Pursuit

At three-thirty the next morning, Sunday, May 17, 1863, the Union force resumed its pursuit of the rebels, with McClernand's corps in the advance. About six miles from where they had spent the night, the lead troops came upon the Confederate fortifications at the Big Black River. Quickly preparing to assault the rebel position, General Carr of McClernand's corps deployed his men to the right of the road, and General Osterhaus of McClernand's corps deployed his column to the left. McPherson's column was on the road in the rear, ready to throw itself into the battle as needed.

Seeing the Union assault carrying the rebel position on the east side of the river, the Confederate troops on the west side set fire to the bridge, stranding their comrades on the east side between the swarming Union troops and the river. Many of the trapped rebel soldiers plunged into the river to escape. Some succeeded; others drowned. By 9:00 a.m. the Confederate position had been captured by McClernand's troops. Also captured were 1,751 Confederate soldiers and eighteen guns. Union losses were thirty-nine killed and 237 wounded. The destruction of the bridge temporarily stalled the Union pursuit of Pemberton's army, and Grant's force had to wait until new bridges—three of them—could be built by his engineers, using felled trees and lumber taken from buildings nearby. By eight o'clock on the morning of Monday, May 18, the new bridges had been completed and the Union troops were marching across them, bound for Vicksburg.

At Vicksburg the dispirited rebel troops were soon organized by their officers and put to work preparing for the arrival of their pursuers, some details repairing the earthworks that had been damaged by the recent heavy rains, and many others laboriously cutting down trees in nearby woods to erect a lengthy abatis outside the perimeter of the earthworks. By the morning of the 19th Vicksburg and its defenders stood ready to face the coming Union assault.

Eager to follow up the staggering blow he had struck at Champion Hill, and believing the rebel defenders were demoralized and weary after the defeat and retreat, Grant ordered an attack on Vicksburg's defenses the day after his army reached the city's approaches, many of his troops having arrived during the night of the 18th. At ten o'clock on the morning of May 19 Grant's artillery commenced a bombardment of the Confederates' earthworks with shot and shell, continuing the thunderous assault until two in the afternoon. As the smoke began to clear, the Union infantry advanced on the rebel entrenchments. Sherman's corps was positioned on the right side of the advancing line; McPherson's corps was in the center; and McClernand's corps was on the left, its troops in a line that stretched to the Mississippi River.

"The rebel parapets were strongly manned, and the enemy fought hard and well," Sherman reported in his account of the fight, and although some Union troops reached the tops of the parapets, they could not cross over. When darkness came, the Union troops drew back and began digging in. The assault had cost Grant's forces 942 casualties, counting killed, wounded and missing. The action had succeeded only in securing more advanced positions, Grant pointed out, putting the best face on the failure.

On May 20, the day after the hurried, failed attack, Grant called his three corps commanders together for a critique. "We compared notes," Sherman related, "and agreed that the assault of the day before had failed, by reason of the natural strength of the position, and because we were forced by the nature of the ground to limit our attacks to the strongest parts of the enemy's line, viz., where the three principal roads entered the city."[90] Unfazed by the failure, Grant on May 21 issued orders for a new general assault on the whole rebel line, commencing at 10 a.m. on the 22nd. Grant recounted the following in his official report:

Promptly at the hour designated, the three army corps then in front of the enemy's works commenced the assault. I had taken a commanding position near McPherson's front, and from which I could see all the advancing columns from his corps, and a part of each of Sherman's and McClernand's.... About 12 m. I received a dispatch from McClernand that he was hard pressed at several points, in reply to which I directed him to re-enforce the points hard pressed from such troops as he had that were not engaged. I then rode around to Sherman, and had just reached there when I received a second dispatch from McClernand, stating positively and unequivocally that he was in possession of and still held two of the enemy's forts; that the American flag then waved over them, and asking me to have Sherman and McPherson make a diversion in his favor. This dispatch I showed to Sherman, who immediately ordered a renewal of the assault on his front.

I also sent an answer to McClernand, directing him to order up [Major General John] McArthur to his assistance, and started immediately to the position I had just left on McPherson's line, to convey to him the information from McClernand by this last dispatch, that he might make the diversion requested. Before reaching McPherson, I met a messenger with a third dispatch from McClernand, of which the following is a copy:

HEADQUARTERS THIRTEENTH ARMY CORPS,
In the Field, near Vicksburg, Miss., May 22, 1863.

Maj. Gen. U.S. Grant:
General,: We have gained the enemy's intrenchments at several points, but are brought to a stand. I have sent word to McArthur to re-enforce me if he can. Would it not be best to concentrate the whole or a part of his command on this point?
John A. McClernand,
Major-General, Commanding

P.S.—I have received your dispatch. My troops are all engaged, and I cannot withdraw any to re-enforce others.

The position occupied by me during most of the time of the assault [Grant continued in his report] gave me a better opportunity of seeing what was going on in front of the Thirteenth Army Corps than I believed it possible for the commander of it to have. I could not see his possession of forts, nor necessity for re-enforcements, as represented by his dispatches, up to the time I left it, which was between 12 m. and 1 p.m. and I expressed doubts of their correctness, which doubts the facts subsequently, but too late, confirmed. At the time I could not disregard his reiterated statements, for they might possibly be true; and that no possible opportunity of carrying the enemy's stronghold should be allowed to escape through fault of mine, I ordered Quinby's division, which was all of McPherson's corps then present but four brigades, to report to McClernand, and notified him of the order. I showed his dispatches to McPherson, as I had to Sherman, to satisfy him of the necessity of an active diversion on their part to hold as much force in their fronts as possible. The diversion was promptly and vigorously made, and resulted in the increase of our mortality list fully 50 per cent, without advancing our position or giving us other advantages.[91]

Grant now determined that McClernand had misrepresented the situation and the facts. What was more, the assault proved another failure. Grant decided he would make no more bloody assaults, but would resort to siege tactics. "The experience of the 22d," he wrote, "convinced officers and men that this was best, and they went to work on the defences and approaches with a will. With the navy holding the river, the investment of Vicksburg was complete. As long as we could hold our position the enemy was limited in supplies of food, men and munitions of war to what they had on hand. These could not last always."[92]

By the morning of the 23rd Grant had decided to relieve McClernand because of his false dispatch stating that he held two of the enemy's forts. Then he changed his mind. He decided it would be better to keep McClernand in his command until the end of the Vicksburg siege; and after that, he would induce McClernand to take a leave of absence. In the meantime, he would closely supervise all of McClernand's operations and would place no reliance on McClernand's reports unless they were corroborated.[93]

Then, before the month was out, McClernand blundered again, this time mortally wounding his military career. On May 30 he issued his General Order No. 72, which purported to be a letter of congratulations to his troops. But as General McPherson interpreted it, "it was written more to influence public sentiment at the North and impress the public mind with the magnificent strategy, superior tactics, and brilliant deeds of the major-general commanding the Thirteenth Army Corps than to congratulate his troops upon their well-merited successes."[94] "Though styled an order," General Sherman concluded, "[it] is not an order. It orders nothing, but is in the nature of an address to soldiers, manifestly designed for publication for ulterior political purposes. It perverts the truth to the ends of flattery and self-glorification, and contains many untruths, among which is one of monstrous falsehood."[95] The so-called order came to Grant's attention by way of Sherman, who sent a published copy of it to him along with an explanatory note dated June 17, 1863:

> On my return last evening from an inspection of the new works at Snyder's Bluff, General [Frank] Blair, who commands the Second Division of my corps, called my attention to the inclosed publication in the Memphis Evening Bulletin of June 13, instant, entitled "Congratulatory Order of General McClernand," with a request that I should notice it, lest the statements of fact and inference contained therein might receive credence from an excited public.... I beg to call his [McClernand's] attention to the requirements of General Orders, No. 151, of 1862, which actually forbids the publication of all official letters and reports, and requires the name of the writer to be laid before the President of the United States for dismissal.[96]

Grant immediately sent a copy to McClernand and asked him if it was what he had written. He replied that it was and blamed his adjutant for its not having been submitted to Grant beforehand: "The newspaper slip is a correct copy of my congratulatory order, No. 72. I am prepared to maintain its statements. I regret that my adjutant did not send you a copy promptly, as he ought, and I thought he had."[97] After reciting, in extravagant detail and fulsome language, all the deeds of the Thirteenth Corps since it left had Milliken's Bend, the "order" went on to criticize, with distortions, the other units of Grant's command:

> On the 22d, in pursuance of the order from the commander of the department, you [McClernand's troops] assaulted the enemy's defenses in front at 10 a.m., and within thirty minutes had made a lodgment and planted your colors upon two of his bastions. This partial success called into exercise the highest heroism, and was only gained by a bloody and protracted struggle; yet it was gained, and was the first and largest success achieved under a scorching sun and destructive fire, you firmly held your footing, and only withdrew when the enemy had largely massed their forces and concentrated their attack upon you. How and why the general assault failed, it would be useless now to

explain. The Thirteenth Army Corps, acknowledging the good intentions of all, would scorn indulgence in weak regrets and idle criminations. According justice to all, it would only defend itself. If, while the enemy was massing to crush it, assistance was asked for by a diversion at other points, or by re-enforcement, it only asked what in one case Major-General Grant had specifically and peremptorily ordered, namely, simultaneous and persistent attack all along our lines until the enemy's outer works should be carried, and what, in the other, by massing a strong force in time upon a weakened point, would have probably insured success.[98]

Grant now had finally had enough of McClernand. On June 18 he issued, through his assistant adjutant general, the following order, Special Order No. 164: "Maj. Gen. John A. McClernand is hereby relieved from the command of the Thirteenth Army Corps. He will proceed to any point he may select in the State of Illinois, and report by letter to Headquarters of the Army for orders. Maj. Gen. E.O.C. Ord is hereby appointed to the command of the Thirteenth Army Corps, subject to the approval of the President, and will immediately assume charge of the same."[99]

McClernand reacted by pulling every political string he could think of, protesting to every political person of influence he knew, from President Lincoln on down to Secretary Stanton, Secretary Chase, Illinois governor Richard Yates, Illinois senator Lyman Trumbull and others. He asked Lincoln for a court of inquiry to investigate the whole matter. Lincoln refused. McClernand's campaign for reinstatement continued for months. Finally, in January 1864, under intense pressure from McClernand supporters and thinking of the coming presidential election, Lincoln agreed to return command of the Thirteenth Corps to McClernand, and McClernand and parts of the corps were shipped off to Louisiana to man the largely useless outposts that General Banks, McClernand's new commander, had established along the Texas gulf coast.

Meanwhile, Grant and his Army of the Tennessee had captured Vicksburg on July 4, 1863, and, with the surrender of Port Hudson on July 9, had opened the Mississippi River, restoring passage on the entire river and splitting the Confederacy in two, a mighty and long-sought achievement, the great objective of the Union's Mississippi River campaign. By his victories Grant had become the Union's preeminent military hero—and was untouchable by McClernand's venomous, vengeful attempts to sully him.

On April 11, 1864, Banks called McClernand back to Louisiana from Texas to take command of the units of the Thirteenth Corps that were participating in Banks's disastrous Red River campaign. Banks had just suffered defeat at Mansfield, and his beaten army had withdrawn to Alexandria, where he ordered his troops to dig in. By April 27 McClernand was again commanding troops in the field, this time from a defensive position that Banks had ordered to protect against the heavily outnumbered Confederates. McClernand, though suffering from malaria, argued for launching an attack against the approaching rebels, but Banks declined.

On May 1, finally giving in to the effects of his malaria, McClernand put Brigadier General Michael Lawler in command of the Thirteenth Corps and went on sick leave. After several days McClernand insisted that he was getting better but at last realized he was not. He left his troops and returned home to Illinois to recuperate. In June, after Grant had become general in chief, the Thirteenth Corps was disbanded, its regiments assigned to other commands in the Department of the Gulf.

McClernand (on right) with President Lincoln. McClernand managed to maintain his connection with the president, as when he visited the Antietam battlefield here with Lincoln and Lincoln's friend Allan Pinkerton. When Grant relieved McClernand of his command, McClernand immediately appealed to Lincoln and to every other political person of influence he knew (Library of Congress).

McClernand's army, like his army life, had come to an end. It took him a while to realize it, however. In July, while still on leave, he wrote to Secretary Stanton proposing a new command embracing the areas along the Mississippi from St. Louis, having in mind being the commander of it. Stanton never responded.

During the 1864 presidential campaign he kept himself busy stumping for George McClellan, the Democrats' candidate, whom Lincoln beat handily. On November 23, after the election, every ray of hope for renewal of his military career having darkened, McClernand resigned from the army. With more candor than kindness, General Grant gave his reaction to the resignation: "I am satisfied the good of the service will be advanced by [his] withdrawal from service."[100]

McClernand returned to the practice of law in Springfield and continued his political activities, serving as chairman of the Illinois State Democratic Committee, making speeches at political rallies, including the 1868 Democratic convention, and serving as chairman of the 1876 national Democratic convention. He later served as commissioner of the Utah Territory, appointed by President Grover Cleveland. In 1895, when he was eighty-three years old and in poor health as well as poor circumstances, the Illinois legislature awarded him a pension of one hundred dollars a month. He died five years later, on September 23, 1900, survived by his wife, Minerva, and three children, to whom he left his estate amounting to eight hundred dollars and a piece of real estate. Dressed in his major general's uniform, he was buried in Oak Ridge Cemetery in Springfield, not far from Lincoln's tomb.

6

Major General Stephen Augustus Hurlbut

Before the War: Born November 29, 1815, in Charleston, South Carolina, son of a Unitarian minister from Massachusetts and a South Carolina mother. Studied law, admitted to the bar in 1837. Became active in Charleston civic organizations and in Whig political organization and campaigns. Escaping financial problems, he moved from Charleston to northern Illinois in 1845 and settled in Belvidere, a county seat, where he opened a law practice and resumed his political activities. Married Sophronie Stevens, the sister of his law partner's wife, in 1847. Children: a son. Political affiliation: Whig, Republican. Was a Whig elector in the 1848 presidential election. Elected to the Illinois House of Representatives in 1859 and in 1861. During the 1848 presidential campaign he met Abraham Lincoln, a fellow Whig who was then a U.S. congressman from Illinois, and campaigned with him on behalf of the candidacy of Zachary Taylor. He tried and failed repeatedly to gain election to the U.S. House of Representatives. Became a Republican and in 1856 campaigned for the Republicans' unsuccessful presidential candidate, John Frémont. Military experience: Served as a sergeant in the South Carolina militia, later promoted to lieutenant and served as regimental adjutant. In 1840 he served with the militia during the Seminole War in Florida but saw no combat. He later served as the elected captain of an Illinois militia company that saw no active service.

When Captain Stephen Hurlbut, commander of the thirty-three member Boone Rifles militia company and a political friend of the president of the United States, saw that he was not going to be rewarded with a plum for his vigorous campaigning in behalf of Lincoln in the 1860 presidential election, he shifted his aspirations toward a presidential appointment as a brigadier general in the volunteer army that President Lincoln had called for following the assault on Fort Sumter in April 1861. Hurlbut had already performed a service for the new president, bravely but fearfully accepting a mission to scope out the political situation in Charleston shortly before the Fort Sumter attack. Knowing that Hurlbut had useful connections in Charleston, Lincoln had asked him to accompany Ward Lamon, Lincoln's troubleshooter and former law partner, on a fact-finding visit to Charleston to see just how bad things were there. (Things were hopelessly bad, Hurlbut and Lamon went back and reported to Lincoln.)

With the support of Illinois' governor and other political influentials, Hurlbut got the appointment. But before the Senate could get around to confirming it, Hurlbut managed to get himself into a position that made his confirmation doubtful. Under orders from Major General George McClellan, commanding the Department of the Ohio, the military district that included Illinois and Missouri, Hurlbut, now a brigade commander pending his Senate confirmation, was to take his troops to Missouri to prevent rebel raiders from harassing the Hannibal & St. Joseph Railroad, which ran across northern Missouri. His apparent anxiety over leading troops in an actual military movement, as opposed to dressing up in colorful uniforms and merely drilling and parading, drove him into binges of heavy drinking, resort to alcohol being one of his persistent weaknesses.

In Chicago, where he was supposed to be preparing his units for their mission in Missouri, he spent much of his time carousing and in so doing spent much of the government money meant for his troops. His flagrant drunkenness drew the attention of the *Chicago Tribune*'s renowned editor, Joseph Medill. When Hurlbut finally departed Chicago, taking the Nineteenth Illinois Regiment with him, Medill observed that Hurlbut left "in a sad condition—scarcely able to walk at all, so drunk was he." Medill wrote to Illinois senator Lyman Trumbull, who would vote on Hurlbut's confirmation: "Will the Senate inflict this confirmed sot upon the army?"[1]

Maj. Gen. Stephen Hurlbut. President Lincoln appointed him a major general despite his reputation as a drunk. The editor of the *Chicago Tribune,* Joseph Medill, protested to Illinois senator Lyman Trumbull, who would vote on Hurlbut's confirmation: "Will the Senate inflict this confirmed sot upon the army?" (Library of Congress).

Nevertheless, Hurlbut carried on, with his orders and with his habits. The mission proved to be truly impossible. In July 1861 the army created a Department of the West, comprising the states west of the Mississippi River as far as the Rocky Mountains, plus Illinois, and appointed Major General John Frémont as its commander, with headquarters in St. Louis. Organizing his command and moving to suppress secessionist forces, Frémont appointed Brigadier General John Pope, a West Point graduate and veteran of the Mexican War, to command the newly created military District of North Missouri, making him Hurlbut's immediate superior. Pope decided the way to protect the railroads in his district was to reduce the number of troops strung out along the rail lines and to cluster them at railway stations and other points. Hurlbut, in attempting to fulfill his mission to guard the rails, would have to function with a reduced force.

That handicap, plus his inexperience at combat and facing a rebel guerrilla army twice the size of his force so frustrated Hurlbut that he once again took refuge in the bottle. A *New York Times* correspondent reported that he had frequently seen Hurlbut so drunk that he couldn't walk and that ordinary soldiers, seeing him fallen on the ground, would pick him up and take him to his quarters. Even so, on August 5 the U.S. Senate confirmed his appointment as a brigadier general.

The enemy that he faced—other than himself—was a rebel force called the Missouri State Guard, commanded by Colonel Martin Green, who consistently outsmarted, outgeneraled and outmaneuvered Hurlbut. In early September 1861, expecting a dreaded confrontation with Green's army, Hurlbut prepared himself for battle by getting drunk en route by rail with 350 men of his Third Iowa Regiment. The plan was to reinforce the regiment of Colonel Nelson Williams, which was holding the town of Shelbina against an assault by Green's rebels. But Hurlbut had so delayed his arrival to reinforce Williams that Williams had to evacuate the town and withdraw, marching toward Macon City, where Hurlbut had stopped the train and learned that Williams had abandoned Shelbina. Hurlbut then decided to sit comfortably on his idled train and wait for Williams to reach Macon City on foot.

It was about eight in the evening when Williams arrived in Macon City, where Hurlbut had been making a drunken spectacle of himself in the town's streets. When Williams reported to Hurlbut, he found Hurlbut too drunk to command, too drunk to stand, and he ordered him arrested, then had him confined in a railroad car until Hurlbut sobered up later that night.

On September 7, having received reports of Hurlbut's drunken behavior, Pope had him arrested and charged with dereliction of duty and incompetence. The matter went to Frémont, who ordered Hurlbut home on furlough. Newspapers in Missouri and Illinois poured out an assortment of editorial opinion on Hurlbut, some supporting him, others expressing outrage over his alleged misconduct. The *Chicago Tribune* declared that if the charges against Hurlbut proved to be true, a clamor for his removal from command should "resound in every hall and chamber of the White House, whence his appointment came."[2] The *Hannibal (Missouri) Messenger* said it hoped that if Hurlbut was found guilty, "this will be the last whisky appointment the President will make."[3]

In the end, President Lincoln, unwilling to have an Illinois Republican general sacked, dismissed the objections made by some of his ordinarily persuasive friends and, heeding the plea of Illinois' Republican governor, Richard Yates, who himself had a reputation as a drunk, returned Hurlbut to active duty in December 1861. In January 1862 he reported, as ordered, to the training camp at Benton Barracks, near St. Louis, and set about drilling new recruits, a job he handled well.

In February he got a new assignment, in the Army of the Tennessee, whose commander, General Grant, had been recently promoted to major general in recognition of his victories at Fort Henry and Fort Donelson. By Grant's appointment, Hurlbut became commander of his army's Fourth Division. Grant had known Hurlbut briefly when he had served under him for three weeks as a regimental commander in Hurlbut's division in Missouri. Grant was not put off by reports of Hurlbut's intemperance. A victim of reports of drunkenness himself, he knew such reports were often more sensational than factual.

Hurlbut received the new command just in time to participate in the Union's major thrust into the heart of the Confederacy. Hurlbut's division and five others, totaling nearly 49,000 men, supported by Navy gunboats, were to move up the Tennessee River deep into Tennessee, and on March 10 they got under way. When Hurlbut's troops disembarked at Pittsburg Landing on March 17 to await the massing of Grant's army for an attack on Corinth, Mississippi, they took a position on what became an irregular line that formed a rough semicircle around the landing, facing mostly south, in the direction of Corinth.

The right side of the line was occupied by Sherman's division, with McClernand's division on Sherman's left, and General Prentiss's division on the left of McClernand's. On Prentiss's left, on the extreme left side of the line, was a brigade of Sherman's division, commanded by Colonel David Stuart. Hurlbut's division was positioned as a reserve behind Prentiss's troops, with its left flank on the bluff of the twisting Tennessee River, upstream of the landing. The division of General C.F. Smith, which was commanded by Brigadier General W.H.L. Wallace after Smith had been become incapacitated by illness, was in reserve on the right side of the line.[4] Altogether, the Union force numbered about 33,000 effectives.[5]

Hurlbut's three brigades were commanded by Colonel James Veatch, Brigadier General Jacob Lauman and Colonel Nelson Williams, the officer who had ordered him arrested in Missouri and confined in a railroad car until he had sobered up. While they awaited the arrival of General Buell, marching from Nashville to reinforce Grant's army, Confederate skirmishers began approaching the Union line in increasing numbers. Hurlbut grew eager to send his troops out to meet them and precipitate a major engagement, but he was restrained by Sherman. And so, like the rest of the troops along the Union line, Hurlbut and his men waited.

Then suddenly, at dawn on Sunday, April 6, 1862, a wave of some 45,000 Confederate attackers crashed against the entire Union front. A private in Company D of the 15th Illinois Infantry Regiment, of Hurlbut's division, described the shock: "The camp was alarmed Sunday morning just as the streaks of red begin to ringe [*sic*] the eastern sky, by the rapid firing of the pickets, who soon came in with the report that the enemy was marching on us in overwhelming numbers and were even now in sight.... There was no time to give orders then.... The enemy was in camp before it had time to arouse and form a line. Some were shot in their sleep, never knowing what hurt them. Terrible and complete was the surprise."[6]

Prentiss's division, in front of Hurlbut's position, absorbed the assault and attempted to hold its line while troops on either side of it fell back, exposing Prentiss's flanks. It was forced to give ground, gradually falling back to a spot in a heavily wooded area where the depression created by an old roadway formed a trench that provided cover for Prentiss's desperately embattled fighters as their general rallied them to maintain their resistance. The struggle went on for hours, Prentiss's stubborn troops repelling eleven rebel assaults on their line and exacting a staggering toll on their attackers. So intense was the prolonged combat the spot became known as the Hornets' Nest.

As units of Prentiss's division fell back, they passed through Hurlbut's position, and Hurlbut's artillery quickly moved into action and opened on the advancing Confederates. Braving the intense fire of muskets and artillery, Hurlbut mounted his horse and rode up to the front to urge his men on as they repelled a rebel bayonet charge with fierce musket fire. When the Confederate advance concentrated on Sherman's division, Hurlbut ordered Veatch's brigade to reinforce Sherman. He later led two of his brigades to reinforce Prentiss.

Eventually, Hurlbut had to give ground, falling back to a new line nearer the landing as the rebels pressed their advance. Grant strengthened the left side of the Union line by moving up fifty artillery pieces to halt the advance while the two Union gunboats, the *Lexington* and the *Tyler*, stood in the river firing broadsides into the rebel ranks. Before the day was done, the Confederates made one more desperate attempt to turn the Union left flank but were repulsed. After thirteen hours of fighting, the troops of both sides were exhausted. General Beauregard, who had assumed command of the Confederate forces after General A.S. Johnston had been mortally wounded, at last ordered his troops to disengage and pull back a short distance, then bivouac for the long, rainy night that was to follow.

Hurlbut and his men, along with Prentiss and his troops, had played an important part in staving off a disastrous defeat by holding the left side of the Union line against repeated strong attacks by the Confederates, allowing time for the right side of the line to fall back toward the landing and form a tight new semicircular perimeter and, at the same time, foiling Beauregard's plan to turn the Union left flank and drive Grant's entire army into the swamps north of the landing. Hurlbut's division had paid a heavy price, as had all the other divisions, especially Prentiss's, which, as Grant reported, "was gone." Valiantly holding on against the rebel attackers till the last minute, Prentiss had at last surrendered to the Confederates, and he and 2,200 of his men, including a Missouri regiment that had reinforced him, had become prisoners.

Grant was bloodied but unbeaten. Overnight his force had swelled with the arrival of the 5,000 men of Lew Wallace's division, which for disputed reasons had failed to reach the battlefield on the 6th, and the timely arrival of General Buell's 20,000 troops during Sunday night, bringing the total Union force to about 40,000 effectives. They would be facing a rebel army now severely diminished by losses and amounting to no more than Buell's troops alone. "So confident was I before firing had ceased on the 6th that the next day would bring victory to our arms if we could only take the initiative," Grant related, "that I visited each division commander in person before any reenforcements had reached the field. I directed them to throw out heavy lines of skirmishers in the morning as soon as they could see, and push them forward until they found the enemy, following with their entire divisions in supporting distance, and to engage the enemy as soon as found."[7]

On the morning of Monday, April 7, shortly after sunrise, Grant's army was on the move. Grant described the battle formation of the Union force, now on the offensive: "General Lew Wallace was on the right, Sherman on his left; then McClernand, and then Hurlbut. Nelson, of Buell's army, was on our extreme left, next to the river; Crittenden was next in line after Nelson, and on his right; McCook followed, and formed the extreme right of Buell's command. My old command thus formed the right wing, while the troops directly under Buell constituted the left wing of the army."[8]

Grant's orders were for his divisions to advance and recapture their original camps. Buell would be commanding his divisions independently over Grant, but would be coordinating his advance with Grant's. Moving forward over the ground that the Confederates had won and from which they had withdrawn when the engagement ended late Sunday afternoon, Sherman's troops soon reached the extreme right of McClernand's former position. Lew Wallace, as ordered, moved west and then south. McClernand moved forward, and with him, Hurlbut. As he led his troops in helping McClernand's division drive the

Confederates back, as ordered by Grant, Hurlbut had a horse shot from under him and was slightly wounded when a rebel bullet grazed his arm.

By ten o'clock Monday morning the sounds of battle from the left side of the Union line revealed that Buell's divisions were advancing as well. As the Union forces drove ahead and converged, the area around Shiloh Church became the focus of their attack, the fighting growing in intensity as the morning wore on. "The battle raged furiously for four hours," one of Beauregard's aides, Colonel Jacob Thompson, related. "About 11:30 o'clock it was apparent that the enemy's main attack was on our left, and our forces began to yield ground to the vigor of his attack."[9]

Sometime after noon, Beauregard realized his situation had undergone a dangerous reversal. It became obvious to him that Grant had received substantial reinforcements overnight and that the Confederate force was now outnumbered and facing fresh troops. He instructed members of his staff to ride out and tell the corps commanders to retire, slowly and in good order, making a graceful exit from the field of battle. He positioned a strong rear guard near Shiloh Church to cover the withdrawal, and by four o'clock Monday afternoon his army was trudging over muddy, rain-soaked roads toward Corinth. "The roads were almost impassable," Grant related. "The enemy carrying his artillery and supply trains over them in his retreat, made them still worse for troops following. I wanted to pursue, but had not the heart to order the men who had fought desperately for two days, lying in the mud and rain whenever not fighting, and I did not feel disposed to positively order Buell, or any part of his command, to pursue."[10]

Reaching Corinth, Beauregard had his troops establish a strong defensive position to protect the town and its rail lines from the Union advance he knew would soon come from Pittsburg Landing. General Halleck, meanwhile, now decided to supersede Grant as commander in the field and he and the Army of the Tennessee slowly, cautiously crept toward Corinth, digging lines of entrenchment every few miles until the Union forces were finally close enough to besiege the town and open an artillery bombardment on it. Outnumbered, threatened by the possibility of a huge Union flanking movement that would cut off his communication, and plagued by widespread disease among his troops, Beauregard decided on a strategic withdrawal, and on the night of May 29–30 he and his army stealthily stole away, leaving to the Union forces the town he had earlier said was crucial to the defense of the entire Mississippi River valley and possibly to the survival of the Confederate cause.

Hurlbut and his division were then ordered by Halleck to march to LaGrange, Tennessee, about thirty-five miles west of Corinth and about forty-five miles east of Memphis, to protect the Memphis & Charleston Railroad. About three months later, in July 1862, command of the Army of the Tennessee was returned to Grant, and he appointed Hurlbut commander of the military District of Memphis, the city of Memphis having been captured by Union forces following the U.S. Navy's victory over the Confederates' River Defense Fleet at the Memphis riverfront on June 6. On July 15 Hurlbut and his division marched into Memphis. He set up a headquarters and remained there until September 5, when he moved to Bolivar, Tennessee, about sixty miles east of Memphis.

On September 17 Hurlbut received a promotion to major general, which Grant had recommended to President Lincoln, and on September 24 he was assigned by Grant as commander of the District of Jackson, with headquarters in Jackson, Tennessee, an important rail center about eighty miles northeast of Memphis.

Hurlbut's next action in the field came in October 1862. Confederate Major General Earl Van Dorn got the idea that he could take Corinth on his way into middle Tennessee to support a rebel thrust into Kentucky. The idea proved a serious miscalculation of the strength of Union defenses at Corinth, commanded by Major General William Rosecrans, and on October 3–4 Van Dorn's army of 22,800 was repulsed in a fierce battle in which Confederate casualties amounted to 20 percent of their force. Van Dorn and his beaten army hastily withdrew to the northwest, toward Ripley, Mississippi, and General Grant quickly moved to intercept and crush them. Grant ordered Major General Edward Ord to march a force from Bolivar and move down the west bank of the Hatchie River, about fifteen miles northwest of Corinth, to prevent Van Dorn from crossing, trapping him on the east side of the river, where Rosecrans would attack the fleeing rebels from their rear. Ord's force would include Hurlbut's Fourth Division of the Army of the Tennessee and a brigade comprising the Sixty-eighth Ohio Regiment and the Twelfth Michigan Regiment. The infantry would be supported by two Ohio cavalry battalions.

The Confederates reached the river first, arriving on the morning of October 5 and intending to cross at Davis Bridge. Their advance unit set up a defensive position to guard the bridge from the heights overlooking the river and was soon challenged by the advance of Hurlbut's brigades, Veatch's brigade in the lead, with skirmishers in front. When the skirmishers encountered fire from a farmhouse on the west side of the river, Hurlbut ordered a battery of the Second Illinois Light Artillery to shell the building, and a few rounds chased off the rebel defenders.

By then, Ord had come up to take command of the situation. Also, the Confederates had established a line of defense on the east side, but determined to meet Hurlbut's advance on the west side of the river, forming a line with about 700 men. After exchanging fire for nearly an hour, the Confederates were running out of ammunition. Noticing the reduced gunfire, Ord ordered Hurlbut's troops to charge the rebel line with bayonets, which sent the heavily outnumbered Confederates running back to the bridge in a rout. Not all made it, including about 200 who were taken prisoner.

While the thin rebel line on the west side had been resisting the Union advance, rebel reinforcements from Van Dorn's column were arriving on the east bank and forming up a battle line supported by artillery. Ord now decided to engage it, rather than merely hold the bridge and prevent Van Dorn from crossing the Hatchie while Rosecrans, according to Grant's plan, approached from Van Dorn's rear. It was a deadly mistake. The advantage that the Union troops had in opposing an army trying to funnel itself into and across a narrow bridge, presenting a narrow front highly vulnerable to defensive fire, was reversed, the advantage shifting to the rebels, who poured volleys of musket and artillery fire into the onrushing Union column. The survivors immediately dispersed to the right and left, seeking cover on the river's east bank. Hurlbut described the desperate situation in his official report:

> The infantry, under orders from Major-General Ord, who was constantly at the front, were thrown across the bridge, together with Bolton's battery. This was done under heavy fire of musketry and canister and was one of the most gallant deeds of record. It unfortunately happened that the peculiarities of the ground on the east side of the Hatchie were not so familiar to the major-general commanding as to those of us who had previously encamped on the very hill we now sought to seize, hence the order to throw the regiments alternately right and left of the road massed six regiments of men

in a triangular space of ground which would have been abundantly occupied by one. They were exposed in this mass to a flanking fire of canister from a battery on their left, and here the great loss of men took place."[11]

Hurlbut Takes Command

Among the casualties was General Ord, who, while rushing across the bridge to try to salvage his army from the disaster he had created, was hit by a blast of canister shot and forced to take himself out of the action, turning command over to Hurlbut. Rather than withdraw from the east bank and expose the men to the dangers of crossing the bridge again, Hurlbut, now on the east side himself, ordered the regiments already on the east bank to quickly extend their line to the left and take the hill that rose north of the road. Within thirty minutes Hurlbut's troops took the hill, gaining a commanding position. "The batteries were rapidly run forward," Hurlbut reported, "and placed by Major Campbell, chief of artillery, in positions of mutual support. Some sharp artillery firing then took place, ending in silencing the enemy's battery.... The battle virtually ceased about 3:30 p.m. the enemy making a strong demonstration at that hour on General Lauman's right, which was met by a change of front by that brigade. Under cover of this movement they hauled off their crippled battery, leaving the caissons, and retreated southward, crossing the Hatchie that night at Crum's Mill, 6 miles up the river."[12]

Hurlbut had wrung victory from disaster. But Grant's plan to trap the Confederates had failed because Rosecrans and his troops didn't show up in time to trap them. Rosecrans received his orders from Grant in the afternoon of October 4, calling for him to move immediately, but he ignored the order for immediacy and didn't move out until the morning of the 5th, much too late to be of any effective use. Once the rebel army had crossed the Hatchie, its flight continued until it had reached Holly Springs, Mississippi, some sixty miles west and south of Corinth. What was more, the victory had come at a stiff price. The Union force had suffered a loss of 570 officers and men, killed, wounded, missing or captured. Ninety-two had been killed.

On October 8 Hurlbut, back in Bolivar, Tennessee, issued a congratulatory message to his troops and, reverting to the loquacity that had served him well as a politician, paid fulsome tribute to those killed in action: "Our dead—our glorious dead! The joy of victory is dimmed when we think of them. But they died as they would wish—died in defense of the Union and the laws; died bravely on the red field of battle with their unconquered banner over them." He ended the message by urging his troops on, attempting to inspire them with a self-serving exhortation: "Officers and men, continue to deserve your lofty reputation, and then as heretofore you will receive the approbation of your general and strengthen his hands in the performance of his duties."[13]

Despite having demonstrated that he had some ability on the battlefield, Hurlbut earned no new opportunities to display it. In a reorganization of the Army of the Tennessee on October 26, 1862, Grant appointed him commander of a new Thirteenth Corps, a promotion from division commander, but kept him assigned to the District of Jackson, to Hurlbut's keen annoyance. On November 25 Grant came up with a new assignment for him, appointing him commander of the military District of Memphis, another administrative job, in which

Memphis in the 1860s. Although Hurlbut displayed some military ability on the battlefield, Grant shifted him into an administrative job, making him commander of the military District of Memphis, with headquarters in Memphis. Here he gained a reputation for abusing his power and enriching himself and returned to his drinking habit (Library of Congress).

he succeeded Sherman. In Memphis Hurlbut's combat was not in the field but was with smugglers, profiteers and a host of other opportunists making the most of the demand for cotton and other goods. By his procedures of enforcing trading restrictions, including confiscations, Hurlbut gained a reputation for abusing his power and enriching himself. He also returned to his drinking habit.

In December the Army of the Tennessee underwent another reorganization and was formed into four corps, one of which, the Sixteenth, would be commanded by Hurlbut, with his headquarters remaining in Memphis. In that role Hurlbut sent out troops to suppress the operations of Van Dorn's army and the raids executed by Nathan Bedford Forrest and his cavalrymen in west Tennessee, but he had little success. Following Grant's capture of Vicksburg in July 1863 Hurlbut resigned his commission, claiming that Vicksburg's fall would lead to the end of the Confederacy in the West and that therefore his services were no longer needed. Grant approved the resignation, but President Lincoln refused to accept it, intending Hurlbut to direct the reconstruction of Arkansas. His efforts at that task also fell short of success, while his administration of Memphis's affairs grew scandalous and included the licensing of brothels for a fee.

At last Hurlbut got to see action in the field once more. In November 1863 Sherman, as commander of the Division of the Mississippi, came to Memphis to prepare for a campaign into eastern Mississippi, a campaign that included Hurlbut and the 16th Corps. In February 1864 Hurlbut led a force of 20,000 troops from Vicksburg on a drive through central Mississippi to capture Meridian, an important railroad center, tearing up tracks and burning trestles as they swept across the state, encountering only token resistance from Confederate skirmishers and offering no further test of Hurlbut's military ability. It was a mission easily accomplished, prompting Sherman to tell Grant that the campaign had taken on "more of the character of a pleasant excursion than of hard military service."[14]

Hurlbut returned to Memphis in late February, only to create more controversy for his administration and himself. In the field, his failed efforts to suppress Forrest's marauders led to his ultimate blame for Forrest's atrocities at Fort Pillow, where soldiers of the Union garrison, particularly black soldiers, were cruelly massacred on April 12. Hurlbut came under heavy criticism from the press and elsewhere for holding a large force at Memphis while Forrest was ranging west Tennessee, committing such horrors as the Fort Pillow massacre.

Exasperated by what he perceived as Hurlbut's timidity in prosecuting the war in west Tennessee, Sherman complained to Grant, and Grant finally decided it was time for Hurlbut to go. On April 16, 1864, Hurlbut was relieved of his duties, and Grant ordered him to return to Belvidere to await further orders. In August, however, after a visit by Hurlbut, who would be an Illinois delegate to the 1864 Republican convention, where Lincoln hoped to again receive his party's nomination, President Lincoln returned him to active duty. His new assignment was as commander of the army's Department of the Gulf, succeeding Nathaniel Banks, with headquarters in New Orleans.

Though unable to withstand temptations to enrich himself through abuse of his authority, making enemies in Louisiana's reconstruction government in the process, Hurlbut managed to avoid prosecution and remained in that job until the end of the war. He was honorably discharged from the army on June 20, 1865.

As president, Grant in 1869 appointed him minister to Colombia. In 1872 he was elected an Illinois representative to the U.S. Congress and was reelected in 1874. Defeated in a third try for Congress, he was appointed by President Garfield as ambassador to Peru in 1881. He died in Lima on March 27, 1882, at age 66 and was later buried in Belvidere.

7

Major General Lewis Wallace

Before the War: Born April 10, 1827, in Brookville, Indiana, son of a West Point graduate who became governor of Indiana in 1837. Moved with his family to Indianapolis. Studied law, admitted to the bar in 1849. Opened law office in Covington, Indiana, 1850. Elected prosecuting attorney for Indiana's Eighth Judicial Circuit, 1851, 1852. Resigned as prosecuting attorney in 1853 and moved to Crawfordsville, Indiana, where he began a law practice. Met Abraham Lincoln at a storytelling competition in Danville, Illinois. Married Susan Elston, 1852. Had one child, a son. Political affiliation: Democrat. Served as secretary of the Montgomery County (Indiana) Democratic convention in 1856. Ran unsuccessfully for the Indiana Senate in 1856, ran again in 1858 and was elected. Served one term. Military experience: Recruited men for the Marion Volunteers, an Indiana militia company, during the Mexican War, served as second lieutenant in the unit, which was activated as H Company of the First Indiana Volunteer Infantry Regiment. He later served as colonel of the regiment, which helped guard the Rio Grande and occupied Matamoros and later Monterrey, but saw no combat. After the war, in 1856, he was appointed by Indiana's governor as captain of the Crawfordsville Guards, a militia company.

Wallace liked the name "Lew" better than "Lewis," and that's what he called himself when he put his name on his first novel, *The Fair God*, and later on *Ben-Hur*, the novel that made him famous. Old-timers who knew him as a youngster remembered him as being wild as a March hare, exhibiting a restlessness caused probably by being too smart for the schools he attended. There was an oddly romantic side to that wild young man, though, which spawned dreams of living a soldier's life, a life as he imagined it, in desperate battle, fighting his way to glory. Tall, slender, with dark hair and dark, soulful eyes set in a bony face that in later years became partly obscured by a bushy goatee and oversized mustache, he described himself in his autobiography as having "an all-abiding confidence in myself hard to distinguish from vanity."[1]

He thought he had got his chance for a soldier's glory when his militia unit, the Marion Rifles, was called to service in the Mexican War. The war, for him, turned out to be a big disappointment. He saw no action, no opportunities to be the hero of his imaginings. He blamed the failure not on the vicissitudes of military service, but on his commanding general, Major General Zachary Taylor, who seemingly purposely excluded units of volunteers from service at the front, preferring to have men of the regular army do the fighting.

But in early 1861, with the Civil War looming, Wallace the romantic would get another chance at glory. When President Lincoln issued his call for 75,000 new troops following the Confederacy's assault on Fort Sumter, Wallace immediately answered the call, which came to him in the form of an assignment from Indiana's governor, Oliver Morton, who placed Wallace in charge of Indiana's response to the president's urgent request. Wallace would become Indiana's adjutant general, an administrative position, and organize the volunteers who also were answering the president's call. He agreed to serve in that job only until six regiments, Indiana's assigned quota, were raised. "I will not remain in the rear," he allowed, "while there is work to be done at the front."[2]

By April 23, 1861, the six regiments had been raised—plus enough additional recruits to form another five regiments. That done, Wallace resigned as adjutant general and was commissioned by Governor Morton as a colonel in command of the Eleventh Indiana Volunteer Infantry, one of the newly formed regiments. The Eleventh Indiana was mustered into the army on April 25, eleven days after the fall of Fort Sumter.

Wallace drilled his men and trained them in fighting Zouave style, the outstanding tactic of which was to advance on the run, fire and drop prone to the ground to reload. The regiment's first assignment was to Evansville, Indiana, on the Ohio River in the southwestern corner of the state. There they were to keep an eye on river traffic and prevent the movement of contraband goods to the rebels. Wallace—and his men as well—quickly tired of that chore, and he appealed to his brother-in-law, U.S. senator Henry Smith Lane of Indiana, for help in getting the Eleventh a new assignment. The help resulted in Wallace and the Eleventh Indiana being moved in early June to Cumberland, Maryland to guard the Baltimore & Ohio Railroad's vital bridges there. Taking a B&O train from Indianapolis to Cumberland, the Eleventh, composed of some 800 troops, crossed the Ohio River and passed into western Virginia approaching the area where most of the war's action was going on. At Grafton, Virginia (now West Virginia), where the train made a stop, Wallace learned from the commander of Union troops posted there that a Confederate force of as many as 1,500 troops had been

Maj. Gen. Lew Wallace, son of a former governor of Indiana, served as Indiana's adjutant general at the beginning of the war and entered federal service as a colonel commanding the Eleventh Indiana Volunteer Infantry Regiment. In September 1861 he was promoted to brigadier general, commanding a brigade. Following the capture of Fort Donelson he was promoted to major general (Library of Congress).

reported to be at Romney (now West Virginia), some 80 miles east of Grafton and 20 miles south of Cumberland, just a day's march from the bridges Wallace was being sent to guard.

When his train reached Cumberland on the morning of June 10, Wallace received the orders sent to him by the commander of the Department of Pennsylvania, Major General Robert Patterson, now Wallace's commanding officer, instructing him that if he discovered hostile armed bodies of men to "capture or rout them by surprise, if possible, and seize and hold as prisoners of war all parties injuring the lines of communication, or arrayed or plotting against the peace of the United States,"[3] which Wallace apparently had already decided he would try to do.

Informants told him that there were two roads into Romney, one being the main highway from Cumberland, and the other a mountainous route coming from the west. The informants said the rebels were not patrolling the mountain road, and Wallace decided that was the route he would use to advance on the Confederate encampment. Under the cover of darkness on the night of Wednesday, June 12—the day after an assembly of Virginia Unionists met in a convention in Wheeling to organize a new state that would break away from Virginia and remain loyal to the Union, resulting in the creation of West Virginia—Wallace took all but two companies of his regiment from Cumberland by train to Piedmont (West Virginia), where at about 11:00 p.m. the Eleventh Indiana left the train and began its march to Romney. A member of the Eleventh, a soldier named Gookins, gave a concise account of the expedition:

> Camp M'Ginnis (Cumberland, Md.)
> June 14, 1861
>
> On the evening of the 12th of June Colonel Lewis Wallace, commanding the Eleventh (Zouave) Indiana Regiment, stationed at this place, having received intelligence of a camp of secessionists at Romney, Virginia, where they were said to be assembled in considerable numbers, well armed and equipped, also having erected a battery of two pieces of cannon, headed a detachment of four hundred men, of whom your correspondent was one, and leaving this place at nine p.m., proceeded by rail to Piedmont, twenty-one miles distant from here; there debarking, marched over a rugged mountain road twenty-three miles to Romney, arriving there at 9 1/2 a.m. June 13. On coming within a mile of Romney we were fired on by the picket-guard of the rebels, while passing through a defile walled in by tremendous cliffs. At the sound of the first gun, however, we deployed as skirmishers, and being scattered thus no one was hurt on our side.
>
> We returned their fire and killed one of the picket. He was seen to fall and slide down the side of the mountain about twenty feet, when his body lodged against a tree. We then ran forward, and passing out of the defile came to a long covered bridge. On the other side of the river the rebels had planted their cannon and trained them upon the bridge; our men, however, dashed forward through the bridge with a yell, when the cowards (of whom there was quite a large body posted on the hills) fled without firing a shot from their cannon.
>
> On reaching the farther end of the bridge our advance was again fired on by a body of rebels who were posted in a brick house about seventy-five yards away from the bridge. Here the orderly-sergeant of Company A of our regiment was slightly wounded—not at all dangerously. The men ran forward, firing as they ran, riddling the house with Minie balls. The rebels, however, escaped by the back entrance into the hills

back of the house. One more was killed here, and another very badly wounded in the thigh. While this was going on we were again fired on from the mountains back of us. No one was hurt. We then moved forward to the town, where we learned for the first time, the number of secession soldiery; there were five companies of them in the aggregate—over four hundred men, well armed with Derringer rifles and United States muskets. In their retreat they were so pushed that they left behind their baggage, some rifles, tents, swords, pistols, etc., etc. We took seven officers' marquees, a quantity of uniforms, and large quantities of clothing, a secession flag, four horses (one of which was the rebel colonel's riding-horse), four large chests of ammunition, camp equipage, and a great variety of other articles. Three wagons were laden with the best part of things taken, and the rest were destroyed.

We learned that the rebels had received information of our approach an hour before we arrived. This enabled them to prepare for a retreat, and, much to our chagrin, they thus succeeded in saving their cannon.[4]

In his official report Wallace gave additional details from his perspective, providing an account best told by him, an account given without boast, exaggeration, self-congratulation or spin, which distinguished it from the embroidered reports filed by other political generals, particularly Butler and McClernand:

In approaching the place, it was necessary for me to cross a bridge over the South Branch of the Potomac. A reconnaissance satisfied me that the passage of the bridge would be the chief obstacle in my way, although I could distinctly see the enemy drawn up on the bluff, which is the town site, supporting a battery of two guns, planted so as to sweep the road completely. I directed my advance guard to cross the bridge on the run, leap down an embankment at the farther entrance, and observe the windows of a large brick house not farther off than seventy-five yards. Their appearance was the signal for an assault. A warm fire opened from the house, which the guard returned, without other loss than the wounding of a sergeant. The firing continued several minutes. I led a second company across the bridge, and by following up a ravine got them into a position that soon drove the enemy from the house and into a mountain to its rear.

My attention was then turned to the battery on the hill. Instead of following the road, as the rebels expected, I pushed five companies in skirmishing order, and at double-quick time, up a hill to the right, intending to get around the left flank of the enemy, and cut off their retreat. Hardly had my companies deployed and started forward, and got within rifle range, before the rebels limbered up and put off over the bluff in hottest haste.[5]

Concluding the report, he signed it, as he did his novels, "Lew. Wallace."

Not taking a chance that the rebels would regroup and ambush his regiment as it made its way back to the railroad, Wallace had his troops get some food at Romney and then hurried back across the rough mountain road to reboard their train, reaching the railroad about 11 o'clock on the night of the 13th.

News of the successful action set off a huge wave of good feeling among Northerners eager for a victory, even as small as the one Wallace and the Eleventh Indiana had won at Romney. Wallace became something of a national hero, as did the members of the Eleventh Indiana, when reports of their success were quickly published in newspapers around the nation. In its comments on the Romney fight, the *Evening Star* of Washington, D.C., spelled out the victory's significance to the people of western Virginia:

View of Romney, Virginia, in the 1860s. Here Wallace first made a name for himself on June 13, 1861, initiating a successful assault on a Confederate outpost from which the rebels had been harassing Union loyalists (Library of Congress).

> At half a dozen points in Northwestern Virginia, the conspirators in Richmond have stationed small bodies of their followers in arms, numbering from one hundred to fifteen hundred men each. They were so placed as to overawe the Unionists of the surrounding country, who, though greatly in the majority, were almost wholly unarmed. Their [the rebels'] mission was to prevent them from organizing in defence of their liberties, and to compel them to do military service in the disunion cause. They were instructed to enforce there the general draft to take place throughout the State to-day [June 14, 1861].
>
> The force at Romney, though comparatively small, (between four and five hundred) had been carrying matters with a high hand, robbing, oppressing, and browbeating the Unionists at will.... [T]he duty of dispersing them was devolved on Col. Wallace and his Indiana Zouaves, and it has been thoroughly performed.... The leading Unionists ... freely stated that with the disunion force at Romney driven away, a large portion of the men sought to be drafted there into the disunion service, would gladly, instead, enroll themselves in the service of the cause of the Union.[6]

There was strategic significance as well. Harpers Ferry, the town where the Baltimore & Ohio Railroad crossed the Potomac River and where the Confederates had posted an occupying force in May, had a branch rail line that ran through Romney to a terminus in Winchester, Virginia. By that branch line the Confederate force at Harpers Ferry was sustained and was allowed communication with Richmond and the rest of Virginia. After suffering Wallace's rout of the rebel force at Romney, fearing that Wallace's attack was the beginning of a larger drive and seeing that Harpers Ferry could be cut off by an interdiction of the road to Winchester, Confederate brigadier general Joseph Johnston pulled his troops out of Harpers Ferry, handing the town back to U.S. forces.

Back in Cumberland, Wallace, as General Patterson had instructed, formed a reconnaissance patrol that rode over the area to scout out the nearby Confederates and their movements. One of the patrols led to an engagement with a detail of Captain Turner Ashby's cavalry on Kelly's Island in the Potomac River in late June, Wallace's scouts repelling the rebels in a fierce fight that ended with Ashby's men pulling away and retreating. That fight, small as it was and with Wallace having done nothing to direct it save sending two companies to reinforce the scouts, resulted in more public adulation for Wallace and the Eleventh Indiana, troops, attracting even the attention of President Lincoln, who complimented them in a conversation with Indiana representative Schuyler Colfax, which Colfax reported to Wallace.[7] Other compliments came to Wallace from General Patterson and General McClellan, commander of the army's Department of the Ohio.

On July 5 Wallace received orders to take the Eleventh to Martinsburg, Virginia (now West Virginia), to join Patterson's army, which was assembling there to commence a drive on Winchester, Virginia. A Confederate force under General Beauregard was deployed in northern Virginia to defend the strategic railroad junction at Manassas, Virginia, a vital link in the Confederates' line of communication for the movement of troops and supplies. The War Department was preparing to attack that Confederate force with the 35,000 troops posted in and around Washington, and Patterson's assignment was to move against Winchester and threaten it in order to prevent General Joseph Johnston, commanding a force of 10,000 rebel troops at Winchester, from reinforcing the Confederate army at Manassas.

On July 19 Wallace wrote to his wife expressing gleeful anticipation of a big, significant battle, saying he was about to realize his lifelong wish of participating in a dramatic struggle of arms and that he "would not miss it on any account."[8] He did miss it, however, because General Patterson received information that Johnston was laying a trap for him and, fearful that the report was true, Patterson decided to proceed with extreme caution. He marched southward to Bunker Hill, within fifteen miles of Winchester, on July 15, bivouacked there, then moved eastward to Charles Town, hoping those movements would be enough to alarm Johnston and force him to keep his army at Winchester. Johnston was undeterred. He put his men on a train bound for Manassas, about thirty-five miles southeast of Winchester, where they reinforced Beauregard and on July 21 helped him defeat a Union army commanded by Major General Irvin McDowell at the First Battle of Bull Run (or Manassas), the first great battle of the war and a humiliating loss for the U.S.

On July 23, 1861, the Eleventh Indiana and its colonel were sent from Virginia back to Indiana with a hearty farewell from General Patterson (who was subsequently relieved of his command, apparently for failing to prevent Johnston's movement and thereby contributing to the Union defeat at Manassas). Patterson lauded Wallace and his troops, especially those men who had agreed to stay on for several more days of critical service despite their three-month enlistment having expired. Once the Eleventh was back home in Indiana, Wallace began a recruiting campaign to enlist men for his regiment who would sign up for three years instead of three months. In August he established a training camp just outside Indianapolis for his recruits, including some who earlier had served with him.

On August 31 Wallace's new Eleventh Indiana Regiment was mustered into the U.S. Army. On September 5 he was ordered to take it to St. Louis, whence it moved back across the Mississippi River to Kentucky and then on to Paducah, arriving there on September 10. Three days later he learned he had been promoted to brigadier general. He now would command a brigade, three regiments instead of one. They were the Eleventh and Twenty-third

Indiana regiments and the Eighth Missouri. Also included in his command were Battery A of the First Illinois Light Artillery Battalion and a company of the Fourth U.S. Cavalry Regiment. Events then began to move slowly for Wallace, the man who hungered for action, with many weeks occupied by little more than seemingly endless drilling and keeping his men out of trouble with the residents of Paducah they were ostensibly protecting. Then, early in the new year of 1862, the ice jam of inactivity began to crack.

By early January Grant's military jurisdiction had been shifted eastward from southeast Missouri to an area designated the District of Cairo, which included the mouths of the Tennessee and Cumberland rivers. The Confederate line of defense ran through Kentucky from Columbus, where it was anchored on the bluffs above the Mississippi River, eastward to Bowling Green and on to Mill Springs, and a U.S. War Department plan was drawn to burst through it. Brigadier General Don Carlos Buell, spearheading the movement, was expected to encounter a large, opposing Confederate force, commanded by Major General Simon Bolivar Buckner, at Bowling Green. On January 6 Grant received orders to make menacing moves to prevent Buckner's being reinforced by troops from Columbus or from the rebel forts that guarded the Cumberland and Tennessee rivers, forts Heiman, Henry and Donelson.

Responding to his instructions, Grant ordered Brigadier General Charles F. Smith, Wallace's commander, to take a force from Paducah up the west bank of the Tennessee River to threaten Fort Heiman and Fort Henry, the Tennessee's guardian fortresses. Other units of Grant's command were to make threatening moves toward Columbus. General Smith had already made a reconnaissance up the west bank of the Tennessee and had reported to Grant that from what he had seen of Fort Heiman, which was still under construction, he thought it could be captured. It stood on high ground on the west bank of the river, commanding Fort Henry on the east side of the river, and its possession by Union forces would likely ensure the capture of Fort Henry as well.

Smith's report confirmed what Grant had already concluded—that "the true line of operations for us," as he said, "was up the Tennessee and Cumberland rivers. With us there, the enemy would be compelled to fall back on the east and west entirely out of the state of Kentucky."[9] Grant, with persistence, eventually got a reluctant go-ahead from Major General Henry Halleck, commander of the army's Department of the Missouri and Grant's commanding officer, to launch an expedition to capture the three forts. The expedition would include seven of the gunboats commanded by Flag Officer Andrew Foote, which would escort the transport steamers that would carry Grant's 15,000 troops.

On the morning of Sunday, February 2, 1862, the expedition force started out from Cairo, Illinois, steaming up the Ohio River toward Paducah, where it would embark Wallace's brigade and the rest of General Smith's division, and continue up the Tennessee to forts Heiman and Henry. Grant wanted to land the troops as close to Fort Henry as possible but still stay beyond the range of its guns. He particularly wanted to put the men ashore on the fort side of a stream that emptied into the Tennessee north of the fort, a stream now swollen by weeks of rain, presenting a significant obstacle to the troops.

Once all of Grant's troops had been brought up to the vicinity of the forts, Grant planned to move them against the two forts simultaneously, in concert with an artillery assault by Foote's gunboats. "The plan," Grant explained, "was for the troops and gunboats to start at the same moment. The troops were to invest the garrison and the gunboats to attack the fort at close quarters. General Smith was to land a brigade of his division on the west bank during the night of the 5th and get it in the rear of [Fort] Heiman."[10]

Fort Henry stood in a dog-leg bend of the Tennessee River on its east bank in Stewart County, Tennessee, and was connected to Fort Donelson, eleven miles away on the west bank of the Cumberland River, by a road that led also to the town of Dover, about two miles south of Fort Donelson. Built on low, marshy ground, Fort Henry was subject to flooding when the Tennessee River rose out of its bank, as it had now, engorged by rainwater. Part of the ground on which the fort stood was now two feet deep in water. Below the fort, the floodwater extended from the river into woods for a distance of several hundred yards. The fort was a strong, skillfully built, five-sided earthwork covering ten acres, with ramparts about twenty feet thick at their base and tapering up to a thickness of ten feet at their top. Its five bastions were four to six feet high, and its artillery embrasures were stoutly framed with sandbags. Six of its seventeen heavy guns were placed to protect the fort from an assault by land. The eleven others protected the river, commanding the Tennessee for a distance up to two miles. Commanding Fort Henry was Confederate Brigadier General Lloyd Tilghman, a forty-six-year-old native of Maryland and a graduate of West Point.

The morning of Thursday, February 6 dawned cold and wet, and the movement of troops and gunboats began as planned. General McClernand's division advanced up the east side of the Tennessee to be in position to attack Fort Henry from the rear and to block the flight of the rebel garrison if they attempted to retreat toward Fort Donelson. Wallace's brigade was one of two brigades of General Smith's division that started moving up the west side of the river to capture Fort Heiman and turn its guns on Fort Henry. The troops on both sides of the river had to march about five miles to reach the forts, and their progress, through mud and water, was much slower than expected. The rainstorm had turned every stream into a torrent, repeatedly forcing the troops to halt long enough to build hastily erected bridges for the artillery to cross the raging water.

At half-past noon, after vainly waiting for the arrival of Grant's troops, delayed by the floodwater, Foote's gunboats at 1,700 yards opened fire with their bow guns. Fort Henry's guns quickly responded. Steaming to within 600 yards of the fort's batteries, the ironclads let loose their broadside guns while the fort's gunners vigorously answered. Wallace, encountering such a thunderous exchange for the first time, recounted the awesome experience: "The guns of the fleet opened while we were yet quite a mile from our objective. Our line of march was nearly parallel with the line of fire to and from the gun-boats. Not more than seven hundred yards separated us from the great shells, in their roaring, fiery passage. Without suffering from their effect, we had the full benefit of their indescribable and terrible noise. Several times I heard the shots of the fort crash against the iron sides of the boats. You can imagine the excitement and martial furor the circumstances were calculated to inspire our men with."[11]

The ironclads took a heavy pounding, but it was Fort Henry that took the heaviest beating. With devastating accuracy the gunboats' unceasing fire of shot and explosive shell smashed through the earthworks and sandbags, dismounting and crippling the fort's big guns, crumpling buildings and setting others ablaze, toppling trees within the fort's compound, relentlessly raining shot and shrapnel down onto the fort's defenders.

An hour and fifteen minutes after the gunboats' assault had begun, General Tilghman decided it was time to end it. "It is in vain to fight longer," he is reported to have said to his men. "Our gunners are disabled, our guns dismounted. We can't hold out five minutes longer."[12] He ordered the Confederate flag lowered and a white flag of surrender raised in its place. When the crewmen of Foote's gunboats saw it, they broke into "the wildest excitement," as one account has it, and loud cheers. It was their victory, the U.S. Navy's victory, stunning in its achievement. The gunboats drew up to the fort and received a deputation from General Tilghman, soon followed by Tilghman himself, formally surrendering the battered and crippled fort and what was left of its bloodied garrison, most of the fort's troops having fled up the road to Fort Donelson during the assault.

On the other side of the river, when Wallace and the other brigade finally reached Fort Heiman, ready to fight their way into it, they found the fort deserted, its garrison having joined the hasty flight toward Fort Donelson. If Wallace was disappointed at having missed another fight, he didn't reveal the disappointment in the letter he wrote to his wife three days later, expressing instead elation over the triumph of the navy's gunboat crews.

On the day after the capture of Fort Henry, General Grant and his staff, escorted by a detachment of cavalry, made a reconnaissance to within a mile of the fortified perimeter of Fort Donelson, guardian of the Cumberland, and there he began to plot the next assault on the Confederates' defenses.

Before launching it in haste, however, Grant called his commanders together in a council of war, the only such meeting he ever held. It was held in the ladies' cabin of the dispatch steamer *Tigress*, on which Grant had made his headquarters. To Wallace the meeting of generals seemed as uncomfortably cold as the weather, "probably," he wrote, "because, like myself, they were mostly new to the business.... [T]here was not the slightest pretense of sociability, no introductions, no bowing, no hand-shaking, no conversation."[13] From Wallace's description, it was easy to see why Grant called no more such councils. "After a little," Wallace related, "General Grant stepped to the table and said, ever so quietly: 'The question for consideration, gentlemen, is whether we shall march against Fort Donelson or wait for reinforcement. I should like to have your views.'"

As they remained standing, the generals spoke in the order of their seniority, General Smith, a former instructor at West Point, going first. He was in favor of attacking immediately. Then McClernand pulled from his pocket and read a lengthy paper that Wallace thought was offensive, perhaps insulting, to Grant, setting forth his ideas about the proposed assault on Fort Donelson. When he finished reading, he announced that he also favored an immediate attack. "It had been better for him, probably," Wallace wrote, "had he rested with a word to that effect.... The proceeding smacked of a political caucus, and I thought both Grant and Smith grew restive before the paper was finished; then as if in haste to preclude argument instantly that the reading ended, Grant turned to me, nodding, and I said, 'Let us go, by all means, the sooner the better.'"[14]

Wallace Gets Guard Duty

Wallace soon learned that he had been given an assignment that would prevent his participating in the fight to take Fort Donelson. Someone had to stay behind with a force to guard the newly captured forts. Grant left the selection of that someone to General Smith, who chose Wallace, setting off an explosive reaction from Wallace. He dashed off a quick note to Grant protesting the assignment, to which Grant responded by promising Wallace a division of his own. Grant's aide, Captain William Hillyer, wrote back to Wallace on February 11 to reassure him: "I was surprised to hear that you were to be left behind, and so was Grant.... Let me beg of you as your friend that you keep quiet for a day or two—and you will have a position that will suit you in every particular—having no intermediate commander."[15] That note was followed by orders from Grant to Wallace: "You will hold your brigade in readiness to follow the advance and to assume command of a Division, which will be composed of new arrivals, six regiments of which have already been sent around by the Cumberland, where orders may reach you."[16] The first of the six promised regiments, the First Nebraska, commanded by Colonel John M. Thayer, arrived on February 12.

Around midnight on the 13th Wallace got the orders he wanted. He was instructed to march immediately to Fort Donelson with two regiments of his new division. He chose his favorite—the Eleventh Indiana—and the Eighth Missouri and brought along Battery A of the First Illinois Light Artillery, escorted by Company A of the Thirty-second Illinois Regiment. Grant described the situation into which Wallace and his men were marching:

> I started from Fort Henry [on February 12] with 15,000 men, including eight batteries and part of a regiment of cavalry, and, meeting with no obstructions to detain us, the advance arrived in front of the enemy by noon. That afternoon and the next day were spent in taking up ground to make the investment as complete as possible. General Smith had been directed to leave a portion of his division behind to guard Forts Henry and Heiman. He left General Lew. Wallace with 2,500 men. With the remainder of his division he occupied our left, extending to Hickman Creek. McClernand was on the right and covered the roads running south of the village. The troops were not intrenched, but the nature of the ground was such that they were just as well protected from the fire of the enemy as if rifle-pits had been thrown up. Our line was generally along the crest of ridges. The artillery was protected by being sunk in the ground. The men who were not serving the guns were perfectly covered from fire on taking position a little back from the crest. The greatest suffering was from want of shelter. It was midwinter and during the siege we had rain and snow, thawing and freezing alternately. It would not do to allow camp-fires except far down the hill out of sight of the enemy, and it would not do to allow many of the troops to remain there at the same time. In the march over from Fort Henry [in temporarily warmer weather] numbers of the men had thrown away their blankets and overcoats. There was therefore much discomfort and absolute suffering.[17]

In his account of the Fort Donelson expedition Wallace characterized the Confederate officers charged with defending the fort. General Albert Sidney Johnston was the commander of the Confederate army's Western Department, but he was not on the site.

> Having taken to defend Nashville at Donelson, he intrusted the operations to three chiefs of brigade—John B. Floyd [a former U.S. secretary of war, under indictment by a grand jury in Washington, D.C.], Gideon J. Pillow, and Simon B. Buckner [an old friend of Grant]. Of these, the first was the ranking officer.... The second officer had a genuine military record; but it is said of him that he was of a jealous nature, insubordinate, and quarrelsome.... All in all, therefore, there is little doubt that the junior of the three commanders [Buckner] was the fittest for the enterprise intrusted to them.... [A]s a soldier, in all the higher meanings of the word, he was greatly their superior.[18]

Manning the fort on the morning of the 13th, Wallace reported, was a garrison of twenty-eight infantry regiments, plus two independent battalions, a regiment of cavalry and enough artillerymen to service six light batteries and seventeen heavy guns, making a total of about 18,000 effectives. Buckner's division—six infantry regiments and two artillery batteries—formed the right wing of the Confederate line and was posted to cover the land approaches to the fort's water batteries. The left wing was composed of six brigades, with four batteries distributed among them.[19]

Shortly after receiving his midnight orders to hasten to Fort Donelson, Wallace ferried his troops across the Tennessee River and reported with them at Grant's headquarters before noon the next day, Friday, February 14, 1862. He was instructed by Grant to place his newly formed division at the center of the Union line and to allow the two divisions on his flanks to close up and strengthen their positions. "The plan," Grant explained, "was for the troops to hold the enemy within his lines, while the gunboats should attack the water batteries at close quarters and silence his guns if possible. Some of the gunboats were to run the batteries, get above the fort and above the village of Dover.... That position attained by the gunboats it would have been but a question of time—and a very short time, too—when the garrison would have been compelled to surrender."[20] With luck, Grant figured, the besieged fort, once its commanders could see that their communications and escape route on the river were cut off, would surrender without further loss to the troops of either side.

The first of the ironclad gunboats, the *Carondelet*, arrived to take position on the 12th. Flag Officer Foote arrived with three more ironclads and two timberclads shortly before midnight of the 13th. In daylight on the 14th, as Foote pressed his vessels closer and closer to the fort, the fort's guns opened fire with terrible effect, the *Carondelet* especially taking a heavy beating, suffering two severely damaging shots into the pilothouse. The tiller ropes of the ironclad *Louisville* were shot away by rebel fire, and the tiller ropes of the *St. Louis*, Foote's flagship, were severed by an errant shot from the timberclad *Tyler* (or *Taylor*, as it had been renamed). Among the casualties on the *St. Louis* was Flag Officer Foote, who suffered wounds to his left arm and left foot. The battered gunboats, three of them unable to steer, then drifted down the river, out of the furious action.

That night, the evening of February 14, General Floyd, commanding Fort Donelson's defenders, held a council of war in the hotel on the waterfront at Dover, calling together his general officers and regimental commanders. He told them that despite the Confederates' heroic repulse of Foote's gunboat flotilla, he considered the defenders' position untenable, in the face of what Floyd and others believed was an overwhelming and growing U.S. Army. Floyd had earlier been instructed by General Johnston to fall back to Nashville by way of Charlotte, Tennessee, if the situation at Fort Donelson became hopeless. To Floyd it now seemed hopeless. He suggested an attack on the right side of the Union line to recapture the road to Charlotte and force open a path for a massive withdrawal of the rebel forces from Fort Donelson.

Floyd's plan was for General Pillow to launch an assault against the right side of the Union line at dawn on the 15th, with Buckner supporting Pillow by attacking the right center of the Union line and taking a position beyond the rebel trenches to cover Fort Donelson's retreating garrison. Floyd's proposal was unanimously accepted by the officers at the meeting.

During the frigid night of February 14–15 the rebel commanders took 10,000 or more of their troops—infantry, cavalry and artillery—out of the snow-covered rifle pits and massed them on the Confederate left, moving so quietly that Union sentries did not detect them. "The pickets of the Federals were struggling for life against the [wintry] blast," Wallace later recounted, and probably did not keep good watch."[21] Wallace, the novelist, surely the most eloquent of all the Civil War's generals, described the rebels' surprise attack on the morning of the 15th:

> Here and there the musicians were beginning to make the woods ring with reveille, and numbed soldiers of the line were rising from their icy beds and shaking the snow from their frozen garments, As yet, however, not a company had fallen in. Suddenly the pickets fired, and with the alarm on their lips rushed back upon their comrades. The woods on the instant became alive.
>
> The regiments formed, officers mounted and took their places; words of command rose loud and eager. By the time Pillow's advance opened fire on [regimental commander Colonel Richard] Oglesby's right [positioned on McClernand's extreme right], the point first struck, the latter was ready to receive it. A rapid exchange of volleys ensued.... An hour passed, and yet another hour, without cessation of the fire. Meantime the woods rang with a monstrous clangor of musketry, as if a million men were beating empty barrels with iron hammers.
>
> Buckner flung a portion of his division on McClernand's left, and supported the attack with his artillery.... McClernand, watchful and full of resources, sent batteries to meet Buckner's batteries.... The roar never slackened. Men fell by the score, reddening the snow with their blood. The smoke, in pallid white clouds, clung to the underbrush and tree-tops as if to screen the combatants from each other.
>
> The pressure on the front grew stronger.... At last he [Colonel Oglesby] realized that the end was come. His right companies began to give way, and as they retreated, holding up their empty cartridge-boxes, the enemy appeared emboldened, and swept more fiercely around his flank, until finally they appeared in his rear. He then gave the order to retire the division....
>
> My division in the center was weakened by the dispatch of one of my brigades to the assistance of General McClernand.... When General McClernand perceived the peril threatening him in the morning, he sent an officer to me with a request for assistance. This request I referred to General Grant, who was at the time in consultation with Foote. Upon the turning of Oglesby's flank, McClernand repeated his request, with such a representation of the situation that, assuming the responsibility, I ordered Colonel Cruft to report with his brigade to McClernand. Unfortunately a guide misdirected him, so that he became involved in the retreat, and was prevented from accomplishing his object.[22]

By eleven o'clock that morning, Saturday, February 15, General Pillow held the road to Charlotte, as well as the entire position that McClernand's division had occupied. The way out of Fort Donelson was now clear for its Confederate defenders.

Meanwhile, Grant, who was absent from the field during the rebel assault on the right side of his line, had returned from a meeting that Flag Officer Foote had requested. Unable to come to Grant because of his wounds, Foote had asked Grant to come to him on his flagship, anchored in the river below the fort. At that meeting Foote had suggested that Grant entrench while he himself returned to Mound City, Illinois, with his disabled boats so he could have repairs made. He said he thought he could be back at Fort Donelson in ten days.

Grant had agreed to that new course of action, then had departed Foote's flagship and was rowed back to shore. Just as he landed, he was met by Captain Hillyer, his aide, who reported that the rebels had come out of their lines in full force and attacked and scattered McClernand's division, which was in full retreat. As he passed along his line, moving from its left side toward its right, he found, as he said, "everything favorable." Then, during a lull in the battle, he reached the right side. Wallace recounted the next events:

> Even the cannonading ceased, and everybody was asking, "What next?" Just then General Grant rode up to where General McClernand and I were in conversation. He was almost unattended. In his hand were some papers, which looked like telegrams. Wholly unexcited, he saluted and received the salutations of his subordinates.... He was then informed of the mishap to the First Division, and that the road to Charlotte was open to the enemy.... His face flushed slightly. With a sudden grip he crushed the papers in his hand.... In his ordinary voice he said, addressing himself to both officers [Wallace and McClernand], "Gentlemen, the position on the right must be retaken." With that he turned and galloped off.[23]

Grant decided that although some of his men were demoralized, the rebel troops must feel worse. They, he reasoned, had attempted to force their way out, but had fallen back. "The one who attacks first now," he told a member of his staff, "will be victorious."[24] Grant quickly decided he would immediately make an assault on his left, sending General Smith's troops against the section of the rebel line commanded by General Buckner. "It was clear to my mind," Grant recalled, "that the enemy had started to march out with his entire force, except a few pickets, and if our attack could be made on the left before the enemy could redistribute his forces along the line, we would find but little opposition except from the intervening abatis."[25] Riding swiftly to Smith's command post, Grant explained the situation to Smith and ordered him to charge the rebels' works in front of him with his entire division, telling him that he would find only a thin line to oppose him.

Almost immediately Smith had his units on the move. Once past the thick, fearsome abatis, they overran the Confederates' position, the rebel soldiers in their rifle pits hurriedly clambering out and fleeing toward the fort as Smith's regiments planted their colors on the rebel breastwork. Later in the day, Buckner sent his men back to try to retake the lost ground, but all their efforts failed. Wallace's dramatic account detailed the action on the right side of the Union line:

> Riding to my old regiments—the 8th Missouri and the 11th Indiana—I asked them if they were ready. They demanded the word of me. Waiting a moment for [brigade commander Colonel] Morgan L. Smith to light a cigar, I called out, "Forward it is, then!" They were directly in front of the ascent to be climbed. Without waiting for his supports, Colonel Smith led them down into a broad hollow, and catching sight of the advance, [Colonel Charles] Cruft and [Colonel Leonard] Ross also moved forward. As the two regiments began to climb, the 8th Missouri slightly in the lead, a line of fire ran along the brow of the height. The flank companies cheered while deploying as skirmishers. Their Zouave practice [of loading their weapons while lying prone on the ground] proved of excellent service to them. Now on the ground, creeping when the fire was hottest, running when it slackened, they gained ground with astonishing rapidity, and at the same time maintained a fire that was like a sparkling of the earth. For the most part the bullets aimed at them passed over their heads and took effect in the ranks behind them.

Colonel Smith's cigar was shot off close to his lips. He took another and called for a match. A soldier ran and gave him one. "Thank you. Take your place now. We are almost up," he said, and, smoking, spurred his horse forward.

A few yards from the crest of the height the regiments began loading and firing as they advanced. The defenders gave way. On the top there was a brief struggle, which was ended by Cruft and Ross with their supports.

The whole line then moved forward simultaneously, and never stopped until the Confederates were [back] within the works. There had been no occasion to call on the reserves. The road to Charlotte was again effectually shut, and the battle-field of the morning, with the dead and wounded lying where they had fallen, was in possession of the Third Division, which stood halted within easy musket-range of the rifle-pits. It was then about half-past 3 o'clock in the afternoon.

I was reconnoitering the works of the enemy preliminary to charging them, when Colonel Webster, of General Grant's staff, came to me and repeated the order to fall back out of cannon range and throw up breastworks. "The general does not know that we have the hill," I said. Webster replied: "I give you the order as he gave it to me." "Very well," said I, "give him my compliments, and say that I have received the order." Webster smiled and rode away. The ground was not vacated, though, the assault was deferred. In assuming the responsibility, I had no doubt of my ability to satisfy General Grant of the correctness of my course; and it was subsequently approved.

When night fell, the command bivouacked without fire or supper. Fatigue parties were told off to look after the wounded; and in the relief given there was no distinction made between friend and foe. The labor extended through the whole night, and the surgeons never rested. By sunset the conditions of the morning were all restored. The Union commander was free to order a general assault next day or resort to a formal siege.[26]

Confederate Commanders Agree to Surrender

All of that occurred on Saturday. On Saturday evening the three chief Confederate commanders conferred in the old hotel on the Dover riverbank and after some expression of bravado by Floyd and Pillow and a recital of the actual situation by Buckner, the three generals agreed the fight was hopeless and that they would capitulate, Floyd and Pillow being given time to flee and Buckner being left holding the bag of formal surrender. Command of the fort and its defending troops passed to Buckner, who called for a bugler, a pen, ink and paper. When the articles were brought to him, he sat down at a table and wrote his message of surrender to Grant.

Grant received Buckner's message shortly before daylight on Sunday, February 16. In it Buckner asked Grant to appoint commissioners who would work out the terms of the surrender. Grant replied swiftly and succinctly: "No terms except an unconditional and immediate surrender can be accepted. I propose to move immediately upon your works."

Irritated but resigned to defeat, Buckner responded to Grant's demand: "The distribution of the forces under my command, incident to an unexpected change of commanders, and the overwhelming force under your command, compel me, not withstanding the brilliant success of the Confederate arms yesterday, to accept the ungenerous and unchivalrous terms which you propose."[27] Even before he had received Grant's reply, Buckner had dispatched notes to the rebel commanders along the line of entrenchment, notifying them he had sent the capitulation proposal to General Grant and ordering the commanders to "refrain from hostile demonstrations with a view to preventing a like movement on the enemy's part."[28] White flags soon began appearing along the Confederate line.

Wallace's division, at the center of the Union line, was up early that Sunday morning, getting into formation in preparation for an attack on the Confederate breastworks south of Dover. "In the midst of the preparation," Wallace related, "a bugle was heard and a white flag was seen coming from the town toward the pickets. I sent my adjutant general to meet the flag half-way and inquire its purpose. Answer was returned that General Buckner had capitulated during the night, and was now sending information of the fact to the commander of the troops in this quarter, that there might be no further bloodshed. The division [Wallace's Third Division] was ordered to advance and take possession of the works and of all public property and prisoners."[29]

From his command post Wallace then rode to Dover, encountering no challenges as he passed the Confederate positions. "I found General Buckner with his staff at breakfast," Wallace wrote. "He met me with politeness and dignity. Turning to the officers at the table, he remarked: 'General Wallace, it is not necessary to introduce you to these gentlemen; you are acquainted with them all.' They arose, came forward one by one, and gave their hands in salutation. I was then invited to breakfast, which consisted of corn bread and coffee, the best the gallant host had in his kitchen. We sat at the table about an hour and a half, when General Grant arrived and took temporary possession of the tavern as his headquarters. Later in the morning the army marched in and completed the possession."[30] If General Grant thought it inappropriate for Wallace to precede him to Buckner's headquarters at the Dover Hotel, he didn't reveal his feelings in his memoirs. "As soon as the last letter from Buckner was received I mounted my horse and rode to Dover," Grant wrote. "General Wallace, I found, had preceded me an hour or more. I presume that, seeing white flags exposed in his front, he rode up to see what they meant and, not being fired upon or halted, he kept on until he found himself at the headquarters of General Buckner."[31]

Grant went on to observe that the victory at Fort Donelson "caused great delight all over the North"—including, apparently, in Washington, D.C., where rewards for the commanders' good service were given out. "I was promptly promoted to the grade of Major-General of Volunteers and was confirmed by the Senate," Grant wrote. "All three of my division commanders [Smith, McClernand and Wallace] were promoted to the same grade and the colonels who commanded the brigades were made brigadier-generals in the volunteer service."[32]

McClernand was placed in command of the newly captured Fort Donelson, and Wallace, on the same day that Fort Donelson fell, was ordered to return with his troops to Fort Henry and again assume command there. Although eager to press on to the next objective, Grant was abruptly thwarted by his commander, General Halleck, who seemed to suffer from a painful jealousy of Grant, now the army's rising star in whose brilliance Halleck's bright light became barely visible. With the blessing of General McClellan, Halleck relieved Grant of his command on trumped-up charges but soon had to back down when President Lincoln intervened, firing McClellan as general in chief at the same time.

Grant reassumed command of the Army of the Tennessee on March 17 and found that while he had been sidelined, his army had been on the move. Continuing its penetration into the Confederacy's heartland, it had moved up the Tennessee River as far as Pittsburg Landing. About half of the army was encamped on the east bank of the river at Savannah, Tennessee, Wallace's division being positioned at Crump's Landing on the west bank about four miles farther up the river, and the remainder of the six divisions having been posted at Pittsburg Landing, five miles above Crump's Landing. Grant immediately ordered the troops at Savannah to move to Pittsburg Landing, knowing, he said, that the rebels were massing an army at Corinth under the command of General Albert Sidney Johnston.

Grant's routine was to spend the day at Pittsburg Landing, then return to his headquarters in Savannah in the evening. He intended, he wrote in his memoirs, to shift his headquarters to Pittsburg Landing, but he was expecting General Buell, marching from Nashville to reinforce Grant, to arrive at any time and he expected him to come first to Savannah, where Grant expected to meet him.[33] During the day on April 5, 1862, the first of Buell's troops, the division commanded by Brigadier General William Nelson, arrived in Savannah, and Grant ordered Nelson to take a position on the east bank of the river, where his division could be quickly ferried to Pittsburg Landing or to Crump's Landing, both of which, Grant believed, were threatened by the Confederates, who were only a day's march away in Corinth.

Early the next morning—Sunday, April 6—Grant was at breakfast in Savannah, intending to meet with Buell later in the day, when in the distance he heard sounds of heavy firing coming from the direction of Pittsburg Landing. He dashed off a hurried note to be delivered to General Buell, explaining that he would be unable to meet with him in Savannah, then swiftly made his way to Savannah's river landing and boarded his dispatch steamer and headed upriver. His first stop was Crump's Landing, where he met with General Wallace, who was aboard the steamer he used as his headquarters and was waiting for Grant, having anticipated his coming in response to the noise of battle. Grant instructed him to form up his troops and be ready to execute whatever orders he might be given. Wallace replied that his men were already under arms and were prepared to move out.[34] Grant later related the following:

> Up to that time, I had felt by no means certain that Crump's landing might not be the point of attack. On reaching the front, however, about eight a.m., I found that the attack on Pittsburg was unmistakable, and that nothing more than a small guard, to protect our transports and stores, was needed at Crump's. Captain Baxter, a quartermaster on my staff, was accordingly directed to go back and order General Wallace to march immediately to Pittsburg by the road nearest the river. Captain Baxter made a memorandum of this order. About one p.m., not hearing from Wallace and being much in need of reinforcements, I sent two more of my staff, Colonel McPherson and Captain Rowley, to bring him up with his division. They reported finding him marching towards Purdy, Bethel, or some point west from the river, and farther from Pittsburg by several miles than when he started.[35]

Rowley wrote a detailed—and revealing—report on his mission to fetch Wallace and his division:

> Shortly after the hour of 12 o'clock m., as we were riding towards the right of the line, a cavalry officer rode up and reported to General Grant, stating that General Wallace had positively refused to come up unless he should receive *written* orders. After hearing the report General Grant turned to me, saying, "Captain, you will proceed to Crump's Landing and say to General Wallace that it is my orders that he bring his division up at

once, coming up by the River road, crossing Snake Creek on the bridge (which General Sherman would protect), and form his division on the extreme right, when he would receive further orders; and say to him that it is important that he should make haste." Adding, "It has just been reported to me that he has refused to come up unless he receives a *written* order. If he should require a written order of you, you will give him one," at the same time asking me if I had writing materials in my haversack. I started at once, when the general called to me again, saying, "You will take with you the captain (referring to the cavalry officer before mentioned, who was still sitting there on his horse—his name I do not recollect), and two orderlies, and see that you do not spare horse flesh." This was at the hour of 12.30 o'clock m., as near as I can recollect.

I proceeded at once to General Wallace's camp, back of Crump's Landing, and being well mounted, it took me but a short time to reach it. Upon arriving there I found no signs of a camp, except one baggage wagon that was just leaving. I inquired of the driver as to where General Wallace and his troops were; he replied that they had gone up to the fight. I inquired what road they took; to which he replied by pointing to a road, which I understand to be the Purdy road.

While sitting there upon my horse I could hear the firing upon the battle-field quite distinctly. I then took the road pointed out by the teamster and rode a distance of between 5 and 6 miles, as I judged, when I came up with the rear of General Wallace's division; they were at rest, sitting on each side of the road, some with their arms stacked in the middle of the road. I passed the entire division (except the cavalry), all being at a halt. When I reached the head of the column I found General Wallace sitting upon his horse, surrounded by his staff, some of whom were dismounted and holding their horses by the bridles.

I rode up to General Wallace and communicated to him General Grant's orders as I had received them, and then told him that it had been reported to him (*i.e.*, General Grant) that he had refused to march without written orders; at which he seemed quite indignant, saying that it was a "damned lie!" that he had never refused to go without a written order, in proof of which he said, "Here you find me on the road." To which I replied that I had certainly found him on a road, but I hardly thought it the road to Pittsburg Landing. It certainly was not the road that I had come down from there on, and that I had traveled farther since I had left his camp than I had in coming from the battle-field to the camp, and, judging from the sound of the firing, we were still a long distance from the battle-field. To which the general replied that this was the road his cavalry had brought him, and the *only road* he knew anything about. He then ordered one of his aides to ride ahead and bring the cavalry back.

I then asked him where this road came into Pittsburg Landing; to which he replied that it crossed the creek at a mill (I think he called it Veal's Mill) and intersected the Corinth and Pittsburg Landing road in front of where General McClernand's camp was. I then told him that I thought it would be impossible for him to get in upon that road, as the enemy now had possession of those camps, and that our line of battle was to the rear of them. At this moment his cavalry came back and General Wallace rode forward to communicate with them. When he came back he remarked that it was true that the enemy was between us and our army; that the cavalry had been close enough to hear the musketry. The order was then give to counter-march; upon which I remarked to General Wallace that I would ride on and inform General Grant that he was coming; to which he replied, "No, captain; I shall be obliged to keep you with me to act as guide, as none of us knew the River road you speak of." I accordingly remained.

The march toward the old camp was continued to a point about one-half mile north of it, where the troops filed to the right and came into the River road. At the point filing off we were met by Lieutenant Colonel (now Major-General) McPherson and Major Rawlins, members of General Grant's staff, who had also come to look after General Wallace. The march continued up the River road until the battle-field was reached, which was just as it was getting dark and after the fighting of the day was over.

Of the character of the march after I overtook General Wallace I can only say that to me it appeared intolerably slow, resembling more a reconnaissance in the face of an enemy than a forced march to relieve a hard-pressed army. So strongly did this impression take hold of my mind, that I took the liberty of repeating to General Wallace that part of General Grant's order enjoining haste. The same idea seemed to have taken possession of the minds of Colonel McPherson and Major Rawlins, as on the march from the camp to the battle-field Major Rawlins on several occasions rode back for the purpose of trying to hurry up the troops and to ascertain what was the cause of the delay. I have no means of judging as to what distance General Wallace was from the battle-field when I found him, except that I could hear the firing much more distinctly at the camp he had left than I could at the point where I found him.[36]

Wallace Absent from the Day's Battle

Wallace thus missed the entire, disastrous first day of the battle while U.S. forces at Pittsburg Landing were sore-pressed for reinforcements. His excuse that he didn't know about the river road, over which Rowley had rushed to him without obstruction or delay, makes Wallace appear either awkwardly incompetent—not to have scouted out and discovered, after days of opportunity to do so, the nearby roads and the routes to Pittsburg Landing—or a blatant liar. Grant at first formed an opinion not favorable to Wallace but one short of implying incompetence. "I never could see and do not see now," he wrote in his memoirs, "why any order was necessary further than to direct him to come to Pittsburg landing.... I presume his idea was that by taking the route he did he would be able to come around on the flank or rear of the enemy, and thus perform an act of heroism that would redound to the credit of his command, as well as to the benefit of the country."[37]

However, with further information revealed in a letter that Wallace wrote on April 5, Grant later changed his opinion. "This letter shows," he wrote, "that at that time General Lew. Wallace was making preparations for the emergency that might happen for the passing of reinforcements between Shiloh and his position, extending from Crump's landing westward, and he sends it [the reinforcements] over the road running from Adamsville to the Pittsburg landing and Purdy road." Grant concluded that that road, which Wallace had designated as the route to be taken by the reinforcements, the same one on which Rowley had found Wallace moving, was probably in truth the only road to the U.S. position near Pittsburg Landing that Wallace knew about, as he told Rowley. "The mistake he made," Grant wrote, "was that of advancing some distance after he found that the firing, which would be at first directly to his front and then off to the left, had fallen back until it got very much in rear of the position of his advance.... If the position of our front had not changed, the road which Wallace took would have been somewhat shorter to our right than the River road."[38]

Grant's comment seems generous, for the more serious mistake Wallace apparently made was in failing to exercise due diligence to inform himself about the routes beforehand, which he had several days to do. Even if he had turned around when the sounds of battle indicated the front had changed, he would not have reached the Union position since, according to his statement made to Rowley, he knew no other route to Pittsburg Landing. If indeed Baxter's relation of Grant's oral order specified that he take the River Road to hasten to Pittsburg Landing, a detail about which there was—and is—much dispute, Wallace would not have known which road that was or where it was, according to the statements he made to Rowley. Wallace's official report detailed much of his division's actions on the crucial second day of the battle:

> About 1 o'clock at night [on the morning of Monday, April 7] my brigades and batteries were disposed, forming the extreme right, and ready for battle. Shortly after daybreak Captain Thompson opened fire on a rebel battery posted on a bluff opposite my First Brigade, and across a deep and prolonged hollow, threaded by a creek and densely wooded on both sides. From its position and that of its infantry support, lining the whole length of the bluff, it was apparent that crossing the hollow would be at heavy loss, unless the battery was first driven off. Thurber was accordingly posted to assist Thompson by a cross-fire and at the same time sweep the hiding place of the rebels on the brow of the hill. This had the desired effect. After a few shells from Thurber the enemy fell back, but not before Thompson had dismounted one of their rifled guns. During this affair General Grant came up and gave me my direction of attack, which was formed at a right angle with the river, with which at the time my line ran almost parallel.
>
> The battery and its supports having been driven from the opposite bluff, my command was pushed forward, the brigades in echelon—the First in front, and the whole preceded by skirmishers. The hollow was crossed and the hill gained almost without opposition.

Wallace's account went on in detail, describing the fight up till 4:00 p.m. when the action faded. "About 4 o'clock," he wrote, "the enemy to my front broke into rout and ran through the camps occupied by General Sherman on Sunday morning. Their own camp had been established about 2 miles beyond. There, without halting, they fired tents, stores, &c. Throwing out the wounded, they filled their wagons full of arms (Springfield muskets and Enfield rifles) ingloriously thrown away by some of our troops the day before, and hurried on. After following them until nearly nightfall I brought my division back to Owl Creek and bivouacked it."[39]

General Beauregard, who had taken command of the rebel army after General Albert Sidney Johnston had fallen mortally wounded on Sunday afternoon, had at last ordered his weary and worn troops to retire from the field, and Grant decided not to pursue, but to bury the dead of both sides instead. Their remains still lie today in graves on the field of battle.

Writing his official report on the battle, Grant cited Sherman's actions for particular praise, but followed his comments concerning Sherman with the statement that "in making mention of a gallant officer [Sherman] no disparagement is intended to the other division commanders, Maj. Gens. John A. McClernand and Lewis Wallace, and Brig. Gens. S.A. Hurlbut, B.M. Prentiss, and W.H.L. Wallace, all of whom maintained their places with credit to themselves and the cause."[40] He was at that time apparently satisfied with his political generals' performance.

When Beauregard learned that General Halleck, who was unhappy with the way Grant had conducted the battle (as was much of the country when the casualty numbers were published), was coming with reinforcements to take command himself, he began planning to abandon Corinth. Seven weeks after the Pittsburg Landing fight and the rebel retreat to Corinth, Beauregard and his army slipped away from Corinth and moved fifty miles south to Tupelo, Mississippi. "Beauregard published his orders for the evacuation of Corinth on the 26th of May," Grant reported, "and fixed the 29th for the departure of his troops, and on the 30th of May General Halleck had his whole army drawn up prepared for battle and announced in orders that there was every indication that our left was to be attacked that morning. Corinth had already been evacuated and the National troops marched on and took possession without opposition."[41]

Having avoided battle, and thus missed again a test of his ability in the field, Halleck resorted to the tasks of administration, something with which he was more comfortable and capable. He figured out a way to remove two of his political generals from action. He created within his command a reserve, comprising the divisions of Wallace and McClernand, with McClernand in command of both. Wallace and his division were then posted at Bolivar, in west Tennessee, and assigned to guarding the railroad.

On June 6 a flotilla of U.S. gunboats steamed down the Mississippi River to confront the Confederates' River Defense Fleet, a collection of steamers, many of them towboats, converted hastily into rams and given the woeful task of stopping the Union's advance down the Mississippi from St. Louis and Cairo. The rebel fleet was no match for the U.S. vessels and was swiftly swept from the river, destroyed or captured, save for one ram that managed to escape. The city of Memphis, in front of which the battle was fought, then fell open to capture by an infantry force put ashore from the U.S. gunboats.

On June 17, acting on a report that a Confederate force was threatening the U.S. occupation of Memphis, Wallace, on his own initiative, marched his troops into the captured city and took command of it. His reign as Memphis's lord was short-lived. On June 21 Halleck ordered Grant to move his headquarters to Memphis, which he promptly did, arriving there on June 23 and nudging Wallace out. Wallace put in for a leave of absence, which Grant quickly approved, allowing him twenty days and permission to take his staff with him. Command of the Third Division, Wallace's division, then passed to Major General Alvin Hovey. Wallace never returned to reclaim it.

Before Wallace's twenty days were up, his old friend the governor of Indiana, Oliver Morton, called him to Indianapolis and asked him to lend a hand at recruiting efforts in the state. When Wallace resisted, Morton handed him a telegram from secretary of war Stanton ordering Wallace to report to Morton. Wallace made a stab at helping recruiting efforts by giving a speech in Evansville and when that was over, he received new orders from Stanton, directing him to go home to Crawfordsville and await further instructions. He was clearly now in the army's doghouse and out of a job. Henry Halleck, who bore an intense dislike for Wallace—an antipathy aggravated by Wallace's ridicule of Halleck in remarks made unknowingly to members of Halleck's staff—in July had become general in chief of the U.S. Army and he seemed determined to keep Wallace out of action. Wallace urged Governor Morton to ask President Lincoln to intercede in his behalf, but Morton declined to do so, apparently having decided Wallace had become persona non grata in Washington.

In August, while still in Crawfordsville, Wallace was again summoned to Indianapolis by Governor Morton. Word had reached Morton that a Confederate army commanded by Major General Edmund Kirby Smith was driving northward through Kentucky, headed toward the Ohio River and an invasion of Indiana and Ohio. Morton asked Wallace's help in defending his threatened state. Welcoming the chance to get back into action, Wallace leaped at the opportunity, taking a temporary reduction in rank—to provisional colonel—so that he could join the fight. En route to Lexington, Kentucky, to assume his new command, he was stopped and given new orders for a more urgent mission—defending Cincinnati against that advancing rebel army. He quickly responded to the daunting challenge, rounding up four artillery pieces and calling for civilian volunteers to construct a ten-mile-long earthworks fortification on the Kentucky side of the Ohio and a pontoon bridge to span the river. The response to his appeal for volunteers to man the fortification was so successful that he was able to post some 55,000 men, armed mostly with muzzle-loading hunting rifles, on the line facing the rebel advance from Lexington.

Confederate brigadier general Henry Heth, commanding the 21,000-man wing of Kirby Smith's force marching on Ohio, after scouting out Wallace's imposing fortification bristling with 55,000 rifles and a battery of artillery, decided to cancel his plans. On the night of September 11 he and his troops withdrew back toward Lexington and then southwestward toward Bardstown, Kentucky. Recognized as the hero of the battle that was avoided, Wallace received an outpouring of thanks and congratulations from the grateful—and greatly relieved—citizens of Cincinnati and others across the nation as well. The brass in Washington, however, seemed unimpressed.

His next opportunity for action came again from Governor Morton. Confederate cavalry raiders commanded by John Hunt Morgan had crossed the Ohio from Kentucky into Indiana and captured the town of Corydon, then slashed through the Indiana countryside on a terrifying campaign of pillaging and destruction. They were now threatening the capital, Indianapolis. Morton wired Halleck asking him to order Wallace to do what he could to stop Morgan, and an order soon was issued by Secretary Stanton instructing Wallace to come to the aid of his home state. The mission quickly ended when Morgan, finished with his depredations in Indiana, moved into Ohio, becoming someone else's problem. Morgan eventually ran out of luck and was captured near Salineville, in northeastern Ohio, on July 26, 1863. He later managed to escape from imprisonment, but on September 4, 1864, he was killed by Union cavalrymen at Greeneville, Tennessee.

On March 12, 1864, three days after Halleck had been superseded by Grant as general in chief, Wallace was placed in command of the army's Middle Department, which encompassed Maryland as far west as the Monocacy River, near Frederick, Maryland, as well as the entire state of Delaware. Included in his command was the Eighth Army Corps. The job was essentially administrative, and Wallace performed well in it, exercising his power as sternly and effectively as had Benjamin Butler in Baltimore. Then, in July 1864, Wallace got another longed-for opportunity to command in the field.

Weeks before, on Thursday, June 23, Confederate lieutenant general Jubal Early had ordered his troops, those of the Army of Northern Virginia's Second Corps, formerly Stonewall Jackson's command, to begin a long march from their position near Gaines' Mill, Virginia, just east of Richmond, westward into the Shenandoah Valley, taking the road that led through Charlottesville. They were to strike the Union army commanded by Major General David Hunter, which was advancing up the valley, and destroy it or drive it out of the valley. After that, they were to march northward down the valley, cross the Potomac River around Leesburg or around Harpers Ferry and then march on Washington City, as the U.S. capital was then called. The idea was not to capture Washington, but merely to threaten it and force General Grant to shift troops to defend it, easing Grant's pressure on the rebels' beleaguered army at Petersburg, Virginia, outside Richmond. On July 4 two of General Early's divisions attacked the Union garrison at Harpers Ferry and drove it back to a defensive position on Maryland Heights, where it was joined by the troops of Major General Franz Sigel. Seeing the strong defensive position of the Union force commanding the Potomac River crossing at Harpers Ferry, Early decided to cross the Potomac at Shepherdstown, east of Martinsburg, and march eastward on Frederick. Driving Union skirmishers before it, Early's main column moved into Frederick and took over the town on July 9.

Early's movements quickly set off an alarm in Washington—and in the headquarters of General Grant, the army's new general in chief. On July 3 Halleck, now chief of staff under Grant, from Washington had wired Grant, then encamped at City Point, Virginia, below Richmond, that Early was moving toward the Potomac. Halleck let Grant know the danger, telling him, "The three principal officers on the line are Sigel, Stahel, and Max Weber. You can, therefore, judge what probability there is of a good defense if the enemy should attack the line in force."[42] Until July 3 Grant had thought Early was at Petersburg. Now, though, made aware of Early's threat to Washington, he had replied to Halleck, saying that if the Confederates crossed the Potomac, he could send an army corps from Petersburg to meet them or cut off their return south.[43]

With the army of General Hunter having been chased out of the Shenandoah Valley, leaving a long, shameful trail of ashes behind it (Hunter being better at burning houses than at fighting rebel armies), and thus unavailable for immediate help, responsibility for defending the northern end of the valley—and the nation's capital—fell to Lew Wallace, commanding the military department in which the lower Shenandoah Valley lay. Grant described Wallace's response: "His surplus of troops with which to move against the enemy was small in number. Most of these were raw and, consequently, very much inferior to our veterans and to the veterans which Early had with him; but the situation of Washington was precarious, and Wallace moved with commendable promptitude to meet the enemy at the Monocacy. He could hardly have expected to defeat him badly, but he hoped to cripple and delay him until Washington could be put into a state of preparation for his [Early's] reception."[44] And while Wallace would be stalling Early's advance, Grant would be speedily sending more troops to Washington.

Monocacy, also known as Monocacy Junction and Frederick Junction, was a community three miles southeast of Frederick. Beside it the Monocacy River flows southwestward to the Potomac, forming a natural barrier that lay across the southeastward path of Early's army as it advanced on Washington. The river was spanned by three bridges near Monocacy, one carrying the Baltimore & Ohio rail line, one the turnpike to Washington and one the road to Baltimore. Monocacy, Wallace decided, was the place to confront Early's army. Wallace's force numbered about 5,800 men, and he positioned them at the bridges and fords, presenting a six-mile front to the advancing rebels. Wallace realized that the best he could hope for was to delay Early and allow time for Grant's reinforcements to arrive to defend Washington. After positioning his troops, Wallace himself, on July 7, took a position in Frederick to wait for events to unfold, satisfied, he said, they would not be long delayed:

Monocacy railroad bridge. Here on July 9, 1864, Wallace and his troops held off the invading army of Gen. Jubal Early long enough to allow Union reinforcements to reach Washington, D.C. Grant gave Wallace credit for saving the nation's capital from possible capture by Early's army (Library of Congress).

About 6 o'clock in the afternoon, Colonel Catlin telegraphed me that a heavy force of rebel infantry was moving toward Urbana by the Buckeystown road. This threatened my lines of retreat and the position at Monocacy bridge. What was more serious, it seemed to disclose a purpose to obtain the pike to Washington, important to the enemy for several causes, but especially so if his designs embraced that city, then in no condition, as I understood it, to resist an army like that attributed to Early by General Sigel.

I claim no credit for understanding my duty in such a situation; it was self-apparent.

There was no force that could be thrown in time between the capital and the rebels but mine, which was probably too small to defeat them, but certainly strong enough to gain time and compel them to expose their strength. If they were weak, by going back to the bridge I could keep open the communication with General Sigel; on the other hand, if they were ever so strong it was not possible to drive me from that position, except by turning one of my flanks; if my right, retreat was open by the Washington pike; if my left, the retirement could be by the pike to Baltimore. I made up mind to fight, and accordingly telegraphed General Halleck: "I shall withdraw immediately from Frederick City, and put myself in position to cover road to Washington, if necessary." This was done by marching in the night to the railroad bridge, where Brigadier-General Ricketts was in waiting.[45]

More of Wallace's troops continued to arrive throughout the next day, July 8. Early on the morning of Saturday, July 9, Wallace deployed his army along his lines in expectation of meeting the advancing rebels.

About 8 a.m., [Wallace related] the enemy marched by the pike from Frederick, and threw out skirmishers, behind whom he put his guns in position, and began the engagement. His columns followed a little after 9 o'clock. Passing through a field, just out of range of my pieces, without attempting to drive in my skirmishers, they moved rapidly around to the left, forced a passage of the river at a ford about mile below Ricketts. From 9 o'clock to 10.30 the action was little more than a warm skirmish and experimental cannonading, in which however, the enemy's superiority in the number and caliber of his guns was fully shown. Against my six 3-inch rifles, he opposed not less than sixteen Napoleons.

In this time, also, the fighting at the stone bridge assumed serious proportion; Colonel Brown held his position with great difficulty.... So great was the rebel front, also, that I was compelled to order the whole division into one line, thus leaving it without reserves. Still the enemy's front was greatest.... Finally, by burning the wooden bridge and the block-house at its further end, thus releasing the force left to defend them, I put into the engagement every available man.... The enemy's first line was badly defeated. His second line then advanced and was repulsed, but after a fierce and continuous struggle.... One o'clock came, but not the [expected] re-enforcements; and it was impossible to get an order to them. My telegraph operator, and the railroad agent, with both his trains, had run away. An hour and a half later I saw the third line of rebels move out of the woods and down the hill, behind which they made their formation; right after it came the fourth. It was time to get away. Accordingly, I ordered General Ricketts to make preparations and retire to the Baltimore pike. About 4 o'clock he began the execution of the order.

The stone bridge held by Colonel Brown now became all important.... I rode to the bridge and ordered it to be held at all hazards by the forces then there, until the enemy should be found in its rear, at least until the last regiment had cleared the country road by which the retreat was being effected. This order General Tyler obeyed. A little after 5 o'clock, when my column was well on the march toward New Market, an attack on his rear convinced him of the impracticability of longer maintaining his post. Many of his men then took to the woods, but by his direction the greater part kept their ranks, and manfully fought their way through.[46]

Early decided not to pursue farther than the stone bridge. "Wallace's entire force had taken the road towards Baltimore," Early explained in his account, "and [besides] I did not want prisoners."[47] All of Early's troops crossed the Monocacy River that night, to be ready to resume their march toward Washington the next day.

The rebels' march toward Washington resumed at daybreak on Sunday, July 10. Traveling the Georgetown pike, Early's army covered some twenty miles and at the end of the day bivouacked about four miles west of Rockville. At dawn on the 11th the rebel column was again on the move. As it neared the ring of fortifications around Washington, Early and his troops could see a cloud of dust behind the defenders' works and then watched as a column of U.S. troops filed into the fortification, turning to the left and right, and then sending out a line of skirmishers. Within minutes the defenders' artillery opened on the Confederates. "This defeated our hopes of getting possession of the works by surprise," Early reported, "and it became necessary to reconnoitre."[48]

What the reconnaissance revealed was the extent of the Union fortifications, which Early decided were too formidable and forbidding for his reduced force. The toils of the road on his troops' long, rapid march, plus the losses in battle on the way, particularly at Monocacy, had shrunk his infantry, he reported, "to about 8,000 muskets. Of those remaining, a very large number were greatly exhausted by the last two days marching, some having fallen by sunstroke, and I was satisfied, when we arrived in front of the fortifications, that not more than one-third of my force could have been carried into action." Even so, stubborn as he was, Early determined to make an assault on the enemy's works at daylight the next day, unless, he said, "some information should be received before that time showing its impracticability."[49]

During the night, he received that information. He learned that two corps of Grant's army had arrived in Washington. "As soon as it was light enough to see," he related, "I rode to the front and found the parapets lined with troops. I had, therefore, reluctantly, to give up all hopes of capturing Washington, after I had arrived in sight of the dome of the Capitol, and given the Federal authorities a terrible fright."[50] Early would have to be satisfied, for all the misery and danger he had put his troops through, with having given U.S. officials that terrible fright. After dark on July 12 he began withdrawing, his bold hopes dashed, his thwarted army starting a long trudge back to the Shenandoah Valley in defeat.

General Grant readily gave Wallace due credit for having thwarted Early and his army and perhaps having saved the nation's capital from capture. "There is no telling," he wrote in his memoirs, "how much this result was contributed to by General Lew Wallace's leading what might well be considered almost a forlorn hope. If Early had been but one day earlier he might have entered the capital before the arrival of the reinforcements I had sent. Whether the delay caused by the battle amounted to a day or not, General Wallace contributed on this occasion, by the defeat of the troops under him[,] a greater benefit to the cause than often falls to the lot of a commander of an equal force to render by means of a victory."[51]

From the bridges at Monocacy Wallace rode back to Baltimore with his retreating troops, there to resume his administrative duties, at which he excelled. In January 1865 Grant ordered him to west Texas to investigate the military situation there and along the Rio Grande, where a possible collaboration between Confederates and the French occupation forces in Mexico was believed to be a threat to the United States in a cause that petered out about four months later.

Wallace's next notable assignment was as a member of the military commission that in May and June 1865 tried the conspirators in the murder of President Lincoln, finding all eight of them guilty. His final assignment was as a commissioner in the court-martial of Confederate army Captain Henry Wirz, commandant of the notorious Andersonville prisoner-of-war camp, who was charged with thirteen counts of murder. The trial lasted from late August until October 24, 1865. Wirz was found guilty on eleven counts of murder, sentenced to hang and was executed on November 10 at the Arsenal Penitentiary in Washington, where four of the Lincoln assassination conspirators had been hanged four months earlier.

Three weeks later, on November 30, 1865, Wallace resigned his commission and left the army. During the 1870s and 1880s he held a number of political positions, including that of governor of the New Mexico Territory. During that time he also returned to his writing, and in 1880 his best-selling novel, *Ben-Hur: A Tale of the Christ*, was published. His other books include his lengthy, two-volume autobiography, published in 1906, which his wife, Susan, completed following his death. Lew Wallace died in Crawfordsville, on February 15, 1905, at age seventy-seven. He was buried in Oak Hill Cemetery in Crawfordsville.

Chapter Notes

Introduction

1. Catton, *Grant Takes Command,* page 139.
2. *Official Records of the Union and Confederate Armies,* Series 1, Vol. 34, Part 3, page 333.
3. Grant, *The Personal Memoirs of Ulysses S. Grant,* page 548.
4. Sherman, *Memoirs of General William T. Sherman,* Vol. 2, page 86.
5. Grant, page 548.

Chapter 1

1. Butler, *Butler's Book,* page 179. Other accounts vary on the number of cars that got through.
2. Ibid., page 194.
3. Ibid.
4. Ibid., page 195.
5. Ibid., page 202.
6. Ibid., page 199.
7. Ibid., pages 199–200.
8. Ibid., page 221.
9. Ibid., pages 200–201.
10. Ibid., page 230.
11. Ibid., page 232.
12. Ibid., page 233.
13. Ibid., page 235.
14. Ibid.
15. Ibid., pages 240–241.
16. Ibid., page 239.
17. Ibid.
18. Ibid., page 245.
19. Parton, *General Butler in New Orleans,* page 127.
20. Ibid., pages 128–129.
21. Ibid., page 129.
22. Ibid., page 131.
23. Butler, pages 259–260.
24. Parton, page 141.
25. Butler, page 270.
26. Ibid., page 275.
27. West, *Lincoln's Scapegoat General,* page 96.
28. Philadelphia *Inquirer,* June 21, 1861. Quoted in West, page 96.
29. Butler, page 279.
30. Ibid.
31. Quoted in West, page 206.
32. Butler, page 281.
33. David D. Porter, *The Naval History of the Civil War,* page 44.
34. Butler, page 282.
35. *Official Records,* Series 1, Vol. 4, page 579.
36. Ibid.
37. Ibid., page 580.
38. Ibid.
39. David D. Porter, page 46.
40. Ibid.
41. *Official Records,* op. cit. page 583.
42. *Wikipedia,* "Battle of Hatteras Inlet Batteries," page 1. Other sources vary.
43. David D. Porter, page 47.
44. Butler, page 286.
45. Ibid., pages 286–287.
46. Ibid., page 288.
47. Ibid., pages 285–286.
48. Ibid., page 289.
49. Ibid., page 288.
50. Ibid., page 294.
51. Parton, pages 179–180.
52. Johnson and Buel, eds., *Battles and Leaders of the Civil War,* Vol. 2, page 25.
53. Butler, page 324.
54. Ibid., page 325.
55. Ibid.
56. Ibid., page 333.
57. Parton, page 191.
58. Ibid.
59. Ibid., page 192.
60. Ibid.
61. Butler, pages 333–334.
62. Ibid., page 334.
63. Ibid., page 335.
64. Ibid.
65. Ibid., pages 335–336.
66. Ibid., page 336.
67. Parton, pages 193–194.
68. Ibid., page 208.
69. Butler, pages 351–352.
70. Ibid., page 355.
71. Ibid.
72. Ibid., page 360.
73. Ibid., page 361.
74. Ibid.
75. David D. Porter, page 185.
76. Butler, page 358.
77. Ibid., page 367.
78. Ibid., page 368.
79. David D. Porter, page 186.
80. Butler, pages 368–369.
81. Parton, page 270.
82. Ibid., page 272.
83. Ibid., page 274.
84. Ibid., page 275.
85. With the skies threatening rain, one of the crew had removed the guns' firing wafers to avoid their being ruined by the rain. The guns would not fire without them.
86. Parton, page 276.
87. Dufour, *The Night the War Was Lost,* pages 312–313.
88. Butler, page 371.
89. In his autobiography, *But-*

ler's Book, Butler states that he got to New Orleans on the day after the mint flag incident, which would have him arriving on Monday, April 28, and he states that he learned about the incident while aboard the *Wissahickon* (page 370). Other accounts vary.

90. Parton, page 279.
91. Ibid., pages 280–281.
92. Ibid., page 281.
93. Ibid., page 283.
94. Butler, pages 375–376.
95. Ibid., pages 376–377.
96. Parton, page 290.
97. Ibid., page 292.
98. Ibid., page 295.
99. Ibid., page 291.
100. Ibid., pages 295–296.
101. Parton, page 296.
102. Ibid., pages 296–297.
103. Ibid., page 298.
104. Ibid., page 300.
105. Ibid., page 323.
106. Ibid., page 327.
107. Ibid., page 331.
108. Ibid.
109. Ibid., pages 327–328.
110. Ibid., page 328.
111. Butler, page 419.
112. Hearn, *When the Devil Came Down to Dixie,* page 105.
113. Butler, pages 392–393.
114. Ibid., pages 393–394.
115. Yellow fever, also called Yellow Jack, is transmitted to humans by female mosquitoes, principally the *Aedes aegypti,* found in tropical and subtropical areas. It was not until 1881 that Cuban physician Carlos Finlay proposed that yellow fever was transmitted by mosquitoes, not by unsanitary conditions or by direct contact with other humans. Later tests proved Doctor Finlay correct.
116. Seymour, *The Civil War Memoirs of Captain William J. Seymour,* footnote 71, page 38.
117. Parton, page 518.
118. Ibid., page 523.
119. Ibid., page 524.
120. Ibid., page 346.
121. Butler, page 439.
122. Ibid., page 440.
123. Ibid., page 443.
124. Ibid., page 441.
125. Ibid., pages 441–442.
126. www.executedtoday.com/2009/06/07/1862-william-b-mumford-flag-desecrator/.

127. Parton, page 356.
128. Ibid., pages 355–356.
129. Ibid., page 357.
130. Butler, page 529.
131. Ibid., page 530.
132. Ibid., pages 533–534.
133. Ibid., page 534.
134. Ibid., page 535.
135. Ibid., page 550.
136. Ibid.
137. Ibid., pages 550–551.
138. Ibid., page 617.
139. Badeau, *Military History of Ulysses S. Grant,* Vol. 2, pages 246–247.
140. Grant to Butler, April 16, 1864. Quoted in Badeau, Vol. 2, page 46.
141. Butler, pages 630–631.
142. Badeau, Vol. 2, page 47.
143. William Farrar Smith, "Butler's Attack on Drewry's Bluff," in Johnson and Buel, eds., *Battles and Leaders,* Vol. 4, page 208.
144. Ibid., pages 208, 206.
145. Ibid., pages 208–209.
146. Badeau, Vol. 2, pages 253–255.
147. Smith, op. cit., page 212.
148. Ibid.
149. Horace Porter, *Campaigning with Grant,* pages 146–147.
150. Badeau, Vol. 2, page 258.
151. Grant reported the date as June 10.
152. Badeau, Vol. 2, pages 343–344.
153. Ibid., page 345.
154. Ibid., pages 463–464.
155. Grant, page 570.
156. David D. Porter, page 684.
157. Ibid., page 692.
158. Ibid.
159. Butler, page 775.
160. David D. Porter, page 692.
161. Ibid.
162. Butler, page 775.
163. Ibid., page 783.
164. Ibid.
165. Grant, page 572.
166. Ibid., pages 572–573.
167. Ibid., pages 573–574.
168. Ibid., pages 574–575.
169. Ibid., page 575.
170. Gragg, *Confederate Goliath, The Battle of Fort Fisher,* page 104.
171. Butler, page 782.
172. Horace Porter, op. cit, page 373.
173. Gragg, page 104.

174. Foote, *The Civil War, Red River to Appomattox,* page 740.

Chapter 2

1. Hollandsworth, *Pretense of Glory, The Life of General Nathaniel P. Banks,* page 15.
2. Ibid., page 50.
3. Ibid., page 19.
4. Worthing G. Snethen was the Baltimore correspondent for the *New York Daily Tribune.*
5. *Official Records,* Series 1, Vol. 2, pages 138–139.
6. Ibid., page 139.
7. Ibid., page 140.
8. *Official Records,* Series 1, Vol. 5, page 18.
9. Ibid., page 56.
10. Ibid.
11. Kernstown casualty estimates are drawn from Cozzens, *Shenandoah 1862,* page 215; Eicher and Eicher, *Civil War High Commands,* page 211; and Robertson, *Stonewall Jackson: The Man, the Soldier, the Legend,* page 346.
12. *Official Records,* Series 1, Vol. 12, part 3, pages 111–112.
13. Ibid., page 112.
14. Ibid., page 118.
15. Ibid., page 122.
16. Ibid., page 129.
17. Ibid.
18. Ibid., page 140.
19. Ibid., page 142.
20. Ibid., page 150.
21. Ibid., page 151.
22. Gordon, *From Brook Farm to Cedar Mountain,* page 196. Quoted in Hollandsworth, page 60.
23. *Official Records,* Series 1, Vol. 12, part 1, page 528.
24. National Park Service, http://www.cr.nps.gov/hps/abpp/battles/va104.htm.
25. Letter from Banks to Mary Banks, May 28, 1862, Banks Collection, Library of Congress. Quoted in Hollandsworth, page 69.
26. *Official Records,* Series 1, Vol. 12, part 1, page 529.
27. Ibid., page 530.
28. *Official Records,* Series 1, Vol. 12, part 2, pages 177–178.
29. Ibid., pages 183–184.
30. Ibid., pages 27.

31. Ibid., pages 25–26.
32. Ibid., pages 26–27.
33. Ibid., page 28.
34. Johnson and Buel, eds., *Battles and Leaders,* Vol. 2, page 496.
35. *Official Records,* Series 1, Vol. 15, page 590.
36. Hollandsworth, page 86.
37. Butler, page 530.
38. Ibid., page 531.
39. *Official Records,* Series 1, Vol. 15, pages 590–591.
40. Winters, *The Civil War in Louisiana,* page 206.
41. *Official Records,* Series 1, Vol. 15, page 639.
42. Quoted in Hollandsworth, page 89.
43. Butler, pages 531–532.
44. Hollandsworth, page 96.
45. *Official Records,* Series 1, Vol. 15, pages 639–640.
46. Ibid., page 256.
47. Butler, page 532.
48. Richard B. Irwin, in Johnson and Buel, eds., *Battles and Leaders,* Vol. 3, pages 588–589.
49. Lawrence Lee Hewitt, *Port Hudson,* page 39.
50. Ibid., page 40.
51. Mahan, *Admiral Farragut,* page 222.
52. Ibid., page 213.
53. Ibid., page 224.
54. Shea and Winschel, *Vicksburg Is the Key,* page 88.
55. Ibid., page 96.
56. Hewitt, page 127.
57. Ibid.
58. Irwin, op. cit., page 597.
59. Shea and Winschel, page 197.
60. Hewitt, page 131.
61. Irwin, op. cit., page 597.
62. *Official Records,* Vol. 26, part 1, page 624. Quoted in Shea and Winschel, page 203.
63. Irwin, op. cit., page 598.
64. Ibid.
65. *Official Records,* Series 1, Vol. 26, part 1, page 672.
66. Ibid.,
67. *Harper's Weekly,* October 10, 1863.
68. *Official Records,* Series 1, Vol. 26, part 1, page 288.
69. Ibid., pages 290–291.
70. Irwin, op. cit., page 346.
71. *Official Records,* Series 1, Vol. 26, part 1, page 785.
72. Ibid.

73. Quoted in Hollandsworth, page 143.
74. Irwin, op. cit., page 346.
75. Sherman, Vol. 1, pages 396–397.
76. Ibid., page 393.
77. Grant, page 418.
78. Brooksher, *War Along the Bayous,* page 34.
79. Irwin, op. cit., page 350.
80. Grant, page 412.
81. Thomas O. Selfridge, in Johnson and Buel, eds., *Battles and Leaders,* Vol. 4, pages 362–363.
82. Ibid.
83. Ibid., pages 363–364.
84. Ibid., pages 364–365.
85. Irwin, op. cit., page 358.
86. Ibid.
87. Ibid., page 359.
88. Ibid.
89. Selfridge, op. cit., page 365.
90. Irwin, op. cit., pages 361–362.
91. Brooksher, page 228.
92. *Official Records,* Series 1, Vol. 34, part 3, page 293.
93. Ibid., page 331.
94. Ibid.
95. Ibid., page 332.
96. Ibid., page 409.
97. Ibid., page 490.
98. Ibid., page 491.
99. Banks to Mary Banks, May 13, 1864, Banks Collection, Library of Congress. Quoted in Hollandsworth, page 200.

Chapter 3

1. William M. Wherry, "Wilson's Creek, and the Death of Lyon," in Johnson and Buel, eds., *Battles and Leaders,* Vol. 1, page 291.
2. Ibid.
3. Ibid., page 292.
4. Ibid., pages 293–295.
5. Texas Rangers formed a part of General McCulloch's army.
6. Franz Sigel, "The Flanking Column at Wilson's Creek," in Johnson and Buel, eds., *Battles and Leaders,* Vol. 1, pages 305–306.
7. Wherry, op. cit., pages 296–297.
8. "The Opposing Forces at Wilson's Creek," in Johnson and Buel, eds., *Battles and Leaders,* Vol. 1, page 306.
9. William Garrett Piston and Richard Hatcher, *Wilson's Creek,* pages 305–306.
10. Franz Sigel, "The Pea Ridge Campaign," *Battles and Leaders,* Vol. 1, pages 315–316.
11. *Official Records,* Series 1, Vol. 8, pages 471–472.
12. Ibid., page 461.
13. Ibid., page 462.
14. *Official Records,* Series 1, Vol. 3, pages 94–95.
15. Ibid., pages 95–96.
16. "The Civil War in Arkansas, The Battle of Pea Ridge," civilwarbuff.org/Places/Benton/pea_ridge.html, page 8.
17. *Official Records,* Series 1, Vol. 12, part 2, page 21.
18. Ibid.
19. Ibid., page 25.
20. Ibid., page 26.
21. Ibid., page 47.
22. Franz Sigel, "Sigel in the Shenandoah Valley in 1864," in Johnson and Buel, eds., *Battles and Leaders,* Vol.4, page 487.
23. Grant, pages 412–413.
24. Sigel, "Sigel in the Shenandoah Valley in 1864," in Johnson and Buel, eds., *Battles and Leaders,* Vol. 4, page 488.
25. John D. Imboden, "The Battle of New Market, Va., May 15th, 1864," in Johnson and Buel, eds., *Battles and Leaders,* Vol. 4, page 480.
26. Ibid.
27. Ibid., pages 480–481.
28. Ibid., page 481.
29. Sigel, in Johnson and Buel, eds., *Battles and Leaders,* Vol. 4, page 488.
30. Imboden, op. cit., page 481.
31. Sigel, in Johnson and Buel, eds., *Battles and Leaders,* Vol. 4, page 488.
32. Ibid.
33. Ibid.
34. Imboden, op. cit., page 482.
35. Ibid., page 483.
36. Ibid.
37. Ibid.
38. Colonel George D. Wells, report addressed to Massachusetts Governor John A. Andrew dated May 21,1864. Published online at civilwarhome.com/wellsnewmarket.htm.
39. Sigel, in Johnson and Buel, eds., *Battles and Leaders,* Vol. 4, pages 489–490.

Chapter 4

1. Frémont, *Memoirs of My Life*. Quoted in Nevins, *Frémont, Pathmarker of the West*, page 477.
2. Sherman, Vol. 1, pages 195–196.
3. *Official Records*, Series 1, Vol. 3, pages 416–417.
4. John C. Frémont, "In Command in Missouri," in Johnson and Buel, eds., *Battles and Leaders*, Vol. 1, pages 279–280.
5. Hansen, *The Civil War*, pages 97–98.
6. Ibid., pages 98–99.
7. Catton, *Terrible Swift Sword*, page 31.
8. www.longcamp.com/proc3.html, page 2.
9. www.civilwarstlouis.com/HistoryFrémont.htm, page 2.
10. Catton, page 50.
11. Frémont, in Johnson and Buel, eds., *Battles and Leaders*, Vol. 1, page 280.
12. Ibid., page 281.
13. Frémont Memoirs, Bancroft Library, University of California, pages 240–241. Catton, page 27.
14. McElroy, *The Struggle for Missouri*, Rule, ed., www.civilwarstlouis.com/History/Frémont.htm, page 10.
15. Foote, *The Civil War, A Narrative: Fort Sumter to Perryville*, page 98.
16. Catton, page 50.
17. Cox, "West Virginia Operations Under Frémont," in Johnson and Buel, eds., *Battles and Leaders*, Vol. 2, page 278.
18. Ibid.
19. Ibid., pages 279–280.
20. Ibid., page 280.
21. Imboden, "Stonewall Jackson in the Shenandoah," in Johnson and Buel, eds., *Battles and Leaders*, Vol. 2, page 291.
22. Ibid.
23. Ibid.
24. Rolle, *John Charles Frémont, Character as Destiny*, page 225.
25. Ibid., page 255.

Chapter 5

1. *Official Records*, Series 1, Vol. 4, page 197.
2. Grant, page 161.
3. Ibid., page 163.
4. Ibid., pages 163–164.
5. Ibid., page 166.
6. Ibid., pages 166–167.
7. *New York Herald*, November 19, 1861, page 1.
8. *Official Records*, Series 1, Vol. 53, pages 506–507.
9. Ibid., Vol. 3, page 271.
10. Grant, pages 168–169.
11. Ibid., page 169.
12. McClernand to Lincoln, January 28, 1862, Lincoln Collection. Quoted in Kiper, *Major General John Alexander McClernand*, page 65.
13. *Official Records*, Series 1, Vol. 5, page 41.
14. Grant, page 169.
15. Ibid., page 170.
16. Hoppin, *Life of Andrew Hull Foote*, page 194.
17. Grant, page 172.
18. Jesse Taylor, "The Defense of Fort Henry," in Johnson and Buel, eds., *Battles and Leaders*, Vol. 1, pages 369–370.
19. Ibid., pages 371–372.
20. Hoppin, page 205.
21. *Official Records*, Series 1, Vol. 7, page 130.
22. Ibid.
23. Ibid.
24. Wallace, *Lew Wallace, An Autobiography*, pages 376–377. Quoted in Kiper, page 73.
25. Lew Wallace, "The Capture of Fort Donelson," in Johnson and Buel, eds., *Battles and Leaders*, Vol. 1, page 406.
26. Ibid., pages 407–409, 414–415.
27. Ibid., page 415.
28. Ibid., pages 415–417.
29. Ibid., page 422.
30. McFeely, *Grant, A Biography*, page 102. Lew Wallace, *Autobiography*, Vol. 1, page 412.
31. Grant, page 181.
32. Ibid.
33. Wallace, in Johnson and Buel, eds., *Battles and Leaders*, Vol. 1, page 423.
34. Grant, page 182.
35. Wallace, in Johnson and Buel, eds., *Battles and Leaders*, Vol. 1, page 425.
36. Gideon J. Pillow, "Siege and Capture of Fort Donelson, Tennessee," Report No. 2, page 3, www.civilwarhome.com/pillow1fortdonelson.htm.
37. Grant, pages 183–184.
38. *Official Records*, Vol. 7, pages 180–181.
39. Ibid., page 179.
40. Ibid., page 170.
41. McClernand letter to Grant, dated February 26, 1862, McClernand Collection. Quoted in Kiper, page 92.
42. *Official Records*, Series 1, Vol. 7, pages 679–680.
43. Ibid., page 680.
44. Ibid., Vol. 10, part 2, page 3.
45. Grant, page 193.
46. *Official Records*, Series 1, Vol. 10, part 2, page 4.
47. McClernand to Grant, March 6, 1862, McClernand Collection. Quoted in Kiper, page 94.
48. Force, *From Fort Henry to Corinth*, page 95.
49. Ibid.
50. Grant, page 195.
51. Ibid., pages 196–197.
52. McClernand to Grant, March 27, 1862, McClernand Collection. Quoted in Kiper, page 101.
53. Quoted in Williams, *P.G.T. Beauregard*, page 126.
54. Ulysses S. Grant, "The Battle of Shiloh," in Johnson and Buel, eds., *Battles and Leaders*, Vol. 1, pages 472–473.
55. *Official Records*, Vol. 10, part 1, page 145.
56. Ibid., page 118.
57. Grant, in Johnson and Buel, eds., *Battles and Leaders*, Vol. 1, pages 473, 474–475.
58. *Official Records*, Vol. 10, part 1, pages 119–120.
59. Grant, page 207.
60. *Official Records*, Vol. 10, part 1, page 121.
61. Ibid., pages 113–114.
62. Grant, pages 209–210.
63. *Official Records*, Vol. 10, part 1, page 114.
64. Ibid., Vol. 17, part 2, page 282.
65. David Dixon Porter, *Incidents and Anecdotes of the Civil War*, page 14.
66. Grant, pages 252–253.

—— Chapter 4 notes continue ——

40. Grant, page 424.
41. Eby, ed., *A Virginia Yankee in the Civil War*, page 230.

67. Ibid., page 253.
68. Ibid., page 254.
69. Ibid., page 255.
70. Sherman, Vol. 1, page 296.
71. Ibid., pages 296–297.
72. Porter, page 288.
73. Sherman, page 298.
74. Porter, page 291.
75. Sherman, page 301.
76. Ibid., page 303.
77. Porter, page 292.
78. Grant, page 260.
79. Ibid., page 261.
80. Basler, ed., *The Collected Works of Abraham Lincoln*, page 70.
81. Grant, page 261.
82. Ibid., page 264.
83. Ibid., pages 264–265.
84. Bearss, *The Campaign for Vicksburg*, Vol. 2, page 345.
85. Grant, page 286.
86. Ibid., pages 298–299.
87. Ibid., page 299.
88. Ibid., page 302.
89. *Official Records*, Series 1, Vol. 24, part 1, page 53.
90. Sherman, page 325.
91. *Official Records*, Series 1, Vol. 24, part 1, pages 55–56.
92. Grant, page 312.
93. *Official Records*, Series 1, Vol. 24, part 1, page 87.
94. Ibid., page 164.
95. Ibid., page 162.
96. Ibid.
97. Ibid.
98. Ibid., page 161.
99. Ibid., pages 164–165.
100. Simon, ed., *The Papers of Ulysses S. Grant* Vol. 13, page 16. Quoted in Kiper, page 292.

Chapter 6

1. Quoted in Lash, *A Politician Turned General*, page 69.
2. Ibid., page 85.
3. Ibid.
4. Grant, "The Battle of Shiloh," in Johnson and Buel, eds., *Battles and Leaders*, Vol. 1, page 469.
5. Ibid., page 485.
6. Denney, *The Civil War Years, A Day-by-Day Chronicle*, page 151.
7. Grant, *Battles and Leaders*, Vol. 1, page 476.
8. Ibid.
9. Williams, *Grant Rises in the West*, page 383.
10. Grant, *Memoirs*, pages 209–210.
11. *Official Records*, Series 1, Vol. 17, part 1, page 306.
12. Ibid.
13. Ibid., page 309.
14. Quoted in Lash, page 134.

Chapter 7

1. Wallace, *Autobiography*, Vol. 1, page 77.
2. *Crawfordsville Weekly Journal*, April 13, 1893. Quoted in Stephens, *Shadow of Shiloh*, page 18.
3. *Official Records*, Series 1, Vol. 2, page 668.
4. *Harper's Weekly*, July 6, 1861.
5. *Official Records*, Series 1, Vol. 2, pages 123–124.
6. Washington *Evening Star*, June 14, 1861.
7. Stephens, page 28.
8. Ibid., page 30.
9. Grant, page 169.
10. Ibid., page 172.
11. Hoppin, page 200.
12. Ibid., page 203.
13. Wallace, *Autobiography*, Vol. 1, page 376. In Wallace's account published in *Battles and Leaders*, Vol. 1, page 404, Wallace says the meeting was held on the *New Uncle Sam*, a steamboat that was afterward converted into the gunboat *Blackhawk*.
14. Ibid., pages 376–377.
15. William S. Hillyer letter to Wallace, February 11, 1862, Wallace Papers. Quoted in Stephens, page 48.
16. Grant to Wallace, February 12, 1862, Simon, ed., *The Papers of Ulysses S. Grant*, page 198. Quoted in Stephens, page 48.
17. Grant, page 176.
18. Wallace, "The Capture of Fort Donelson," in Johnson and Buel, eds., *Battles and Leaders*, Vol. 1, page 401.
19. Ibid., pages 403–404.
20. Grant, page 178.
21. Wallace, in Johnson and Buel, eds., *Battles and Leaders*, Vol. 1, page 415.
22. Ibid., pages 417, 419.
23. Ibid., page 422.
24. Grant, page 181.
25. Ibid.
26. Wallace, op. cit., pages 423–425.
27. Texts of the notes are from Grant, pages 183–184.
28. Pillow, op. cit.
29. Wallace, op. cit., page 428.
30. Ibid.
31. Grant, page 184.
32. Ibid., page 187.
33. Ibid., page 197.
34. Ibid., page 198.
35. Ibid., pages 198–199.
36. *Official Records*, Series 1, Vol. 10, part 1, pages 179–180.
37. Grant, page 199.
38. Ibid., pages 208–209.
39. *Official Records*, Ibid., pages 170, 173.
40. Ibid., page 226.
41. Grant, page 226.
42. Bushong, *Old Jube*, pages 197–198.
43. Catton, *Grant Takes Command*, page 310.
44. Grant, page 521.
45. *Official Records*, Series 1, Vol. 37, part 1, page 195.
46. Ibid., pages 196–197.
47. Early, *A Memoir of the Last Year of the War for Independence, in the Confederate States of America*, page 55.
48. Ibid., page 57.
49. Ibid., page 59.
50. Ibid., page 61.
51. Grant, page 522.

Bibliography

Badeau, Adam. *Military History of Ulysses S. Grant,* Volume 2. Bedford, MA: Applewood Books, 2008. Originally published by D. Appleton and Company, New York, 1881.

Brooksher, William Riley. *War Along the Bayous: The 1864 Red River Campaign in Louisiana.* Dulles, VA: Brassey's, 1998.

Butler, Benjamin F. *Butler's Book: Autobiography and Personal Reminiscences of Major-General Benj. F. Butler.* Boston: A.M. Thayer, 1892.

Catton, Bruce. *Grant Takes Command.* Boston: Little, Brown, 1969.

_____. *Terrible Swift Sword.* New York: Pocket Books, 1960.

Chaffin, Tom. *Pathfinder: John Charles Fremont and the Course of American Empire.* New York: Hill & Wang, 2002.

Denney, Robert E. *The Civil War Years: A Day-by-Day Chronicle.* New York: Gramercy Books, 1992.

Dufour, Charles L. *The Night the War Was Lost.* Lincoln: University of Nebraska Press, 1994.

Early, Jubal Anderson. *A Memoir of the Last Year of the War for Independence, in the Confederate States of America.* Lynchburg, VA: Charles W. Button, 1867. Photocopy reprint published by Nabu Press, 2010.

Engle, Stephen D. *Yankee Dutchman, The Life of Franz Sigel.* Baton Rouge: Louisiana State University Press, 1999.

Foote, Shelby. *The Civil War: A Narrative, Fort Sumter to Perryville.* New York: Random House, 1958.

_____. *The Civil War: A Narrative, Red River to Appomattox.* New York: Vintage, 1986.

Force, M.F. *From Fort Henry to Corinth.* New York: Charles Scribner's Sons, 1903.

Goss, Thomas J. *The War Within the Union High Command: Politics and Generalship During the Civil War.* Lawrence: University Press of Kansas, 2003.

Gragg, Rod. *Confederate Goliath: The Battle of Fort Fisher.* Baton Rouge: Louisiana State University Press, 2006.

Grant, Ulysses S. *The Personal Memoirs of Ulysses S. Grant.* Old Saybrook, CT: Konecky & Konecky, 1993.

Hansen, Harry. *The Civil War.* New York: New American Library, 2001.

Harrington, Fred Harvey. *Fighting Politician, Major General N.P. Banks.* Philadelphia: University of Pennsylvania Press, 1948.

Hearn, Chester G. *When the Devil Came Down to Dixie: Ben Butler in New Orleans.* Baton Rouge: Louisiana State University Press, 1997.

Hewitt, Lawrence Lee. *Port Hudson: Confederate Bastion on the Mississippi.* Baton Rouge: Louisiana State University Press, 1987.

Hollandsworth, James G., Jr. *Pretense of Glory, The Life of General Nathaniel P. Banks.* Baton Rouge: Louisiana State University Press, 1998.

Hoppin, James Mason. *Life of Andrew Hull Foote, Rear Admiral United States Navy.* New York: Harper and Brothers, 1874.

Johnson, Robert Underwood, and Clarence Clough Buel, eds. *Battles and Leaders of the Civil War,* Volume I. South Brunswick, NJ: Thomas Yoseloff, 1956.

_____, eds. *Battles and Leaders of the Civil War,* Volumes II, III and IV. Secaucus, NJ: Castle, 1982.

Joiner, Cary Dillard. *One Damn Blunder from Beginning to End: The Red River Campaign of 1864.* Wilmington, DE: SR Books, 2003.

Kiper, Richard L. *Major General John Alexander McClernand, Politician in Uniform.* Kent, OH: Kent State University Press, 1999.

Lash, Jeffrey N. *A Politician Turned General: The Civil War Career of Stephen Augustus Hurlbut.* Kent, OH: Kent State University Press, 2003.

Mahan, A.T. *Admiral Farragut.* London: Sampson Low, Marston, 1892.

McFeely, William S. *Grant: A Biography.* New York: W.W. Norton, 1981.

Morseberger, Robert E., and Katharine M. Morseberger. *Lew Wallace: Militant Romantic.* New York: McGraw-Hill, 1980.

Nevins, Allan. *Frémont, Pathmarker of the West.* Lincoln: University of Nebraska Press, 1992.

Parton, James. *General Butler in New Orleans.* New York: Mason Brothers, 1864.

Porter, David D. *The Naval History of the Civil War.* Mineola, NY: Dover, 1998.

Porter, Horace. *Campaigning with Grant.* New York: Mallard Press, 1991.

Rolle, Andrew. *John Charles Frémont: Character as Destiny.* Norman: University of Oklahoma Press, 1991.

Seymour, William J. *The Civil War Memoirs of Captain William J. Seymour: Reminiscences of a Louisiana Tiger.* Baton Rouge: Louisiana State University Press, 1991.

Shea, William L., and Terrence J. Winschel. *Vicksburg Is the Key: The Struggle for the Mississippi River.* Lincoln: University of Nebraska Press, 2003.

Sherman, William Tecumseh. *Memoirs of General William T. Sherman,* Volume 2. Originally published by Henry S. King & Co., London, 1875. Photocopy reprint published by Nabu Press, 1998.

Stephens, Gail. *Shadow of Shiloh, Major General Lew Wallace in the Civil War.* Indianapolis: Indiana Historical Society Press, 2010.

Wallace, Lew. *Lew Wallace: An Autobiography.* 2 volumes. New York: Garrett Press, 1969.

West, Richard S., Jr. *Lincoln's Scapegoat General: A Life of Benjamin F. Butler, 1818–1893.* Boston: Houghton Mifflin, 1965.

Williams, T. Harry. *Lincoln and His Generals.* New York: Vintage, 1952.

Winters, John D. *The Civil War in Louisiana.* Baton Rouge: Louisiana State University Press, 1963.

Index

Numbers in ***bold italics*** indicate pages with photographs.

Alexandria, La. 78, 81, 82, 88, 93, 94, 95, 97, 99, 183
Algiers, La. 27, 36
Andrew, John 6, 23
Andrews, George L. 87
Annapolis, Md. 7, 8, 10
Army of the James 51, 52, 55, 57
Army of the Potomac 51, 52, 53, 55, 66, *67*, 72, 118, 119, 120, 147, 158
Army of the Tennessee 2, 183, 188, 191, 192, 193, 194, 210
Army of Virginia 118, 119, 138
Augur, Christopher C. 77, 82
Averell, William W. 120

Babcock, O.E. 62
Badeau, Adam 52, 56
Bailey, Joseph 98, 99
Baltimore, Md. 5, 6, 10, 11, 18, 23, 65, 216, 219, 220
Baltimore & Ohio Railroad 5, 127, 197, 200, 217
Banks, Nathaniel 2, 49, 50, 118, 137, 183, 195; background 64; death 101; description 64–65; in New Orleans 75–77; Port Hudson campaign 79–88; Red River campaign 91–99; relieved of command 99–101; Shenandoah valley campaign 66–75; Texas campaigns 88–91
Baton Rouge, La. 27, 41, 77, 78, 79, 81, 82, 173
Baxter, A.S. 211, 214
Bayou Sara, La. 80
Beall, William N.B. 83
Beauregard, P.G.T. 36, 44, 54, 55, 160, 161, 162, 164, *165*, 165, 166, 190, 191, 201, 214, 215

Belmont, Mo. 142, 145
Benton, Thomas Hart 128
Bermuda Hundred, Va. 53, 54
Big Bethel *16*, 17, 23
Blair, Frank 2, 3, 133, 178, 182
Blair, Montgomery 18, 21, 133
Blue Wing 169
Bowen, John S. 176
Bowling Green, Ky. 146, 147, 202
Bragg, Braxton 162
Brashear City, La. *see* Morgan City, La.
Breckinridge, John 120, 122, 123, 124, 126
Brownsville, Texas 90, 91
Bruinsburg, Miss. 175, 176
Buckner, Simon B. 153, 154, 155, 156, 157, 202, 205, 206, 207, 208, 209, 210
Buell, Don Carlos 146, 160, 164, 165, 166, 189, 190, 191, 202, 211
Bull Run 18, 23, 119, 158
Butler, Andrew Jackson 46
Butler, Benjamin F. 2, 199, 216; Annapolis occupation 7–12; background 5, *6*; Baltimore occupation 10–11; Big Bethel disaster 15, 17; confiscates escaped slaves 13–15; death 63; Fort Fisher campaign 57–63; Hatteras Inlet campaign 19–22; new assignment offers made after New Orleans 50–51; New Orleans campaign 24–28, 30, 31; New Orleans occupation 35–49; relieved of command by Grant 62; relieved of New Orleans command 49–50; service under Grant 52–63

Cairo, Ill. 131, 133, 140, 142, 144, 145, 146, 147, 148, 152, 167, 202, 215
Cameron, Simon 11, 12, 15, 23, 66, 134
Canby, Edward R.S. 100, 101
Carr, Eugene 176
Carthage, Mo. 104, 105, 111
Cedar Creek 120, 126
Cedar Mountain, Va. 73, 74, 119
Champion Hill, Miss. 179, 180
Charleston, S.C. 54, 186
Chase, Salmon 166, 183
Cherokee Indians 115
Chicago, Ill. 187
Chicago Tribune 187, 188
Churchill, Thomas J. 95, 170
City Point, Va. 53, 54, 59
Clarksville, Tenn. 146, 156, 157
Colfax, Schuyler 201
Columbus, Ky. 141–144, 146, 147
Commercial Bulletin 45
Corinth, Miss. 158, 160, 161, 162, 166, 189, 191, 192, 193, 211, 212, 215
Cox, Jacob 136, 137
Crook, George 120
Crump's Landing, Tenn. 160, 161, 211, 212, 213
Culpeper, Va., Culpeper Court House 75, 118, 119
Curtis, Newton M. 61
Curtis, Samuel 109, 110, 112–118, 134

Dana, Charles A. 56
Dana, Napoleon 90
Davis, David 134
Davis, Jefferson (CSA president) 9, 17, 43, 44, 48, 82, 113

Davis, Jefferson C. (U.S. Army officer) 115, 116
Davis Bridge 192
Dodge, Grenville 116
Dover, Tenn. 149, 153, 203, 206, 209, 210
Dowling, Richard 89
Drewry's Bluff, Va. 54
Dry Fork, Mo. *see* Carthage, Mo.
Duncan, Johnson K. 29, 31
Dwight, William 83, 85

Early, Jubal 73, 127, 216, 217, *218*, 218, 219, 220
Eighth Massachusetts Infantry Regiment 6, 7, 8, 9
Elkhorn Tavern, Ark. 113, 115, 116, 117
Emory, William H. 77, 81
Evening Star 199
Ewell, Richard 69, 70, 71

Farragut, David G. 24, 28, 29, 30–35, 43, 77, 79, 80, 88, 175
Floyd, John B. 154, 156, 205, 206, 209
Foote, Andrew 24, 148, 151, 152, 153, 155, 202, 203, 204, 206, 207
Forrest, Nathan Bedford 157, 168, 194, 195
Fort Clark 18, *20*, 20
Fort DeRussy 94
Fort Donelson 146, 149, 150, 152, 153, *157*, 158, 160, 188, *197*, 202, 203, 204, 205, 206, 210
Fort Fisher 57–63
Fort Griffin 89
Fort Hatteras 18, *20*, 20
Fort Heiman 146, 147, 149, 151, 153, 202, 203, 204
Fort Henry 146, 147, 148, 149, *150*, 150, 151, 152, 160, 188, 202, 203, 204, 205, 210
Fort Hindman 169, 170, *171*, 171
Fort Jackson 24, 30, 31, 46, 75
Fort Livingston 27
Fort Massachusetts 28
Fort McHenry 11, 66
Fort Monroe 11, 12, *13*, *14*, 18, 23, 25, 28, 52, 53, 62, 66, 70, 147
Fort Morgan 76
Fort Pillow 195
Fort St. Philip 24, 30, 31, 46, 75
Fort Sumter 1, 5, 146, 186, 197
Fox, Gustavus 21, 24
Franklin, William B. 89, 90, 91, 93, 98
Frederick, Md. 216, 217, 219
Fremont, Jessie Benton 128, 132, 134, 136, 139
Fremont, John 64, 72, 109, 118, 141, 187; background 128; death 139; description 128; in St. Louis 129–136; in Shenandoah valley 136–139
Front Royal, Va. 70, 71
Frost, Daniel 103

Galveston, Texas 88, 90, 91
Gardner, Franklin 82–88
Gillmore, Quincy A. 53, 54, 55, 56
Gordon, George H. 70, 71
Gordonsville, Va. 73, 75, 118, 119
Grand Gulf, Miss. 175, 176, 177
Grant, Ulysses S. 2, 3, 51, 52, 53, 55–62, 78, 82, 84, 86, 88, 91, 93, 94, 99, 100, 120, 126, 133, 138, 140, 142–146, 147, 148, 149, 151, 152, 153, 155, 156, *157*, 158, 159, 160, 161, 162, 163, 164, 165, 166, 167, 172, 173, 174, 175, 176, 177, 178, 179, 180, 181, 182, 183, *184*, 185, 188, 190, 191, 192, 193, *194*, 194, 202, 204, 205, 206, 207, 208, 209, 210, 211, 212, 213, 214, 215, 217, *218*, 220
Grover, Cuvier 77, 78, 81, 84, 85

Haggerty, Peter 10
Hahn, Michael 91, 92
Halleck, Henry 2, 3, 49, 50, 52, 56, 76, 77, 78, 80, 81, 88, 89, 90, 91, 93, 99, 100, 109, 110, 112, 113, 119, 126, 146, 147, 148, 158, 159, 160, 166, 167, 172, 191, 202, 210, 215, 216, 217, 219
Hamburg Landing, Tenn. 160, 161
Hannibal Messenger 188
Hardee, William 162
Harney, William 128
Harpers Ferry, W.Va. 10, 66, 121, 126, 200, 217
Harris, Isham 164
Harrisburg, Va. 68, 70, 137, 138
USS *Hartford* 28, 29, 30, 32, 79, 80
Hatch, John 71
Hatchie River 192
Hicks, Thomas 7, 8
Hill, A.P. 73, 119
Hillyer, W.S. 155, 205, 208
Hinks, Edward 54
Hoke, Robert F. 61, 63
Hollandsworth, James Jr. 65
Hornets' Nest 189
Houston, Texas 88, 90
Hovey, Alvin 173, 179, 215
Hunter, David 109, 126, 134, 135, 216, 217
Hurlbut, Stephen A. 161, 162, 163, 164, 172, 214; background 186; Battle of Hatchie River 192–193; Battle of Shiloh 189–191; death 195; discharged 195; promotion to major general 191; service in Missouri 187–188

Imboden, John D. 120, 121, 122, 123, 124, 126, 137
Irwin, Richard B. 78, 83, 86, 88, 91, 97, 99

Jackson, Claiborne 103, 104, *105*, 105
Jackson, Thomas (Stonewall) *67*, 67, 68, 70, 71, 72, 73, 75, 137, 216
Jackson, Miss. 82, 177, 178
Jefferson Barracks 103
Jefferson City, Mo. 104, 109, 129
Johnson, Edward 70
Johnston, Albert Sidney 160, 161, 162, 163, 164, 166, 190, 205, 206, 211, 214
Johnston, Joseph 51, 66, 72, 82, 177, 178, 179, 201

Kansas City, Mo. 109, 132
Kautz, August 54
Kelly's Island 201
Kimball, Nathan 68

Lake Providence, La. 80
Lamb, William 61
Lamon, Ward 186
Lane, Henry Smith 197
Lawler, Michael 183
Lee, Robert E. 1, 51, 52, 53, 55, 72, 73, 75, 121
Lefferts, Marshall 9
Lexington, Mo. 132, 133, 135
Lincoln, Abraham 1, 2, 3, 5, 12, 17, 21–22, 23, 24, 25, 26, 44, 49, 50, 51, 52, 57, 58, 59, 62, 64, 66, 69, 72, 75, 78, 81, 88, 89, 92, 100, 109, 120, 128, 129, 130, 131, 132, 133, 134, 135, 136, 138, 139, 140, 147, 148, *150*, 151, 152, 159, 166, 167, 168, 172, 183, *184*, 185, 186, 188, 191, 194, 195, 196, 197, 201, 210, 215, 220
Lincoln, Mary Todd 140
Logan, John A. 2, 3, 176, 179
Loring, William 178, 179
Louis Napoleon 88
Lovell, Mansfield 31, 37, 40
Lyon, Nathaniel 103–107, 111, 112, 131, 132

Mahan, A.T. 79
Mansfield, La. 95, 99, 183
Marcy, Randolph 26
Martinsburg, W.Va. 71, 72
Maximilian, Archduke 88
McClellan, George B. 24, 25, 26,

Index

27, 52, 64, 66, 67, 68, 72, 146, 158, 159, 185, 187, 210
McClernand, John A. 2, *171*, 189, 190, 199, 203, 204, 207, 208, 210, 212, 214, 215; background 140; Battle of Belmont 143–145; Battle of Shiloh (Pittsburg Landing) 161–166; death 185; Fort Donelson campaign 152–158; Fort Henry campaign 148–152; Fort Hindman assault 169–172; promotion to major general 159, 210; relieved of command 183; Vicksburg campaign 172–183, *184*
McCulloch, Benjamin 104, 107, 109, 111, 112, 113, 114, 115
McDowell, Irvin 68, 69, 70, 72, 118, 137, 201
McPherson, James 2, 80, 82, 173, 175, 176, 177, 178, 179, 180, 181, 211, 213
Meade, George 51, 52, 120
Medill, Joseph 187
Memphis, Tenn. 86, 167, 168, 169, 172, 191, 193, *194*, 194, 215
Memphis Evening Bulletin 182
Mobile, Ala. 27, 76, 88, 93, 101
Monocacy, Md. 217, 220
Monocacy bridge *218*, 218, 220
Monroe, John T. 31–33, 37, 38, 41, 43, 44
Morgan, G.W. 169
Morgan, John Hunt 216
Morgan City, La. 78, 93
Morton, Oliver 197, 215, 216
Mosby, John S. 122
Mower, Joseph 94, 96
Mumford, William *33*, 33, 46–48
Muscle Shoals, Ala. 146

Nashville, Tenn. 52, 153, 157, 158, 189, 206
Nelson, William 211
New Carthage, La. 173, 174, 175
New Market, Va. 68, 70, 122, 123, 126
New Orleans, La. 24, 25, 27, 28, 30–32, 35, 40, 43, 44, 48, 49, 76, 77, 78, 79, 81, 82, 89, 90, 91, 93, 101, 167, 195
New Orleans Bee 41
New York, N.Y. 49, 102, 119, 128, 139
New York Herald 145

Oglesby, Richard 142, 154, 207
Opelousas, La. 81, 90, 91
Ord, Edward 120, 183, 192, 193
Osterhaus, Peter 115, 116, 176

Paducah, Ky. 141, 142, 147, 148, 201, 202

Paine, Halbert 85
Parton, James 28, 48, 49, 50
Patterson, Robert 66, 198, 201
Pattersonville, La. 81
Pea Ridge, Ark. 113, *117*, 117
Pemberton, John C. 80, 168, 177, 178, 179
Petersburg, Va. 53, 54, 55, 56, 57, 217
Phelps, John W. 24, 28, 31, 36
Picayune 33
Pierce, Ebenezer 17
Pillow, Gideon 130, 133, 153, 154, 155, 156, 157, 205, 206, 207, 209
Pittsburg Landing, Tenn. 160, 161, 162, 163, 164, *165*, 189, 191, 211, 212, 213, 214, 215
Pleasant Hill, La. 95, *96*, 96
Polk, Leonidas 142
Pope, John 72, 73, 74, 75, 118, 119, 130, 133, 138, 187
Port Gibson, Miss. 176, 177
Port Hudson, La. 50, 77, 78, 79, 80, 81, 82, *83*, 84–87, 173, 177, 183
Porter, David D. 18, 20, 24, 29, 30, 31, 57–61, 63, 79, 82, 92–96, 99, 167, 168, 169, 170, *171*, 171, 172, 173, 174, 175
Porter, Horace 55, 62
Prentiss, Benjamin M. 130, 131, 140, 162, 163, *165*, 189, 190, 214
Price, Sterling 104, 105, 106, 109, 111, 112, 113, 114, 116, 131, 135, 142
Proctor's Creek *see* Drewry's Bluff

Rawlins, John 213
Red River 78, 79, 80, 81, 82, 88, 92, 93, 94, 95, 99, 100, 173, 183
Reynolds, Joseph J. 100
Richmond, Va. 52, 53, 54, 57, 66, 69, 72, 118, 200, 216, 217
Romney, W. Va. 198, 199, *200*, 200
Rosecrans, William 192, 193
Rowley, William A. 211, 213, 214

Sabine Pass, Texas 88, 89, 90
St. Louis 102, 103, 104, 108, 109, 113, 118, 128, 129, 130, 133, 134, 135, 136, 147, 185, 188, 215
Savannah, Ga. 3, 128
Schofield, John 103, 110, 112
Scott, Winfield 1, 10, 11, 12, 15, 18, 24, 64, 65, 66, 133
Selfridge, Thomas O. 94, 95, 96
Seward, William 44, 48, 49, 50
Shenandoah valley 66, 72, 118, 120, 216, 220
Sheridan, Philip 55

Sherman, Thomas W. 77, 82, 84, 85, 120, 129, *171*, 181
Sherman, William T. 2, 23, 51, 52, 62, 77, 91, 93, 99, 161, 162, 163, 164, 168, 169, 170, *171*, 171, 172, 175, 177, 178, 180, 182, 189, 190, 194, 195, 212, 214
Shields, James *67*, 67, 68, 69, 70, 138
Shiloh 161, 163, *165*, 165, 166, 191, 213
Ship Island, Miss. 25, 28, 29
Shreveport, La. 81, 91, 95, 96
Sigel, Franz 2, 72, 74, 217, 218, 219; background 102, *103*; Battle of Pea Ridge 114–118; death 127; description 102; relieved of command 127; service in Missouri 103–112, 118; service in Shenandoah valley 118–127, 139, 216, 217
Sixth Massachusetts Infantry Regiment 5, 6, *7*, 10
Slaughter Mountain, Va. *see* Cedar Mountain
Smith, A.J. 93, 95, *96*, 96, 99, 101, 170, 171, 176
Smith, Charles F. 142, 147, 148, 149, 150, 151, 152, 153, 155, 156, *157*, 158, 159, 162, 189, 202, 203, 204, 210
Smith, Edmund Kirby 81, 216
Smith, Francis H. 121
Smith, Morgan 208, 209
Smith, Thomas Kilby 94
Smith, William F. 52, 53, 54, 55, 56
Soule, Pierre 34, 40, 41
Springfield, Mo. 104, 105, 106, 107, 108, *108*, 111, 112, 131, 132
Springfield Landing, La. 95
Stanton, Edwin 2, 25, 26, 50, 52, 56, 57, 59, 62, 66, 68, 69, 70, 71, 72, 100, 119, 120, 166, 167, 168, 183, 185, 216
Staunton, Va. 68, 120, 121, 137
Steele, Frederick 93, 94, 101, 170
Strasburg, Va. 67, 68, *69*, 69, 70, 71, 72, 120, 121, 126, 137
Stringham, Silas H. 18, 22
Strother, David H. 126
Stuart, David 170, 189
Sturgis, Samuel 105, 107, 108

Taylor, Jesse 149, 151
Taylor, Richard 81, 95, *96*
Terry, Alfred Howe 62
Thayer, John M. 205
Thomas, George H. 147
Thomas, Lorenzo 134
Thompson, Jacob 191
Tilghman, Lloyd 151, 179, 203
Trent Affair 25

True Delta 36, 37
Trumbull, Lyman 140, 183, 187

Van Dorn, Earl 13–117, *117*, 192, 194
Vicksburg, Miss. 24, 50, 78, 79, 80, 82, 86, 91, 92, 94, 160, 167, 168, 169, 173, 175, 176, 177, 178, 180, 181, 183, 194

Walke, Henry 144
Wallace, Lew 2, 152, 153, 154, 155, 156, *157*, 159, 160, 164, 190, 210; background 196; Battle of Fort Donelson 205–210; Battle of Monocacy Bridge 217–220; Battle of Romney 198–199; Battle of Shiloh 211–214; death 221; promotion to brigadier general 201; promotion to major general 210; resigns commission 221; writes *Ben-Hur: A Tale of the Christ* 221
Wallace, W.H.L. 162, 163, 189, 214
Washington, D.C. 5–10, 18, 21, 22, 23, 25, 27, 49, 58, 59, 63, 66, 67, 70, 71, 78, 92, 99, 118, 119, 120, 126, 127, 128, 131, 132, 135, 140, 166, 167, 199, 210, 217, *218*, 218, 219, 220
Webster, J.D. 155, 209
Weitzel, Godfrey 27, 57, 58, 59, 61, 78, 81, 83, 84
Welles, Gideon 22, 24, 57, 79, 173

Wells, George D. 124
West Point 9, 29, 54, 59, 77, 100, 103, 110, 113, 147, 187, 203
Wheeling, W. Va. 136, 198
Wherry, William 106, 107
Williams, Alpheus 71
Williams, Nelson 188, 189
Wilmington, N.C. 57, *58*, 62
Wilson's Creek, Mo. 105, 106, 108, *108*, 111, 132
Winchester, Va. *67*, 67, 68, 71, 120, 121, 122, 137, 200, 201
Wirz, Henry 221
Woodstock, Va. 121, 122
Wool, John E. 17, 18, 19, 21, 22

Yates, Richard 151, 166, 183, 188

www.ingramcontent.com/pod-product-compliance
Ingram Content Group UK Ltd.
Pitfield, Milton Keynes, MK11 3LW, UK
UKHW050532150426
5217IPUK00026B/1908